The Logic of Governance in China

Drawing on more than a decade of fieldwork, *The Logic of Governance in China* develops a unified theoretical framework to explain how China's centralized political system maintains governance and how this process produces recognizable policy cycles that are obstacles to bureaucratic rationalization, professionalism, and rule of law. The book is unique for the overarching framework it develops; one that sheds light on the interconnectedness among apparently disparate phenomena such as the mobilizational state, bureaucratic muddling through, collusive behaviors, variable coupling between policymaking and implementation, inverted soft budget constraints, and collective action based on unorganized interests. An exemplary combination of theory-motivated fieldwork and empirically-informed theory development, this book offers an in-depth analysis of the institutions and mechanisms in the governance of China.

XUEGUANG ZHOU is Kwoh-ting Li Professor of Economic Development, Professor of Sociology and senior fellow at Freeman Spogli Institute of International Studies at Stanford University. He publishes widely on topics related to governance, state-making, government bureaucracy, and social inequality in contemporary China.

The Logic of Governance in China

An Organizational Approach

XUEGUANG ZHOU
Stanford University

CAMBRIDGE
UNIVERSITY PRESS

CAMBRIDGE
UNIVERSITY PRESS

University Printing House, Cambridge CB2 8BS, United Kingdom

One Liberty Plaza, 20th Floor, New York, NY 10006, USA

477 Williamstown Road, Port Melbourne, VIC 3207, Australia

314–321, 3rd Floor, Plot 3, Splendor Forum, Jasola District Centre, New Delhi – 110025, India

103 Penang Road, #05-06/07, Visioncrest Commercial, Singapore 238467

Cambridge University Press is part of the University of Cambridge.

It furthers the University's mission by disseminating knowledge in the pursuit of education, learning, and research at the highest international levels of excellence.

www.cambridge.org
Information on this title: www.cambridge.org/9781009159425
DOI: 10.1017/9781009159418

© Xueguang Zhou 2022

First published 2022

A catalogue record for this publication is available from the British Library.

Library of Congress Cataloging-in-Publication Data
NAMES: Zhou, Xueguang, 1959– author.
TITLE: The logic of governance in China : an organizational approach / Xueguang Zhou.
DESCRIPTION: Cambridge, United Kingdom ; New York, NY : Cambridge University Press, 2022. | Includes bibliographical references and index.
IDENTIFIERS: LCCN 2022020686 (print) | LCCN 2022020687 (ebook) |
ISBN 9781009159425 (hardback) | ISBN 9781009159401 (paperback) |
ISBN 9781009159418 (epub)
SUBJECTS: LCSH: Bureaucracy–China. | Political culture–China. | Politics, Practical–China. |
BISAC: SOCIAL SCIENCE / Sociology / General
CLASSIFICATION: LCC JQ1512 .Z8868 2022 (print) | LCC JQ1512 (ebook) | DDC 352.6/
30951–dc23/eng/20220701
LC record available at https://lccn.loc.gov/2022020686
LC ebook record available at https://lccn.loc.gov/2022020687

ISBN 978-1-009-15942-5 Hardback
ISBN 978-1-009-15940-1 Paperback

Contents

Figures and Tables

Figures

Tables

Preface

This book reports my decade-long research effort to understand this basic question: How China has been and is governed. And this intellectual journey that led to this book also witnessed the dramatic changes that China experienced during this period. This research began in 2004, when a colleague friend introduced me to an agricultural township in northern China and I got acquainted with local officials and villagers there.

Between 2004 and 2015, I visited this township several times each year, staying one week to a few weeks each time. During my visit, I stayed in a guest room in the township government courtyard together with other township cadres and staff members, and interacted with them from early mornings into evenings. I went with local cadres on their daily routines: attending meetings, implementing policies, responding to crises, or carrying out village elections. I also went to nearby villages and got to know many villagers and village cadres there. Through these activities I gradually gained firsthand experience in and a deeper understanding of policy implementation at local levels and the practice of local governance. During this period, I also worked with several graduate students and other colleagues on government behaviors in other areas.

This research experience offers me a bottom-up perspective to examine larger issues about interactions between policy making and implementation; between the central and local governments; and among state policies, local officials, and grassroots society, and ultimately the logic of governance in China.

The journey of my research took place amidst tremendous changes that China has experienced over the last two decades. I was especially fortunate that I conducted my fieldwork in those years when China was experiencing the grand trend of opening up to the outside world, after China joined the World Trade Organization (WTO) in 2001. This larger environment provided the favorable opportunity for my research and facilitated my interactions with the local cadres and villagers.

In those years when I immersed myself in my fieldwork, I began to publish most of my research findings in academic journals in China, as I wanted to engage in discussions and debates in a striving research community on government behaviors. I collected these publications and integrated them into a book manuscript in the Chinese language in 2013, and in the following year it was accepted for publication at Sanlian Shudian, a prestigious academic press in Beijing. The book manuscript had to wait for three more years before it got approval and went into print in March 2017. The first printing of 7,000 copies were sold quickly, and the press was planning to reprint by May. But the reprint was halted for undisclosed reasons, and eventually my book was "unselfed," a coded term meaning that it was not allowed to be reprinted or circulated. And the press returned all copyrights associated with this book to me.

This book, now in the English language, is based on the aforementioned book in Chinese published in 2017. But most of the materials are revised and rewritten into English for the first time.

Throughout this research process, I have accumulated many debts to many friends, colleagues, and institutions that helped me along the way. I am most grateful to those villagers and local cadres in the township of my fieldwork. When I first arrived, I was a stranger and an outsider to them. Over the years, we got to know one another well, and I gained their acceptance, trust, and friendship. They helped me in many ways and educated me about their everyday life experience, their views of the world, and the actual processes of problem-solving and policy implementation at the grassroots level. Regrettably, to protect their anonymity I cannot record their names here and express my gratitude to them.

Over the years, I received valuable comments, critique, and support from many colleagues and friends in China. They are Cai He, Cao Zhenghan, Chen Guoquan, Chen Jiajian, Chen Nabo, Di Jinhua, Feng Shizheng, He Yanling, Huang Jin, Huang Xiaochun, Li Lianjiang, Li Lulu, Li Qiang, Li Youmei, Liu Shiding, Liu Yuzhao, Ma Jun, Ouyang Jing, Qu Jindong, Qiu Haixiong, Shen Yuan, Shi Puyuan, Tian Kai, Tian Xianhong, Zhang Jing, Zhang Xiang, Zhang Yonghong, Zhao Dingxin, Zhao Shukai, Zhe Xiaoye, Zhou Feizhou, and Zhou Li-an. On the other side of the Pacific Ocean, I presented my work at various conferences and workshops at Columbia University, Harvard University, the University of

Michigan, Stanford University, the University of California's Berkeley, Los Angeles, and Irvine campuses, and so on. I thank the participants at those presentations and especially Karen Eggleston, Mark Granovetter, Kevin O'Brien, Jean Oi, Leonard Ortolano, Minxin Pei, Scott Rozelle, Andy Walder, and Yingyu Ye. I am especially indebted to my mentors James March and John Meyer, who had strong intellectual influence upon the organizational approach adopted in this book.

I want to especially thank Ai Yun at Central University of Finance and Economics in Beijing and Lian Hong at Sun Yat-sen University in Guangzhou. They are my former students, now colleagues and friends. My research project intersected with their dissertation research, and I have learned a great deal from their research. Some findings reported in this book were first jointly published with them.

My intellectual journey spans several institutions that have provided a great academic environment for my research: Hong Kong University of Science and Technology, Duke University, and Stanford University, as well as a fellowship year at the Stanford Center for Advanced Studies in Behavioral Sciences (2008–2009). Over the years, my fieldwork research has been supported by several funding sources at Stanford: the Asia Pacific Research Center (APARC) in the Freeman Spogli Institute for International Studies, Center for East Asia Studies (CEAS), Presidential Fund for Innovation in International Studies, Hewlett Faculty Fund, China Fund, and UPS Fund. In addition, I am grateful to Nancy Hearst for her superb copyediting assistance. I thank Sara Doskow, my editor at Cambridge University Press, and editorial assistant Jadyn Fauconier-Herry, who guided me through the publishing process.

I am grateful to my wife, Zhaohui Xue, who has supported my intellectual journey, tolerated my long absence from home, and always shared my excitement and curiosity in research. Without her encouragement and persuasion, there would not be the English version of this book. Finally, I thank my mother, Tang Xiulan, who nurtured my intellectual curiosity as I grew up and set the example for me in her life of continuous learning, and to whom I dedicate this book.

Abbreviations

CCP   Chinese Communist Party
CEPB   County Environmental Protection Bureau
COD   chemical oxygen demand
CSM   campaign-style mobilization
ISBC   inverted soft budget constraint
MEP   Ministry of Environmental Protection
MEPB   Municipal Environmental Protection Bureau
PEPB   Provincial Environmental Protection Bureau
PREV   Paved Road to Every Village
SBC   soft budget constraint
SLCP   Sloping Land Conservation Program
SO_2 sulfur dioxide
TVE   township village enterprise

I

Introduction: The Logic of Governance in China

But the one thing communist governments can do is to govern; they do provide effective authority. Their ideology furnishes a basis of legitimacy, and their party organization provides the institutional mechanism for mobilizing support and executing policy.

Samuel Huntington (1968, p. 8)

It was China's unique destination to preserve as a civilization long after other ancient civilizations had perished; and this perseverance involved not fossilization but a series of rebirths.

Philip A. Kuhn (1980, p. 11)

[Technological revolutions] Why Europe and the West, and why not China?

David S. Landes (2006, p. 3)

Contemporary China presents many puzzles for social-science inquiries. On the one hand, as Huntington writes, one is impressed with the commanding role of the Chinese state in governing its diverse regions of uneven development and in engineering rapid economic growth since the 1980s (Brandt, Ma and Rawski 2014, Naughton 1996). On the other hand, contemporary China has witnessed large-scale political turbulence and economic disasters, such as the Great Leap Forward and the Great Famine of 1959–1962, when more than thirty million perished (Dikotter 2010, Yang 2013a), and the political persecution and turmoil of the "Cultural Revolution" that caused great suffering for millions (Su 2011, Walder 2019), to name but a few. In a less dramatic but equally profound manner, during the short seventy-year history of the People's Republic of China, cycles of centralization and decentralization have characterized the relationship between central and local governments, and top-down political campaigns have periodically generated policy twists and turns. At the micro-level, problems of policy implementation, such as selective implementation, deviation, and collusion among local officials, have been rampant and resilient, as demonstrated by the sizable literature on the Chinese bureaucracy (Gobel 2011, Heberer and Schubert 2012, Kung and Chen 2011, O'Brien and Li 1999, Zhou 2010a).

Similar phenomena are manifested under specific circumstances and in specific areas, such as environmental protection (Kostka and Nahm 2017, Rooij 2006, Zhang 2017b, Zhou et al. 2013), economic development, or urbanization processes (Bulman 2016, Lee and Zhang 2013, Oi 1999, Whiting 2000), each with its own particular form and its own rhythm of occurrence. As such, each can be examined in its own right. Indeed, there are separate literatures on these specific issues – central–local government relations, regional development, policy implementation, and so forth.

Yet, the persistence and recurrence of these phenomena raise a larger issue: Are there some common, stable mechanisms and processes that underpin and interconnect such occurrences taking place in different areas? Put another way, are there some larger, fundamental mechanisms and processes that systematically produce and reproduce these phenomena across areas? A further, related question is the following: Is there a broader perspective, or a theoretical framework, that sheds light on the interconnectedness and the underlying logic among these apparently diverse issues and phenomena – in different forms, across different arenas, and at different points in time – such that, so to speak, we can see the forest beyond the trees, and we can uncover the sources by tracing the streams?

These questions motivate the theme of this book: an inquiry into the logic – the institutional logic – of governance in China. By *institutional logic*, I refer to those recurrent, predictable, and often causal relationships based on stable institutional arrangements. Here, the term *governance* refers to those patterned practices in the exercise of authority organized by and around the Chinese state. Sociologist Charles Tilly (1995, p. 1601) describes the mechanisms in political processes as follows: "They consist of recurrent causes which in different circumstances and sequences compound into highly variable but nonetheless explicable effects." This depiction fits well with my view of institutional logic. That is, those diverse, apparently disparate, but recurrent phenomena are in fact manifestations of the same underlying institutional logic. The goal of this book is to uncover those stable institutional arrangements and processes that shape the larger, variable, but recognizable and predictable patterns of behavior in China's governance.

This book reports on my decade-long journey of inquiry into these questions. Between 2004 and 2015, I conducted fieldwork in an agricultural township in northern China. By adopting a microscopic lens, my goal was to gain a deeper understanding of the behavior and interactions among local officials, villagers, and state policies, and to make sense of larger issues about how China is governed. I visited this township several times every year, one week or several weeks at each time, and conducted participatory observations of how local cadres carried out their daily work – implementing top-down official policies, solving local problems, and responding to crises. During this process, I immersed myself in different streams of events: village elections, the provision of public goods, policy implementation, and bureaucratic behavior in everyday work environments.

Over time, my fieldwork led me to broaden my inquiry in two directions: First, the observed patterns of practice at local levels resonated with patterns in China's past, thus taking me on a journey to search for recurrent governance issues and their underlying causes in Chinese history. Second, local responses to top-down state policies directed my attention from micro-events to macro-processes and larger issues about principal–agent problems in the Chinese bureaucracy, tensions between policymaking and policy implementation, and ultimately the institutional logic of governance in China. This book is the result of these interrelated lines of research.

In this introductory chapter, I outline the main theme of this book to highlight the key issues, institutions, mechanisms and their interconnectedness, so as to provide a roadmap on the specific topics covered in the remainder of the book.

Let me first summarize the central theme in this volume (see Figure 1.1). I argue that there exists a fundamental tension in governing China, that is, a tension between the all-encompassing role of the centralized authority on the one hand and effective, local governance on the other. The fundamental tension can be characterized as follows. On the one hand, the centralized authority has a tendency to move decision rights and resources upward toward the center; in so doing, it weakens the capacity of local authorities – local governments or traditional authorities – for problem solving, and hence it undermines effective governance at the local levels. On the other hand, strengthening effective, local governance requires the allocation of

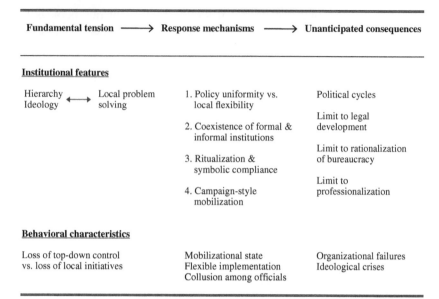

FIGURE I.I The conceptual framework

decision rights and resources downward toward lower levels where there is better information. But in so doing, local authorities have a tendency – or are perceived as having a tendency – to deviate from the center and to cause the loss of control and to undermine the legitimacy of the centralized authority. A fragile equilibrium between the two can be reached only temporarily, will be frequently disrupted, and must be readjusted over time.

Over the course of Chinese history, a set of mechanisms and corresponding institutions have emerged in response to this fundamental tension, inducing and reinforcing distinctive behaviors and practices in the political process, in the evolving authority relationships within the Chinese bureaucracy, and in interactions between the state and society. These mechanisms and institutions have been selectively retooled and reshaped by the Leninist ruling party, the Chinese Communist Party (CCP), since it took power in 1949. This book is about institutional responses in contemporary China to the age-old challenges of governance and their consequences.

I highlight four distinct response mechanisms and the corresponding institutional arrangements: first, a variable-coupling between state policies and local implementation based on stable institutional arrangements. That is, the extent of coupling between the centralized authority and local officials varies over time; sometimes it is tight and rigid under heightened political pressures and at other times it is loose and flexible, allowing the latter to adapt to local circumstances. Second, stable and resilient informal institutions coexist with and complement formal institutions, allowing substantial variations in the Chinese bureaucracy. Third, the political rhetoric and the ritualization of the official ideology play an important role in maintaining symbolic compliance by local officials and making loose-coupling practices tolerable to the centralized authority. Fourth, top-down campaign-style mobilization, often in the form of political campaigns, provides an important political weapon for the central authority to reassert its authority, to redefine the boundaries of local flexibility, and to tighten the variable-coupling between the central and local authorities.

In contemporary China, these stable institutional mechanisms were activated from time to time in the practice of China's governance, helping to maintain a delicate balance and to rebalance between the two sides of the fundamental tension during the course of continuous fluctuations and adjustments. As a result, they induced and reproduced systematic behavioral patterns by those involved in the interactions, which in turn engendered consequences, such as institutional limits to, and stagnation in, the rationalization of bureaucracy and the rule of law, as indicated in the last column of Figure 1.1. These issues will be examined in greater detail in the remainder of this book.

By focusing on these institutional mechanisms, I aim to develop a new analytical framework, together with a set of middle-ranged theoretical models and concepts, to make sense of the stable institutional logic of governance in China. Extensive and in-depth research on China's governance during the past four decades has led to a much deeper understanding of the actual processes and mechanisms at work in China's governance. This book is my effort to provide a major update of our knowledge about how China has been and is being governed based on my decade-long research as well as cumulative evidence in the literature.

The remainder of this introductory chapter is organized as follows. I first explicate the fundamental tension between the centralization of authority and effective, local governance, and the two pillars of governance, that is, the bureaucracy and ideology. I then turn to discuss the four response mechanisms and related institutional arrangements that have characterized the practice of governance in China both historically and today: (1) the variable-coupling between centralized policy making and flexible policy implementation, (2) the complementary roles of formal and informal institutions, (3) the ritualization of the official ideology, and (4) campaign-style mobilization as a political mechanism to regulate the extent of coupling between central and local governments. I then briefly discuss the organizational approach adopted in this study. I end this chapter with a précis of the topics to be covered in this book.

CENTRALIZED AUTHORITY AND LOCAL PROBLEM SOLVING: THE FUNDAMENTAL TENSION

Establishing the Context

All nation-states confront the challenges of competition for survival, and these challenges have been especially acute for the Chinese state, both during its long history as well as today, because of the formidable scale of governing a vast territory and a large population characterized by diverse local cultures and uneven economic development.

Here, the scale of governance refers to both the territorial size and the specific responsibilities assumed by the state. In comparative institutional analyses, scholars often treat nations as the unit of analysis and make broad strokes of comparison without paying careful attention to the scale of governance that is involved across these nation-states. For example, Singapore has a territory and a population roughly only that of a medium-sized Chinese city. The size of South Korea is about that of Jiangsu province in China, but with only two-thirds of the population of the province. Indeed, the territorial size of China today is roughly that of all of Europe, with twice the population and with as diverse cultures and uneven regional development as in Europe (Skinner 1964). In other words, the challenges of governing China are comparable to those of governing all of Europe under one centralized authority.

The scale of governance is also related to the institutional details of governance, that is, *what* is being governed and *how* governance is carried out. Therefore, both the scale of governance and the mode of governance should be considered in tandem. Different modes of governance embody variations in the authority relationships across areas and localities in a society. Contrast the mode of centralization with the mode of federalism in governance. In the former, all localities are under the control of the central authority, which takes on comprehensive responsibility for all localities and over all matters, often through the intermediate and local governments. This means that the central government must respond to problems and pressures that come from all corners and all arenas in a society. In constitutional federalism, in contrast, local governments take responsibility for those issues and problems within their respective jurisdictions, and, as a result, the scale and scope of governance become decentralized accordingly.

Transaction cost economics sheds light on the choices among the various modes of governance. Economist Ronald Coase (1937, 1960) asks: If market mechanisms are efficient in the allocation of resources, why do we observe the presence of formal organizations in a society? Business historian Alfred Chandler (1994), in his celebrated book *Scale and Scope*, argues that the rise of managerial capitalism plays an important role in the throughput – organizational processes – to increase the efficiency and competitiveness in returns to scale and scope. Nevertheless, the other side of the same coin is this: If formal organizations are advantageous for organizing, why have we not observed an increasing scale of organizations that eventually encompasses the entire national economy (Williamson 1975, 1985)? Such a model of a planned economy was indeed attempted in the state-socialist countries of the Soviet Union, Eastern Europe, and China in the twentieth century, and it failed miserably in all these places.

There are distinctive transaction costs of scale and scope associated with formal organizations as well as nation-states. Economists Alesina and Spolaore (2003) examine the size of nations and its implications for economic development, public goods provision, and national security. On the one hand, large countries incur higher costs of national integration amid the diverse interests and cultures within the national boundaries. On the other hand, large countries benefit from the scale of market activities and the fixed costs of public goods provision, such as defense. At the organizational level, McAfee and McMillan (1995) point out that members of organizations have private information due to their specific roles and positions, and they tend to use that information advantage for rent seeking and bargaining. Although "rents . . . are the lubricants that make it possible for a hierarchy to function" (p. 402), there is nevertheless a loss of efficiency. The authors develop a proposition on organizational diseconomies of scale: Along with an increase in scale of governance, the chain of command lengthens, the distribution of private information becomes more dispersed, and problems associated with information asymmetries worsen, leading to a disproportionately increasing loss of efficiency in organizations.

Institutions arise and evolve in response to challenges and crises. The preceding discussion offers a somber reminder that to understand China's institutional foundations and the ways in which it is governed, one needs to keep in mind the kind of challenges that China has faced, and has responded to, from which path-dependent patterns of institutional practice have emerged. The emphasis on the importance of scale in governance directs my focus to the key role of bureaucratic organizations and moves the organizing mechanisms to the central stage of my inquiry.

The Fundamental Tension

There has been, and still is, a fundamental tension in governing China: a tension between the centralization of authority on the one hand and effective, local governance on the other. Here, the *centralization of authority* means that the central authority at the very top – be it the emperor in Chinese history or the ruling CCP in contemporary China – has legitimate, unlimited, and all-encompassing authority in all areas and over all affairs of the society. The centralized authority is embodied in everyday institutional practices: the top-down policy-making processes, the power over resource allocation and personnel management on the basis of the Chinese bureaucracy, and the arbitrary power of the top leaders to intervene at any time, at any level, and in any process. *Effective governance* refers to the problem-solving capacities, such as policy implementation, public goods provision, and conflict resolution, of the *local* authority within its respective jurisdictions.

In contemporary China, the fundamental tension between the two can be depicted as follows: The centralized authority has a tendency to move upward the decision rights and resources, away from those local administrations (e.g., the county and township offices) that have richer and better information, thus weakening their problem-solving capacity at the local levels, and therefore incurring the *loss of initiative* (Qian 1994). Conversely, the strengthening of local-governance capacities implies the expansion of local authority, which often leads to – or is interpreted as – deviations from the center and incurs a *loss of control*, thereby undermining the legitimacy of the central authority and presenting an acute threat to the latter.

The fundamental tension is built into the institutional arrangements. In the contemporary era, the two pillars of the institutional arrangements are the bureaucracy and the ideology.

Organizational Basis of Governance: The Chinese Bureaucracy

Modern states are built on bureaucratic organizations. According to Weber (1978), the bureaucracy is a distinct form of organization, characteristic of a clear delineation of authority in a hierarchical order, whose directives are carried out by rules and procedures. Personnel in the bureaucracy receive professional training and embark on professional careers. Such institutionalized practices increase precision, punctuality, and efficiency to achieve the organizational goals. In contrast to the traditional organizational form, such as the family, kinship, or community, bureaucratic organizations are the central organizing mechanisms in contemporary society. Sociologist James Coleman (1982) observes that, along with the rise of corporate persons in contemporary society, a large amount of public affairs is carried out by bureaucratic organizations that make and implement public policies; deliver social welfare, public safety, and other public goods; and regulate market transactions, contracts, and capital flows. Indeed, modern society has a tendency, in developed as well as developing countries, to gradually transfer political power to bureaucratic organizations (Wilson 1975).

China has been governed by a large, multilayered bureaucratic organization on territorially based prefectural and county institutions – the so-called *junxianzhi* – since the Qin dynasty (221 BC). In formality, Chinese bureaucracy in ancient times shares many similarities with the contemporary Weberian bureaucracy (Li 2008). Nevertheless, it is noteworthy that the former took shape some 2,000 years before Max Weber first identified its modern counterpart in Europe in the early twentieth century, a somber reminder that we should exercise caution in comparing the Chinese bureaucracy to the Weberian bureaucracy. Historically, there have been two kinds of power in the Chinese polity (Kuhn 1990): One is the *bureaucratic power* based on administrative positions, rules, and procedures; the second is the *arbitrary power of the supreme leader(s)*, who can intervene into the bureaucratic processes at any level and at any time. At the core of the centralization of authority in China, the latter always trumps the former. The central authority holds supreme and ultimate power over the bureaucracy in all areas and processes.

This defining characteristic has been greatly strengthened on the basis of the Leninist Communist Party in contemporary China – the extent of its reach, the scope of its coverage, and the scale of its mobilization all dwarf that of other rulers in Chinese history. Power is especially centralized in the areas of resource allocation and personnel management. For example, the central government, through its representatives, holds authority in personnel management, in rule making, and in decision rights for the selection, evaluation, and mobility of officials throughout the entire nation. In terms of resource allocation, the central government has tremendous power to extract, mobilize, and allocate resources. Throughout Chinese history, the bureaucracy has played a pivotal role in governance, implementing top-down policies and integrating diverse regions in the direction of the center, both symbolically and organizationally.

For any ruler, however, the bureaucracy is a double-edged sword. As Weber (1978) observes, a bureaucracy often has a mind of its own and evolves toward its own interests for survival. In the language of contemporary social science, bureaucratic organizations are plagued with agency problems in principal–agent relationships, such as the cost of political influence and negotiation within organizations (Milgrom and Roberts 1988, Wilson 1989).

These problems are especially acute for a large-scale government bureaucracy such as that in China. The challenge of scale is not merely related to physical size but also is related to the scope and content of governance, both of which have expanded significantly since the founding of the People's Republic of China in 1949 to reach all corners of the society. A case in point is the evolution of rural governance in the People's Republic. In the era of the People's Communes from the late 1950s to the late 1970s, the Chinese state assumed control of the planning and procurement of agricultural activities in the rural areas, placing all farming decisions under the planned economy. An elaborate organizational apparatus was developed in the rural areas, from the People's Commune, to the production brigades, and to the production teams, which incurred tremendous organizational, coordination, and incentive costs and led to a stagnation of agricultural productivity. During the post-Mao decollectivization era, since the late 1970s, villagers have been given decision rights over farming and over the sale of their produce. As a result, agricultural productivity soared (Perkins 1988), and, at the same time, the organizational burden of rural governance upon the state was greatly alleviated (Zhou 2006).

The fundamental tension is first and foremost embodied in the process of top-down policy implementation of central–local government relationships. On the one hand, the very nature of the authoritarian state dictates the centralization of policymaking, reinforced through top-down inspections and evaluations of the bureaucratic processes. On the other hand, as the central authority becomes more rigid and inflexible, the extent of the centralization of resources and personnel management becomes greater, and it is less likely that the policies of the central authority will fit the diverse local circumstances, thereby undermining the effectiveness of local governance. In many instances, such centralized institutional arrangements not only incur huge costs that are not sustainable but also cause great disasters, as during the Great Leap Forward and the Cultural Revolution (Yang 1996, Zhou 2009). The vast territory, uneven economic development, and diverse local circumstances all present serious challenges to, and put constraints upon, the will and arbitrary power of the centralized authority.

A second and related aspect of the fundamental tension is the limit of bureaucratic organizations. Formal organizations incur their own transaction costs (Williamson 1975, 1985), including the costs of coordination and the provision of incentives. As the degree of complexity increases in a society, the costs of management and coordination increase exponentially. Organization research has long examined various problems and costs in bureaucratic organizations: Bounded rationality leads to problems in goal setting, organizational processes, and incentive design (Cyert and March 1963, March and Simon 1958); principal–agent problems are manifested in the separation of authority, accountability, and incentives among the agents, such that they cannot take a long-term view of their responsibilities and goals. At the same time, asymmetric information in principal–agent relationships gives the informed party, usually the local officials, an advantage in negotiations, leading to their considerable autonomy in real operations (Jensen and Meckling 1976, Wilson 1989). These issues are present in all kinds of bureaucratic organizations, but they are intensified in the Chinese bureaucracy due to problems in organizational size, managerial capacity, and informal relations, a theme to be elaborated upon in the following chapters.

As a result, the burden of centralization inevitably led to various degrees of loose-coupling between policy making at the center and policy implementation at the local levels in response to the aforementioned fundamental tension between the centralization of authority and effective, local governance.

Official Ideology and Political Education

Facing diverse local conditions and institution-based or organized interests, the Chinese bureaucracy – or any other form of organization – on its own cannot effectively carry out the will of the centralized authority. Other mechanisms are needed to reach out to and integrate different levels and corners of the society. The official ideology provides just such a mechanism.

Historically, Confucian culture long played a role in cultivating deference and obedience to authority (Chen 1992, Huang 1981, Wang 1981 [1948]). Because of the civil-service examination institution (*keju*), many potential officials underwent a "professionalization" process by learning the Chinese classics and acquiring shared knowledge, behavioral norms, and role expectations (Elman 2013, Zhou 2019b). At the societal level, the peasants' everyday lives were infused with cultural expectations of hierarchical relations between father and son and, by analogy, between emperor and subjects (Yan 2006). The limited reach of the Chinese state and the active role of the local gentry class created institutions for "two-track politics" that played a complementary role in diffusing tensions at the local levels and between the state and grassroots society (Fei 1992 [1948]).

Fast forward to the People's Republic of China. As Schurmann (1968) puts it, organization and ideology are the two pillars of the Chinese Communist state. During the early years of the People's Republic, the state temporarily but effectively replaced the role of Confucian culture with Marxist ideology as the unifying mechanism within the ruling party and extended it further as the official ideology to govern China. Contemporary China has undergone various kinds of "political education" campaigns. At times, these activities took place within tightly controlled party organizations or in a specific area; at other times, they took the form of mass mobilization in different corners of the society. Although the areas being affected may have differed and the specific targets may have varied, these top-down political campaigns can be seen as efforts to establish, maintain, and reinforce a shared value system that upholds the centralized authority. The official ideology of the People's Republic has been maintained and renewed through a series of thought reforms, political campaigns, and other types of large-scale mass mobilization (Chen 2013, Yang 2013b, Zhang 2017a).

Nevertheless, both the Chinese bureaucracy and the official ideology encountered serious crises by the end of the Mao era in the late 1970s. Government organizations, under attack by the Red Guards, were paralyzed, and bureaucratic authority was no longer effective in organizing everyday social life; the official ideology also faced a deep crisis in the aftermath of the Cultural Revolution as citizens became disillusioned because of the political violence and economic stagnation. These crises induced the institutional response in the form of the so-called "opening up and reform" policy reorientation that signaled the beginning of the post-Mao era.

INSTITUTIONAL MECHANISMS IN RESPONSE TO THE FUNDAMENTAL TENSION

The tremendous variations across arenas and regions of China, in terms of economic development, resource distribution, and local institutions, pose a formidable challenge to the centralization of authority in governing China. By the very nature of the centralization principle, top-down policymaking is characterized by imposing some uniform directives that do not give due attention to local variations. In other words, the aforementioned fundamental tension is inherent in the centralized political regime in China.

To cope with the pressures and ensuing crises induced by this fundamental tension, there emerged a series of response mechanisms and corresponding institutions in the evolution of the practice of governance in China. I highlight four key institutional mechanisms below, which will be elaborated upon throughout this book.

Variable-Coupling between Centralized Policy Making and Flexible Implementation

The ideal type in the Weberian bureaucracy is a tightly coupled system, in which behaviors are conducted based on rules and procedures; administrative directives are transmitted and implemented in a timely and precise manner; and the links across bureaucratic levels are tight and responsive to ensure efficiency, reliability, and predictability. But students of organizations have identified an alternative mode of organization, the so-called loosely coupled system, in which different parts of the organization have considerable autonomy and whereby they are connected only loosely and occasionally; and they are slow to respond to one another (March and Olsen 1979, Orton and Weick 1990, Weick 1976). While tight-coupling yields high coordination and mobilizational capacities, loose-coupling has an advantage in flexibility and local adaptation. Loose-coupling may take different forms, as between different subunits, between rhetoric and action, between formal and informal authorities, and between behavior across different points in time.

In essence, the patterns of practice as identified by the fragmented authoritarian model (Lieberthal and Lampton 1992) are characteristic of a loosely coupled system, where top-down directives are implemented only loosely and selectively, official rhetoric and behavior are often loosely connected, and considerable autonomy is built into everyday institutional practices. This loose-coupling system serves a dual purpose: It can hold on to the appearance of symbolic compliance in deference to the centralized authority and, at the same time, it can allow flexible, local adaptation and it can alleviate institutional rigidity. Economist Li-an Zhou's "administrative subcontract" model (Zhou 2014, 2017) captures similar patterns of institutional practice, in which the central government puts different kinds of administrative affairs (employment, economic development, public goods provision, etc.) into one package and delegates them to the lower-level governments, and, at the same time, delegates local officials' appointment, evaluation, and management to their immediate supervisory agencies.

In the eyes of the centralized authority, however, loose-coupling has its own costs because it gradually erodes the basis of the centralized authority: If local problems can be successfully addressed in a loosely coupled system, the very legitimacy of the central authority is challenged in these areas. Thus, loose-coupling is often perceived as causing the loss of control and as a threat to the central authority. From time to time, the higher authority tightens up these loosely coupled parts by means of political campaigns – to be discussed below – and produces a highly coupled system. The tightly coupled system incurs the loss of initiative in local problem solving and development. Predictably, over time the tightly coupled system becomes too costly for the central authority, thus triggering a shift back to a loosely coupled system.

In practice, loose-coupling practices are not stable; they vary with the circumstances and with the interactions between the central and local governments. The logic behind the centralization of authority is that the central government (or the supervising agency) has arbitrary power to intervene in the implementation process. The central government may redirect the attention of local officials through formal or informal means, such as campaign-style mobilization, personnel mobility, and sponsored project arrangements, thus disrupting or rearranging priorities on the agenda of lower-level governments. For example, Skinner and Winckler (Skinner and Winckler 1969, Skinner 1985) observe that, between the 1950s and the 1970s, the central government imposed eleven rounds of top-down policy intervention. Zhou Feizhou (2009) finds that, in promoting the Great Leap Forward campaign, Mao Zedong forced local officials to follow his directives through a series of efforts to replace provincial leaders. During the post-Mao era, local officials are still under tremendous pressures to follow all kinds of top-down directives in their routine work (Ouyang 2011, Wu 2007, Zhang 2018, Zhao 2010). The administrative subcontract does not imply a binding contract between the central and local governments, and it cannot provide an effective buffer from top-down arbitrary interventions.

Over time, we observe a perpetual cycle between tight-coupling (centralization) and loose-coupling (decentralization). I characterize the observed patterns as *variable-coupling*, which may take place in different forms between various levels of the hierarchy, between symbolic compliance and behavioral deviations, and over time. At times, it may operate as a loosely coupled system, but at other times there are mechanisms of top-down mobilization and it reverts to a tightly coupled system. Variable-coupling results less from rational planning than from haphazardly responding to pressures and crises generated by the fundamental tension.

Recognition of these observed patterns is the beginning, rather than the end, of my inquiry into the institutional logic of governance in China. Over time, variable-coupling has induced, and become intertwined with and sustained by, a set of distinctive institutional mechanisms, to which I now turn.

Complementarity of Formal and Informal Institutions

Variable-coupling between the Chinese state and the Chinese bureaucracy and within the Chinese bureaucracy is made possible in part by the complementary role of formal and informal institutions in China's governance. Here, the formal institutions reflect the established state apparatus, including the legal and normative apparatuses, for the exercise of power by the central authority. The hierarchical order of the bureaucracy fits this mission well, with the imposition of a top-down authority relationship across levels and localities. But the fundamental tension implies that, in general, a top-down directive that is both specific *and* enforced has serious consequences, for example, in the area of environmental regulation. If the policy directive is specific, the problem inevitably arises that one size does not fit all and enforcement is likely to trigger resistance and crises. If the top-down directive lacks specifics, then it cannot be enforced, thereby providing *de facto* delegation of authority to and flexibility in implementation at local levels.

The Chinese bureaucracy responds to this dilemma by loose-coupling between the formal, administrative directives and informal implementation practices. On the one hand, the stable, formal institutions give the appearance of a tightly coupled system, where policies from the central government are adopted and implemented effectively and satisfactorily.

On the other hand, students of the Chinese bureaucracy have long observed the prevalence of informal social relations in political processes and bureaucratic practices that suggest a loosely coupled system. Walder's (1986) early work on new traditionalism points to a hybrid of Communist ideology and patron–client relationships in the workplace. Shue (1988) highlights the honeycomb structure of segmented, localized cell-like structures that resist intervention from without. Oi's (1995) work shows the importance of patron–client relationships during the reform era. Scholars have called attention to the pervasive, informal relationships in workplaces and social life in China (Bian 2018, 2019, Lin 2001, Yang 1994).

During the last three decades, substantial knowledge has been accumulated on local government behavior. This is the case especially in Chinese-language literature because Chinese scholars have had better access to the inner workings of the bureaucracies through their participation in policy-making and policy implementation at different levels. We can make sense of the salient behavioral characteristics of local governments. For example, scholars note *"biantong"* – flexible adaptation – in policy implementation (Wang, Liu and Sun 1997). These efforts reflect the initiatives by local officials that deviate from the official rhetoric or formal institutions, as semi-formal ways of operation between formal and informal processes, or the informal operation of formal institutions (Sun and Guo 2000, Ying 2001). To a great extent, the effectiveness of local governments in problem solving is reflected in the use of those tactics that are local, social, and informal (Ai 2011, Chen, Zhang and Hu 2015, Gobel 2011, Lee and Zhang 2013, Wang and Wang 2018).

I argue that informal institutions are an indispensable component of the institutions of governance in China. That is, formal institutions of higher authority and informal institutions coexist in a symbiotic relationship, and they are complementary in the sense that the strong, formal rhetoric often goes hand in hand with the equally robust presence of informal institutions that allow flexible, local adaptation. As the policy-making process becomes more centralized, the implementation process has to become more flexible. The logic is straightforward: With a more centralized decision-making process, the gap between its policy targets and local circumstances becomes larger, and hence greater flexibility has to be allowed for local implementation. In his relentless critique of Chinese bureaucratic institutions throughout history, political economist Wang Ya'nan (1981 [1948]) points out a salient characteristic of Chinese rulers' taxation practice: "Stand firmly by the principle, but be flexible in enforcement." This expression reveals the essence of state governance in China: Formal institutions are firm and stable, whereas informal institutions allow enforcement flexibility in implementation.

We can also understand the collusive behavior among local governments. Zhou (2010a) highlights the prevalent phenomenon of collusive behavior among local officials in covering up problems and in falsifying records in response to inspections by the higher authority. Given the diverse economic, historical, and institutional conditions across localities, such behavior can be reinterpreted as an effective, adaptive strategy under the protection of the immediate supervising agencies (Heberer and Schubert 2012). Seen in this light, "collusion" creates local flexibility in implementation, which has strategic implications for understanding the coexistence of a symbolically strong state and effective governance at the local level. On the one hand, we witness a symbolically strong state, where all major decisions have to be made by a centralized authority; on the other hand, collusion at local levels may act as a corrective and countervailing force to the problems that plague the centralized decision-making process.

Be it flexible adaptation or collusion, such behavior implies a challenge to the centralized authority because it gives prominence to those mechanisms outside the realm of the formal institutions, and it undermines the effectiveness of the central authority in its everyday presence and replaces it with local, informal relations. In this sense, effective governance is achieved at the expense of the centralized authority.

Ritualization of the Official Ideology as Symbolic Compliance

No organizational apparatus alone, be it the formal bureaucracy, administrative subcontracting, or flexible adaptation, can govern successfully. The limitations of organizing capacities give importance to the official ideology, which has always, from the early days of Confucian culture to the Communist ideology, played a major role in the integration of the Chinese nation. If local officials are given real authority in governance and flexible implementation, then it is ultimately critical to ensure that they follow the will and intentions of the higher authority in their discretionary behavior.

"Governance by morality" (*daode zhiguo*) was a central pillar of the institutions of governance in Confucian China (Chu 1965, Levenson 1965). This logic has been extended to contemporary China in the form of political education and indoctrination to shape the behavior of local officials (Shambaugh 2007). Throughout the history of the People's Republic, all kinds of political rectification and thought reform campaigns have continually taken place in waves, reflecting the top leaders' tireless efforts to strengthen and to repair the deterioration of the shared values that sustain the centralized authority. During the early days of the Mao era, the Communist Party used ideology effectively to incorporate different social groups in the nation-building project (Schurmann 1968). The role of ideology reached its height during the Cultural Revolution when Mao's little red book was seen everywhere, in every hand and on every occasion, and political-study sessions became routine practice in everyday life.

After the Cultural Revolution when the formal, bureaucratic authorities were attacked and paralyzed, efforts to create a new authoritarianism were greatly weakened (Kipnis 2015). In the era of "opening up and reform," the banal preaching of political doctrines met uncomfortably with the increasing pluralistic values infused in the daily life of individuals, with new forms of horizontal organizations and active informal institutions in everyday life. As a result, the authority has had to increasingly rely on formal, organizational regulations, such as officially dictated time slots in political studies and other formal gatherings, to carry out political education (Shambaugh 2008, Tsai and Dean 2013). These organization-based activities have little relevance to the daily life and behavior of individuals, and they have become rituals in which individuals are required to participate from time to time.

Another source of the ritualization of political participation is the local officials' need to demonstrate their compliance with top-down directives. As noted above, local officials must adopt various strategies, such as collusive behavior in policy implementation, that incur considerable political risks. Therefore, it is critical for their risk management to demonstrate political allegiance to the central authority. As one local official put it, "When the central government issues directives, it is important for us to show a receptive attitude, but it is less important to follow through in implementation . . . . . . we need to take seriously those directives from our immediate supervising authorities." At a countywide meeting of all village cadres, a county party secretary tried to help his local cadres see the significance of these symbolic activities: "Nowadays there are many top-down dictated projects and tasks. You need to make reference to these projects and tasks when you report on your work to your superiors. If you say a great deal about what you have done, but you make no reference to these designated tasks, it is not a good report. To link your work to what the superiors advocate here and now is the key to your report. You have always carried out your daily work the same way, but you need to make connections to those tasks that the top leaders advocate at the moment when you report on your routine work." In so doing, the prevailing, unifying official ideology is transformed into a ritualistic practice in everyday life.

What are the implications of such ritualistic activities for the centralization of authority? Ritualistic practices do not produce shared values, but they do produce synchronized behavior in response to top-down political mobilization. In this sense, such activities are akin to drill practices in military training. Such practices perpetuate and reinforce symbolic compliance with the centralized authority, under whose shadow local flexibility and behavioral deviation can be carried out without being seen as a threat to the central authority.

Moreover, such ritualistic activities not only have symbolic value but also have substantive implications for the exercise of control by the authoritarian state. As individuals follow ritualistic practices, these activities reveal obedience to and acceptance of the authority relationship. In other words, such ritualistic behavior maintains and reinforces awareness and recognition of the central authority in everyday life. These mobilization practices test and re-test the authority's legitimacy and effectiveness in these processes; they discipline and condition the participants' habitual behavior of following marching orders. As a result, when political mobilization takes place, obedient behavior is activated accordingly. To put it simply, these ritualistic activities cultivate shared knowledge in obedience to authority and maintain a ready-state for activation upon political mobilization. In this sense, such rituals and ceremonies in effect are the basis of power (Chwe 2001).

Both the administrative-subcontracting institution and the prevalence of informal institutions have eased tensions in the centralization of authority, while mechanisms of ritualistic political education have sustained symbolic compliance with the centralized authority. But for the top leaders, such response mechanisms have their own perils. When the central authority acquiesces to or encourages flexible adaptation by local governments, the latter may interpret state policies based on their own interests and their ensuing behavior may lead to further deviations from the intentions of the top leaders and become challenges to the central authority. Therefore, a key concern in the institutional arrangements is that the central authority must retain ultimate, arbitrary power to intervene, with the capacity to rein in local deviations and to redraw the boundaries of what is appropriate behavior by the local officials. A corresponding mechanism of governance – the mechanism of campaign-style mobilization – arose in the political processes in China, as we shall discuss below.

Campaign-Style Mobilization

If there is variable-coupling between the central and local governments, what are the mechanisms that lead to the shifts across the different modes of governance, that is, the shifts between tight-coupling and loose-coupling? There are many organizational mechanisms at work, such as attention allocation, bureaucratic milestones, and other practices that regulate the rhythms of coupling between the two. But one key mechanism, campaign-style mobilization, especially in the form of political campaigns, deserves special attention.

Campaign-style mobilization has been a key mechanism in China's governance in different arenas, from political rectification to economic development (Feng 2011). From an organizational perspective, its central feature is the political mechanism used in mobilization, such as the criteria for evaluation and the manner in which penalties and rewards are administered. Campaign-style mobilization often reveals arbitrariness and non-routine characteristics that create high uncertainty and place political pressures upon officials. This is in sharp contrast to routine mechanisms based on rules and procedures in bureaucratic administration, which cultivate stable, predictable, rule-following behavior. Political and routine mechanisms are often in tension with each other, as the exercise of the former disrupts the operation of the latter, and the effectiveness of the latter imposes constraints upon the former.

Political campaigns serve as an important mechanism to respond to the tensions between the centralization of authority and local adaptation. As discussed earlier, potential crises may result from such tensions, and they are manifested in the form of deviations by local officials from top-down policies. A key characteristic of campaign-style mobilization is that it temporarily disrupts the routine bureaucratic processes, replacing them with political mobilization processes, in order to overcome bureaucratic inertia and to achieve the effects of redrawing or reinforcing the boundaries of appropriate behavior. Political campaigns are used as a mobilizational mechanism in various areas, from the anti-corruption campaigns and the poverty alleviation campaigns to those targeting financial order or safety in production process, to achieve the effect of activating the officials' attention, shaking up bureaucratic inertia, and swiftly transmitting top-down intentions and signals to different levels of the bureaucracy. In so doing, the agenda and pace of the bureaucracy are shifted into different gears and directions.

To put this in perspective, I argue that flexibility and deviation in policy implementation are often the same phenomenon, but with different labels. That is, the same behavior may be interpreted in diagonally different ways. Once local flexibility reaches above a certain threshold, it will touch the nerves of the central authority and become a threat. However, it is commonly observed that, in the process of political campaigns, both the choice of targets and the penalties imposed are often selected arbitrarily, with the aim of deterring others rather than seeking to resolve these so-called bureaucratic problems. The purpose of these political campaigns is not to eliminate such flexibility; rather, it is an instrument deployed to redefine the boundaries of flexibility through such campaigns so as to maintain over time dynamic equilibria in the interplay between the state and local authorities.

The prevalence of campaign-style mobilization has created a distinctive feature of the Chinese bureaucracy: the delegation of arbitrary power at each administrative level so as to facilitate the mobilization of resources across areas and levels in the bureaucracy. Above all, the basis of political campaigns is distinct from that of the bureaucracy or the rule of law, with the former predicated on top-down arbitrary power. That is, the higher authority can change the rules of the game at any time without being questioned or challenged. But to do so requires that the higher authority has ultimate and arbitrary authority as well as the capacity for political mobilization, all these rely on the particular mode of domination and legitimation bases, which will be discussed in Chapter 2.

The Dynamics of Governance: Shifts between Tight-Coupling and Loose-Coupling

Thus far, I have discussed a series of mechanisms that respond to the fundamental tension between the centralization of authority and effective, local governance. How are these response mechanisms interrelated? In terms of a variable-coupling process, we can look into the interactions among these mechanisms during the cycle of tight-coupling (centralization) and loose-coupling (decentralization) of decision rights between central and local governments over time, which may be depicted as follows.

The starting point of our observation is the routine stage of state governance, that is, the phase of loose-coupling between uniformity in policy making and flexibility in implementation. At this phase, the central government directs the activities of local governments through general policy guidelines, but it leaves a large proportion of the decision rights to the local level or leaves considerable room for flexible implementation, often in the mode of "administrative subcontracting." Local governments symbolically follow the top-down directives to gain legitimacy and at the same time they take initiatives in problem solving within their respective jurisdictions for effective governance. Therefore, their behavior is often informal, or collusive with their immediate supervisory offices, in order to meet, through flexible implementation, the targets set by the top-down directives. As a result, diverse tendencies emerge from policy implementation across localities, with increasing variations in experimentation and flexibility.

Such local variations threaten the authority of the central government, leading to a "loss of control" on the part of the central government over the local governments, thereby triggering a corrective response by using top-down political campaigns. The central government uses political campaigns to recentralize decision rights (personnel, resources, etc.) upward, reinforces norms and behaviors on the basis of political lines, and generates a tightly coupled system. To reorient the bureaucratic machinery, the central government imposes intensive political pressures to promote its new policies as well as harsh penalties to overcome bureaucratic inertia and resistance. All of these efforts tilt the balance of power in the direction of centralization.

Tight-coupling has its own costs. Because of the arbitrariness of political campaigns, these corrective measures often generate unintended consequences, such as immobilism among local officials (Harding 1981, Li and Bachman 1989). That is, because of the arbitrariness of political campaigns in terms of their targets of suppression, local officials are extremely cautious and risk-averse, incurring costs in the "loss of initiatives." Although this phase stabilizes and reinforces the authority of the central government, it reduces the problem-solving capacity of the local governments. Moreover, a high level of political mobilization may be effective in the short run but costly to sustain over an extended period. Under the high pressures of political campaigns, local officials are limited in terms of flexible implementation and local problem solving. Over time, local problems and tensions accumulate, and crises loom large.

Facing the tensions and crises resulting from the loss of initiatives at the local levels, the central government has to readjust and reorient its policies toward decentralizing decision rights and resources to the lower levels in

order to strengthen the problem-solving capacity of the local governments. During this process, a series of new reforms emerge, such as
regional experimentation, special policies, directed reforms, and so forth.
In order to eliminate the political pressures from the last round of centralization, a different kind of political campaign, in the opposite direction,
takes place to encourage local innovation and experimentation in different directions, such as that occurred during the early stage of the post-
Mao era in the late 1970s. The balance of power was then tilted toward
loose-coupling. As a result, the relationship between the central and local
governments returned to the phase of loose-coupling between uniformity
in policy making and flexibility in implementation, thereby completing
the entire political cycle.

Not surprisingly, the response mechanisms outlined above – variable-
coupling among central–local relationships, complementary roles of
formal and informal institutions, political rituals, and political campaigns – are interrelated. The organizational basis of ritualistic activities
is linked to political campaigns by incorporating individuals into routine
compliance, thereby preparing a ready-state for political mobilization. At
the same time, the interactive processes between formal and informal
institutions provide a mechanism for shifting between tight-coupling
(formal compliance) and loose-coupling (behavioral deviations). All these
mechanisms contribute to the variable-coupling between the central and
local governments, either alleviating or exacerbating the fundamental
tension depending on the occasion, thereby contributing to the cyclic
dynamics.

CONSEQUENCES OF THE FUNDAMENTAL TENSION AND THE INSTITUTIONAL RESPONSE

Over the course of history, institutional mechanisms arose in response to
challenges and crises created by the fundamental tension. With hindsight,
we can see a clearer picture: The resulting institutional arrangements
produced significant and often unanticipated consequences that shaped
the future trajectory of change in governance.

In particular, the institutional arrangements imposed a limit on the
extent of institutional transformation in terms of the rule of law and in
the rationalization of the Chinese bureaucracy. During the post-Mao era,
establishment of the rule of law has been a proclaimed goal of the Chinese
state, but this frustratingly slow process has stagnated and in recent years
has been reversed. Formally, the legal system has been in place for a long

time, with an ever-elaborate body of rules and regulations, but substantial progress in terms of the independence of judicial authority has been stalled from the outset. Rationalization of the bureaucracy, in the form of rule-following and universalism in public goods provision, and the development of professionalism are key mechanisms of legal–rational governance to regulate and coordinate behavior in different areas, such as health, education, or journalism, to name a few. Unfortunately, development in these areas has been severely limited and has experienced many setbacks (Chan and Gao 2018, Munro 2012). Why?

I argue that these constraints are the logical consequences of the fundamental tension that exists between the centralization of authority and effective governance and the existing institutions that respond to this tension. These new institutions, such as the rule of law, the rationalization of bureaucracy, and professionalization, undermine the current political configuration of the centralized authority. First, these new mechanisms of governance induce autonomy and multi-centered governance that present a threat to the centralization of authority and to the higher authority's arbitrary power to intervene at the local levels. Second, the rule of law and bureaucratic rationalization impose standardized practices across different regions and areas, thereby greatly reducing the flexible-implementation capacity of the local governments, hence lowering the effectiveness of governance at the lower levels. These new institutions are at odds with the existing institutions of governance in China today and the vested interests associated with such institutions. I will revisit this set of issues in the concluding chapter of this book.

OUTLINE OF THE BOOK

I begin this chapter with quotes by Samuel Huntington, Philip Kuhn, and David Landes, who all call attention to the striking characteristics of Chinese governance and its body politic. As outlined in the preceding discussion, there is a fundamental tension in China's governance, and a set of institutional mechanisms and practices, with distinctive Chinese characteristics, have arisen and evolved in response. It is against this larger background that the institutional logic of governance in contemporary China has encountered fundamental challenges because of its increasing incompatibility with the diverse, pluralistic society, both domestic and international.

The chapters in the remainder of this book further elaborate and extend the key arguments developed in this chapter, and report on the empirical evidence from my fieldwork, to substantiate and inform these arguments.

The Organizational Approach

In this book, I examine the institutional logic of governance in China from an organizational perspective. The Chinese state is, above all, based on bureaucratic organizations, involving institutional arrangements of authority relationships, resource allocations, and personnel management. These stable institutional arrangements produce predictable behavior by government officials and by those with whom the government officials interact.

Why an organizational approach? A focus on the institutional logic of governance gives prominence to the role of the Chinese bureaucracy. Issues such as information flows, incentive designs, and decision-making and implementation processes in the Chinese bureaucracy can be examined using the analytical tools of organizational research. Moreover, organizational research is an interdisciplinary field intersecting with active research activities by sociologists, economists, political scientists, and psychologists. It provides a broad lens to examine the research issues outlined in this chapter, as described below.

First, one characteristic of formal organizations is their stable structures, authority relationships, and incentive apparatuses such that organizational behavior is stable and predictable. A key task of a bureaucracy is to design appropriate incentives to align the interests of its members with the organizational goals. The presence of bounded rationality and interest compatibility of multiple principals (Cyert and March 1963, Simon 1947) implies that an inappropriate incentive design often induces unintended organizational behavior that deviates from organizational goals. In light of organizational analysis, we can ask a series of questions: How are authority relationships established and at work among government offices and across levels in the Chinese government? How are residual control rights in policymaking and implementation allocated across different levels of the bureaucracy?

Second, informal institutions are an important dimension to understand organizations and organizational behavior (Blau 1963, Crozier 1964, Gouldner 1964, Merton 1968a). Social relations are not only derived from formal authority relationships, but they also stem from informal, social interactions or from other arenas, such as alumni relations, hometown origins, or kinship ties. In the Chinese context, shared norms and expectations at different levels of the bureaucracy, or within bureaus and offices, provide stable institutional bases for collusive behavior to resist top-down intervention. It is in the context of the informal institutions that we see most clearly the operation and limits of the formal institutions.

Finally, organizational analysis directs our attention to the relationship between organizations and their social environments. All organizations must exchange resources with their environments to survive. In this sense, formal organizations are embedded in the larger societal and cultural environment (Stinchcombe 1965). At the macro-level, the mode of domination must be based on a certain type of legitimacy, the specific form of which shapes the distinctive institutional arrangements.

The theoretical ideas and analytical tools outlined above help me interpret and make sense of the empirical observations; conversely, the fieldwork observations help me to develop and clarify the theoretical concepts and to sharpen their analytical strength. I weave these ideas and concepts into my analyses of China's governance practices and intertwine these analyses with the narrative of the observed governance practice.

A Roadmap

There are two main themes in the Chinese configuration of governance: One is the relationship between the central and local governments; the other is the relationship between state and society. This book is organized around these two themes. The first two parts of the book focus on the first theme, that is, the relationship between the central authority and local governments. The third part focuses on the patterns of interaction between state and society, as mediated by government bureaucracies, and the implications for understanding the logic of governance in China. The chapters are organized as follows.

The three chapters in Part I – "The Logic of Governance: Institutions and Mechanisms" – further elaborate and extend the key institutional arrangements and the response mechanisms outlined in this introductory chapter. Chapter 2, "The Chinese State and the Chinese Bureaucracy: A Weberian Lens," develops a Weberian interpretation of the distinct mode of domination in China and the location of the Chinese bureaucracy therein. I discuss the relationship between the Chinese bureaucracy and the top authorities and the resultant organizational forms and behavioral characteristics as the stable organizational basis of state governance. Chapter 3, "Modes of Governance in the Chinese Bureaucracy," proposes a "control rights" theory on the allocation of different decision rights across hierarchical levels, which gives rise to different modes of governance in the Chinese bureaucracy. Chapter 4, "Campaign-style Mobilization," contrasts this distinct mechanism of mobilization with that of bureaucratic routines to highlight a key characteristic of governance practices in China. I pay particular attention to the distinctive institutional and organizational arrangements upon which campaign-style mobilization is based.

Part II – "The Logic of Governance and Government Behavior" – focuses on the processes and behaviors of local governments to make sense of the micro-processes and mechanisms in policy implementation and problem solving at the local levels. In this series of studies, I focus on the commonly observed organizational phenomena and government behavior, and examine their connections to and implications for the institutional logic of governance in China.

Chapter 5, "Bureaucratic Bargaining in the Chinese Bureaucracy," adopts a game-theoretic framework to sort out the different patterns of bargaining practice between supervisory and subordinate agencies at different stages of the policy-implementation process. This conceptual framework is then applied and illustrated in a case study of policy implementation in the environmental protection area. Chapter 6, "Collusion Among Local Governments," examines the institutional foundation of collusive behavior and related informal institutions among local officials in response to higher-level directives and inspections, especially their implications for understanding variable-coupling between the state and local officials. Chapter 7, "Muddling Through in the Chinese Bureaucracy," applies the behavioral model in organization research to interpret the multiple logics that affect local officials in their daily work environments and their strategies and behaviors in response to multi-faceted environments and pressures. Chapter 8, "Inverted Soft-Budget Constraints," focuses on the downward extraction of resources by local governments, and analyzes this organizational phenomenon in light of changes in the institutional environment, the incentive design, and the bureaucratic response to transitions from the planned economy to the post-Mao era of decentralization.

Part III – "The Logic of Governance and Chinese Society" – turns to the second theme, that is, the relationship between state and society. Chapter 9, "The Road to Collective Debt," offers a case study of a road pavement project in two villages to understand the interaction between the bureaucratic logic of policy implementation and the rural logic of resource mobilization in local problem solving. Chapter 10 looks into the evolution of village elections in a township over the course of more than a decade to make sense of the multiple institutional logics in the interaction and evolution of state policies, local bureaucracies, and rural society, placing governance and institutional change in a broader context.

Chapter 11 examines a distinctive phenomenon in China, that is, collective action on the basis of unorganized interests and the underlying state-society relationship. These studies reveal that Chinese society stubbornly insists on a role in the governance process, in its own way and its own manner, thereby contributing to the dynamics of governance in China.

In the concluding chapter (Chapter 12), I summarize the main findings from the studies reported in this book and discuss the emerging patterns of interactions among state power, the Chinese bureaucracy, and social groups, and the challenges in China's future transformation.

PART I

THE LOGIC OF GOVERNANCE: INSTITUTIONS AND MECHANISMS

2

The Chinese State and the Chinese Bureaucracy:
A Weberian Lens

Only bureaucracy has established the foundation for the administration of a rational law.

Max Weber (1946, p. 216)

Cadres are a decisive factor, once the political line is determined . . .

Mao Zedong (1991, p. 526)

To examine the logic of governance in China, we begin with an inquiry into the relationship between the Chinese state and the Chinese bureaucracy. As outlined in Chapter 1, governance in China has been characterized by the encompassing role of the central authority, whose power is uninhibited and whose reach is unlimited over its people and its vast territory. In Chinese history, the Chinese bureaucracy provided the organizational basis for the state to exercise its power. In the People's Republic of China since 1949, the Chinese bureaucracy has undergone considerable transformation to become the organizational weapon of the party-state and to become entrenched in all corners of the society. For ordinary citizens today, the Chinese bureaucracy *is* the Chinese state.

Yet, if we take a closer look at the political rhetoric and practice in China, we can discern some blurred yet recognizable boundaries as well as distinct dynamics between state power at the center and the bureaucratic apparatus as the instrument of policy implementation. Indeed, the relationship between the Chinese state and the bureaucracy has been at the very center of the tensions in governing China. The mechanisms of governance, as outlined in Chapter 1, have arisen in response to the tensions between the state and the bureaucracy, in that the centralized authority has to rely on the bureaucracy to govern and to pursue its policy goals and, at the same time, it has to guard against deviations from its prescribed course of action by the bureaucracy. Tensions between the emperor's power and bureaucratic power, often cloaked in the rhetoric of struggles between "centralism and localism" or between "unity and separatism," have been a recurring theme throughout Chinese history.

In this chapter, I draw on Weber's comparative, institutional perspective to examine the mode of domination and its basis of legitimacy in Chinese society, and the location of the Chinese bureaucracy therein. My premise is that the Chinese bureaucracy as a distinct organizational form has its own logic and internal mechanisms of action, but the bureaucracy does not stand alone; rather, it is embedded in a specific institutional context, evolving over time and exhibiting strong path dependency. The institutional analysis in this chapter calls attention to fundamental issues about the basis of legitimacy for the exercise of power that results in the particular kind of authority relationships and the distinct mode of domination in China's governance structure. Only after these fundamental premises are clarified can we make sense of the principal–agent relationships and the bureaucratic behavior observed in everyday work environments.

This chapter is organized as follows: I first introduce Weber's concepts and arguments on the bases of legitimacy, types of authority, and modes of domination, and the relationships among them. I will then use the Weberian lens to discuss and locate the role of the Chinese bureaucracy in the mode of domination found in imperial China. Following this, I extend this line of argument to examine the role and location of the Chinese bureaucracy and the resultant bureaucratic behavior in the mode of domination in contemporary China.

BASES OF LEGITIMACY, TYPES OF AUTHORITY, AND MODES OF DOMINATION: WEBER'S THEORY

Contemporary social-science research emphasizes the importance of the Weberian bureaucracy for governance and economic development (Acemoglu and Robinson 2012, Evans and Rauch 1999, Fukuyama 2004). China scholars have, either explicitly or implicitly, examined the Chinese bureaucracy in light of the Weberian bureaucracy and have discussed similarities and differences between the two (Lieberthal and Lampton 1992, Rothstein 2015, Shirk 1993, Walder 1986, Whyte 1973). On the surface, the Chinese bureaucracy appears to be markedly similar to the Weberian bureaucracy, with its clearly delineated hierarchical structures, elaborate rules and written documents, and professional training and careers therein. There is a tendency in the social-science literature to treat the Chinese state as a kind of gigantic bureaucracy, with the central authority as the headquarters at the top and the local governments governed by the same bureaucratic logic as the subsidiaries at different levels (Lieberthal and Lampton 1992). In this picture, issues such as principal–agent relationships, information asymmetry, the provision of incentives, discretion and delegation, among others, become important analytical issues (Landry 2008, Oi 1992, Qian, Roland and Xu 1999, Qian, Roland and Xu 2006, Walder 1995a, Xu 2011, Zhou 2007).

From a Weberian perspective, however, the Chinese bureaucracy differs from the Weberian bureaucracy in significant ways. Weber was the first to point out these striking contrasts in his historical comparative study, *Religion in China*. According to Weber (1968: p.152), the Chinese bureaucracy "was grafted upon a base which, in the West, had been essentially overcome with the development of the ancient polis." It is worth noting that the Chinese bureaucracy has grown to its full-fledged form at least since the Han dynasty (206 BC–220 AD) (Li 2008; Yan 1996), about 2,000 years before Max Weber introduced his concept of bureaucracy to contemporary social sciences. In contrast to the Weberian bureaucracy that arose in response to international competition and to the capitalist economies that demanded promptness, precision, and efficiency, the Chinese bureaucracy took a different path, in tandem with the historical evolution of the Chinese state (Zhao 2015) and, in modern times, it was molded in the organizational form of the Leninist political party (Schurmann 1968).

This is not to suggest that Weber's analysis of bureaucracy is irrelevant to our understanding of the Chinese bureaucracy. On the contrary, a Weberian comparative perspective provides insights into the key features of the Chinese bureaucracy, especially regarding the locus of the bureaucracy in the mode of domination and the implications thereof for the relationship between the bureaucracy and the Chinese state, whether the monarchies in history or the party-state in contemporary China.

Weber's Comparative, Institutional Framework

Central to his comparative institutional analyses is Weber's insight that distinct bases of legitimacy engender different types of authority, which give rise to different modes of domination. "[T]he continued exercise of every domination ... always has the strongest need of self-justification through appealing to the principles of its legitimation" (Weber 1978, p. 954). In Weber's view, no power can be built for long on the basis of coercion or violence; instead, power must be exercised on the basis of legitimate claims. Different bases of legitimacy – traditional, charismatic, and legal–rational – have shaped the corresponding types of authority: traditional, charismatic, and legal–rational.

Weber further extends these three types of authority to develop three corresponding modes of domination: patrimonial, charismatic, and legal–bureaucratic. According to Weber, "*domination* will thus mean the situation in which the manifested will (*command*) of the ruler or rulers is meant to influence the conduct of one or more others (the *ruled*) and actually does influence it in such a way that their conduct to a socially relevant degree occurs as if the ruled had made the content of the command the maxim of their conduct for its very own sake. Looked upon from the other hand, this situation will be called *obedience*" (p. 946). At the macro-level, then, modes of domination refer to the foundations of the authority relationships between the ruler and the ruled in a society. Weber's notion of the mode of domination fits nicely with the theme of this book, namely, the institutional logic of governance in a society.

Bases of legitimacy, types of authority, and modes of domination are three interrelated pillars in Weber's comparative institutional analysis (see Figure 2.1). Weber's contribution is not only his delineation of these ideal types but also his development of a set of analytical concepts and theoretical ideas to shed light on the relationships among the three, together with the corresponding institutional arrangements and societal contexts.

From a Weberian perspective, the different modes of domination are founded on their respective bases of legitimation. A powerholder must be

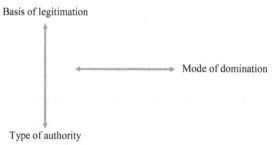

FIGURE 2.1. Three pillars in Weber's comparative, institutional analysis

able to justify his/her exercise of power on specific claims of legitimacy and to make use of the corresponding institutions to substantiate this set of legitimacy claims. The patrimonial mode of domination, for instance, is built on the basis of respect and acceptance of the traditional authority. As a result, norms, ceremonies and rituals, and related cultural practices based on ancestral lineages are central institutions that sustain the legitimate claims for the patrimonial mode of domination. Charismatic authority is built on the followers' belief in the charisma of the leaders; hence, those institutions that can ensure direct interactions between the charismatic leader and his followers as well as the manifestation of "miracles" by the charismatic leader are central. In the legal–bureaucratic mode of domination, there is a close relationship between formal procedures and legal–rational authority; as a result, key institutions that arise are organized around due process, procedural rationality, and equal rights before the law (Hamilton 1984).

In Weber's framework, the three pillars are interrelated such that a particular mode of domination rests on a specific type of authority associated with the corresponding type of legitimacy basis, which may be incompatible with the other bases of legitimacy. For example, traditional authority, once it is placed in a legal–rational environment (i.e., one person, one vote), will experience tensions such that its basis of legitimacy becomes problematic and its mode of domination will no longer be stable. By the same logic, a legal–rational authority can hardly be built on the legitimacy claim of traditions or the legitimacy claim of the leader's charismatic appeal.

Of course, as Weber recognizes, domination in the real world may take the main characteristics of one ideal type but be mixed with characteristics of other ideal types. In other words, real authority may have mixed bases of legitimacy, with one dominant basis of legitimacy but also intertwined with other types inherited from the historical legacies or some transformation of the ideal types, such as the routinization of charisma in office, which combines both the legal and the charismatic (Eisenstadt 1968). For example, it is often observed that the key institutions of legal–rational authority, such as popularly elected officials or the Supreme Court in the USA, acquire some characteristics of charisma. These multiple elements of legitimacy, though drawn from different sources, may coexist as they alternately become salient on different occasions and at different points in time. But on some occasions, these elements may become so incompatible that they create tensions and conflicts, inadvertently exposing their distinct relationships and the nature of domination in a society.

Locus of the Bureaucracy in the Mode of Domination

For my research interests, it is instructive to take a closer look at Weber's view of bureaucracy in the different modes of domination. Weber develops his theory of bureaucracy at two levels. At the level of organizational analysis, he focuses on the bureaucracy as an organizational form and on its key characteristics, such as the hierarchical structure, rule-based conduct, and professional education and career (Weber 1946). At this level Weber's attention is on the structural features and the internal mechanisms of formal organizations. At the second level, that of comparative, institutional analysis, Weber treats the bureaucracy as the basis of a particular mode of domination and he contrasts it with other modes of domination to highlight different types of societal organizations, authority relationships, and bases of legitimacy. These two levels are interrelated: Authority relationships within the bureaucracy are built on a particular basis of legitimacy claims, which in turn provides the institutional basis for the mode of legal–rational domination in a society.

In this light, the Weberian bureaucracy is itself a set of institutional arrangements characteristic of distinct and interrelated internal structures, types of authority, and bases of legitimacy. In contrast to traditional forms of organization, such as family, kinship, villages, or small craft shops, bureaucracies – formal organizations – are characterized by clear lines of authority, hierarchical structures, communications through written documents, and rule-based conduct. Officials have their own professional training and careers, and their mobility and promotion are governed by formal rules and procedures (Weber 1978, pp. 956–1005).

Weber (1978) further argues that the basis of legitimacy of a bureaucracy is such that "The 'validity' of a power of command may be expressed, first, in a system of consciously made *rational* rules (which may be either agreed upon or imposed from above), which meet with obedience as generally binding norms whenever such obedience is claimed by him whom the rule designates ... [H]is power is legitimate insofar as it corresponds with the norm" (p. 954). That is, the bureaucratic authority is consistent and compatible with the legal–rational mode of domination, with an impersonal orientation and rule-based behavior as the core features.

The following is Weber's insight into the bureaucracy as the basis of democratic governance:

Bureaucracy inevitably accompanies modern *mass democracy*, in contrast to the democratic self-government of small homogeneous units. This results from its characteristic principle: the abstract regularity of the exercise of authority, which is a result of the demand for "equality before the law" in the personal and functional sense – hence, of the horror of "privilege," and the principled rejection of doing business "from case to case." (p. 983)

In other words, democracy and bureaucracy share similar bases of legitimacy in terms of rule following and equality before the law. In contrast, traditional authority rests on the hierarchical order and cultural legacies and charismatic authority is based on the leaders' charisma, both of which are at odds with legitimacy that is based on "abstract rules."

To Weber's discussion we may add the proposition that the Weberian bureaucracy is hardly compatible with the mode of domination based on charismatic authority. Central to charismatic authority is the appeal of the charisma of the leader to the followers, where a close, intensive relationship between the leader and the follower is crucial. The Weberian bureaucracy, with its emphasis on rules and rule-following behavior, is part of the larger process of rationalization and disenchantment in history, which undermines the very basis of legitimacy for charismatic leaders.

Yet, if we stop here, we would have missed the key insight in Weber's comparative, historical analysis, for, at the same time, Weber points out: "Patrimonial officialdom may develop bureaucratic features with increasing functional division and rationalization, especially with the expansion of clerical tasks and of authority levels through which official business must pass" (p. 1028). That is, the bureaucracy may also rest on an entirely different basis of legitimacy, serving as an efficient instrument of control in other modes of domination. Compare the bureaucracy in the legal–rational mode of domination with that in the patrimonial mode. In the former, bureaucratic power stems from procedures and rules that are accepted and seen as legitimate. But in the latter,

submission to the ruler, and his position vis-à-vis the subjects is merely the external aspect of this relation. Even when the political official is not a personal household dependent, the ruler demands unconditional administrative compliance. For the patrimonial official's loyalty to his office is not an impersonal commitment ... to impersonal tasks which define its extent and its content, it is rather a servant's loyalty based on the strictly personal relationship to the ruler and on an obligation of fealty which in principle permits no limitation. (pp. 1030–31)

Empirically, this observation is not surprising, as we find similar bureaucratic forms of government and officials in all kinds of societies with different modes of domination. But their actual operations and characteristics are shaped by the particular mode of domination in which they are situated.

It is in this larger, institutional context that we examine the locus of the Chinese bureaucracy in the specific mode of domination in history and in contemporary China.

BUREAUCRATIC MONARCHY: A DETOUR ON THE HISTORICAL PATH IN CHINA

The Chinese bureaucracy is one of the historical legacies of Chinese civilization, providing the stable organizational basis of the Chinese empire and having an impact that is still felt keenly today.

In Weber's historical comparative framework, the Chinese bureaucracy was used to illustrate different modes of domination in history. In Weber's view, the traditional Chinese bureaucracy was firmly located in the patrimonial mode of dominance, as described by Weber in the following: "We shall speak of a *patrimonial state* when the prince organizes his political power over extrapatrimonial areas and political subjects – which is not discretionary and not enforced by physical coercion – just like the exercise of his patriarchal power" (Weber 1978, p. 1013). Different from the Weberian bureaucracy, the Chinese bureaucracy was not built on legal–rational legitimacy but rather it was under the arbitrary power of the emperor. Historian Philip Kuhn echoes this characterization, calling it a bureaucratic monarchy (Kuhn 1990). In this mode of domination, the emperor's power and bureaucratic power coexist for governance, but imperial power is the highest power, and the bureaucracy serves as an instrument for governance.

The Weberian approach helps us to decipher the inner logic of the bureaucratic monarchy. First, the emperor's power and bureaucratic power have their distinctive bases of legitimacy. The emperor's power is exclusive and unlimited, and, as such, it does not tolerate other competing sources of power. That is, the monarchic power rested on the ultimate power of the emperor, which was above and beyond all institutions and laws (Zhu 2006). The emperor's power was built on a mixture of both traditional authority and charismatic authority, from royal ancestries and as the son of heaven. These legitimate claims were sustained and reinforced in cultural institutions as well as in the way of everyday life, such as the Confucian classics, the civil service-examination institutions, bureaucratic offices, emperor–bureaucrat relationships, and ancestral worship and ceremonies. To the people, the imperial power became a natural order (Chen 1992, Isamu and Zhang 2010 [1991], Jin and Liu 2011).

In contrast to the basis of legitimacy for the emperor's power, bureaucrats acquired their legitimacy from a top-down process, embodied in an upward accountability system. That is, the basis of legitimacy for the Chinese bureaucracy was fundamentally different from that for the Weberian bureaucracy. On appearance, many characteristics of the Chinese bureaucracy show marked similarities with the Weberian bureaucracy, such as merit-based recruitment, a hierarchical order, and elaborate rules and procedures, and so forth. But in the bureaucratic monarchy, the bureaucracy was not independent nor were the bureaucrats rule-following; rather, they were subordinate to the imperial power. Moreover, as Weber's description of the patrimonial domination suggests, officials in the Chinese bureaucracy had a personal dependence upon the emperor. We can discern these characteristics through a series of institutional arrangements (Chu 1962): (1) The selection, promotion, mobility, and demotion of officials were ultimately in the hands of the imperial power; (2) all officials exercised their authority as the agent of and in the name of the emperor; (3) although there existed an elaborate set of rules and regulations, the emperor had arbitrary and ultimate power to intervene at every step. In other words, the emperor's power was above and beyond the bureaucratic rules and procedures.

Second, in this mode of domination, the emperor's power and bureaucratic power were interrelated but at the same time there were tensions. As Levenson (1965) writes: "From their very beginnings the traditional Chinese bureaucratic and monarchical institutions had existed in a state of mutual and ambivalent attraction-repulsion" (Vol. 2, p. 10). This relationship originated from the political culture of Confucianism, in which governance by morality treated the emperor as the embodiment of morality and, as such, the emperor's behavior was constrained by moral preaching. The charismatic authority and the traditional authority elevated the status of the emperor's power, upon which bureaucratic power acquired legitimacy. At the same time, it was the behavior of the officials that made it possible to exercise imperial rule, to extract resources, and to demonstrate the emperor's moral leadership. The emperor's power had to be exercised through the bureaucrats, and tensions were built into the organizational apparatus interlocking the two. On the one hand, bureaucratic power was based on a top-down process of delegation; on the other hand, the bureaucracy had its own internal mechanisms and routines that tended to buffer external interventions. In this sense, the emperor's power met with resistance from the entire bureaucracy (Huang 1981). As Levenson puts it, it is in this tension that the bureaucratic monarchy gained its vitality.

These tensions were also reflected in the pervasiveness of informal authority that undermined the emperor's power. Informal authority refers to the alternative sources of power outside of the formal structure, derived from interpersonal relations and behavior. Informal relations were pervasive in the traditional Chinese bureaucracy (Zhou 2019a). A striking characteristic of the Chinese bureaucracy is the irony of elaborate, formal rules on recruitment, mobility, evaluation, and promotion on the one hand, and pervasive social networks on the other.

We can trace two sources of the prevalence of informal social ties. First, this was the unavoidable product of the bureaucratic monarchy, where the bureaucracy could never reach the extent of rationalization and move its authority on the basis of legal–rational legitimacy, as in the Weberian bureaucracy. Doing so would imply a weakening or a denying of the emperor's arbitrary power. This would not be acceptable to the emperor, nor could the bureaucrats find a legitimate basis for making such a claim. Furthermore, to ensure the effectiveness of the arbitrary power of the emperor, officials at each level of the bureaucracy had to possess similar arbitrary power in order to implement the top-down decrees. In other words, without such arbitrary power at each level of the bureaucracy, officials would not be able to pursue the will of the emperor and disrupt the routines of the bureaucratic machine.

Once the bureaucracy is not founded on formal procedures, it opens the door to informal rules and social relations, for several reasons. First, the upward accountability system produced high uncertainty for the bureaucrats. As is well known, outcomes of managerial efforts are difficult to evaluate because such work is highly contingent on a large number of factors. The real authority of evaluation was in the hands of their immediate supervisors who had better information and knowledge of the circumstances. Therefore, informal relations among subordinates and supervisors became critical for bureaucratic career advancement. Second, top-down pressures in implementation often induced collusive behavior among the lower-level bureaucrats for self-protection (Zhou 2011). As a result, patron–client relationships were historically pervasive in the Chinese bureaucracy and often became a great threat to the emperor's power.

Thus far, I have discussed Weber's arguments on types of authority, bases of legitimacy, and modes of domination, and their relevance to understanding the mode of dominance in the bureaucratic monarchy in Chinese history, and the location of the Chinese bureaucracy and the tensions between the emperor and the bureaucrats therein. The institutional tensions in this mode of domination imply that the relationship between the two was critical and subtle. When the emperor's power was imposing, the bureaucrats were forced to be submissive, but this was not a stable equilibrium. When the emperor's power became weak, eroded by the fundamental tension or in the face of crises, the bureaucracy rebounded and regained its vitality. Political and institutional changes were often made through these arduous readjustments of the state-bureaucracy relationship. The contemporary Chinese bureaucracy is the outcome of this long historical evolution.

FROM BUREAUCRATIC MONARCHY TO BUREAUCRATIC PARTY-STATE: CONTINUITY AND CHANGE IN CONTEMPORARY CHINA

As we turn to contemporary China after 1949, it may appear that it is no longer relevant to dwell on the contrast between the emperor's power and bureaucratic power. On the contrary, however, I submit that in contemporary China the basic political architecture and the coexistence of the two powers – the arbitrary power of the rulers, now in the form of the party-state and its top leaders, and the bureaucratic power of officials – remain largely the same. In fact, the top leaders of the CCP have made tremendous efforts to maintain such a distinction. In official CCP documents, for example, the former is typically referred to the impersonal "the party and the state," whereas the latter is referred to as the humanly "officials at different levels of the bureaucracy" ("cadres at different levels" or "local cadres"). While the official rhetoric has upheld the "greatness, glory, and invincibility" of the CCP, critiques and rectification of bureaucratic problems have been a recurrent theme in the political process. The repeated attacks by Mao Zedong on the bureaucracy, through waves of political campaigns that climaxed in the Cultural Revolution, indicate that there have been persistent tensions between those at the top of the party-state and those officials who exercise bureaucratic power.

To make sense of the role of the Chinese bureaucracy in the People's Republic, let us ask the following two questions from the Weberian lens: (1) What is the mode of domination in the People's Republic? (2) What is the location of the Chinese bureaucracy in this larger institutional structure? Just like any other power holder, the CCP, as the ruling party, needs to justify its power on some legitimate basis. By looking into its basis of legitimacy, we find clues to the mode of domination in the party-state, the corresponding institutional arrangements, and the role of the bureaucracy in this configuration.

Starting from Weber's three ideal types of authority, I argue that the legitimacy of the contemporary Chinese state rests on a mixture of legal–rational legitimacy in form but charismatic authority in practice, giving rise to what I call a *mode of party-state domination*. The intertwining of legal–rational legitimacy with charismatic authority is often present in contemporary societies (Eisenstadt 1968, Shils 1975). In China, this mix has not been ironed out smoothly; rather, the legal–rational basis has been weak and tentative, whereas the charismatic authority has been forceful and relentless, refusing to be contained within the bounds of the former. Such tensions have existed from the inception of the People's Republic in 1949, sometimes appearing as undercurrents of political tension and sometimes in open and violent confrontations, such as those that occurred during the Cultural Revolution. Let us take a closer look at the key characteristics of the mode of domination in contemporary China.

Before the mid-twentieth century when the CCP took power, China underwent several waves of political and social movements after the collapse of the Qing Empire, namely, the 1911 Xinhai Revolution, the New Culture Movement, and the Communist revolution. Through these political movements, both the traditional authority and the charismatic authority associated with imperial rule were fundamentally shaken, and the legitimacy of the loyal ancestry totally collapsed. Under attack by the Communist revolution, the Confucian-based traditional authority could no longer provide a legitimate basis for governance. Worldwide, the legal–rational authority became the indisputable legitimate form of the modern state in the twentieth century (Finer 1997). The People's Republic chose the legal–rational form almost by default, as reflected in the formality of electoral rules and procedures and in the representative institutions such as National People's Congress.

However, the party-state after 1949 is far from a legal–rational authority. That is, in the actual process of governance, the ruling party has not built its legitimacy on the basis of a legal–rational authority. Rather, it has exerted tremendous energy and effort to build its legitimacy largely on the basis of charismatic authority.

As Weber (1978) discusses, at the core of the charismatic authority is the leader whose extraordinary character gains recognition and acceptance by his followers. The charismatic leader demonstrates his qualities and legitimacy through "miracles" and performance. The CCP and Mao Zedong made great efforts to establish Mao's charismatic leadership position during the Yan'an era (Gao 2000). The unexpected, impressive victory over the Nationalist Party in the 1940s showed inklings of such miracles (Chen

1998). The early success of the People's Republic on other fronts then considerably strengthened the charismatic authority of the top leaders.

The distinctive characteristics of the Chinese Communist revolution and of the CCP facilitated the rise of a charismatic authority. A charismatic authority requires recognition and acceptance by its followers, a characteristic that also fits the CCP's style of governance. The so-called "mass line" has long been a salient practice in CCP history. After 1949, Mao strengthened this relationship by repeated mass mobilizations in different areas (Feng 2011), such as the Great Leap Forward in the economic arena, the anti-rightist campaign in the political arena, and so forth.

A charismatic authority has an inherent instability problem of leadership succession, and it may undergo a process of routinization, such that the personal character of the leader is transferred to the stable organizational apparatus, which then acquires sacredness and permanence (Weber 1978). After 1949, the ruling CCP underwent such a process, with elaborate political propaganda, indoctrination, and political rhetoric of the self-proclaimed representative of the working class, with its great, glorious, and invincible character, and Mao Zedong became the symbol of this charismatic authority. The routinization of charisma in the ruling party was weaved into a series of institutional arrangements, such as the dominance of party organs over the administrative apparatus; the red-expert personnel selection criteria; and the dual process of routine-based operations and campaign-based mobilization on the basis of the party apparatus (see Chapter 4). After the routinization of charisma, as Weber (1978, p. 1121) observes:

When the tide that lifted a charismatically led group out of everyday life flows back into the channels of workaday routines, at least the "pure" form of charismatic domination will wane and turn into an "institution"; it is then either mechanized, as it were, or imperceptibly displaced by other structures, or fused with them in the most diverse forms, so that it becomes a mere component of a concrete historical structure. In this case it is often transformed beyond recognition, and identifiable only on an analytical level.

As a result, a mix of charismatic authority in substance and legal–rational authority in form emerged as a distinct mode of party-state domination in the People's Republic.

With regime change and the new organizational form of a Leninist party, the relationship between the state and the bureaucracy acquired new characteristics.

First, domination of the state over the bureaucracy was greatly strengthened. As often noted, in the traditional bureaucratic monarchy scholar-officials played a dual role of exercising bureaucratic power and practicing Confucian doctrine, and hence their behavior was constrained by both the bureaucratic authority and the Confucian morality and expectations, which in turn constrained the emperor's power, as reflected in a series of institutional practices, such as official positions for criticism (*yanguan*), court debates (*tingyi*), and the emperor's declaration of self-critiques (*zuijizhao*).

After 1949, the mode of domination abandoned the traditional authority and the associated political culture; the institutional constraints on the top leaders were also thrown out of the window. In the formal institutions, the top leaders adopted the organizational form of a Leninist political party, characteristics of charismatic authority, and tightened discipline, with much stronger constraints and control over the bureaucracy. Take the personnel system as an example. In traditional China, scholar-officials could easily move between their official positions and their roles as scholars (Yan 1996). But in the contemporary bureaucracy, officials are placed in bureaucratic positions and on hierarchical ladders, and their entire careers are confined to the internal, closed bureaucratic system, with almost no available exit option. In other words, the dependency relationship between the bureaucrats and the state is much stronger than it was in traditional China.

Second, along with the routinization of charisma in the party-state, the Chinese bureaucracy has greatly expanded, reaching all corners of society. The charismatic authority is not built in a vacuum; rather, it must rest on the central value system of the society, accepted and respected by its followers. As Eisenstadt (1968) points out: "The search for meaning, consistency, and order is not always something extraordinary, something which exists only in extreme disruptive situations or among pathological personalities, but also in all stable social situations even if it is necessarily focused within some specific parts of the social structure and of an individual's life space" (p. xxvi). The new basis of legitimacy in contemporary China must constantly strengthen ties between the state and its followers through different kinds of activities in order to reinforce the consciousness of the followers' obedience to the charismatic authority. This is an important departure from the bureaucratic monarchy in history, when the reach of the state to society was limited (Huang 1974, Kuhn 2002, Skinner and Baker 1977). In traditional China, the relationship between the state and society relied heavily on the traditional authority and on the role of the Confucian values that were infused in everyday life (Fei 1992[1948]). The charisma of the emperor was embodied in complicated ceremonies and rituals. But in the People's Republic, the close relationship between the state and the people has been the basis of legitimacy for the charismatic leadership, hence the basis of the legitimacy for the party-state.

The bureaucracy provides strong support for this legitimacy claim in two ways. First, it is done by a monopoly over all channels of expression and by the official ideology. The charismatic authority is based on the followers' conviction about the superiority of the top leaders. It is not difficult to understand that any challenge to the charismatic leaders is likely to undermine their basis of legitimacy. A monopoly over expression is essential to safeguard the charismatic authority. Since 1949, the party-state, through the organizational weapon of the bureaucracy, has reached to and eventually monopolized all areas related to ideological control: education, media, the press, and so forth. These institutional arrangements are a logical extension of the mode of party-state domination based on charismatic authority.

Second, the party-state put individuals from all walks of life into the web of organizations under the bureaucracy, thereby establishing a stable organizational link between the masses and the charismatic leader. Here, organizational discipline serves as an important means to ensure bureaucratic practices. As Weber (1978) points out, discipline is an effective means for the charismatic leaders to secure the blind obedience of subjects. In the People's Republic, this organizational form has reached a historically unprecedented extent: All aspects of the society have been organized, from urban to rural, from work to family life. Imposition of the official ideology and the organizational society reinforce each other. The party line has offices and officials who specialize in propaganda and political education to draw the masses into the process of political indoctrination through a variety of political activities: political study sessions, performance appraisals, and political campaigns. In contrast to the traditional values that were diffused through everyday life and rituals, in contemporary China political education is directly imposed by the force of the bureaucratic organizations.

Charismatic leaders must demonstrate their superior ability to convince their followers. In contemporary China, this is reflected in state efforts to develop the economy and to provide public goods (Zhao 2001). Here again, the Chinese bureaucracy provides the vehicle to organize the masses in pursuit of the top leaders' policy goals (Feng 2011). The central role of the bureaucracy, with its tremendous mobilizational capacity, is manifested in all the political and economic campaigns, such as the nationalization of enterprises in the urban areas, the agricultural collect-ivization of the rural areas, the Great Leap Forward campaign, and so forth. Simply put, the Leninist political party, with its tight organizational structure and discipline, has provided a solid organizational foundation for the mode of party-state domination in the People's Republic.

CHARACTERISTICS OF THE BUREAUCRACY IN THE PARTY-STATE MODE OF DOMINATION

Drawing on the Weberian perspective, I make a conceptual distinction between the Chinese state and the Chinese bureaucracy. The former refers to the collective top leaders in the party-state today or the imperial monarchy in history, and the latter refers to those bureaucrats who are subordinate to the former.

This conceptual distinction is important, for it directs our attention to identify the distinctive basis of the legitimacy of the Chinese state and of the bureaucracy, and the relationship between the two. In the patrimonial mode of domination in Chinese history, the legitimacy of the monarchy rested on the patrimonial lineage as well as on the charisma of the "son of heaven" (Brandt, Ma and Rawski 2014, Schwartz 1985). Significant changes took place after the collapse of the Qing dynasty in the early twentieth century. In short, contemporary China is governed by a mode of party-state domination with a mixed basis of legal–rational and charis-matic authority, the former being echoed in institutions such as the People's Congress and other forms of representative institutions, and the latter through the "routinization of charisma" in the ruling Chinese Communist Party and its top leaders.

In both modes of domination, both today and historically, the Chinese bureaucracy's basis of legitimacy has remained the same: It acquires its authority from the delegation of power from the Chinese state; hence, it can only exercise its power on behalf of the state, and it is subject to the arbitrary power of the state. This basis of legitimacy dictates that the bureaucracy is no more than a political instrument of the party-state, or its "organizational weapon," as Selznick (1952) aptly puts it.

This distinction leads us to revisit the two types of power and their relationships in this distinct mode of domination, that is, the arbitrary power of the Chinese state and bureaucratic power based on positions and organizational routines. The role of the Chinese bureaucracy in the Chinese mode of party-state domination has not fundamentally changed today as compared with its counterpart under the imperial monarchy: It has served, and still continues to serve, as the tool of domination for the Chinese state, and the relationship between the emperor, or today the top leaders, and the bureaucrats to a great extent depends on institutionalized personal dependency and loyalty.

Despite the fact that power has changed hands and the party-state has replaced the monarchy, the shift from the mode of domination in the bureaucratic monarchy to that of the party-state has not altered the fundamental authority relationships. Not surprisingly, the dependency relationship between the emperor and his servants continues in a similar manner in the relationship between the top leaders of the party-state and the bureaucrats in contemporary China.

Nevertheless, bureaucratic organizations also have their own mechanisms and their own minds. The hierarchical structure, the system of written communications, professional careers, and formal and informal authorities, all unavoidably shape the thinking and behavior of those officials who work in this bureaucratic environment. As the organization expands and becomes more complex, the power configuration, incentive design, and structural arrangements are all amplified and become more prominent (Crozier 1964, Merton 1968a, Wilson 1989). On the one hand, the Chinese bureaucracy today shows many similarities and parallels to its counterpart in history, as dictated by the mode of domination; on the other hand, the mode of party-state domination promotes new characteristics of the Chinese bureaucracy. I outline these key features as follows.

First, the monopoly of power is replicated across different levels of the hierarchy. The charismatic authority relies on officials at different levels of the hierarchy to transmit and implement its directives and instructions. One important consequence is that in this process of policy implementation, the same kind of arbitrary power associated with the charismatic leadership has to be delegated to those at each level of the hierarchy. In other words, the logic of arbitrary power for the emperor has to be extended to the top officials at each level such that they can exercise the same power on behalf of the charismatic leader. As a result, the upward accountability of the Chinese bureaucracy exhibits a tremendous organizational capacity. The high efficiency in the top-down implementation process is accompanied by weak capacity in the transmittal of information from the bottom-up. The same organization may be charged with both top-down implementation and bottom-up feedback tasks, but these two tasks will produce tensions that reduce the efficiency and organizational capacities of the former. This is consistent with the logic of charismatic authority that does not derive from the delegation of power from the bottom-up. Rather, the masses are merely followers, who readily accept the charismatic authority.

Second, in actuality upward accountability rests on accountability to the next immediate authority. In the charismatic authority mode of domination, officials derive their authority from a top-down delegation of power. As noted above, the immediate leaders at each level of the hierarchy hold arbitrary power to evaluate the performance of subordinate officials and they hold decision-making power for promotion. With the lengthening of the chain of command, the information costs for performance evaluation, incentive administration, reliability of indicators, and diversity of circumstances inevitably lead to the delegation of decision-making power, including personnel decisions, to the lower levels. Even in those situations where the immediate authority does not have decision-making power for the subordinates' promotions, she may affect their everyday work environment through task assignments, rotations, or other means. The upward accountability system becomes accountability to the next immediate authority, encouraging segmented, closed local networks based on locality or work units.

Third, organizational rules are situated in an awkward position in this picture. In the bureaucratic monarchy, the emperor struggled to impose rules to regulate the officials' behavior and at the same time to avoid becoming trapped in a web of rules. Rules are the enemy of the charismatic authority. First, the charismatic authority rests on the superiority of the leader and the respect and conviction of the followers. The relationship between the leader and the followers tends to be direct, non-routine interactions beyond conventional rules. Bureaucratic institutions tend to be rule-following and procedure-oriented and, as a result, they often impose constraints on the charismatic leaders and become barriers between the charismatic leader and his followers. Second, to a great extent a rule-following bureaucracy imposes constraints on the arbitrary power of the charismatic leaders, thereby transferring power from the leader to the bureaucrats.

Because of this inherent tension, charismatic leaders cannot tolerate bureaucratic constraints, and from time to time they disrupt the routines and inertia of the bureaucratic institutions in order to exercise their arbitrary power. Critiques of bureaucratism, factionalism, and departmentalism appear frequently in the writings of Mao Zedong (Whyte 1973, 1980). Political campaigns were launched from time to time to disrupt the rules and processes in the bureaucracy.

As formal rules and procedures are unstable, informal institutions become prevalent. In the Chinese bureaucracy, social relations become salient in part in response to the tensions in the nature of the charismatic authority. On the one hand, the dependency relationship and environmental uncertainties prompt officials to make great efforts to cultivate informal relations for career advancement and for self-protection. On the other hand, such informal relations also serve as a means to implement policies and to diffuse top-down pressures because getting things done often requires the use of informal relations to mobilize resources and to solve problems. Flexible adaptation (*biantong*) becomes a common practice in the policy-implementation process (Tian and Zhao 2008, Wang, Liu and Sun 1997), and such flexible adaptation is often at odds with the formal institutions, thus requiring collusion among local officials (Zhou 2010a). The interactions among the formal processes, informal relations, articulation of interests, and factional alliances all facilitate and reinforce the diffusion and entrenchment of informal institutions within and without the bureaucracy. Such apparently abnormal behavior is in fact rooted and reinforced in the mode of domination and the authority relationships therein.

Fourth, there is a dilemma in the interactions among the charismatic leaders, the bureaucrats, and the masses. In the charismatic authority, the relationship between the leader and the followers acquires particular significance because the followers' acceptance and conviction provide a basis for the legitimacy of the charismatic authority, and this relationship must be reinforced through miracles by the leaders and through responses by the followers. In other words, there must be close interactions between the leaders and the followers. In China, the party-state is directly involved in organizing as well as in imposing discipline upon the followers. The bureaucracy becomes a double-edged sword in this relationship: On the one hand, it helps establish a stable basis for this relationship; on the other hand, bureaucratic operations lead to rules and procedures that regulate the coupling between the leader and the followers, with the tendency to distance the two and to replace the charismatic authority with hierarchical links.

During the nation-building process in contemporary China, the leaders of the ruling party attempted to address these tensions. One practice that developed was to separate the impersonal party from the bureaucrats in action, portraying the former with charismatic sacredness and distancing the charismatic leader from those problems arising in the actual processes. In his critique of bureaucratic problems, Mao Zedong made a conscious distinction between the party and those bureaucratic problems that he argued deviate from the party line, and he activated waves of political rectification to combat them (Mao 1977a, pp. 36, 401). These tactics may have alleviated the tensions in the short run, but they were by no means solutions to these tensions. As bureaucratic practices were present everywhere and all the time, bureaucratic problems were also widespread, casting doubt about the charismatic leaders, weakening the followers' convictions, and undermining the basis of legitimacy.

Another tactic with which Mao experimented was to make use of the bureaucracy and the mass movement as two interrelated and mutually countervailing forces. On the one hand, the bureaucracy developed techniques and skills to mobilize the masses to participate in all kinds of top-down political campaigns; on the other hand, the masses were mobilized to tame the bureaucracy. In many instances, mass mobilization took place in tightly controlled organizational processes. As a result, mass mobilization entered the arena of formal governance in contemporary China, for instance by inviting workers to become involved in party rectification or during the Cultural Revolution, and so forth. But this strategy has its own perils. The bureaucratic logic and the mass mobilization logic are not always compatible, and it is difficult to maintain a stable equilibrium between the two. In reality, the mass movement often disrupted routine organizational processes, or the latter led to the silence of the former. A mass movement organized by the bureaucratic process can hardly address bureaucratic problems, but once a mass movement can no longer be controlled by the bureaucracy, it becomes difficult to tame, even by Mao (Walder 2009, Wang 1995).

In short, it was difficult to find an equilibrium for the tensions among the masses, the bureaucracy, and the charismatic leaders within the mode of party-state domination. As time went on, the dwindling of mass enthusiasm led to a decline in charismatic authority; the bureaucracy was weakened due to the disruption of its routines; the enthusiasm of the masses wore off as the charisma of the leaders was no longer effective. The three interacted with one another and became increasingly disconnected, leading, toward the end of the Mao era, to a legitimacy crisis.

During the post-Mao years, the charismatic authority faced challenges on multiple fronts and experienced even deeper crises. As China opened up to the world and entered the global community, economic and social developments were constantly being evaluated through a comparative lens, and it was difficult to maintain the basis of legitimacy for the charismatic mode of domination. The basis of charismatic authority

– acceptance by and conviction of the followers toward the leaders – could hardly be continued. More importantly, along with the diverse developments in Chinese society, both the organizational apparatus and the official ideology – the two pillars of the centralization of authority – were greatly weakened in the post-Mao era. Before the Xi Jinping era of the mid-2010s, post-Mao leaders made considerable efforts in search of a new basis of legitimacy, from term limits for party and government officials to the proclaimed goal toward the rule of law. All these signaled an attempt at shifting from a mode of domination based on charismatic authority to a mode of domination based on legal–rational authority.

In recent years, it has become clear that the vested interests, existing institutions, as well as the ideology, fought forcefully to repair the existing institutions, and many such efforts were manifested in the form of a strengthening of the charismatic authority, such as the tightening of control over propaganda, ideology, and political education. The great economic development of the past four decades, as well as the impressive improvements in living standards, were all portrayed as giving testimony to the achievements of the charismatic party-state, thereby renewing efforts by the top leaders to justify and maintain their charismatic authority.

SUMMARY

Drawing on the Weberian argument on the bases of legitimacy, types of authority, and different modes of domination, this chapter examines the mode of party-state domination in contemporary China, and the place of the Chinese bureaucracy in this larger picture and its relationship to the party-state.

There has been a significant transition in the mode of domination, from the bureaucratic monarchy in history to the mode of party-state domination that is characterized by a mix of legal–rational authority in form but charismatic authority in substance. But the role of the bureaucracy has not undergone a substantive transformation, nor has its relationship as a subordinate to the charismatic authority and its basis of legitimacy by top-down delegation been altered. Nevertheless, the bureaucracy as a particular organizational form has its own structures and processes as well as its own behavioral attributes, which are often in tension with the state. It is the interdependence and mutual constraints between the state and the bureaucracy that has shaped the logic of governance in contemporary China.

The preceding discussion leads us to a recognition that the Weberian bureaucracy and the Chinese bureaucracy, with 2,000 years separating their inceptions, experienced two strikingly different historical paths of evolution. Consequently, they each play distinctive roles in the legal–rational mode of domination and in patrimonial or party-state domination, as the quotes by Weber and Mao Zedong at the beginning of this chapter make clear.

The Weberian lens highlights two inherent tensions within the Chinese bureaucracy and between the Chinese bureaucracy and the Chinese state: First, there is a tension between the arbitrary power of the state and the routine-based power of the bureaucracy. Second, there is a tension between the formal rules and rule-based behavior on the one hand and personal dependence and loyalty, and the consequent informal institutions, on the other. Both tensions point to the limits of the rationalization of the Chinese bureaucracy. That is, there has been a strong resistance, built into the institutional arrangements, to the enforcement of formal rules for all and to the principle of equality before the law, which is the very essence of the Weberian bureaucracy. These tensions and the ensuing organizational responses are themes that run through the following chapters of this book.

3

Modes of Governance in the Chinese Bureaucracy:
A Control Rights Theory

In Chapter 2, I situate the role of the Chinese bureaucracy in the larger institutional context of patrimonial and party-state domination, whereby bureaucratic power acquires legitimation from, and is subordinate to, the arbitrary power of the emperor or the ruling party. However, the authority relationship is neither static nor rigid; rather, it is realized through a process of constant readjustment. In this chapter, I take a closer look at the internal processes and develop a middle-ranged theory on the allocation of control rights across hierarchical levels and the resultant distinct modes of governance in the Chinese bureaucracy. The proposed theoretical model is intended to shed light on a defining characteristic of the institutional mechanisms in China's governance, namely, the variable coupling across hierarchical levels and across central and local governments.

As a motivation for the proposed theory, let me begin with the following observation. Considerable progress has been made in the study of the Chinese bureaucracy, especially regarding the micro-behavior of street-level bureaucrats in local governments or in specific areas (e.g., environmental protection). Yet, what emerges from these studies are multiple, contradictory images of the Chinese bureaucracy. Let us consider a recurrent theme in this literature – tensions between policymaking and policy implementation. Some studies document in vivid detail how local governments, in the process of implementing state policies, often impose even higher goals and stronger measures upon subordinate officials, adopt various strategies, legitimate or illegitimate, and exercise their power to ensure that policy targets are met (Deng and O'Brien 2013, Rong 1998, Wang and Wang 2009). Expressions such as "pressure-centered government" (*yalixing tizhi*) and "downward acceleration of implementation pressures" (*cengceng jiama*) have entered the lexicon in the literature on the Chinese bureaucracy. Other research shows the extensive efforts by local bureaucrats to cope with these pressures through strategies of selective attention, evasion, distortion, sabotage, and collusion (Chung 2016, Gobel 2011, O'Brien and Li 1999, Schubert and Ahlers 2012). Even the same bureaucracy may exhibit these contradictory behavioral tendencies when working on the same task (Zhou and Ai 2010).

There are also diverse, even conflicting, findings in similar bureaucratic settings. Take for example, principal–agent relationships in the Chinese bureaucracy. Central to this line of argument is a recognition of information asymmetry and incongruence of goals between the principal and the agent, which call for appropriate incentive provisions so as to motivate the agent to take appropriate action (Jensen and Meckling 1976). Some studies show effective organizational designs to address principal–agent relationships and incentive provisions (Oi 1992, 1999, Walder 1995a, Whiting 2000), and cadre management (Heberer and Trapple 2013, Pang, Keng and Zhong 2018), as well as impressive implementation (Ahlers and Schubert 2015, Edin 2003, Gobel 2011). Others uncover serious problems in incentive provision, coordination, and political manipulation (Eaton and Kostka 2014, Sun 2015, Zang 2017). In some cases, incentive provision plays a minor role in the face of multiple policy goals (Zhou et al. 2013).

How do we reconcile these disparate and contradictory images and behavioral patterns in the Chinese bureaucracy? These contradictory images, I submit, result from the fact that principal–agent relationships and the ensuing agency problems vary with different modes of governance in the Chinese bureaucracy. We need to move down to the concrete, analytical level to first specify the kind of game being played before we can meaningfully analyze the rules of the game and the specific principal–agent relationships that are involved.

This is the goal of this chapter. I propose a theoretical model to take a fresh look at authority relationships and modes of governance in the Chinese bureaucracy. The proposed theory aims to explicate different modes of governance in the Chinese bureaucracy, the variable-coupling across hierarchical levels, and the ensuing principal–agent relationships and their behavioral implications. I draw on recent ideas in the economics of incomplete contracts, to conceptualize authority relationships in organizations as a function of the allocation of control rights among the principal, the supervisor, and the agent. By analyzing the allocation of control rights across levels of the bureaucracy, the theory provides a unified theoretical framework, together with a set of analytical concepts and empirical implications, to shed light on a wide range of interrelated bureaucratic phenomena, rather than treating them as disparate, individual cases.

This chapter is organized in two parts: First, I develop a theoretical model based on the allocation of control rights in organizations, which provides a unified theory to account for the different modes of governance in the Chinese bureaucracy. Second, I apply the proposed model to analyze and make sense of bureaucratic practices in the area of environmental protection over a five-year-plan period.

A THEORY ON THE ALLOCATION OF CONTROL RIGHTS AND MODES OF GOVERNANCE

In developing a theoretical model on authority relationships in the Chinese bureaucracy, I will focus on the allocation of control rights among the principal, the supervisor, and the agent. I take three steps to introduce and elaborate the proposed model. First, I set up the organizational context to situate the research issues for analysis. Second, I draw on the economic theory of incomplete contracts to introduce key ideas on property rights, control rights, and authority relationships in organizations. Third, I then extend this line of argument to develop a unified model to account for variations in the allocation of control rights and the resultant modes of governance in the Chinese bureaucracy.

The Organizational Setting

Authority relationships in an organization refer to the legitimate power in command and responsibility associated with hierarchical positions, which are central to the design of organizational processes and practices. The term "mode of governance" refers to the specific way in which an authority relationship is specified. In an organizational setting, principal–agent relationships and ensuing agency problems are mostly associated with the formal, authority relationships.

Let us consider a three-level bureaucracy involving a principal, a supervisor, and an agent (see Figure 3.1). The labels for these three levels reflect the conventional images of the authority relationship in a hierarchy. In this model, the principal has ultimate authority in policymaking and in organization design, such as incentive provisions and performance evaluations, among others. The agent is responsible for following administrative fiats and for implementing top-down policies. The principal

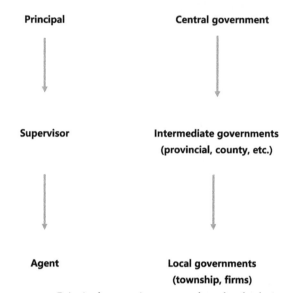

FIGURE 3.1. Principal–supervisor–agent three-level relationships

assigns certain aspects of his authority to the supervisor, whose primary responsibility is to supervise the agent's implementation of the directives established by the principal. In a concrete setting of the Chinese bureaucracy, in this model one may consider the central government as a principal, the provincial government as a supervisor, and the municipal (or prefectural) government as an agent.

Even in this simple organizational setup, a variety of issues emerge in different organizational designs. For example, in a strictly hierarchical structure, the intermediate government (e.g., the provincial government) plays a "supervisory" role to ensure the implementation of state policies at lower levels. But, as we know, the intermediate government may also play a different role in another area (i.e., urban management) and may act as a principal in establishing its own goals. These roles may also vary on different occasions and over time. For example, environmental regulation was largely delegated to the local level in early years before the 2010s, but there has been a trend to recentralize it toward the center in later years (Kostka and Nahm 2017). As a result, the role of the principal, supervisor, and agent varies with the specific relationships specified in an organizational setting.

In summary, while principal–agent problems are pervasive and ever-present in all organizations, the particular forms of manifestation vary with the specific relationship between the principal and the agent as well as with the distribution of information and the organizational design. This recognition invites further investigation into the ways in which principal–agent relationships are specified in concrete organizational settings and the ensuing behavioral consequences. My analyses below primarily focus on issues related to principal–supervisor relationships in a three-level bureaucracy model.

From Incomplete Contracts, Property Rights, to Control Rights

Starting from the premise that it is not feasible to sign complete contracts that specify all contingencies between firms or within a firm (e.g., between the employer and the employee), the economic theory of incomplete contracts (Grossman and Hart 1986, Hart and Moore 1988, Hart 1995) focuses on issues related to the allocation of property rights among economic actors. This line of argument is predicated on the premise that when contracts are incomplete and not all uses of an asset can be specified in advance, any contract negotiated in advance must leave some discretion over the use of the assets to the "owner" who has the residual rights of control over the assets. In this conceptualization, a firm is a collection of assets over which the owner has residual rights of control. Different allocations of the control rights give rise to different incentives and powers to the various involved parties.

In the context of industrial organizations, this incomplete contract framework leads to a focus on the allocation of property rights and on the boundaries of the firm; that is, under what conditions one should integrate an asset or an activity within the organization or leave it to market transactions. This question is crystalized in the strategic choice of different modes of organizations (i.e., firms or markets) in economic analysis. Consider two alternative forms of governance: an employment relationship versus subcontracting, a favorite contrast used in economic analysis. In the case of an employment relationship, the principal retains firm control over both decision making and implementation through the hierarchical structure. That is, the higher authority retains all the control rights for the organization of production, incentive design, and performance evaluation, among others. In the "subcontracting" mode, however, in a particular area (e.g., economic growth) or over a particular policy goal (e.g., the quota in pollution reduction), the principal may subcontract the tasks to an outside subcontractor (or to the supervisor), with specific, contractual stipulations about the targets to be met or services to be delivered, but the principal will leave all other control rights – how the tasks are to be carried out, the resources allocated, and incentives administered – to the subcontractor. That is, in those areas beyond explicit contract stipulation, the subcontractor will have real authority – the residual control rights within his jurisdiction. Note that principal–agent problems are involved in both employment relationships and subcontracting modes, but the specifics of these problems vary significantly with the ways that the control rights are allocated.

This line of argument can be applied to the study of authority relationships in a public bureaucracy. In this framework property rights can be reframed in terms of control rights over the use of "assets" (or activities related to a task or project) beyond those specified in the "contract" (in the specific policy stipulation). While I use the conventional principal–supervisor–agent labels to characterize the hierarchy, the roles of the three may vary significantly in different organizational settings, as may their relationships and behavioral patterns. In the "employment relationship" mode, the principal (e.g., the central government) stipulates policies, and the supervisor (e.g., the provincial government) plays the role of "supervising" the local governments to carry out policy implementation. In the "subcontracting" mode, however, the principal delegates policy targets to the supervisor, along with part or all of the control rights for the implementation process, including decision rights *for actual implementation and incentive provision*. In so doing, the authority relationship between the principal and the supervisor undergoes subtle but critical changes. That is, in the "subcontracting" mode, the supervisor acts as a "subcontractor" who retains a significant type of control rights over how to carry out the delegated tasks or projects as well as the control rights over incentive provision within its own jurisdiction. I use the term "supervisor-as-subcontractor" to capture this specific role of the supervisor in this subcontracting mode of governance.

One central issue in light of the incomplete contract approach is the strategic allocation of the residual rights of control among the different parts of an organization, which leads to variations in the authority relationships in different modes of governance as well as to different types of principal–agent problems. The same logic can also be applied to government organizations, as Tirole (1994, p. 16) puts it, "one can view the government as a distribution of control rights over various kinds of decisions. This division is determined by constitutions, laws and traditions."

The allocation of control rights can take more subtle forms. Drawing on Weber, Aghion and Tirole (1997) distinguish formal and real authority in organizations in this framework. Formal authority is prescribed by the formal structure of the organization, whereas real authority rests with those who have more information. As the authors argue, given the cost of time and effort, the principal may strategically delegate real authority to the supervisor. To wit, the party that has real authority is the one who has *de facto* control rights over the use of an asset (or activities) beyond the explicit stipulation of the contract or customary practice in power sharing. The distinction between formal and informal authority has long been recognized in the literature on organizations (Blau 1963, Crozier 1964), and the focus on the allocation of control rights makes these distinctive phenomena analyzable. An important implication of the distinction between formal and real authority is that the modes of governance can undergo significant changes even without an explicit alternation of formal authority. For example, even if the formal authority of the principal is intact, it may become vague and symbolic when actual control rights are shifted to other parties (e.g., the supervisor). Here we can see a clue to the interplay between formal and informal institutions and its implications for variable coupling across hierarchical levels.

To sharpen the analytical power of control rights theory for the study of the Chinese bureaucracy, I now propose to further differentiate the control rights along the following three dimensions:

- *Control rights over goal setting*: the control right to set goals/targets for subordinates within the organization. This is the core of the hierarchical authority relationship. The process of goal setting may take the form of a top-down process or of negotiations among the involved parties, as in contract agreements that are negotiated in the marketplace.
- *Control rights over inspection*: the control right to inspect and evaluate the performance of the agents on the basis of the goal-setting right. Clearly, the "inspection" right is secondary to the "goal-setting" right. It is separable from the "goal-setting" right in that the principal may set up goals but leave the inspection right to another party (e.g., the supervisor). It is important to note that the control right to inspect is distinct from the control right for incentive provision (see below). That is, the main purpose of inspection is to ensure that goals are accomplished and policy targets are met, and it is not for the purpose of evaluating the agent's performance.
- *Control rights over incentive provision*: the control right to design and implement incentive mechanisms to reward or penalize the agent, whose performance is subject to appraisal. The distinct control right in providing incentives to agents implies that there may be a separation of

inspection and incentive provision. Control rights in incentive provisions, including performance evaluation, may be allocated to the supervisor; or, alternatively, they may be retained in the hands of the principal.

By differentiating and conceptualizing control rights along these dimensions, I put forth a key theoretical proposition: Decision rights (including property rights) as a bundle of control rights are decomposable, separable, and hence can be allocated, with costs, among the parties in an organization. Different allocations of the control rights give rise to different modes of governance.

I submit that such a separation of control rights is not only desirable under certain conditions, but it is also unavoidable for any large-scale organization. To illustrate this point, let us revisit the three-layer bureaucracy involving the central government (the principal), the intermediate government (the supervisor), and the local government (the agent). Given both the scope and the distance among the three, the separation of these control rights is both necessary and inevitable. Consider a concrete example. In the case of SO_2 reduction, one of many environmental regulatory arenas governed by the Ministry of Environmental Protection, there are dozens of projects and facilities involved in each county. At a municipal level, hundreds of such items are involved, and at each provincial level, there are thousands of them. At the national level, this amounts to hundreds of thousands of projects in this particular area, which is just one of many areas under environmental regulation. It is mind boggling to imagine the task load for the central government (e.g., the Ministry of Environmental Protection) to exercise control rights in all three dimensions. Similarly, the cost is prohibitively high for the central government to exercise control rights for incentive provision for lower-level agents, which requires accurate information about the agent's efforts, the state of nature, and other contingencies. Even the exercise of the control right for inspection has to be highly selective because it is simply too costly to conduct a comprehensive inspection of all involved items.

It is not surprising, then, that the separation and delegation of these rights are commonplace in the Chinese bureaucracy. Indeed, there is a variety of control-right configurations in different arenas and among governments at different levels. By considering these distinct dimensions of control rights and how they are allocated across levels of the hierarchy, we are able to discern and examine distinctive modes of governance and variable-coupling in the Chinese governments with considerable analytical power, as we will see in the example below.

Control Rights and Modes of Governance in the Chinese Bureaucracy: A Unified Framework

In the aforementioned three-layer bureaucracy, different allocations of control rights among the principal, supervisor, and agent give rise to a variety of modes of governance. Before turning to the specific modes, recall the pair of concepts introduced in Chapter 1, *tight-coupling versus loose-coupling*, which were developed in organization research to characterize distinct organizing processes. The extent that different elements in an organization are coupled with one another varies greatly. In a tightly coupled system, these elements are coupled through dense, tight linkages such that they are sensitive to and respond to one another. The ideal type of hierarchy is one in which directives from the higher authority are responded to and implemented by lower levels in an efficient manner. In contrast, elements in an organization may be loosely coupled in that different parts of the organization retain their own identities, and responses among them are slow, imprecise, and variable (Weick 1976, 1982). In many respects, the tight-coupling versus loose-coupling states are analogous to the "centralization" versus the "decentralization" scenarios in organizations. But notions of centralization and decentralization have acquired multiple and often confusing meanings and interpretations in the literature (Treisman 2007). The notions of tight-coupling versus loose-coupling are used here to avoid unnecessary complications.

Table 3.1 summarizes the different modes of governance produced by the different allocations of control rights along the three proposed dimensions.

- *The tight-coupling mode.* The principal retains all three control rights for goal setting, evaluation, and incentive provision, and enforces his directives through supervisors, resulting in a mode of tight-coupling and hence high responsiveness, among the three layers of the bureaucracy. In the Chinese bureaucracy, this is often accompanied by a heightened mobilizational state of policy implementation.
- *The subcontracting mode,* in which the principal establishes goals and targets, but "subcontracts" these tasks to the supervisor, or the goals may be negotiated and agreed upon by the principal and the subcontractor. The principal holds the control rights for inspection to evaluate the policy outcomes. But the control rights for implementation, enforcement, and incentive design are left entirely in the hands of the supervisor. In this case, the supervisor acts as a subcontractor, with his own control rights for organizing activities within his jurisdiction.

TABLE 3.1. *A framework for control rights and modes of governance*

	Modes of governance			
	Tight-coupling	Subcontracting	Loose-coupling	Federalism
Control rights				
Goal setting	Principal	Principal/ Negotiated	Principal/ Negotiated	Supervisor
Inspection	Principal	Principal	Supervisor	Supervisor
Incentive provision	Principal	Supervisor	Supervisor	Supervisor
Behavioral consequences				
Principal	Mobilization	Inspection strategies	Symbolic authority Loss of control	Absent
Supervisor	Loss of local initiative	Implementation pressures Collusion	Acting as principal	Acting as principal

- *The loose-coupling mode,* in which the principal retains the control rights for goal setting, or the goals may be negotiated between the principal and the agents. Both the right of inspection and the right of incentive provision are allocated to the supervisor. In this scenario, the principal becomes a figurehead, his authority is formal or symbolic, and the supervisor retains real authority for both inspection and incentive provision.
- *The federalism mode,* in which the principal delegates all three control rights to the supervisor in certain areas or functions. In this scenario, then, the supervisor has both formal and real authority.

The proposed conceptual framework adds considerable analytical power to the study of the Chinese bureaucracy. First, by focusing on specific control rights and the allocation of these rights among the principal, supervisor, and agent, we are able to be much more analytical in pinpointing the specific relationships between the principal and the supervisor and in deriving the implications for their behavioral patterns. For example, the principal–supervisor relationship in the "tight-coupling" mode is akin to the conventional "employment relationship" discussed above; however, the nature of this relationship changes significantly in the "subcontracting" mode, as the intermediate government assumes a supervisor-as-subcontractor role.

Second, we are able to discuss the behavioral implications in a more specific and meaningful way and to pin down the specific mechanisms that give rise to the different modes of governance. Take, for example, the phenomenon of collusion between the supervisor and the agent, which reflects a strategic alliance between the two in response to fiats and intervention by the principal (Zhou 2010a). Table 3.1 indicates that such an organizational phenomenon is most likely to take place in the "subcontracting" mode, where the principal exercises inspection rights but lacks enough information to carry out evaluations. Collusive behavior is unlikely to occur in other modes of governance for the following reasons: First, in the "tight-coupling" mode, collusion is costly – it is more likely to be caught and to be severely penalized in a heightened mobilizational state such as a political campaign. Second, in the "loose-coupling" mode of governance the supervisor acts like the principal and exercises inspection rights, so there is no incentive for the supervisor to engage in collusion. Clearly, by focusing on the allocation of control rights, we can be much more specific and analytical in discussing the relationship between incentive mechanisms and behavioral patterns among the different involved parties.

Third, different modes of governance in the Chinese bureaucracy can be analyzed in a unified framework, on the same analytical bases, and in relation to one another, rather than being treated as disparate and isolated cases. For example, the "tight-coupling" mode may generate a highly responsive bureaucracy across different levels or functional lines, but it is extremely costly to maintain the mobilizational state for a sustained period of time. Moreover, there is also the cost of the "loss of local initiative" which weakens the effectiveness of problem solving at the local levels. Therefore, the "tight-coupling" mode is inherently unstable and is likely to shift to other modes of governance through formal or informal reallocations of control rights across bureaucratic levels. The mode of tight-coupling may shift to the subcontracting mode, when the principal relaxes its tight grip and allows the supervisor to have real authority for incentive provision. Or it may further shift to a "loose-coupling" mode when control rights for both inspection and incentive provision are delegated to the supervisor.

For example, the policy goal of maintaining social stability had long been managed through a subcontracting (or, at times, a loose-coupling) mode, with local authorities in charge of this area. But in the last two decades the central government's efforts to take command in this area, wielding control rights for both inspection and incentive provision (e.g., penalties) have led to a tightly coupled system among the principal, the supervisor, and the agent. Changes in different conditions lead to a reallocation of control rights, sometimes explicitly, other times informally, that induces a shift from one mode of governance to another.

Note that the three-layer bureaucracy outlined above may apply to other analogous settings in the Chinese bureaucracy, such as central–provincial–prefecture levels, prefecture–county–township levels, or ministry–bureau–section office levels, and so forth. Indeed, the same theoretical logic can be applied to a variety of settings with specific scope conditions, therefore uncovering the interconnectedness of apparently disparate phenomena and the underlying mechanisms.

To sum up, I have drawn insights from the economics of incomplete contracts to develop my proposed model of authority relationships in the Chinese bureaucracy based on the allocation of distinct control rights along three dimensions. The proposed model provides a new theoretical lens as well as a set of analytical tools to make sense of different modes of governance in the Chinese bureaucracy. I now apply this model to interpret local government behavior and the changing modes of governance in the area of environmental regulation.

GOVERNING ENVIRONMENTAL REGULATION: A CASE STUDY

Between 2008 and 2011 our research team conducted fieldwork in a municipal Environmental Protection Bureau in northern China. Figure 3.2 depicts the formal authority relationship in the field of environmental protection, with the national Ministry of Environmental Protection (MEP) at the top, and the Environmental Protection Bureaus at the provincial, municipal, and county levels. In light of the proposed model, I focus on the Municipal Environmental Protection Bureau (MEPB) at the prefecture level as the supervisor, with the MEP and the Provincial Environmental Protection Bureau (PEPB) as its principals, and the County Environmental Protection Bureaus (CEPBs) as the agents. Whenever possible I will treat both the PEPB and the MEP as if they are the same principal for the MEPB. This simplifying assumption allows us to focus on the key issue about the allocation of control rights between the MEPB on the one hand and the higher authorities on the other.

Our research team tracked the MEPB's implementation of policy targets during the period of the five-year plan from 2006 to 2010. We gathered information and data retrospectively for the first two years of

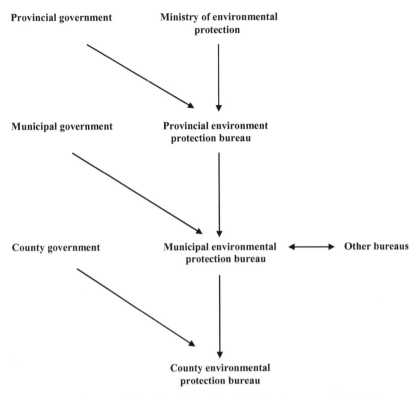

FIGURE 3.2. Structural location of the Municipal Environmental Protection Bureau (MEPB)

the five-year plan before our fieldwork began. Meeting policy targets in the five-year plan was the central focus of the MEPB among the numerous tasks that it carried out during this period. Both the MEP and the PEPB conducted their respective inspections twice a year in the form of semi-annual and annual inspections to ensure satisfactory progress toward meeting the targets. Our fieldwork provides us with a rare opportunity to observe the allocation of control rights in this area and the corresponding behavioral patterns. In line with the proposed model, the analytical focus is on the allocation of control rights for goal setting, inspection, and the provision of incentives during the implementation process.

Below, I first provide a brief sketch of the allocation of the three control rights among the MEP (and PEPB), the MEPB, and the CEPBs. I then add institutional and behavioral details in the actual exercise of these control rights.

The Allocation of Control Rights for Environmental Regulation:
A Brief Sketch

Control rights for goal setting. The policy goal set for the five-year plan period was a reduction of pollution levels in two areas: chemical oxygen demand (COD, related to water pollution treatment) and sulfur dioxide (SO_2, related to air pollution treatment). The MEP established specific policy targets for each province in accordance with the national five-year plan of the central government. Once the province received its policy targets, the PEPB had full control rights to decompose these targets among the MEPBs within its jurisdiction, making the PEPB the *de facto* principal for the MEPBs. For the MEPB in our study, the goals were set as an eighteen percent reduction in COD and a nine percent reduction in SO_2 over the five-year-plan period. The MEPBs and CEPBs were not involved in this goal-setting process. It is obvious that control rights for goal setting were firmly in the hands of the principal (i.e., the MEP and the PEPB). In a similar manner, once the policy targets were subcontracted to the MEPB, the supervisor-as-subcontractor, the control rights for the allocation of quotas within the jurisdiction and for meeting these policy targets were given to the MEPB. In other words, once the goals are set, the control rights for implementation are largely in the hands of the MEPB, who acts as the supervisor-as-subcontractor.

The MEPB also sets its annual targets to ensure the incremental completion of the policy targets in the five-year plan. These goal-setting practices are in accordance with the policy targets in the five-year plan and the annual goals set by the PEPB. Therefore, goal-setting behavior is subject to the same kind of analysis conducted here.

Control rights for inspection. In the field of environmental regulation, the principal (the MEP and the PEPB) exercises its control rights for inspection mainly through the annual inspection procedure, taking the following steps: First, on an annual basis the agents (the CEPBs) and their supervisor (the MEPB) assembled documentation on all efforts and outcomes of pollution reduction in specific areas, projects, and facilities within their respective jurisdictions; second, the MEP and PEPB sent out inspection teams to review and assess documentation at the CEPB level to accept or reject, item by item, decisions and proportions of the CEPBs' claimed accomplishments. The officially accepted outcomes of all CEPBs were aggregated at the municipal level as the certified policy outcome for the MEPB – the subcontracted "policy outcome" delivered to and accepted by the principal. In addition, the inspection team conducted selective onsite inspections during the review process to ensure the quality of the delivered "policy outcomes." There were also other occasions throughout the year when the MEP sent out special inspection teams to targeted facilities and projects and conducted onsite inspections. There were considerable negotiations during the inspection process regarding the accuracy of the measurement, the reliability of the evidence, and the various interpretations. But the principal had ultimate authority in deciding when, where, and how the inspections were to be conducted and in accepting or rejecting the final decisions, and in what proportions, of the claimed accomplishments.

Control rights for incentive provision. Incentive provision within the MEPB is mainly related to the performance evaluation of the CEPBs. Although the MEP/PEPB inspections directly scrutinized all claimed achievements by the CEPBs, it is notable that the MEP/PEPB show no interest in providing incentives at the CEPB level. Instead, real authority for the performance evaluation of the CEPBs resides with the CEPBs' immediate supervisor, the MEPB, which spends a great deal of time and effort in organizing the implementation process to meet the policy targets. In so doing, rich information is passed on to the MEPB to evaluate the relative performance of the CEPBs in their respective jurisdictions, as I will detail below.

To summarize, the brief sketch above shows that the allocation of control rights in the field of environmental protection is consistent with the main characteristics of the *subcontracting model*: The principal (the MEP and the PEPB) holds control rights for goal setting and inspection, but the supervisor-as-subcontractor (the MEPB) holds control rights for the provision of incentives. By specifying the concrete "subcontracting" mode of governance, we can go much further than the general description of principal–agent relationships to pin down the specific information and authority problems involved in the three-level hierarchy. In a typical subcontracting model, the goals are negotiated between the firm and its subcontractor, whereas in the Chinese bureaucracy, goal setting is largely imposed in a top-down process. However, as we will see below, considerable negotiations during the inspection process effectively compromise the principal's control rights for goal setting, in effect making the actual practice a subcontracting model. I now turn to the actual implementation process to make sense of the exercise of these control rights among the three layers of the bureaucracy.

The Principal's Authority in Action: Control Rights for Goal Setting and Inspection

From the MEPB's point of view, the policy targets for the five-year plan were imposed from above, with no room for negotiation. This is in stark contrast to the typical subcontracting process between firms in the marketplace, where the goals (i.e., the terms of the contract) are set based on mutual agreement; hence, they are feasible and binding. In the Chinese bureaucracy, there are considerable variations in negotiation and manipulation between the principal and the supervisor-as-subcontractor during the inspection process, which may either soften or harden the control rights for goal setting. Therefore, it is instructive to consider the exercise of control rights for goal setting and for inspection *jointly* to understand the specific principal–agent problems involved and the principal's authority in action.

As noted, one key element in the MEP/PEPB inspection process is the inspection team's review of the records that document the accomplishments to meet the policy targets, such as the closing of pollution sources, the addition and operation of new water treatment facilities, and so forth. For each round of inspection, this review process usually takes place over a period of several days, during which the inspectors audit the documents and demand explanations and justifications from the MEPB officials on their statistics and calculations. This is the most critical moment for the "supervisor-as-subcontractor," whose year-long efforts depend on the outcome of this inspection process. As a result, on the eve of the inspection process, the MEPB and the CEPBs work together, spending much time and effort, to prepare the documents and to conduct their own inspections of the pollution-treatment facilities to ensure that the principal's inspection proceeds smoothly.

From the perspective of the MEPB officials, the inspection process is characterized by high unpredictability, and the outcomes are often surprising, even to the seasoned MEPB officials. At times, as in the PEPB inspection in 2008, the inspection team conducted extensive and thorough auditing and stubbornly refused the bargaining efforts by the MEPB. These practices resulted in the rejection of a large proportion of the achievements claimed by the MEPB. According to an estimate by an MEPB official, for some key items related to pollution reduction, the inspection team accepted only ten percent to fifty-eight percent of the achievements claimed by the MEPB, resulting in many complaints and much frustration. In other years, the review process proceeded smoothly,

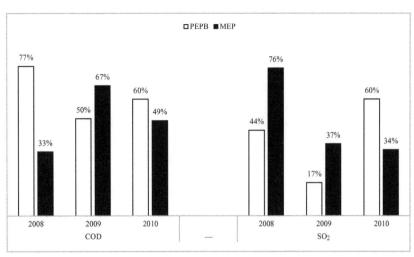

FIGURE 3.3. Proportion of acceptance of the MEPB claims by the Provincial Environmental Protection Bureau (PEPB) and the Ministry of Environmental Protection (MEP)

with a level of acceptance much higher than MEPB officials had expected. During one episode of an MEP inspection that we observed, the MEPB officials engaged in extensive preparation for the inspection. The inspection proceeded uneventfully with no need for serious bargaining or justification, and, as a result, the MEPB officials were disappointed that their extensive preparatory work was not put to use.

Figure 3.3 reports the acceptance level by the MEP and PEPB respectively during the last three years of the five-year plan. The MEP and PEPB conducted each of their respective inspections separately, but both assessed the same pile of records prepared by the local CEPBs and coordinated by the MEPB. The sequence of these inspections varied. Sometimes a "local" office (e.g., the MEPB) conducted its own inspection before the higher authority to ensure the policy outcomes were prepared to the finest detail. Sometimes the "local" office (e.g., the MEPB) conducted its inspection later in order to adjust the rate of acceptance of the policy outcomes based on the outcome of the inspection from above. For example, the PEPB's acceptance decision was in part based on the acceptance decisions by the MEP for the entire province. As Figure 3.3 shows, the acceptance rate varied greatly across years between the MEP and the PEPB and also between the COD and SO$_2$ areas. This is partly due to changes in the criteria used during the inspection process. But at times the inspection decisions were based on other factors that had little to do with the actual quality of the policy outcome. For example, the very low seventeen percent acceptance rate for SO_2 had little to do with the MEPB's actual performance.[1] Instead, this was largely because by that year the MEPB had already met the policy targets of the five-year plan, so the PEPB deliberately lowered its accomplishments to make room for other MEPBs to catch up.

Throughout the inspection process, there was intensive bargaining. In fact, the formal process was designed to provide occasions for both sides to explain, interpret, and discuss these findings, thereby providing a legitimate forum for bargaining and resolving any serious problems uncovered during the process (Zhou, Ai and Lian 2012). That is, although the goals were imposed by the principal, inspection of the policy outcomes was negotiated between the principal and the supervisor. Negotiation flexibility in the inspection process amounted to compromising the control rights for goal setting, resulting in effect in a negotiated goal-setting process.

How do we make sense of these practices in the exercise of control rights for inspection? Our observations suggest that the inspection process is only loosely coupled with the actual outcomes of the implementation efforts. Indeed, it is commonly observed that the inspectors' disposition of either a "tight" or a "loose" inspection was adopted prior to the actual process regardless of the actual performance by the supervisor-as-subcontractor. One way to interpret such behavior is that the inspection process is intended to exert pressures *ex ante* on the subcontractor's implementation efforts in the future, but it is only loosely coupled with the actual implementation process *ex post*. In the larger scheme of things, the principal uses an inspection mainly as a deterrent strategy to put pressure on the subcontractor so as to induce appropriate efforts during the implementation process rather than during the final stage of the inspection.

The Supervisor-as-Subcontractor's Authority in Action: Control Rights for the Provision of Incentives

As noted above, control rights for the provision of incentives are largely in the hands of the supervisor (the MEPB). But in actual practice there is one

---

[1] For all the policy outcomes on SO_2 reduction claimed by the MEPB, only seventeen percent was formally accepted as a completed policy outcome, and the rest (eighty-three percent) of the MEPB's claimed SO_2 reduction was not recognized as a policy accomplishment.

complication. The inspections conducted by the MEP/PEPB are based on the documented achievements provided by each CEPB – the agent at the bottom of the administrative hierarchy. In other words, each MEP/PEPB inspection in effect generates a ranking order of performance scores, from low to high, for all CEPBs within the jurisdiction of the MEPB. If this rank order is taken seriously as the CEPBs' performance evaluations, the MEPB's control rights for the provision of incentives will be largely taken away or seriously compromised.

Interestingly, this was never the case. Instead, each year after the MEP/PEPB inspection was completed and acceptance of the outcomes was known, the MEPB would make considerable efforts to internally reallocate quotas and accomplishments among the CEPBs. Sometimes such adjustments were made in subtle ways. For example, by carefully redistributing the newly added pollution volumes (resulting from adjustments in economic development or population growth) among the counties would increase or decrease a CEPB's level of accomplishment in that year. At times, the reallocation efforts were made openly. During an episode in 2008 a large water treatment facility in operation could contribute significantly to meeting the COD targets for three CEPBs in the region. Instead of measuring the accurate volume of water being treated among the three CEPBs, the MEPB reallocated more volume to the two CEPBs that lagged behind to help increase their achievement levels. In another case, in 2009, the MEPB deliberately underreported the volume of water treatment by a large facility in an effort to lower the performance level of five counties that benefited the most so as to keep a balance of the performance levels among the CEPBs. The MEPB had exercised extensive rights in reallocating the quota, accomplishments, and tasks among the CEPBs such that the link between inspection outcomes and the provision of incentives became tenuous (see Chapter 7).

As a result of these performance (re)evaluation efforts, the rank order of performance among the CEPBs often departed significantly from that which emerged during the MEP/PEPB inspection. Figures 3.4 and 3.5 show the CEPBs' level of accomplishment in terms of COD and SO_2 reduction, first accepted by the PEPB and later readjusted by the MEPB, in 2008. There were similar patterns in other years as well. As one can see, there are considerable discrepancies between the inspection assessments made by the PEPB and the report card on performance issued by the MEPB. For example, several CEPBs were short of meeting the annual target of six percent reduction in COD based on the PEPB inspection (see Figure 3.4), but all met the annual target after the MEPB's readjustment.

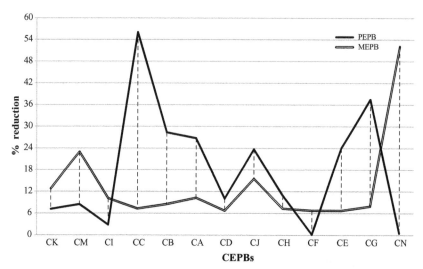

FIGURE 3.4. Chemical oxygen demand (COD) reduction level accepted by the PEPB and readjusted by the MEPB for each county, 2008

We observe the same pattern in the area of SO_2 reductions (see Figure 3.5). Note also that these readjustments often significantly altered the rank order of the CEPBs based on the inspections – further evidence of the decoupling between the MEPB's performance evaluation and the inspection outcome. For example, during the PEPB inspection the CEPB labeled "CN" fell short of meeting the annual target in COD reduction, but it had the best performance after the readjustment made by the MEPB. This was because the MEPB officials tried hard to re-adjust the quota so that this CEPB was able to meet its target for the five-year plan. Occasionally, the MEPB would file a written petition with the PEPB and formally request a reallocation of the task quota or achievement level. But more often than not, such adjustments were made quietly and internally, and the principal never cared. Indeed, throughout the five-year plan period and especially during the last few years, the MEPB repeatedly and deliberately made adjustments and reallocations in its own perform-ance evaluations of the quotas among the CEPBs.

How do we interpret the MEPB's readjustment of the performance evaluation among the CEPBs? On the surface, it may be interpreted as collusion between the supervisor and the agents in defiance of the princi-pal's own inspection. However, the proposed model offers a qualitatively different interpretation. That is, these efforts may be instances in which the subcontractor resists outside interference and exercises his/her control

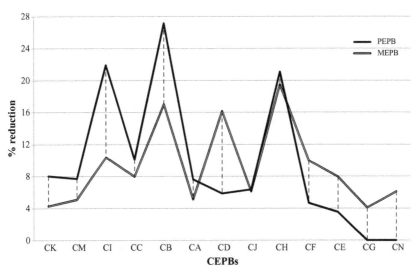

FIGURE 3.5. SO$_2$ reduction level accepted by the PEPB and readjusted by the MEPB for each county, 2008

rights for the provision of incentives on a more informed basis. The enforcement and implementation of environmental regulation involve many parameters; different CEPBs are located in different areas and face different challenges. The MEPB has much richer information about the CEPBs' efforts and the challenges they face, so to a large extent these adjustments reflect informed performance evaluations of their efforts. As will be discussed in Chapter 7, another important consideration is governed by the logic of political coalitions: The MEPB must work with the CEPBs (and the county governments) to implement these policies, thus it is politically critical to help the CEPBs meet their policy targets to ensure future cooperation. That is, the main driving force behind these adjustments and the reallocation of the achievement levels is to ensure that all CEPBs within the jurisdiction are able to meet their policy targets on an annual basis and eventually to meet the targets in the five-year plan.

The MEPB officials do care about motivating its agents, similar to all good managers in other organizations. Whenever possible, they try to link the performance evaluation with rewards for their efforts, and to some extent the readjustments are based on such principles, especially on those occasions when the political coalition is well-protected (i.e., there is no prospect of the CEPBs failing to meet the targets), and they also use the inspection pressures from above to motivate the CEPBs. One common strategy is a proportional reduction strategy that keeps intact the rank order in accordance with the acceptance level by the MEP or the PEPB such that those CEPBs lagging behind in rank order feel pressure to catch up.

One may wonder why the CEPBs tolerate such readjustments and reallocations *ex post*? One important reason is that the CEPBs and the MEPB are interdependent and these readjustments are part of a continuing process of social exchange, or "give and take" that benefits all of them collectively (Ellickson 1991). Moreover, a CEPB's accepted outcome in the inspection process may result from artificial manipulation through collusion between the MEPB and the CEPB. Therefore, the CEPBs have to accept the more informed MEPB's readjustment based on their true performance. At times, the MEPB also withheld information from the CEPBs about the inspection outcomes so as to make room for readjustments.

In contrast to the MEPB's extensive efforts and practices in administering the performance evaluations, the MEP and PEPB show little interest in the performance evaluations at the CEPB level. Even in those cases where the inspections uncover serious problems (distortions or implementation failures), the principal will demand that the problems be corrected and the personnel be penalized, but they will leave decisions about the penalty in the hands of the immediate supervisor. In one 2008 case, a special inspection team uncovered a serious distortion of the data by a CEPB. The PEPB issued a stern warning and demanded that the MEPB investigate and penalize the involved party. The MEPB complied, notifying the PEPB of the steps taken to correct the problems. But, as far as we are aware, these were largely symbolic gestures, with no real consequence. These instances indicate that the principal's main concern is about the quality of the "goods" delivered, that is, meeting the policy targets; thus, the principals focus on the supervisor-as-subcontractor and have no real interest in micro-management within the subcontractor's jurisdiction. In this light, the real consequence of uncovering problems during the inspection process is likely a tightening of the evaluations in this area during the next round, which is consistent with the main purpose of the inspections – to tighten the screw on the subcontractor's future performance.

To sum up, the evidence and the discussion above show that actual practice in the authority relationships in the environmental regulation area is consistent with the subcontracting model where the principal cares only about overall fulfillment of the goals of the MEPB, leaving the MEPB to link rewards/penalties with the actual performance of the agents. Nevertheless, there were also considerable variations over the five-year period that shed light on the changes in the authority relationships during the policy-implementation processes. These variations were largely caused by a reallocation, often informally, of the control rights among the involved parties. Consider the inspection efforts by the principal. During the first year, 2006, the lack of experience by the inspection team led to a loose inspection process and the acceptance of a large proportion of the claimed achievements. This can be interpreted as delegating real authority to the supervisor who was better informed. However, in the next year, 2007, the principal exerted tight control over the inspection process and rejected a large proportion of the claimed achievements by the MEPB. This had serious implications for the performance evaluation of the CEPBs. These actions amounted to a shift in the subcontracting mode toward tight-coupling. In later years, as the policy targets were steadily met over time, pressures were considerably relieved, even though the inspections were still formally conducted and a large proportion of the claimed tasks was not accepted.[2] In this sense, policy implementation shifts to a mode of loose coupling, where control rights for inspection and the provision of incentives are largely left to the supervisor. My proposed model provides a framework and analytical concepts to analyze and make sense of the variations and shifts among the different modes of governance in the Chinese bureaucracy.

To what extent is our case generalizable to other settings or areas in the Chinese bureaucracy? Needless to say, specific tasks, inspection processes, and goal-setting processes vary enormously across different areas. But I believe the structural context in which control rights are allocated is similar across different functional lines and different regions in the Chinese bureaucracy. In this sense, the behavioral patterns observed in our fieldwork are likely to have broader relevance in other areas and localities.

REINTERPRETING THE PRINCIPAL–AGENT RELATIONSHIP IN
THE AREA OF ENVIRONMENTAL REGULATION

The above case study on environmental regulation situates the analysis in a "subcontracting" organizational setting where the allocation of control rights has the following elements: (1) The principal exercises the right of goal setting and then subcontracts the expected policy targets to the

---

[2] A common practice by the principal is to not certify full completion of the tasks or to change the criteria in terms of a tournament competition so that there is still an incentive for the agent to improve during each round of inspection.

subcontractor who is responsible for fulfilling the terms of the subcontract;[3] (2) the principal retains control rights to inspect upon the delivery of the "goods" (i.e., the policy outcomes); and (3) the principal leaves the control rights for the provision of incentives to the subcontractor, within his jurisdiction, together with other control rights to organize and enforce the implementation process. Clearly, this subcontracting model specifies a principal–agent relationship different from that in a conventional employment relationship in a bureaucracy.

Applying this model to the three-layer Chinese bureaucracy, I can recast the policy-implementation processes in the case study of environmental regulation as follows. First, through formal or informal negotiations, the central or provincial government (the principal) sets up specific policy goals or targets in an area (e.g., the level of pollution reduction), and then "subcontracts" (through task allocations) to the intermediate government (e.g., the MEPB). That is, the supervisor-as-subcontractor retains the control rights over the specifics for policy implementation and incentive provision for its agents within the boundaries of the subcontracts. The central government then exercises its inspection right to periodically review and evaluate the policy outcomes to ensure that the supervisor-as-subcontractor has met the policy targets. With the clear delineation of the control rights along these three dimensions, we can interpret the observed behavior in a specific and meaningful way.

Let us first consider the behavior of the principal. In this model, the principal only cares about policy outcomes, so he exercises control rights for goal setting by formulating specific policy targets for the supervisor-as-subcontractor, and he retains control rights for inspection to ensure the quality of the delivered policy. In contrast, control rights for the provision of incentives are delegated to the supervisor-as-subcontractor for good reason. First, the principal only cares about policy outcomes, not the actual process of implementation, so it is logical to allocate "control rights" to the party that has the most incentives to ensure that the implementation process works. Second, given the size of a large organization, it is simply infeasible or too costly for the principal to acquire accurate information to provide incentives for the agents. The supervisor-as-subcontractor works with the agents in policy implementation;

[3] Or, in a variant of the model, the goals may be negotiated between the principal and the supervisor. An implication of such a case is that contractual terms negotiated in this way tend to be feasible and hence binding on both sides.

hence, he has more accurate information about their efforts and perform-ance for the provision of incentives.

This model also entails clear behavioral implications for the ways in which the principal exercises his inspection rights. As noted above, the principal cares about the contracted "policy outcome" to be delivered by the supervisor-as-subcontractor. But because of the high costs of compre-hensive inspection, he adopts a strategy whereby he selectively inspects "patches" of the delivered policy outcomes (e.g., onsite inspections of *selected* sites related to environmental regulation) to ensure the truthful-ness and the quality of the policy outcomes claimed by the supervisor-as-subcontractor. This provides a clue about the observed variations in the inspection processes, which reflect a selective sampling process. Moreover, because the inspection is selective, it is important for the principal to keep the inspection process unpredictable – sometimes loose and sometimes tight – and for the selection of localities to remain random so as to keep the supervisor-as-subcontractor and the agent on their toes. Moreover, because the principal's interest is not to administer the provision of incen-tives but to ensure the quality of the policy outcomes, the inspection process typically is not linked to incentive decisions (i.e., imposing rewards or penalties for the agents at the local levels). These behavioral implications are markedly consistent with our fieldwork observations of behavior during the inspection process.

Now consider the observed MEPB behavior in light of its role as supervisor-as-subcontractor in the proposed model. The main goal for the supervisor-as-subcontractor is to ensure the delivery of the contracted policy outcome to the satisfaction of the principal. To accomplish this goal, the supervisor-as-subcontractor is expected to undertake three types of action. First, to ensure the successful delivery of the policy outcome, he has an incentive to create and maintain pressures on the agents to exert efforts to do their job well. This explains the commonly observed phe-nomenon that the intermediate governments adopt a strategy of "down-ward acceleration of the implementation pressures" by adopting more stringent policy targets for their subordinates in order to minimize the risk of falling short in terms of accomplishment of the tasks. In our case, the MEPB revealed similar behavior. Second, the supervisor-as-subcontractor also exercises control rights for incentive provision to induce the right behavior by the agents within his jurisdiction. That is, as predicted in this model, it is the supervisor-as-subcontractor, not the principal, who cares about the appropriate provision of incentives to link rewards with efforts. Finally, during the inspection process conducted by the principal, both the supervisor-as-subcontractor and the agent share common interests to make sure that the contracted "policy outcomes" are acceptable to the principal. Collusive behavior between the two is most prevalent during the "inspection" phase of the policy-implementation process, which is consistent with the predictions derived from the proposed model.

By focusing on the allocation of control rights, the proposed model provides an analytical lens to examine key features and behavioral implications of the governance structure. The key issue here is the distinctive goals pursued by the principal and the supervisor-as-subcontractor: The principal cares about the quality of the delivered policy outcomes, so the inspection process seeks to ensure that the policy targets claimed by local officials (the agents) on behalf of the subcontractor are true. In contrast, the subcontractor cares about fulfillment of the tasks specified in the subcontracts, not about the truthfulness of the claims as long as they pass the inspection process. Simple as this model may be, it calls attention to several important conceptual distinctions.

First, it is important to make a distinction between the inspection conducted by the principal and the performance evaluation conducted by the supervisor-as-subcontractor. In some circumstances, these two may coincide; that is, the supervisor-as-subcontractor may use the principal's inspection as the basis for the provision of incentives. But more often than not, in reality these are two separate processes and conceptually they should be treated as separate practices. In the former, findings from the inspection process are typically decoupled from considerations about the provision of incentives, as the two decision rights reside with different parties. This recognition sheds light on those familiar, and apparently odd, characteristics of the inspection process. That is, at times the inspection process is very tight and challenging and at other times it is loose and easy; and when problems are uncovered, they are often explained away at the local level with few consequences. The proposed model helps us make sense of such behavior, because, for the principal, the policy outcomes are evaluated and accepted at the aggregate level. Certain off-target problems at a particular local level, just like a small number of defects found in an inspection of a selected batch of goods, do not render the quality of the entire pack problematic as long as such defects are within some permitted range of errors. Variations in the tightness of the inspection process reflect the principal's strategizing in selecting a random sample and in creating a highly uncertain environment to pressure the local agents to make implementation efforts.

Second, it is important to differentiate the types of "deviant" behavior by the local governments. Specifically, we can distinguish three types of implementation behavior that, at an aggregate level, all deviate from the original policy but are qualitatively different. In the first class of phenomena, deviations in implementation and in incentive provisions may merely reflect the supervisor-as-subcontractor's exercise of his control rights within his jurisdiction. As we have seen in the case study, the principal's action in rank ordering the performance of the CEPBs inadvertently intrudes into the supervisor-as-subcontractor's realm of authority in incentive provision. In such cases, the more informed supervisor-as-subcontractor ignores the rank order based on the principal's inspection outcomes. Instead, he exercises his control rights for incentive provision by developing his own rank order of the CEPBs' performance evaluation. In the second class of cases, the supervisor, together with his agents, may adopt various flexible implementation strategies, such as a reallocation of the tasks or accomplishments among the CEPBs, to meet the targets in the implementation process. In the context of the subcontracting model, the supervisor has residual control rights to do this. Indeed, these coping strategies are critical for the supervisor and the agents to fit the policy targets to their local circumstances. In the third class of instances, and especially salient in the inspection process, the supervisor may collude with the agent in order to cover up defective policy outcomes that are to be inspected. As we can see, based on the proposed control rights model, these three classes of implementation deviations have qualitatively different implications. In the first two cases, the supervisor-as-subcontractor's behavior is legitimate in the subcontracting mode of governance since he has residual control rights for providing incentives and for organizing implementation of the subcontract. It is not surprising, then, that the first two types of "deviant" behavior are tolerated, or even encouraged, by the principal. It is only in the third case that we see, from the eyes of the principal, a case of deviations that violates the terms of the subcontract.

Third, this model helps explain two distinct and apparently contradictory types of bureaucratic behavior by the same supervisor. On the one hand, during implementation of the subcontract, the supervisor exerts pressure on his agents so as to ensure that the goods are delivered to the satisfaction of the principal. In this process, then, we observe a salient downward acceleration of implementation pressures across the levels of the bureaucracy. On the other hand, during the inspection process the supervisor adopts various strategies to ensure that the inspection does not uncover problems. Hence, we observe a salient phenomenon of collusion between the supervisor and the agent. These two distinct types of behavior by the same supervisor take place in two distinct phases of the policy cycle (one in implementation and one in inspection), and under two distinct sets of conditions, each of which can be logically analyzed in light of the proposed model.

SUMMARY

As discussed in Chapter 1, one salient institutional response mechanism to the fundamental tension is variable-coupling between the central and local governments – sometimes the relationships are tightly coupled, as in those episodes of heightened political campaigns, and sometimes they are only loosely coupled, as in the many episodes of policy-implementation processes shown in the literature. This chapter develops a control rights theory to account for such phenomena. In so doing, it also adds specifics to the relationship between the bureaucratic power and the arbitrary power of the top leaders in a patrimonial/party mode of domination, as discussed in Chapter 2, by explicating the mechanisms that underlie the authority relationships between the central and local governments and across hierarchical levels.

In the proposed theoretical model, variations in the authority relationships depend on the allocation of control rights over goal setting, inspection, and incentive provision in an organization. On this basis, I conceptualize a range of modes of governance in accordance with the allocation of control rights among the principal, the supervisor, and the agent. At one extreme, the principal may retain all control rights, in effect activating a "tight-coupling" mode of governance. However, maintenance of such a governance structure is costly and is typically accompanied by heightened but temporary mobilizational efforts. At the other extreme, the principal may assign all control rights for a specified area to the supervisor, thereby producing a federalism mode of governance. More often, however, we observe the prevalence of a subcontracting mode of governance, where the principal establishes goals and inspects policy outcomes but leaves to the supervisor the control rights for incentive provision.

The proposed theory is *middle-ranged* in that the three dimensions of control rights are tractable, analyzable, and often observable empirically. Furthermore, they can be effectively applied to empirical research, as illustrated in the case study of the behavioral patterns of the principals and agents and their interactions in the environmental regulation area. The control rights theory provides a unified framework for the interrelatedness of a variety of types of government behavior and their underlying mechanisms.

4

Campaign-Style Mobilization as a Mechanism of Governance

This chapter focuses on an important and prevalent mechanism in Chinese state governance – campaign-style mobilization (CSM), especially in the form of political campaigns and large-scale mass movements. In Chapter 2, I discuss relations between the Chinese state and the Chinese bureaucracy, and their interdependence and tensions. The scale of governance and the long chain of command lead to the plague of bureaucratic problems in China's governance. In Chapter 3, I argue that there are different modes of Chinese governance, ranging from tight-coupling, subcontracting, loose-coupling, to federalism, thus leading to a process of variable-coupling. Campaign-style mobilization, as this chapter will show, is a political tool for the centralized authority to tighten up political control during struggles against bureaucrats and it is an effective mechanism to induce shifts among different modes of governance. This chapter thus provides a conceptual link integrating the first three chapters of this book: interconnections among the mode of domination and the bureaucracy, shifts in different modes of governance in light of control rights, and the role of CSM in the interactive processes.

I examine the phenomenon of political campaigns in the larger context of Chinese history and in the framework of comparative bureaucratic institutions in order to interpret their historical origins and institutional implications. This chapter is organized as follows. First, I situate the political campaign phenomenon in an episode in Chinese history to search for clues about the tensions in the Chinese bureaucracy. I then focus on an institutional analysis of political campaigns, including their basis of legitimacy, their characteristics in contemporary society, and the challenges they face today.

SOULSTEALERS, THE GREAT LEAP FORWARD, AND THE CULTURAL REVOLUTION: CAMPAIGN-STYLE MOBILIZATION REVISITED

To put CSM in a historical perspective, let us first turn to an episode during the Qing dynasty in Kuhn (1990). In the year 1768, during the era of Emperor Hungli, a sorcery crisis called "soulstealing" erupted in southern China and quickly spread to other parts of the country, triggering intensive interactions between the emperor and the bureaucrats.

The soulstealer episode was as dramatic as it was short-lived. It began in March 1768, with some reports or accusations of sorcery acts of soulstealing by unknown travelers that led to hysteria among dwellers in urban and rural areas. These rumors were interpreted by the emperor as a disguise for rebellion against the regime, so local bureaucrats tried to evade their responsibilities by covering up these incidents. Convinced of his suspicions, the emperor launched a political campaign to mobilize all levels of the bureaucracy to engage in a search for the leaders of the rebellion as well as to penalize those officials who shirked their responsibilities. The political campaign quickly reached a climax, with many officials, who were accused of collusion and evasion of responsibilities, being penalized severely. However, by November 1768, it had become clear that there was simply no evidence of rebellion or of an insidious conspiracy. In the end, the emperor had to call off the political campaign and symbolically punish some high-level officials as scapegoats.

This was not an isolated event. From time to time Chinese history has witnessed such political campaigns targeting officials in the Chinese bureaucracy (Levenson 1965). Government responses to other crises such as famines also showed similar patterns of the emperor's direct intervention, of the disruption of routine bureaucratic practices, and of mobilization through political campaigns (Will 1990). As Kuhn (1990, p. 187) puts it: "These stories are layered one upon another, several texts written on a single historical page. Beneath them lies another story, the hardest to read: how local events – including the sorcery scare – served as fuel for running the political system." Such dramas belie the hidden code to decipher the institutional logic of governance in China.

We observe similar instances of political campaigns in contemporary China. In one account, during the twenty-seven years of the Mao era (1949–1976), there were twenty-five political campaigns that took place in different arenas.[1] Zhou Feizhou (2009) examines the political campaign to overcome bureaucratic resistance that Mao Zedong launched during the Great Leap Forward. During the mobilization process, Mao took several steps to replace reluctant officials, launch propaganda campaigns, and induce competition among workplaces, administrative jurisdictions, and different arenas (Li 1999, Song 2002). As a result, local officials at different levels were induced or coerced into the swirl of the fanatic rhythm of mobilization, and their behavior moved in a highly synchronized manner on a national scale (Research Office of CCP History 2006, Research Office of CCP History 2002).

Campaign-style mobilization takes place not only in the political arena but also in areas such as economic development, village elections, and so-called "social stability maintenance," among others (Di 2010, Perry 2011, Wu 2007, Zhe and Chen 2011, Zhou 2010b). Feng (2011) provided an extensive discussion of this type of "national mobilizations" that cover a wide range of areas, including those initiated by government agencies for the purpose of specially targeted political, economic, and other policy goals such as the political campaigns against the "anti-rightists" or the "Cultural Revolution," as well as those related to workplace safety and the cleansing of cities. Indeed, such waves of political campaigns and campaign-style mobilization have occurred off and on, on both large and small scales, and they have never disappeared.

Feng (2011) proposes a "revolutionary indoctrination polity" framework that sees national mobilization since 1949 as the continuation of the revolutionary movements after the CCP took power. In the English-language literature, Whyte (1973) associates the use of CSM with the organizational failures of the Chinese bureaucracy and regards CSM as Mao's critique of the Chinese bureaucracy. CSM is invariably launched by the higher authorities, through top-down processes, and it is often directly based on the will of the top leader. But the outbreak of CSM is by no means arbitrary or random; rather, it is rooted in stable organizational bases and symbolic resources. Moreover, political campaigns, both in history and today, such as the soulstealer episode during the Qing dynasty and CSM during the People's Republic, show so much resemblance that they call our attention to the broader historical, institutional context in which CSM is cultivated and reproduced.

[1] https://en.wikipedia.org/wiki/List_of_campaigns_of_the_Chinese_Communist_Party. Las checked on March 5, 2022.

In the introductory chapter, I argue that there is a fundamental tension between centralization and effective, local governance and that CSM serves as one of the mechanisms in responding to this tension and to the related organizational failures and crises. I will further develop this line of argument in this chapter. My central argument can be summarized as follows: CSM arises in response to the tensions and challenges in the governance of China. In the face of the large scale and huge diversity in governance, a routine-based bureaucratic mechanism is often ineffective, overburdened, and results in a loss of control by the higher authority. CSM plays the role of (temporarily) disrupting and suspending these routine processes and reorienting the course of action at the will of the top leaders.

In this light, CSM and bureaucratic routine are two distinct mechanisms that coexist, but they have a different saliency at different points in time. During most periods and under most circumstances, the routine-based bureaucracy is the prevalent, normal state of governance. But in some specific episodes and under certain circumstances, CSM becomes the key operational mechanism and the routine mechanism becomes subordinate to the former, is suspended, or becomes the target of a CSM. One key proposition to be developed in this chapter is that CSM not only is rooted in history but also rests on the party-state organizations in contemporary China. The frequent appearance of CSM in Chinese history has not been accidental nor has it merely reflected the will of the top leaders. Rather, it has been based on a set of institutional arrangements and it has been an integral part of the institutional logic of governance in China.

ROUTINE VERSUS MOBILIZATION MECHANISMS: THE DUAL BUREAUCRATIC PROCESS

From the lens of organizational analysis, bureaucratic routines and CSM are two distinct mechanisms of organizing, whereby there are tensions, incompatibilities, and substitution effects between the two. Bureaucratic routines are part of a stable organizational structure, with a clear division of labor, with well-defined spheres of activities, and with everyday activities routinized on the basis of rules and procedures. In contrast, CSM takes place in the form of mobilization that goes beyond bureaucratic routines and beyond existing departmental boundaries. For example, CSM is typically associated with rushed organizational processes, the imposition of more restrictive measures, and heightened pressures for attention and penalties for violations. In so doing, the bureaucracy shifts into a different gear and bureaucratic routines are replaced with politics-in-command as the central driving force. To wit, CSM is the antithesis of bureaucratic routines.

Tensions between the routine mode and the mobilizational mode lie in the fact that maintenance of the former strengthens the stability of the organizational structure and a clear delineation of its boundaries, hence imposing barriers on the operation of CSM. In contrast, the CSM mechanism and related processes inevitably disrupt rules and routines and weaken bureaucratic stability. The very significance of CSM is to disrupt the routine and normal pace of the bureaucratic process, forcing it to become a tightly coupled system with a high-response pace. The dual process of routines and CSM and the relationship between the two are not arbitrary; rather, they are the result of specific organizational structures and authority relationships. These observations raise questions about the causes of CSM and the conditions under which it pushes aside the routine bureaucratic mode.

Below I draw on Weber's theory of bureaucracy to highlight the distinctive attributes of the Chinese bureaucracy and the implications for CSM, and I draw on transaction cost arguments to discuss alternative modes of organizing, in particular the shift between routine organization and CSM.

To explore the characteristics of the Chinese bureaucracy and the tensions within, let us revisit the soulstealer episode during the era of Emperor Hungli. As Kuhn (1990) shows, the soulstealer incidents broke out due to rumors and hate crimes by ill-intentioned persons in isolated events and localities and they aroused temporary fears among the people, but they did not cause major disturbances in these localities. They became major political events that shook up the entire bureaucracy only after the emperor's involvement and the resultant, tremendous political pressures in the form of direct decrees, stern reproaches, imposition of penalties, and launch of mobilizational efforts.

Information was central to this process. The soulstealer episode fully exposes the information and communication problems in the Chinese bureaucracy. Kuhn (1990) illustrates in great detail how information regarding those rumors about demon magic was collected, processed, and interpreted, and how such information was transmitted across hierarchical levels at county, region, and provincial levels and eventually to the emperor. Several characteristics stand out.

First, local officials faced the dilemma of how to interpret such incidents and whether to report upward those incidents in their respective jurisdictions. In the bureaucratic hierarchies, it was the local officials who directly dealt with those reported incidents. Compared with high-level officials, these local officials had richer, more accurate information. During the early phase of this episode, local officials made the appropriate judgment that these incidents were isolated cases with no political implications, and they recognized and corrected the coerced confessions. As Kuhn (1990, p. 27) observes, "The way provincial officialdom handled the spring sorcery cases suggests that they felt awkwardly balanced between dutiful caution and agnostic scorn." Yet, whether and how to report to their superiors information about these incidents presented a dilemma: If one reported falsely accused incidents, it could cause trouble for nothing, and the superiors could see these as unjustifiable false alarms that reflected poorly on the officials; however, if one did not report, he may be later accused of covering up problems and hiding critical information from the emperor, and "covering up information was a serious matter between emperor and bureaucrat. The troublesome business of local sorcery could have been kept from Hungli's attention only at some risk of his hearing about it through the rumor network" (Kuhn 1990, p. 77).

Second, there was deep suspicion and mistrust between the emperor and the bureaucrat. "The Throne presumed that the interest of the field official was always to reduce his risk of failure by underreporting the problem at hand" (Kuhn 1990, p. 129). The presence of information asymmetries and manipulation cast a cloud on the motives of local officials and led to overreactions on the part of both sides. It should be noted that information was ambiguous – the emperor and the local officials would have very different interpretations of the same piece of information. The barriers of information flows, diverse interpretations, and mutual distrust led the emperor to conclude that there were serious organizational failures; that is, the local officials were shirking their responsibilities and withholding information about a major crisis. As a result, the emperor disrupted the routine bureaucratic process and turned to a CSM mechanism so as to mobilize attention and pursue an intended crackdown. As high political pressure built up with the top-down directives that defined the incidents as an insidious conspiracy of rebellion, officials at all levels abandoned their own judgments and merely followed the decrees, either enthusiastically or passively, and looked for conspiracy plotters and rebellious leaders, thereby promoting the political campaign and bureaucratic behavior to absurdity.

What caused this major blunder and organizational failure? Let us return to the year 1768; at that time, the Chinese emperor exercised rule over a large country,

By the standards of the eighteenth-century world, Hungli's province chiefs in 1768 ruled immense populations. In the three-province jurisdiction of the Liangkiang governor-general lived more than seventy million people, a population more than twice that of France at the time. The governor of Kiangsu, the largest province in this group and the most populous in the nation ruled perhaps thirty million, at least triple the contemporary population of the United Kingdom. (Kuhn 1990, p. 121)

The Chinese bureaucracy emerged and matured early in history. Since the Qin dynasty (221–207 BC) when the governance system of the county and the prefecture was first established, the polity of centralization was perpetuated over time, running through most of the more than 2,000 years of Chinese civilization (Creel 1964). Historical research has documented an elaborate set of institutions on which such centralization was built, with the civil-service examination system as one of the pillars. Candidates were selected into officialdom by elaborate rules, ceremonies, and hierarchies, and they honed their skills, acquired knowledge about rules and procedures, climbed the bureaucratic ladder, and governed on behalf of the emperor. Officials were appointed, transferred, and allocated nationwide by the central government, serving an important function in sustaining the centralized authority and integration of the territories (Yan 2010).

The Weberian bureaucracy of the nineteenth century emerged in a markedly different historical and institutional context. In Weber's writings, modern bureaucracies arose in response to the demand for precision, promptness, and efficiency in capitalist economies, and they rested on the basis of a legal–rational authority. This is in sharp contrast to the behavior of those bureaucracies under the traditional, informal organizations or those built on personal charisma, as discussed in Chapter 2. In the Weberian organization, the management of employees is largely carried out through formal rules (Gouldner 1964) and employees appeal to the formal rules to resist the arbitrary power of the managers (Crozier 1964). These rule-following characteristics provide routinization mechanisms for the internal operation of formal organizations (Cyert and March 1963).

Stable organizational structures and processes induce corresponding organizational behavior. Sociologist Merton (1968a, p. 252) points out: "The bureaucratic structure exerts a constant pressure upon the official to be 'methodical, prudent, disciplined.' If the bureaucracy is to operate successfully, it must attain a high degree of reliability of behavior, an unusual degree of conformity with prescribed patterns of action." From Merton's point of view, "adherence to the rules, originally conceived as a means, becomes transformed into an end-in-itself; there occurs the familiar process of displacement of goals whereby 'an instrumental value becomes a terminal value' " (p. 253). As a result, routine-based organizations have their own problems, namely, they are risk-averse and trapped in a "iron cage."

As discussed in Chapter 2, unlike the legal–rational basis of the Weberian bureaucracy, the Chinese bureaucracy is based on a patrimonial mode of domination. At the core of this institution is an upward accountability system, that is, officials in different localities exercised their power on behalf of the emperor, and the emperor held arbitrary power to intervene in their decisions and their career development. Moreover, this arbitrary power had to be delegated to top officials at each level of the bureaucracy so that they could intervene in the work of their subordinates in a similar manner. In contrast to the Weberian bureaucracy, to a much greater extent Chinese officials depended on the subjective evaluation of their bosses for performance evaluations and career advancement.

These characteristics of the bureaucracy gave rise to the pervasiveness of informal institutions, where informal social relations played a larger role in performance evaluations and career advancement. As Kuhn points out, there were two types of instructions that regulated officials: The first was formal rules, and the second was particularistic relations. These particularistic relations were an integral part of the bureaucracy rather than a byproduct of the bureaucracy. A striking contrast between the Weberian bureaucracy and the Chinese bureaucracy lies in the role of formal rules. Formal rules are the basis of organizational operations and behavior, and they impose both top-down constraints on bureaucratic behavior and bottom-up protection of employees. As Merton (1968) points out, in the Weberian bureaucracy there is excessive attention to rule following, rule elaboration, and rule enforcement. In contrast, at the core of the Chinese bureaucracy there was upward accountability based on personal loyalty, trust, and patronage relationships. In this sense, the Chinese bureaucracy was not only an organization but also an institution involving multiplex social relations.

On this basis grew the salient characteristics of the contemporary Chinese bureaucracy. First, officials take a risk-averse disposition. Risk-averse attitudes apply to bureaucrats in all kinds of offices, but the same phenomenon may have different sources and different consequences. In the Weberian bureaucracy, rules constrain individual behavior, but in the Chinese bureaucracy, it is the lack of rules for protection that causes officials to be extremely cautious in their behavior so as to avoid stepping on the boundaries imposed by the superior. Second, officials tend to make excessive efforts to cultivate social relations and patronage ties for self-protection because of the lack of formal, protective mechanisms within the organization. As shown in the soulstealer episode, frequent upward reporting ran the risk of leaving the impression that the official lacked judgment or ability; if one did not report, one would be seen as hiding critical information, thus resulting in a serious penalty. In this context, dense social relations can help channel information, soften tensions, and lower potential risks in principal–agent relationships. All these are at the expense of the formal institutions.

Whereas the Weberian lens emphasizes distinct modes of domination and ensuing bureaucratic consequences, contemporary organization theories provide conceptual and analytical tools to make sense of bureaucratic phenomena. In particular, transaction cost theory (Coase 1937, Williamson 1985) sheds light on the shift between routine-based and CSM-based mechanisms in governance. Because parties to a transaction have different interests and different information, any organizational form (i.e., formal organizations, contracts, markets, etc.) has its own specific transaction cost, such as the cost of contract specification and the cost of inspection, coordination, or incentive provision, and so forth (Milgrom and Roberts 1992). Minimizing transaction costs is an important consideration in the choice of an organizational form. If the routine form of organizing encounters serious problems in terms of transaction costs, it will trigger a search for, and the rise of, new, alternative forms of organization in order to lower the transaction costs. This perspective helps us make sense of the shift between routine-based and CSM-based forms of governance.

The routine mode of the Chinese bureaucracy has its own transaction costs, and at times it is overburdened with staggeringly high costs of coordination and incentive design. Let us consider information flows across hierarchies. Problems in information collection, processing, transmission, and interpretation are always present in any organization. Issues related to principal–agent relationships were present between the emperor and the bureaucrat as they are between the supervisor and the subordinate in any organizational setting. The relationship is asymmetric in that one side has more information for strategic use than the other. The

organizational design aims at devising mechanisms to alleviate the negative effect of asymmetric information on organizations. In contemporary
societies, formal organizations, such as firms and other types of organizations, make use of different mechanisms to address these issues
(Hirschman 1970), such as exit, voice, incentive design, and changes in
the authority relationships.

In the Chinese bureaucracy such potential problems tend to be amplified
and intensified. First, the nature of a monopoly and the closeness of the
government bureaucracy render market mechanisms ineffective. Problems
within the bureaucracy cannot be resolved through competition, and over
time these problems accumulate and become more challenging. Second, the
hierarchical structure and the division of labor accelerate the difficulties in
information flows, and these difficulties are amplified due to the large
scale and long chain of command in the Chinese bureaucracy (Deng, Cao
and Pingtianmaoshu 2012). Third, diversity in local conditions produces
flexibility in policy implementation, which leads to deviations, and induces
suspicions between top officials and street-level bureaucrats. Fourth, the
scale of the organization accelerates the burden of supervision and inspection, which can hardly be addressed satisfactorily through monitoring and
surveillance technologies (Qu, Zhou and Ying 2009).

Soon after the establishment of the People's Republic in 1949, these
bureaucratic problems loomed large. As we see in Mao Zedong's repeated
efforts and the ensuing waves of political campaigns – the "three antis" in
1951, anti-bureaucratism in 1953, the party rectification campaign of
1957, to name but a few. During the Mao era, tensions between the
bureaucracy and the top leaders were intense, erupting from time to time,
and bureaucratic rectification was a main theme running through state
governance (Harding 1981).

Not surprisingly, as the routine mechanism of governance became
overburdened and inertia accumulated, associated transaction costs
become too high to continue as usual. These conditions were likely to
induce crises and to trigger a search for an alternative mode of governance
to temporarily disrupt and replace the routine mechanism of the bureaucracy. An alternative mechanism, CSM, arose in response.

The characteristics of routine-based mechanisms and the ensuing organizational failures led to the rise and reproduction of the CSM mechanism.
As noted above, the CSM mechanism takes the form of top-down directives and political means to disrupt and halt routine bureaucratic operations
and to mobilize resources and attention to pursue policy targets. In Chinese
history, we see that these two mechanisms – routines and CSM – coexist

symbiotically, and they take turns in dominating at different points in time. I now turn to examine the origins, forms, and consequences of CSM, and the shift between routine and CSM mechanisms.

CHARISMATIC AUTHORITY, ARBITRARY POWER, AND THE MOBILIZATIONAL MECHANISM

In this section, I continue the theme developed in Chapter 2 and elaborate on the relationship among charismatic authority, arbitrary power, and the role of CSM in the Chinese setting. The key argument is that the mode of domination based on arbitrary power provides the emperor (or the top leaders) with arbitrary power to intervene in bureaucratic processes, to replace a routine mechanism with a political mechanism, and to develop institutional arrangements that facilitate the exercise of arbitrary power.

To address the above issues, let us revisit the soulstealer episode during the Qing dynasty and seek clues from the historical events. Along with the unfolding of this episode, we find an alternating activation of routine and CSM. During the early phase, a routine mechanism was used to attend to these local incidents, and local officials dealt with these cases or pushed them aside as usual. If no unexpected circumstances erupted, these everyday events, both large and small, would disappear quietly in the routine operation of the bureaucratic machinery. Mannheim (1936) observed that the fundamental tendency of all bureaucratic thought is to turn all problems of politics into problems of administration (p. 105). But the persistent social turmoil incited by the soulstealing incidents eventually spilled out of the closed bureaucratic process, touched the suspicious nerve of the Emperor, and triggered the activation of the CSM mechanism. As a result, bureaucratic operations shifted gears from a routine mode to a campaign mode, superiors repeatedly exerted heightened pressures, subordinates followed the directives excessively, and the entire bureaucracy provided a stage on which a fast-evolving drama unfolded, with many careers wrecked and many heads rolling.

Why did the emperor have the power to disrupt the bureaucratic routine and replace it with CSM? Why did Chinese bureaucrats not resort to rules and procedures to resist these interventions? We have already encountered clues to the answer in our preceding discussion. Both routine and CSM mechanisms are derived from the patrimonial mode of domination in the bureaucratic monarchy, whereby the emperor's arbitrary power and bureaucratic power coexist. In this mode of domination, bureaucratic hierarchy and rules shaped the routine process, with an elaborate personnel management system from entry, mobility, and promotion to performance appraisal and evaluation (Chu 1962, Yan 2010, Zhu 2006). Bureaucratic machines, once in operation, had their own pace and rhythm, and they did not always respond to the will of the emperor, thus presenting a threat of loss of control. Moreover, rules, once they were made, may also have constrained the emperor. As Kuhn observes (1990, p. 190): "The monarch had to regulate his thousands of bureaucratic servants by written codes, to ensure that everyone stuck to the administrative procedures that underlay his own wealth and security. At the same time, he was naturally concerned to maintain his own distinctive position, his extra-bureaucratic power and autonomy. Consequently, he had to struggle unceasingly to avoid becoming bureaucratized himself."

CSM was an effective weapon of the emperor in this regard. In the patrimonial mode of governance, the CSM mechanism was at the disposal of the emperor's arbitrary power; that is, the emperor could use CSM to disrupt bureaucratic routines and to shift the bureaucratic machine into a different gear based on his will.

The upward accountability system gave rise to heightened mobilizational capacities. Upward accountability cultivated the dual features of the bureaucrats: on the one hand, the exercise of cautiousness in everyday work, risk-aversion, and responsibility-shirking; on the other hand, once the intentions of the superiors were made clear and opportunities appeared, they were actively followed in order to capitalize on the opportunities and to cultivate or strengthen patronage ties. It is not surprising, then, that the officials were extremely sensitive to their superiors' preferences and followed directives actively and excessively, thereby greatly enhancing the effectiveness of the CSM mechanism.

If routine-based power comes from hierarchical positions and rules and procedures, where does arbitrary power come from? What are the forces that can push the officials to forgo the protection of rules and procedures and to participate in the political processes? In Chapter 2, I argue that the arbitrary power of the bureaucratic monarchy rested on the dual basis of the traditional authority and the charismatic authority as "the son of heaven." Eisenstadt (1968) points out that in the charismatic authority, the role of the followers is critical. It is the followers' recognition and acceptance of this social order, and the expectation and acceptance of this charismatic authority, that provide the basis for its authority. In the relationship between the charismatic leader and his followers, the former does not represent or express the will of the latter but it points out their duties and responsibilities; bureaucratic institutions become a machine that follows the will and directives of the charismatic leader.

But even under a mixed traditional and charismatic authority, the exercise of arbitrary power is not without constraints. This shift from a routine mechanism to CSM requires excuses and opportunities. As Kuhn (1990) observes, a "political crime" provided such an opportunity. A political crime, especially one committed by those officials holding bureaucratic power, indicated the failure of the routine mechanism and provided an excuse to replace it with CSM so as to effectively and speedily implement the will of the charismatic leader. Here, manufacturing a political crime is an important intermediate step in this shift. "Just as the bureaucratic monarchy lived on the economic surplus of China's society, it depended on society for the 'events' that served as raw material for the operation of its internal relationships. The internal machinery of the bureaucratic monarchy processed all such 'events' and transformed them into power and status" (Kuhn 1990, p. 220). The soulstealer episode reflected the activation and operation of the CSM mechanism. As a result, "the overall impetus of a political crime like soulstealing was to shake bureaucrats out of patterns of routine behavior that they used, so effectively, for their own protection; and to give Hungli a context in which to confront his problems with the bureaucracy head-on" (p. 211). Here, the very power to define and convict a political crime came from the arbitrary power based on the charismatic authority.

Fast forward to contemporary society, where the routine mechanism provides the basis for everyday operations of public administration, and the bureaucracy has been expanding and strengthening along with the scale and scope of the nation-state. After the collapse of the Qing dynasty in the early twentieth century, traditional legitimacy withered and gave way to a legal–rational authority. Similarly, the heaven-delegated charismatic authority seemed to have become obsolete with the bygone age of the monarchy.

But this was not the case. During the short history of the People's Republic, there were frequent instances when arbitrary power disrupted and halted the routine-based processes, as evidenced during the Great Leap Forward and the Cultural Revolution as well as during other political campaigns. As we shift our gaze from the late Qing dynasty to contemporary China, we are confronted with the following question: What is the source of CSM in contemporary China in relation to the legitimate basis of domination by the party-state?

ROUTINIZATION OF CHARISMATIC AUTHORITY AND THE CSM
MECHANISM IN THE CHINESE PARTY-STATE

The Routinization of Charisma in Office in Contemporary China

In contemporary China, charismatic authority did not retreat and disappear from the historical stage; rather, it went through a routinization process and survived in new forms during the state-building process. It has continued to play an important role in China's governance. I now discuss how charismatic authority has been routinized to provide a new basis of legitimacy for arbitrary power. The routinization process and the state-building process became intertwined over time, providing clues for us to understand the institutional logic of governance.

Weber points out that an important channel for the routinization of charismatic leadership is the "charisma of office"; that is, some organizational apparatus acquires an extraordinary character and becomes the embodiment of a charismatic authority. Weber uses the concept of charisma of office "to denote the process through which the charismatic characteristics are transferred from the unique personality or the unstructured group to orderly institutional reality" (Eisenstadt 1968, p. xxi). In this process, some designated institutions acquire symbolic representation of the charismatic authority and become the stable foundation for the charismatic authority. In traditional China, Confucian values and the piety-based social order played such a role. Social institutions are reflected partly in these values and norms and partly in the stable organizational basis on which authority is exercised. "It is this double aspect of social institutions – their organizational exigencies on the one hand, and their potential close relations to the realm of meaning on the other – which may provide us with clues as to how the ordinary and the charismatic are continuously interwoven in the process of institution building" (Eisenstadt' xxxviii). Unlike in those traditional societies where the charismatic authority is attached to a single person, in contemporary societies charismatic authority goes through a process of charisma of office and is attached to stable organizations as institutions infused with corresponding values and norms.

In the People's Republic, the party-state has become the embodiment of the routinization of charisma. In symbols, the ruling party has acquired sacred characteristics such as "greatness, glory, and righteousness" that resemble the charismatic authority – an irreplaceable and intrinsic ability in leadership that is invincible, self-correcting, and self-renewing. Moreover, the hierarchical organization, tightened discipline, and mobilizational capacity of the Leninist party have provided a strong organizational basis. When the party-state and its top leaders are projected with a charisma of extraordinary ability and they can recognize and master the law of human society, they naturally acquire a leadership role, the capacity to override routine power, mobilize resources, and develop a top-down design to pursue their goals. Furthermore, they can push aside any alternative form of rational–legal authority and subordinate bureaucratic power as their organizational weapon and disrupt and halt bureaucratic processes at will. The charismatic authority is no longer intertwined with traditional authority; rather, it is built directly on the basis of the bureaucratic organizations, with the charismatic authority of the party-state providing the legitimacy for the exercise of arbitrary power.

This leads us to recognize the importance of ideological control in the hands of the party-state. The routinization of charisma not only requires a stable organizational basis but also needs to be built at the societal center of values and norms. If pluralism and liberalism in the public arena were allowed, doubts about and challenges to the charismatic authority would inevitably arise and undermine its basis of legitimacy. It is not surprising, then, that political indoctrination and ritualization are an important part of the logic of governance under the party-state rule.

Institutional Bases of CSM

The preceding discussion on the routinization of the office of charisma leads us to further consider the institutional basis of CSM, which includes the following elements: the coexistence of party-state dual authority, corresponding red-expert personnel management, and the routinization of mobilizational mechanisms (Schurmann 1968). I discuss these issues below.

First, the party-state dual authority. In contemporary societies the routinization of charismatic authority takes place on a stable organizational basis. We can reinterpret the party-state dual authority structure in this light. The CCP has inherited the charismatic authority in Chinese history, and has updated it to a contemporary version of historical materialism with the Marxist vision of the historical law of human societies. At the same time, the exercise of charismatic authority is routinized in the organizational apparatus of the CCP, parallel to but dominant over the routine power-based government offices. This dual party-state apparatus has established the organizational basis for routine-based versus CSM-based mechanisms; this becomes clear once we put these two side by side. On the "government" side, we observe functional offices, such as those for public health, transportation, energy, education. Such functional lines reflect specialization and division of labor, and their institutional setups are similar to their counterparts in other societies. This organizational apparatus suffers similar organizational problems and transaction costs but these problems and costs tend to be much higher in China due to the scale and the reach of the state apparatus. The CMS mechanism becomes an effective means to addressing these problems by the party-line organizational apparatus, to which we now turn.

Second, as the institutional basis for the chain of command, the party line follows direct directives from the top leader(s) of the ruling party, and its behavior is characterized by political mobilization. Party organizations span the boundaries of the administrative offices in the government line, thereby facilitating coordination and mobilization across boundaries. For example, the party's political and legal commission (*zheng-fa-wei*) at different levels of the party headquarters leads and coordinates all government offices in the legal area. Similarly, the party's agricultural commission plays an anchoring role in all affairs related to the rural areas. Political campaigns and rectifications were often launched to target bureaucratic problems in routine processes. In contemporary China, the dual power of the party and the government alternates over time and across different areas along with the interplay between routine versus CSM mechanisms. During the post-Mao era, the dual authority in functional offices has been largely unified into one leadership, whereas in the territorially based jurisdictions, the party headquarters has its own powerful organizational apparatus in order to enforce top-down directives. In the Xi Jinping era since the early 2010s, the party line has been greatly reenforced and (re)entrenched into different areas and corners of society. In so doing, the top leaders have greatly strengthened the top-down mobilizational capacity and the tools of political campaigns.

Third, the CMS mechanism is also reflected in personnel management practices. The party-state has long adopted the so-called "red and expert" (*you hong you zhuan*) principle. That is, the principle for selecting and promoting officials emphasizes both "red" (loyalty to the party line) and "expert" (competence) qualities, but political loyalty is deemed more important for appointment to positions in party lines (Walder 1995b). In the same government office, party and administrative lines coexist, each attending to their respective responsibilities, but the former overrides the latter. Different career trajectories in the Chinese bureaucracy coexist based on their party and government lines of jobs, which is in sharp contrast to

Weber's emphasis on professional training and careers. In view of the routinization of office discussed above, the red-expert principle ensures the coexistence of routine and CSM mechanisms in the party-government dual authority. An official is expected to perform his/her duties in routine positions and at the same time to be receptive to top-down mobilization.

Fourth, political mobilization and CSM have been weaved into everyday work activities. It is a common observation that CSM is part of routine practice in the party-state at different levels of the government and in different functional areas. For example, during the period of the Beijing Olympic Games in 2008, in the province of my fieldwork, the provincial government dispatched a large number of officials from provincial-level offices to every township in the local areas surrounding Beijing to ensure the so-called "maintenance of social order" (*weiwen*). The county leadership adopted the same mobilizational measures and sent officials from county-level offices into every village in these regions. This mobilization exercise lasted for several months.

To sum up, the coexistence of the party-government dual authority in different types of organizations reveals a contemporary version of the historical coexistence of arbitrary power and routine power in governance. The party line provides the stable organizational basis for CSM, which is sustained by the upward accountability system and the "political crime" ideology and related institutions. These institutional arrangements provide the party-state with an effective mechanism for political mobilization to disrupt routine bureaucratic processes, to pursue its policy goals, and to strengthen political control.

Over time, the party and government apparatus become diffused with each other. In actual bureaucratic processes, personnel move back and forth across party and government lines. For example, in the territorial governments the administrative head of a county or a prefecture is at the same time the vice party secretary of the same administrative jurisdiction, and administrative officials may be promoted into party head positions. In such cases, the "red and expert" principle requires that one must be competent, loyal, and responsive to the arbitrary power of the higher authority. Moreover, the party and government institutions become mirror images of each other. On the one hand, the party organization has become bureaucratized, leading to the ritualization of political mobilization; on the other hand, the administrative offices have become politicized and they make use of CSM mechanisms to get things done.

My discussion above has emphasized the arbitrary power of the highest authority over the routine power of the bureaucracy. But this does not mean that such arbitrary power is unconstrained. The bureaucrats also develop various strategies to respond to and to buffer the arbitrary power of the highest authority, increasing the costs of exercising arbitrary power and the costs of CSM. One such cost is the danger of the loss of control. Once the CSM mechanism is activated, officials may take the opportunity to pursue their own interests and impose their own interpretations, leading to a spillover out of the intended boundaries. Emperor Hungli fully understood this, as he remarked: "When we are lenient in one or two cases in which leniency is appropriate, then all the officials scurry to be lenient. When we are strict in one or two cases that require strictness, then they all scurry to be strict" (Kuhn 1990, p. 199). In the upward accountability system, officials do not take initiatives and they are likely to take the opportunity offered in the CSM process to exercise their own arbitrary power, targeting their opponents, settling scores, and pursuing their own interests. Such instances abound during the episodes of political campaigns in China. They increase the costs of activating the CSM mechanism and they impose constraints upon the top leaders, forcing them to return to the routine mode of operation.

CSM and the Shift in the Modes of Governance in the Chinese Bureaucracy

Thus far, my discussion has focused on the historical origins of CSM, its relationship to the mode of patrimonial and party-state domination, and its institutional basis in contemporary China. I should also point to another important role that CSM plays – in the shift across modes of governance under different allocations of control rights, as discussed in Chapter 3.

Under pressure from the fundamental tension, there is variable-coupling in central–local government relationships or in relationships across levels of the bureaucratic hierarchy, from tight coupling, subcontracting, to loose-coupling or federalism. Chapter 3 discusses the discrete modes of governance associated with the different allocation of control rights along three dimensions: goal setting, inspection, and the provision of incentives. What remains to be addressed is the issue of how the shift across these distinctive modes is possible.

I argue that CSM plays an important role in inducing or pushing such a shift across different modes of governance by mobilizing attention and resources to overcome bureaucratic inertia in a given state. For example, CSM based on the claim of a "political crime" plays the role of producing a tightly coupled system across levels of the bureaucracy such that all control rights are (temporarily) held in the hands of the higher authority. In so doing, the top leaders can shift a loosely coupled routine process to a tightly coupled mode of governance, as Hungli did during the soulstealer episode. We observe a contemporary version during the Peng Dehuai episode during the Mao era and during Xi Jinping's anti-corruption campaign in recent years. In all these episodes, the use of CSM built up tremendous pressures for officials at all levels for "politics to take command" and to adhere to the political logic, resulting in strong and effective implementation of the top leader's agenda.

We should recognize that CSM is not only used for political control but it also is used for the liberalization of political control, as in the case of the early phase of the post-Mao era. The ideological liberation movement of the 1980s allowed the Deng Xiaoping leadership to push for "reform and opening up" policies and for a relaxation of the political control of the Mao era. In this case, CSM induced a shift from a "tight-coupling" to a "loose-coupling" mode of governance in the early 1980s.

Similarly, CSM has been used in the economic arena for top-down efforts to pursue policy targets, such as during the Great Leap Forward or in the advocacy of a market economy during the post-Mao era.

These instances demonstrate the central role of CSM in China's governance and also remind us that CSM has been associated with the political processes in China both historically and in the contemporary era, and it has functioned in different areas and for different policy orientations. We need to gain a better understanding of CSM phenomena within a broader comparative perspective and over a longer historical horizon.

Characteristics of CSM

As an important mechanism of governance in China, various forms of CSM have existed throughout history, but are becoming more prevalent in the mode of party-state domination. I now summarize the key characteristics of CSM in the Chinese setting.

First, one defining characteristic of CSM is its disruption of a routine bureaucratic process and its replacement with a political process and a redefinition of the boundaries of appropriate bureaucratic behavior. CSM is effective in mobilizing attention and resources, but it incurs other risks and costs. As a result, CSM tends to be short term, intermittent, and in that sense "un-routine." But as CSM becomes intertwined with routine processes in the party-state, we observe its occurrences becoming more frequent and more routinized; as a result, it is likely to be transformed by the routine processes and to become less effective as a mobilizational weapon.

Second, recognition of CSM as an institutional response to the failure of routine mechanisms sheds light on the conditions and opportunities for its activation: (1) when there are major exogenous changes, such as crises or disasters to which bureaucratic routines cannot respond effectively; or, (2) when major crises expose problems in bureaucratic routines, which trigger CSM as a corrective mechanism, as in the soulstealer episode; or (3) when there are major endogenous policy reorientations to which the existing bureaucratic routines are ill-adapted; in such cases, CSM is activated to push the bureaucracy toward a new course of action. Much CSM in contemporary China can be understood in this light, such as the Great Leap Forward (Zhou 2009), the ideological liberation movement of the 1980s, and the anti-corruption campaign of Xi Jinping's era since 2012.

Third, a salient characteristic of CSM is its great fanfare in heightened propaganda rhetoric and scale. This is because the key to disrupting the routine rhythm at different levels of the bureaucracy is by mobilizing the attention of officials and changing their dispositions, thereby producing a (temporarily) tightly coupled system so that officials will suspend their habitual responses and shift to a different gear or to a different course of action. In so doing, the CSM mechanism provides an effective mechanism to transmit the intention and the resolve of the higher authorities to all levels of the bureaucracy.

Fourth, an important purpose of CSM is to redefine the boundaries of what is appropriate behavior in response to local initiatives and flexibility, often under the disguise of a "political crime." It is often observed that the penalties for CSM are especially harsh and arbitrary. The main purpose of CSM is to set examples as signals to warn others. In fact, so-called "bureaucratic deviations" and "implementation flexibility" are often different labels for similar behavior. That is, the same type of behavior is interpreted differently under different circumstances. Bureaucratic behavior may be interpreted as a local adaptation in a positive light or as a deviation of the intended policy, depending on the political environment. The latter takes place when the centralized authority sees such behavior as challenging or undermining its authority. But the purpose of CSM is not to eliminate such behavior but to refine its appropriate boundaries from time to time and in the process to reinstate the power of the centralized authority.

SUMMARY

This chapter focuses on a central and prevalent mechanism – campaign-style mobilization – in China's governance practices; it examines its origins, characteristics, and implications. We highlight the coexistence and interplay between routine-based and CSM-based mechanisms in the Chinese bureaucracy and in its practice of governance, and the role of CSM as an integral part of the institutional mechanisms in the logic of governance. The discussion is situated in the larger context of the party-state mode of governance and institutional arrangements in terms of the routinization of charisma.

As the discussion in this chapter shows, CSM arose in part as an institutional response to organizational failures in the overreach of the bureaucracy and the ensuing agency problems and in part as a mechanism for the mobilization of resources and attention to meet policy targets. CSM disrupts bureaucratic routines and reorients their course of action. In many ways, this is indeed an effective means to mobilize attention and resources to achieve policy goals. Moreover, CSM is not arbitrary but built into a set of institutional arrangements, such as the party-state dual authority structure and red-expert personnel management practices. In other words, CSM is a highly institutionalized mechanism of governance and a repair mechanism. Its contemporary version is a major update and qualitative transformation over its historical precedents as a result of the organization of the Leninist party-state. CSM serves as a double-edged sword in alleviating or exacerbating the fundamental tension in Chinese governance and in maintaining or disrupting a delicate balance between the centralization of authority and effective, local adaptation.

This chapter provides a node to connect the themes in the previous chapters. In Chapter 2, I develop an argument about the mode of party-state domination, with a mix of charismatic authority in substance and legal–rational authority in form. The CSM-mechanism is closely related to, or directly built on, the arbitrary power of the party-state and the basis of legitimacy in this mode of domination. In Chapter 3, I discuss different modes of Chinese governance – tight-coupling, subcontracting, loose-coupling, and federalism. In this chapter, I argue that CSM provides a mechanism for a transition across modes of governance, as evidenced in the ideological liberation movement in the early phase of the post-Mao era, which shifted from a tight-coupling system to a loosely coupled system, or in Xi Jinping's anti-corruption campaign that induced a reverse shift from a loose-coupling to tight-coupling system. These major changes and reorientations were accompanied by, indeed pushed by, large-scale CSM.

PART II

THE LOGIC OF GOVERNANCE AND GOVERNMENT BEHAVIOR

5

Bureaucratic Bargaining in the Chinese Government

This chapter is the first of four chapters on bureaucratic behavior in light of the institutional logic of governance in China. Each of the following four chapters will focus on one class of bureaucratic phenomena and its relationship to larger issues of governance practice in China and how these behavioral patterns are shaped by and contribute to the institutional logic. The four chapters share a common approach that blends theoretical analysis with empirical evidence drawn from fieldwork observations.

Here we focus on bargaining practices in order to gain insights into the inner workings of the Chinese bureaucracy. Bargaining practices offer a glimpse into how formal and informal rules operate, and how formal institutions and informal practices interact, to address issues related to information, interests, and political pressures in principal–agent relationships.

Let me first establish the context of our inquiry. A glaring gap exists between the important role of the Chinese bureaucracy and the lack of cumulative knowledge about the processes and inner workings of China's bureaucratic apparatus. On the one hand, the post-Mao era has witnessed the rise of a contemporary, bureaucratic state in China, with an elaborate system of incentives, inspections, and evaluations that shape the behavior of administrative subordinates (Ai 2008, Landry 2008, Yang 2004). On the other hand, knowledge about the Chinese bureaucracy is thin and scattered. To be sure, research on Chinese administrative units is plentiful, including, for example, studies on their roles in economic development and in government-business relationships (Cai and Treisman 2006, Oi 1992, Qian and Weingast 1997, Walder 1995a) and patterns of promotions and personnel management (Chan 2004, Edin 2003, Landry 2008, Li and Bachman 1989, Manion 1985, Pieke 2009, Walder, Li and

Treiman 2000). But most of these studies focus on formal institutions rather than dynamic processes, or on overt behavior in interactions with other groups, such as firms or villages, rather than on the actual workings *within* the Chinese bureaucracy.

Take, for example, the case of bureaucratic bargaining in the Chinese government. Lampton (1992, p. 34) observed: "Bargaining is one of several forms of authority relationship in China ... it has been of central importance in the Chinese policy process throughout the Communist era." Lieberthal and Lampton (1992) propose the fragmented authoritarian model of decision making in the Chinese bureaucracy, whereby bargaining and interest articulation and reconciliation are key properties of China's policy-making processes. Shirk (1993) highlights consensus building through bureaucratic bargaining as a defining characteristic of China's policy-making processes. Bureaucratic bargaining is a recurrent theme in studies on policymaking in the energy sector (Lieberthal and Oksenberg 1986), in policy implementation (Lampton 1987) and in bureaucratic behavior at the street level (Edin 2003, Huang 1995, O'Brien and Li 1999).

Despite the common theme that runs through these studies, little cumulative knowledge on bureaucratic bargaining has been developed in the literature: No well-formulated, analytical concepts or models are proposed, no common or distinct patterns are identified, and there is no empirical research built on previously accumulated knowledge. Lampton (1992) provides the most comprehensive overview of the context, areas, and basic forms of bureaucratic bargaining among Chinese governments, but he focuses on general, institutional bases of bureaucratic bargaining and has little to say about the actual processes. The study of the political logic of reform in the post-Mao era by Shirk (1993) centers on bureaucratic bargaining, but, again, she only deals with this in a general manner. What are the key processes or forms of bureaucratic bargaining? What are the patterns of interaction among bureaus and offices in the bargaining process? What factors contribute to the bargaining power of each side? Twenty years after Lampton's statement quoted above, bureaucratic bargaining in Chinese governments remains a black box.

In this chapter, I take a step to fill this gap. Drawing on insights from game-theoretic models of bargaining and strategic interaction, I develop a conceptual model of bureaucratic bargaining between supervising and subordinate agencies. I use a game-theoretic approach as a heuristic device to help identify research issues and analytical concepts and to outline different elements in the game, or different types of games, that are invoked in the bargaining process. My goal is to gain analytical strength by sorting out the different components that constitute bureaucratic bargaining, clarifying the logical connections among these components, and postulating conditions under which the different forms and processes of bargaining are realized.

Development of the proposed model is informed and inspired by a three-year participant-observation research project, first introduced in Chapter 3, in a municipal environmental protection bureau (MEPB) in northern China between 2008 and 2010. Observations about the behavioral patterns of officials in their daily work and in their interactions with their supervising and subordinate agencies inform the theory building and provide rich material to help identify research issues and to understand the underlying mechanisms of bureaucratic interchange. The conceptual model will be illustrated mainly by the observed interactions between the MEPB and its supervising agency – the provincial environmental protection bureau (PEPB).

Below, I first develop a conceptual model that specifies the rules, structures, and sequences of the bargaining games within the Chinese bureaucracy and propose a set of research issues and analytical concepts. Second, I illustrate the analytical aspects of the bargaining games in the aforementioned research setting – the bargaining process between an MEPB and its supervising agency, the PEPB, in W Province. In a conventional principal–agent context, the PEPB is the principal and the MEPB is the agent.

A MODEL OF BUREAUCRATIC BARGAINING

I develop a model of bureaucratic bargaining in the following steps: First, I introduce the context in which bargaining takes place; then I identify a set of analytical issues and concepts to model the bargaining games; and finally, I locate these analytic considerations in the Chinese bureaucratic context and develop a conceptual model of bargaining between a principal and an agent, and derive a set of empirical implications.

The Institutional Context

Bargaining always takes place in a specific organizational setting and is constrained by institutional rules of the game within that context. To facilitate the substantive discussion below, I start with a description of the authority relationships in a concrete setting, that is, the area of environmental regulation in China in the mid-2000s (Ma and Ortolano 2000).

As discussed in Chapter 3, government agencies in the environmental regulation area are governed by dual authorities. One is the functional, vertical authority relationships among the bureaucratic offices in China's environmental-protection administrative system, with the Ministry of Environmental Protection (MEP) at the top, followed by the provincial, municipal, and county bureaus. The other is the administrative authority of the territorial governments that provides the bureaus with their main resources – annual budgets, staffing, and opportunities for personnel mobility and promotion.

My analytical focus is on the bargaining relationship along functional lines, that is, between the MEPB and its supervising agency, the PEPB. Occasionally, the MEPB may also have direct contact with officials from the MEP as a result of special projects, onsite inspections, or particularistic connections. The Chinese bureaucratic structure stipulates that the local environmental protection bureaus (EPBs) receive policy targets and technical guidance from their supervising functional agencies. In a similar authority relationship, the MEPB also serves as the supervising agency for the county-level EPBs (CEPBs) within its jurisdiction. Here again, the CEPBs are under the same kind of dual authorities, in this case, the authority of the MEPB and the authority of their county governments.

We focus here on the principal–agent relationship between the PEPB as a supervising agency and the MEPB as a subordinate agency. Bargaining takes place between the two when the principal issues a directive that the agent finds objectionable in some respect. In this framework, policy enforcement and bargaining are intertwined in the processes involving principal–agent interactions. I assume that the principal and the agent share the broader goals of environmental regulation. But the agent incurs the costs of implementation.

In addition, the MEPB faces multiple demands, and hence it has multiple, conflicting goals. On the one hand, the MEPB's main function is to enforce environmental policies and regulations; on the other hand, it must also serve the goals of the municipal government. To expand the bases for resource extraction, local governments actively promote economic growth, which is often in tension with the goals of environmental regulation. For example, in the performance-evaluation system issued by the provincial government in W Province, among a multitude of criteria on which the sub-provincial governments are to be evaluated, only six percent of the total weight is given to environmental protection, whereas economic development weighs twenty-five percent.[1] Not surprisingly, the MEPB faces conflicting pressures from the municipal government and the PEPB. The MEPB also depends on other bureaus in the municipal government to carry out its tasks. For example, it must work with the municipal statistical bureau to obtain relevant data; it also must cooperate with the urban management bureau, which implements pollution-control measures in residential areas. In interacting with the PEPB, the MEPB must take into consideration other local authorities that contribute, either directly or indirectly, to the MEPB's environmental-regulation efforts. I will further explore this theme in Chapter 7.

An important characteristic of environmental regulation is that there is considerable ambiguity about the technologies, statistics, measurements, and criteria employed. By ambiguity, I mean that the same information is subject to multiple interpretations (March and Olsen 1979). For example, the same water-quality testing result may be interpreted differently because there may be measurement errors and there may also be suspicions about the results being manipulated or being derived from different testing procedures. The same test results may also be subject to different interpretations because water-quality criteria, the basis for interpretation, may be ambiguous.

The presence of multiple principals, multiple tasks and goals, and ambiguity about information, criteria and technology all suggest that there is much room for bureaucratic bargaining over a number of parameters, including the need for resources, criteria for performance evaluations, workloads, and allocation of blame when things go wrong. The subordinate bureau often has better information and greater technical competence than its supervisory bureau and may thereby be empowered to make legitimate claims and to engage in active bargaining with the supervising unit. Under these circumstances, in spite of formal hierarchies and administrative directives, bureaucratic bargaining permeates the field of environmental regulation.

Analytical Concepts

In the language of contemporary social science, bargaining is usually interpreted as the process of arriving at mutual agreement on the provisions of a contract (Kennan and Wilson 1993). Broadly defined, "nearly all

---

[1] Unless otherwise noted, the empirical evidence in this case study comes from our fieldwork.

human interaction can be seen as bargaining of one form or another" (Binmore, Osborne and Rubinstein 1992, p. 181). Economic models of bargaining typically depict two parties negotiating over division of a "pie," such as between an employer and a labor union over the wage rate. The process involves alternating offers and eventually yields an agreement (or a failure to reach an agreement). Bargaining processes can be formalized in a game-theoretic framework. Admittedly, game-theoretic models are highly stylized and emphasize selected properties of the bargaining process under restrictive assumptions. As a heuristic device, such models add consider- able analytical strength in that they require explication of the assumptions and clarification of the logical connections, and they facilitate the gener- ation of theory-based predictions that can be empirically tested.

Below, I draw on game-theoretic models as a heuristic device to char- acterize distinctive strategies available to the different parties, and the conditions under which one strategy is more likely to be adopted than others. Because different strategic choices may lead to different types of bargaining games, I highlight the rules of the game under different scen- arios. The conceptual framework integrates the rules of the game, the mechanisms involved in the processes, and the expected behavioral pat- terns to provide a explanatory framework for the observed behavioral patterns.

Bargaining in a bureaucratic setting. Unlike bargaining in a market- place, bargaining in a government organization takes place in the presence of formal authority relationships, where agencies or bureaus are intercon- nected in a hierarchical structure. As mentioned, in the functional (vertical) line of the Chinese government (i.e., in this case, the system for environ- mental protection in China), bureaus are organized hierarchically, and administrative orders are transmitted based on formal authority. Bargaining takes place amid interactions in two directions between the supervising agency and the subordinate agency: vertically across hierarch- ical levels of the environmental-protection units, and laterally between an EPB and other administrative units within the same territorial government.

Consider two parties bargaining over the division of some resources (i.e., budgetary allocations, task loads, or share of blame). To make sense of the bargaining processes and the outcomes, the bargaining power associated with the various parties at the table is a key issue. Recent developments in game-theoretic modeling provide analytical concepts useful to organize our theoretical exposition. Game-theoretic models direct our attention to factors affecting the *bargaining power* of the involved parties, the stages of the game, and the kind of strategic maneuvers that may strengthen one's bargaining power. Bargaining power, in this context, can be examined by asking the following question: What does each bargainer believe about the other's willingness to settle and about the other's beliefs? This information is likely to be revealed through alternating offers during stages of the game.

Game-theoretic models of bargaining have largely focused on scenarios involving bilateral bargaining in market-like settings, where participation in the bargaining is voluntary, the parties have exit options, and the parties are of equal status in terms of making and rejecting offers. Market settings are substantively different from bureaucratic settings involving formal authorities and hierarchical relationships. Nevertheless, game-theoretic models provide a basis upon which a conceptual model applicable to the bureaucratic context can be constructed. I now discuss a set of analytical concepts that are central in the bargaining processes: information, deadlines or time pressures, and commitment and credibility.

Information. The distribution of information among bargaining parties is central in game-theoretic models. When all parties have complete information, Pareto-efficient bargaining equilibria generally exist (Rubinstein 1982). However, a particularly challenging aspect of the bargaining process is the presence of incomplete information (about the intention or commitment of the other side), which may be one-sided or two-sided (Fudenberg and Tirole 1983). In the area of environmental regulation, information regarding the level and sources of pollution and the extent of waste reduction being accomplished is typically one-sided in the sense that the MEPB, which is much closer to the sources of pollution and often has disaggregated data, knows more about these details than the PEPB. In addition to this information asymmetry, this type of information is typically incomplete and ambiguous in the sense that data will be missing and, in some cases, data may be manipulated by waste sources. In short, as in a typical principal–agent problem, the agent tends to have richer and more accurate information than the principal. As shown below, these characteristics tend to strengthen the agent's formal bargaining power, and it may lead to signaling, whereby the agent volunteers private information to the principal during the bargaining process.

Deadlines (or time pressures). Patience is an important source of bargaining power (Rubinstein 1985), and the party with more patience has an edge. Deadlines play an important role in bureaucratic settings. Bureaucratic operations have their own rhythms: budget cycles, inspection cycles, policymaking deadlines, and so forth. Since deadlines (for inspection, policymaking, or revision) are set from above, time delays often have a higher cost for the agent. An opportunity not seized in a timely manner may disappear; a resource not fought for in time may be diverted; and a problem not explained away immediately may have negative consequences. Therefore, issues related to time pressures and deadlines provide an important angle to understand strategies and behavioral patterns in the bargaining game.

Commitment and credibility. These factors play an important role in the bargaining process, both intuitively and as demonstrated formally in game-theoretic models. In a bargaining situation, if one side can make a credible commitment, he/she can gain stronger bargaining power. An important aspect of the bargaining process is to reveal, form, or revise beliefs about the opponent's commitment. In an organizational setting, commitment is closely related to the higher authority's resolve. The principal usually has the upper hand in terms of imposing a commitment. However, the principal's commitment is not constant or static. In the Chinese bureaucracy this commitment tends to alternate between two modes: a routine mode and a mobilizational mode, as alluded to in Chapter 4. A model must recognize any changes in the principal's commitment as circumstances shift between the mobilizational and routine modes.

This set of analytical issues – information distribution, time pressures and deadlines and commitment and credibility – are important building blocks in modeling the bureaucratic bargaining game in the Chinese administrative context.

Model Setup

The discussion below outlines a simple, sequential game of bargaining between a principal (the PEPB) and an agent (the MEPB). Several considerations are central to the model specification: First, the sequence of the game captures the rules of the game in the organizational setting; second, the "strategy space" – the strategic choices available – to each side is constructed based on our knowledge of the specific organizational context; third, there are conditions under which certain strategies are likely to be adopted by the principal (with expected payoffs). The model specification provides a basis for reasoning empirically testable propositions. The proposed sequential game is sketched in Figure 5.1, and the discussion below is framed around the sequence in the figure.

Principal

Routine   Mobilization

Agent   **Agent**

Formal bargaining   Informal bargaining   Quasi-exit   Quasi-exit
(Signaling game)   (Alternating offers)   (Implementation game)   (Implementation game)

FIGURE 5.1. A sequential game of bureaucratic bargaining

(1) The Principal's First Move: Choosing between a Routine and a Mobilizational Mode of Implementation

As shown in Figure 5.1, the principal makes the first move, which activates the policy-implementation process in one of the two modes, either routine or mobilizational. The choice between these two modes signals the level of the principal's *commitment* to enforce the policy-implementation process. In the routine mode, established rules, procedures, and expectations regulate the activities of the EPB offices to carry out their tasks. In the mobilizational mode, as discussed in Chapter 4, the higher authority signals a stronger commitment. This is reflected in the heightened attention and resources devoted by the principal (PEPB) to the policy-enforcement process, and its closer scrutiny of the behavior of the MEPB (e.g., by close inspections or by reviewing MEPB data and reports) and imposition of greater penalties for shortfalls in performance.

There are substantive implications of these two modes of policy implementation. Formal organizations operate based on routines, where work is carried out based on established procedures and expectations. In addition, organizational units are loosely coupled and less responsive to one another (Weick 1976), thereby leaving room for the bargaining processes to take place. In contrast, the mobilizational mode signifies a tightly coupled system where different parts (e.g., sub-units, offices) of the organization become highly interconnected and responsive to each other. In this sense, the mobilization mode indicates more rigorous policy enforcement. However, the mobilizational mode is costly. It involves additional resources (attention, funding, frequent inspections, disruption of routine tasks, and so forth). As the mobilization mode cannot be sustained for a prolonged period, in general, policy enforcement is carried out in the routine mode.

The proposed model specification that the supervisor makes the first move underscores three aspects of my argument. First, the principal has the upper hand in initiating and continuing different levels of enforcement intensity. For the agent, the shift between the two modes of enforcement is largely an exogenous factor that he/she does not control and he/she can only respond to in a subsequent move. Second, in initiating the mobilization mode, the principal makes a more credible commitment, thereby gaining stronger bargaining power. Third, as noted, the two modes of policy enforcement define two distinct intra-organizational relationships between the principal and the agent, with distinct costs and implications for their subsequent interactions. Therefore, a critical first step in conceptualizing and modeling the principal's commitment in the bargaining process is to distinguish between the routine and mobilizational modes.

(2) The Agent's Response: Three Types of Strategies

Once the principal makes the first move, which defines the mode of policy enforcement as either mobilizational or routine, the agent responds by selecting one of the strategies available in the strategy space. We first describe the three available strategies and then specify the conditions under which one strategy is more likely to be favored over the others.

Formal, authority-based bargaining. One option available to the agent in a government setting is to invoke formal organizational procedures for bargaining. Specifically, the agent can put forth explanations, petitions, or other types of documentation to the principal in the form of written reports or requests transmitted through formal communication channels. We call this "formal, authority-based bargaining" (formal bargaining. hereafter). In the Chinese bureaucracy as well as in other types of bureaucracies, this is a well-established way of communication and interaction between a supervising agency and a subordinate agency.

A key attribute of formal bargaining is legitimacy based on the logic of appropriateness (March 1994). When an agent puts a formal request or a petition on the table, with the intention of asking the principal to revise its original proposal, this act takes place in the context of formal authority relationships; the formal request is recorded in documents and hence is accessible for evaluation by all relevant actors. Under these circumstances, the claims must take forms that are regarded as legitimate and appropriate.

The formal bargaining strategy is often characterized by "signaling" (Spence 1974). In this context, the agent volunteers "private information" in the interaction so as to strengthen its bargaining power and to convince the principal to accept the proposal. Under certain conditions, the side with private information may have an incentive to signal and thereby gain bargaining advantages. Applying game-theoretic signaling models may shed light on the tendency for the agent to engage in signaling by emphasizing its efforts, accomplishments, or challenges in order to gain a bargaining advantage.

Informal, social relations–based bargaining. One noticeable drawback of formal bargaining is that, within a formal hierarchy, it is typically a one-shot game: The supervisor either "accepts" or "rejects" the subordinate's request. There is not much room for back-and-forth bargaining involving alternating offers. This puts the agent in a disadvantageous position. Thus, the agent may find it desirable to shift from one-shot formal bargaining to a strategy that permits alternating offers; in this way, information and assessments can be revised, bargaining power can be strategically manipulated, and alternating offers can be contemplated. In other words, some mechanisms are needed to bypass the formal authority relationship and to transform the interaction between the principal and the agent into a different kind of game – something close to Rubinstein's (1982) game of alternating offers.

Informal interactions based on social relations can serve such a purpose, particularly in China. As Kornai (1986) observes, an authority relationship in the socialist economy is paternalistic in nature, allowing social relations to play a significant role in supervisor–subordinate interactions. When there are informal interactions between the principal and the agent, such as at the dinner table or at private parties away from the task environment, hierarchical relations recede and informal, back-and-forth exchanges of information prevail. Through this process, alternating offers may unfold, whereby information is questioned and updated, and side offers are made. We call this process "informal, social relations-based bargaining" (informal bargaining, hereafter).

Informal bargaining has some advantages. By moving away from the formal authority setting to an informal social context, a qualitatively different pattern of interactions is triggered, and the commitment of the opponent may soften. Also, assuming time constraints do not preclude it, the agent can extend the bargaining process over a longer time horizon and initiate multiple rounds of alternating offers, with increased bargaining power for the agent.

Informal bargaining is "multidimensional" inasmuch as different forms of capital – economic, social, political, and organizational – can be converted among one another in problem solving (Bourdieu 1986, Geertz 1978). For example, in face of a serious problem uncovered during the principal's inspection of the agent's work, social capital – particularistic social relations – can be mobilized to divert attention, to soften the perceived magnitude of the problem, and to lessen the severity of the penalty. In the Chinese context, formal, organizational processes are infused with informal, social interactions based on generalized kinship relations, social ties, and gift exchanges (Zhou 2019a).

The "quasi-exit" option. In bargaining games that take place in the marketplace, each player typically has an option to exit the game, which obviously affects the bargaining process. Intuitively, the side with a more attractive exit option has a superior fallback plan and hence stronger bargaining power. Game-theoretic models often explicitly take this possibility into consideration. But in a bureaucratic bargaining game, typically neither side has an exit option. For example, neither the agent nor the principal can exit the policy-enforcement process by resorting to external offers. The principal does have the option of replacing or sidelining the agent, thus the principal has an upper hand in this game.

Nevertheless, while exit is impossible, a "quasi-exit" option exists for the agent: In the face of heavy demands by the principal or the agent's inability to respond with an effective formal or informal bargaining strategy (as may occur in the mobilizational mode), the agent's fallback response is to accept the principal's offer but to try to win back the resultant losses during the implementation of whatever agreements were reached at the end of the bargaining process. Instead of merely complying with the principal-imposed demands, the agent can manipulate the results in the subsequent implementation process. I label this response strategy a "quasi-exit" strategy; that is, the agent is forced to accept the offer but he/she chooses to "exit" by not cooperating in the subsequent implementation. Thus, the "quasi-exit" option shifts the bargaining game to the next round, in the implementation process.

The mechanisms of the "quasi-exit" option are similar to those of the "weapons of the weak" proposed by Scott (1985). Unable to resist in the open, the agent resorts to informal, subtle forms of resistance, such as distortion, sabotage, or "collective inaction" (Zhou 1993). These actions undermine the legitimacy and effectiveness of the formal authority, thereby weakening the effectiveness of policy enforcement. Anticipating these potential consequences, then, the principal may either make concessions and continue bargaining or may adopt additional measures, with costs, to curb the agent's resistance in the implementation games.

Another factor that the principal must consider is that, notwithstanding the possibility of getting its way by forcing a quasi-exit when in a mobilizational mode, this mode imposes high costs on the principal.

(3) Conditions for the Agent's Choice of Strategic Responses

The preceding discussion examines the sets of strategic choices available to both the principal and the agent (see Figure 5.1). We now consider the specific conditions under which the agent will choose one or another of the strategies and the specific type of bargaining that such choices may entail.

First, organizations are routine-based. and routine-based implementation can be seen as a default mode. Consider the conditions under which the principal adopts the mobilizational mode of policy enforcement. Use of this mode is often triggered by a top-down process in response to external shocks, new deadlines for meeting or enhancing targets, or crises in other areas. In the context of environmental policy in China, the mobilizational mode may be triggered, for example, by a policy reorientation, media reports of the release of toxic waste, reports of alleged corruption by environmental officials when collecting pollutant discharge fees, or new MEP deadlines for meeting pollution cutback requirements. Or, the choice of mode may be made in anticipation of problems likely to occur in the agent's policy-enforcement work.

The choice of policy-enforcement mode has important implications for the agent's subsequent response. Once the principal makes the first move of adopting a particular enforcement mode (mobilization versus routine), it signals a level of commitment and induces a distinct type of coupling among the sub-units within and across different levels of the administrative hierarchy. Consequently, the selection of enforcement intensity affects the room for bargaining and the probability of success associated with different strategies for the agent. Not surprisingly, the agent will adopt different strategies in response to different enforcement modes.

Adoption of the mobilizational commitment reflects a high degree of intended policy enforcement and substantial deployment of resources for that purpose: Under these circumstances, the agent will recognize that little room is available for bargaining. Moreover, in a mobilizational mode, the agent faces a high risk of adopting behavior that is at odds with the rules imposed by the principal. Based on these considerations, we expect that under such a situation the agent's dominant response strategy is the "quasi-exit" option. In selecting a quasi-exit strategy, the agent's response shifts the principal–agent interactions to the next stage of implementation.

I summarize the preceding discussion with the following propositions.

P1.1 *The "quasi-exit" option is the agent's dominant strategy in response to the principal's choice of a mobilizational mode. Activities associated with formal or informal bargaining become less prevalent in a mobilizational mode than they are in the routine mode of policy enforcement.*

P1.2 *The adoption of a quasi-exit response strategy shifts the bargaining to the next stage of the "policy-implementation game."*

The mobilizational mode is not always the principal's preferred strategy. It incurs high costs and the agent's quasi-exit response does not necessarily imply compliance. As the term implies, routine-based policy enforcement prevails most of the time, and this provides the agent with room to engage in bargaining activities using strategic responses that are different from the quasi-exit response, namely, formal and informal bargaining. Given the principal's choice of a routine mode of implementation, the agent's likely choice depends on additional conditions under which the bureaucratic bargaining takes place.

To further this analysis, first consider "formal bargaining," with its reliance on formal bureaucratic communication channels, characterized by written, formal documents that may include, for example, detailed information, elaborate explanations, and plausible claims. Formal bargaining can be conducted on an open, legitimate basis, at any time, and at different stages of the policy-enforcement process. In addition, formal bargaining often involves lower bargaining costs (in terms of time, energy, and resources) than does informal bargaining. Formal bargaining is likely to be favored under one or more of the following conditions: (1) The agent has private information and by volunteering such information its bargaining power is strengthened, or information is so ambiguous that the issues can be re-framed effectively; (2) the issues involve official matters, such as revisions to the criteria used to evaluate the performance of agents that be made through formal procedures; (3) or the issues to be resolved (e.g., task interdependence, blame shifting, evaluation criteria revision) are such that solutions cannot be obtained privately through bilateral, informal interactions. The previous arguments related to formal bargaining are synthesized in the following propositions.

P2.1 *Formal bargaining is more likely to take place under circumstances in which the agent holds private information that can be used to his/her advantage or in which information is ambiguous to the point that multiple interpretations are plausible so that the agent can convincingly frame an alternative, rational account.*

P2.2 *Formal bargaining is more likely to take place when the decision (e.g., a revision of the criteria to be used in evaluating the agent's performance) is correlated with other competing agencies or in an interdependent task environment.*

P2.3 *If a formal bargaining process is employed, it is likely that the agent will engage in "signaling," in which the agent volunteers private information and/or "framing," in which the agent attempts to change the framing of contentious issues. In either case, the agent believes that it will gain an advantage by publicizing this information.*

Next, consider the conditions associated with informal bargaining. It is a common observation that, given the opportunities, organizations or individuals tend to seek particularistic favors and privileged access to resources, and they also try to redistribute, in their own favor, the blame that follows when things go wrong. However, formal bargaining does not fit these purposes for two main reasons: First, requests for special treatment can hardly be made to appear legitimate if publicly disclosed, and hence they cannot be made through formal channels; second, the formal bargaining process leaves little room for alternative offers to take place, hence that process is unlikely to be effective in the agent's efforts to seek what some might view as special treatment.

In attempts to obtain special treatment, both the principal and the agent will favor a shift to informal bargaining. As mentioned, informal bargaining tends to involve particularistic social ties, and it takes place in informal settings (restaurants, private parties, etc.), where formal relations are put aside, informal social interactions prevail, and alternative offers can be made and considered. However, informal bargaining has its own costs: It requires the possession of other forms of capital, especially social capital such as particularistic ties. The term *guanxi* is commonly used in China to describe such ties, and it is commonly employed in informal bargaining. I develop the following propositions to highlight the conditions under which informal bargaining is likely to occur.

P3.1 *Informal bargaining tends to take place in circumstances when information is unfavorable to the agent (and thus particularistic ties may be used to offset the damaging information), or when the outcomes of formal bargaining will be problematic because bargaining is documented and in the open, and thus it will be highly uncertain for the agent.*

P3.2 *Compared with formal bargaining, informal bargaining generally requires a longer time frame and involves more stages in order to allow alternative offers to take place.*

Finally, let us revisit the "quasi-exit" strategy, this time in the context under discussion, that is, the principal initiates a policy-enforcement process in the routine mode. Recall that using the "quasi-exit" strategy means that the agent accepts the imposed offer and hence exits from the bargaining process. The quasi-exit option is the fallback option for the agent: When the agent does not (or cannot) effectively employ either formal or informal bargaining, he/she has no choice but to take the offer on the table. But, as noted in the earlier discussion, a quasi-exit implies that during subsequent implementation activities the agent may attempt to win back what was lost during the bargaining. As in the other strategies, the selection of a quasi-exit strategy has possible costs to the agent. If distortion and sabotage are used in subsequent policy-implementation activities, the agent runs the risk of being caught. Moreover, in choosing a quasi-exit strategy, the agent's work will not be officially recognized and rewarded on the basis of the terms negotiated by formal or informal bargaining. Whenever possible, the agent would prefer to be able to secure gains through formal or informal bargaining so that its subsequent performance is evaluated in light of an officially recognized platform. These considerations lead us to the following proposition:

P4 *Quasi-exit strategies are more likely to be adopted by those with weak, formal and informal bargaining power or under circumstances involving (perhaps temporarily) tightly coupled relationships between the principal and the agent, with little room for bargaining.*

In summary, the three response strategies by the agent in the routine mode of policy enforcement lead to three different types of bargaining strategies: signaling or framing in the context of formal bargaining, alternative offers in the context of informal bargaining, and implementation games following the adoption of a quasi-exit strategy. As noted, there are different payoffs and costs associated with each of these response strategies and the subsequent interactions. The conditions for choosing between formal and informal bargaining are intuitive: The agent chooses formal bargaining whenever its request or claim is legitimate and can be made in the open, when there is hard evidence to support the agent's request (offer), and/or the outcome is more certain to be favorable. Under these circumstances, formal bargaining is the agent's most efficient means of getting things done. In contrast, when the situation is uncertain, when the request or claim is problematic, or the evidence is unfavorable to the agent, then there is a strong incentive for the agent to rely on informal bargaining. The main advantage of informal bargaining is that it bypasses the formal hierarchical order to allow a negotiation process in which there is a give-and-take exchange of information and there are possibilities for developing a shared understanding of those circumstances or making a side offer that improve the agent's bargaining power.

Compared with informal bargaining, formal bargaining involves lower transaction costs, but the agent can use formal bargaining effectively only under conditions in which he/she can make legitimate claims or gain by offering private information in his/her favor. The quasi-exit option is a last resort since the agent loses the possibility of gaining explicit official approval of the petition or request. In other words, all other things being equal, the agent has a preference ordering in the form of formal bargaining – informal bargaining – quasi-exit. Also, as a matter of expository convenience, we have not considered the possibility of a mixed strategy, for example, a combination of both formal and informal bargaining, which is commonly observed in actual bureaucratic interactions.

Having sketched the sequential bargaining model, I now turn to the empirical data that motivated the development of the above conceptual framework, and I illustrate key elements of the conceptual model and connect these considerations to the larger issues involved in institutional practices of governance.

BARGAINING IN ENVIRONMENTAL REGULATION: EMPIRICAL EVIDENCE

The above conceptual model provides a framework for organizing the empirical observations we have gathered over the three-year participant-observation research in a Chinese MEPB. In the discussion below, I focus primarily on the relationship between the PEPB as the principal, and the MEPB as the agent. In the process of policy enforcement, many issues are subject to bureaucratic bargaining. Here I highlight three categories of issues that appear frequently in this area:

- *Criteria for performance evaluation.* The PEPB proposes a set of explicit measures to rank-order the performance of all MEPBs (and their subordinate CEPBs). This practice triggers bargaining activities over which criteria are to be used and the weights that are to be assigned to these criteria.
- *Meeting policy targets.* At times, a specific policy target is subject to negotiation. Under other circumstances, the extent to which a target is

met is ambiguous and hence it is subject to interpretation
and negotiation.
- *Share of blame.* When an environmental incident occurs (e.g., the accidental release of a chemical dye causing a river to turn orange) or when a
  policy target is not met, who is to blame and how is the blame to be shared
  among the parties, including the environmental authorities?

The Principal's Move: Mobilizational Mode or Routine Mode?

The conceptual model specifies that the principal, the PEPB, makes the
first move by choosing between two different modes of policy enforcement, and this choice signals its levels of commitment, and it also influences the interactions between the principal and the agent during the
subsequent stages of bargaining. Our field research allowed us to gain
first-hand experience regarding each of these two modes. In the routine
mode, policies are enforced through standard procedures carried out by
the municipal and county-level environmental officials on a daily basis:
On-site inspections of firms that discharge waste are conducted, forms are
completed, reports are prepared, and waste discharge permits are issued.
However, when problems arise (e.g., the local municipal people's congress complains that the rate of pollution reduction in the municipality is
behind schedule), bargaining processes are activated in which the various
parties exchange information, interpretations, and accounts, and they
attempt to reach an agreement. This contrasts sharply with the circumstances when external events cause a shift to a mobilization mode, such as
the release of chemicals that leads to public protests by residents. During
such times, the supervising agency and the subordinate agencies are
tightly coupled, with the principal making urgent and stern pronounce-
ments, paying close attention to a particular area of policy enforcement
through intensive inspections and evaluations of the agent's work and
demanding reports and explanations, and with the agent being extremely
sensitive and responsive to those pressures from above. Under such
circumstances, the room for bargaining, either formal or informal,
shrinks drastically.

Consider, for example, the annual inspection in 2008. An annual
inspection, as the name suggests, is a routine practice in the environmental
regulation area, whereby the supervising agency reviews, evaluates, and
certifies the extent to which the subordinate bureaus have carried out their
tasks and met the designated goals for that year. Specifically, the PEPB
reviews the MEPB's data and documentation on pollution reduction,

especially on discharge of the SO_2, air pollutant, and chemical oxygen demand (COD), an indicator of the intensity of wastewater pollution. The PEPB then decides either to accept (or reject) some or all of the MEPB's assertions, and, eventually, it provides its stamp of approval indicating official certification of the MEPB's work for the year. Prior to 2008, such review and inspection processes were carried out on a routine basis, and many of the MEPB's claims were accepted. However, things changed suddenly in 2008, when the PEPB shifted to what we call a "mobiliza-tional mode." In 2008 the PEPB adopted a tougher disposition, made a relatively long (fifteen-day) inspection visit within the MEPB's jurisdic-tion, applied extraordinarily strict criteria to its evaluation, and rejected a much higher proportion of the accomplishments claimed by the MEPB. All MEPBs in the province had similar experiences in that year, and most received a "goals not met" evaluation: Only forty percent of the MEPBs met the designated goals for a reduction of both SO_2 and COD; about half met only one of the two goals; and a few MEPBs failed to meet either goal. These results elicited a resentful and contentious response by the subordinates to the PEPB's inspection practice, but to no avail.

This sudden shift from a routine mode to a mobilizational mode in 2008 was triggered by factors exogenous to the intra-organizational relationships between the PEPB and the MEPBs. In the previous year, 2007, the PEPB's supervisory unit, the MEP, had unexpectedly tightened its evaluation standards for the annual performance evaluation of the PEPB, rejecting a large proportion of its assertions: Only twenty-one percent of the claimed COD reductions and nineteen percent of the claimed SO_2 reductions were accepted by the MEP. As a result, at the end of 2007 the PEPB scrambled to make hasty adjustments to lower the performance evaluation scores for all its subordinate bureaus, causing great confusion and resentment from the subordinate bureaus. To avoid such embarrassment in the future, in the following year, 2008, the PEPB adopted a new strategy by drastically tightening up its own evaluation of the subordinate MEPBs. To signal its commitment and to ensure effective enforcement of this tough new position, the PEPB shifted into a mobiliza-tional mode by marshaling greater resources (personnel, attention, and increased time for inspections); they placed tremendous pressures on the MEPBs to justify their claims, and stubbornly refused bargaining efforts from below. Under these new circumstances, the MEPBs had no choice but to accept the PEPB's "offer" in the form of an unsatisfactory evalu-ation result. In other words, the MEPBs had to use a "quasi-exit" option, thereby exiting from the usual bargaining process.

The PEPB's commitment during the annual evaluation process is an important feature of its strategic bargaining position. The above example shows that the choice of a mobilization mode resulted from both an external shock (the MEP's tightening of its evaluation process) and an endogenous process reflecting the PEPB's desire to induce new behavior by its agents. In a hierarchical context, the principal has formal authority to commit and to make credible threats. However, there are limits to the credibility and commitment of the principal. The authority relationship is neither total nor absolute. In the Chinese administrative system, bureaus have two key principals, which, in the case of the MEPBs, includes the PEPB and the municipal government. The latter is particularly powerful in that it controls key aspects of the MEPBs, such as personnel and budget. In view of the existence of multiple principals of the MEPBs, the PEPB must act appropriately to ensure long-term cooperation from the MEPBs. In addition, the mobilizational mode of enforcement is too costly for the principal to sustain over a long period of time. Given the limits on the principal's effectiveness in using the mobilizational mode, shifts between mobilizational and routine modes are to be expected. Indeed, at most times and under most circumstances, the PEPB selects a routine mode and there are frequent exchanges between the PEPB and the MEPBs involving bargaining over a variety of issues. We now consider the agent's choice of strategies under the routine mode of policy enforcement.

The Agent's Response Strategy: Choosing among Formal, Informal, or Exit Strategies

As specified in the conceptual model, once the PEPB makes its first move in choosing the routine mode of policy enforcement – issuing a directive, setting a goal, or discovering a significant enforcement lapse within the MEPB's jurisdiction – the MEPB has a repertoire of three available response strategies: formal bargaining, informal bargaining, and the "quasi-exit" option. Drawing on examples from our fieldwork, each of these three strategies is illustrated in turn below.

Invoking the formal bargaining process. Formal bargaining involves written requests transmitted through formal organizational channels and recorded upon the sending and receiving at both ends of the official chain of communication. These documents are then directed to the appropriate officials, who typically follow up with official, written responses. In our fieldwork, we frequently observed formal bargaining in the MEPB's dealings with the PEPB. The three examples below, which are typical, are consistent with our conceptual model.

Example 1. In 2007, a large new wastewater treatment plant in the MEPB's jurisdiction failed to operate according to the project design, causing several key pollution indicators to exceed the maximum allowable levels. Facing this major embarrassment and the threat of a poor performance evaluation, the MEPB initiated active communication with the PEPB to reduce its share of blame and to signal its serious efforts to address the matter. The MEPB's written communications made claims to the effect that the problems were caused by extraneous factors well beyond its control: facility upgrading in upstream areas, technical maintenance shortfalls, and the absence of sewers in residential areas. The documents also signaled that the MEPB had worked hard to address these problems. When the PEPB did not accept the MEPB's claims, the MEPB director issued a formal petition in his report to the PEPB: "I suggest that government-sponsored pollution reduction projects be given full recognition, and that investment efforts [by the local governments] be matched with [an acceptance] consistent with the results of the pollution reduction. Only in this way can we expect that the local governments will be willing to make further investments. A poor evaluation will not only slow the progress of the overall pollution reduction effort but also will make it difficult for us local EPBs to justify our push for additional [local government] investments in these projects." The MEPB also took advantage of an on-site visit by a top MEP official to convince him that the wastewater treatment facility was reasonably effective in reducing pollution, despite the violations of the allowable pollution limits. The top official's nodding agreement to this claim was later used by the MEPB to bargain for a better performance evaluation.

These efforts to bargain and to redirect the blame provided an edge for the MEPB during the bargaining process. In the 2009 annual inspection, the PEPB accepted a high proportion of the MEPB's pollution reduction claims, an outcome that far exceeded the MEPB officials' expectations. As one MEPB official said in private: "They [the PEPB's inspection team] have accepted many of the pollution reduction figures we presented. We are very pleased with this outcome."

Example 2. The second example also relates to blame shifting. In 2009, the PEPB found significant water pollution in a river that runs through the MEPB's jurisdiction and it issued violation notices for four consecutive months. In response, the MEPB engaged in formal bargaining to shift the blame to others. In several formal documents sent to the PEPB, the MEPB provided pollutant test results from water samples from the river and argued that the pollution was caused by firms located in an upstream section of the river within a different administrative jurisdiction. These petitions eventually succeeded in exonerating the MEPB for the regulatory failure, although the MEPB's internal document acknowledged that the pollution was mainly caused by some firms within its jurisdiction.

Example 3. The MEPB also bargained with the PEPB over the evaluation criteria that the PEPB adopted to rank-order the performance of all MEPBs in the province. One criterion was related to the effectiveness of government supervision of local businesses. In a formal petition, the MEPB argued that this criterion should be altered to take into account the number of firms involved and the workload required in the different administrative jurisdictions. In some MEPB jurisdictions, the petition argued, there were only a dozen firms requiring close supervision; but in the jurisdiction of this particular MEPB, more than 100 firms were supervised. Throughout our fieldwork, we observed similar requests to modify the evaluation criteria for regulatory effectiveness; these criteria were linked to water quality, air quality, and relative versus cumulative measures of improvement.

In all three examples, the MEPB employed formal bargaining: Formal, written documents and procedures were used to construct a plausible rationale and to provide information to justify the MEPB's claims. In addition, the formal bargaining interactions tended to be one-shot events; the principal either accepted or rejected the agent's request, and that was the end of the game. The one-shot nature of the activity typically was because the hierarchical structure made it inappropriate to use formal communications to engage in a back-and-forth exchange involving alternative offers. Only occasionally, when the subordinate office had strong justifications, or when circumstances permitted, did the formal bargaining develop into a process of repeated petitions by the subordinate office, as seen in Example 2.

As our examples illustrate, formal bargaining processes include signaling. Typically, it was the MEPB that took the initial step to file a written request, with a significant signaling component in its documents. In signaling, the agent uses information previously unknown to the principal to justify its efforts, describes the extent of the difficulties it faced, and/or indicates that it had backing from higher authorities. This involves the agent's provision of private information to gain bargaining power. During our fieldwork, we observed extensive use of formal bargaining by the MEPB. Arguably, the technical nature of the tasks in the area of environmental regulation – typically involving laboratory test results – often makes it possible for the subordinate MEPB to make a legitimate claim based on "objective evidence."

Activating informal bargaining. Our fieldwork showed that bargaining on the basis of informal, social relations is also very common. This is consistent with findings in many other studies in the Chinese context (Ai 2008, Sun and Guo 2000, Wu 2007, Zhang 2018). Our conceptual model provides an analytical basis for understanding the mechanisms that drive the informal bargaining process. As in the case of formal bargaining, we offer examples and draw their implications from the framework of our conceptual model.

Example 4. Rapid response to top-down inspections. Since 2007, the PEPB has adopted a new practice of issuing monthly reports on instances of violations of environmental requirements within the jurisdictions of all MEPBs in the province. MEPB officials take this monthly report seriously because such information, once made public to all MEPBs and their territorial governments, is both an embarrassment and a factor adversely affecting their annual performance evaluations. Interestingly, the usual practice is to first circulate the information in a "preliminary report" ten days before the formal report is issued. This provides the MEPBs with a window of opportunity for maneuvering. In one instance in 2009, a PEPB team came to a polluting firm in the MEPB's jurisdiction and collected wastewater samples. Upon receiving the information, the MEPB officials immediately mobilized for a rapid response. A top MEPB official ordered his staff to gather their own data and the staff, together with the firm's manager, rushed to the PEPB "to work on the [PEPB] inspectors and to touch bases with them informally." The plan was to establish informal contacts with the key PEPB officials even before the preliminary report came out so that once the violation appeared in the preliminary report, these early efforts could pave the way to have this instance removed from the final report. Eventually, the MEPB staff reached the key official in charge through a hometown-based social tie. The problem was quietly resolved and the violation did not appear in the monthly report. This was not an isolated episode. The statistics we gathered show that, month by month, a significant number of violations appearing in the preliminary reports disappeared from the corresponding final reports.

Example 5. Cultivation of guanxi. In our fieldwork, we observed the pervasive presence of informal social relations. When accompanying the inspection teams from the MEP or the PEPB, MEPB officials tried to cultivate informal, interpersonal relationships on the basis of personal friendships, hobbies, or common work experiences. On several occasions, we observed that such informal interactions between the inspection team members and local officials warmed to such an extent that the inspection process became very informal and problems could be easily explained away. On other occasions, a hometown connection with some key officials in the MEP was used strategically to gain special approvals in the performance-evaluation procedures or to persuade the PEPB staff to provide official recognition during the annual review process.

In addition to illustrating the reliance on verbal communications or other symbolic gestures rather than written reports, these examples demonstrate a key feature of informal bargaining in China: extensive reliance on activation of a particularistic, social tie, on the bases of former colleagues, alumni, friends, or hometown connections. In the absence of such direct ties, indirect ties are used as a bridge to reach the person in the strategic location. Indeed, an initial response to a difficulty frequently elicits an intensive search for *guanxi* that can be used to settle things.

Unlike formal bargaining where the rules and structures are already in place, informal bargaining involves improvised actions to suit particular occasions, as was the case in the above-mentioned rapid mobilization of efforts to respond to the preliminary monthly report. That effort extended the bargaining process considerably and allowed several rounds of interactions during which alternative offers could be considered. Such interactions can subtly tilt the bargaining power between the two sides and can often alter the bargaining outcomes.

In the context of our research setting at the MEPB, bargaining processes placed more time pressures on the agent than they did on the principal. The formal authority relationship gives the principal ultimate power to set deadlines and put forth demands, as many bureaucratic clocks are ticking – budget cycles, inspection cycles, reporting cycles, and so forth. For an agent, bargaining over resources, workload, and blame-sharing must generally be conducted in a timely manner. There is a need for timely action by the MEPB, as seen by the extensive advanced preparations for the inspection processes and the rapid-response efforts to modify the PEPB's monthly reports.

Resorting to the "quasi-exit" option. Understandably, choosing the "quasi-exit" option does not involve any visible efforts in negotiation with the superior; rather, wittingly or unwittingly, the passive acceptance of policy targets may imply a "quasi-exit" option in that the imposed tasks are not based on binding contracts between the two sides and the subordinate offices are likely to alter the terms of the imposed contract in the implementation and inspection processes. Instances of selective implementation and collusion during the policy-implementation processes can be understood in this light. Discussions in the following chapters on collusion during the inspection processes (Chapter 6) and "muddling through" behavior during the implementation process (Chapter 7) will further explore this set of issues.

SUMMARY

In this chapter, I develop a conceptual model of bureaucratic bargaining among Chinese government units. By specifying the sequence of the bargaining game and the different response strategies, the model allows us to make sense of the multiple threads in the behavior, responses, and patterns of interaction observed in our participant-observation research. The model also provides an analytical lens to focus on key aspects of the bureaucratic bargaining process in China. For example, our distinction between the different circumstances under which bargaining takes place – routine vs. mobilizational modes of policy enforcement – allows for an analysis of the relationship between the different types of bargaining processes and the level of the principal's commitment. Moreover, recognition of the different types of strategic responses by the agent and the different resultant interactions allow for clarification of the kinds of bargaining processes as well as the rules of the game and the involved mechanisms. Although I illustrate the model in the context of interactions in the environmental regulation area, much of the discussion can be extended to relationships between other supervising and subordinate agencies within the Chinese bureaucracy. This is because government bureaus in China – for instance, the transportation bureau, the bureau of public health, and so forth – are usually in the same structural location under the same type of dual authority associated with the vertical functional line and the lateral, territorial governments as those described for the EPBs.

The proposed model and the empirical cases discussed here also provide clues about the link between bureaucratic practices and the larger institutional logic.

First, formal rules versus informal practice. Given the long chain of command and the considerable variations in local circumstances, formal rules have to be adapted to local circumstances, hence they are limited in terms of regulating behavior by local officials. This gives rise to pervasive informal practices in implementation and bureaucratic bargaining. Without such informal practices that help solve problems and at the same time maintain the appearance of symbolic compliance, the rigidity of the formal rules will encounter serious challenges and crises.

Second, routine versus mobilizational modes. The choice of a routine or a mobilizational mode implies that enforcement by the principal reflects the involved institutional logic. That is, the higher authority always has the upper hand to select the means of implementation and enforcement. However, the bargaining games outlined in this chapter show that the outcome also depends on the response strategies by the agents. As mobilization generates intensive pressures, the agent is likely to adopt a quasi-exit option, shifting interactions to the implementation phase. In other words, we cannot fully appreciate the outcome of the implementation stage without carefully examining the interactions between the principal and the agent during the bargaining stage.

As we will see in the following chapters, bargaining processes of various forms run through the policy-implementation and bureaucratic-inspection processes of the Chinese bureaucracy, permeating the interactions between superiors and subordinates and between governments and urban dwellers or villagers. These practices of bureaucratic bargaining are variations around the larger theme of the governance logic in China.

6

Collusion among Local Governments

A salient phenomenon in the Chinese bureaucracy is the collusive behavior among local officials across offices or hierarchical levels to forge strategic alliances for the purpose of building up administrative achievements to meet the demands of the higher authorities or for covering up problems in the process of policy implementation. As I argue in Chapter 1, variable-coupling between central and local governments and interactions between formal and informal institutions are key mechanisms to respond to these tensions. In fact, collusive behavior among local governments plays a central role in making these variable-couplings feasible.

Shadows of collusive behavior have already loomed in different scenes in the previous chapters. Chapter 3 developed the proposition that collusive behavior is most prevalent during the phase of "inspection" in the subcontracting mode of governance because this is the occasion when the supervisor-as-subcontractor and local agents share the goal of making sure that the policy outcomes in the subcontract are delivered to the satisfaction of the principal. As Chapter 4 shows, campaign-style mobilization is often activated in response to threats of widespread collusive behavior that undermines the central authority. In Chapter 5 on bureaucratic bargaining, I propose that, under the heightened mobilizational pressures, formal or informal negotiations by subordinate agencies are limited and oftentimes they have to accept whatever tasks are imposed from above and adopt a "quasi-exit" strategy. That is, the bargaining process is postponed to the next stage, the stage of policy implementation, when subordinate offices move to center stage. It is on this occasion that collusive behavior among local governments intensifies.

This chapter provides a focused examination of this class of bureaucratic behavior, explicating the institutional mechanisms involved and how it fits into the larger institutional logic of governance. I have two goals in this chapter. First, I will examine the mechanisms and logics that generate and reproduce collusive phenomena as an informal but highly institutionalized practice. Second, I discuss the proposition that collusive behavior serves as a key mechanism to alleviate the fundamental tension. I will illustrate these considerations by drawing on some empirical findings from our research team.

THE COLLUSIVE PHENOMENON IN THE CHINESE BUREAUCRACY

A salient organizational phenomenon in the Chinese bureaucracy is that officials in local governments have a tendency to form strategic alliances (Heberer and Schubert 2012, Zhou 2010a) and develop coping strategies in ways that often sidetrack or sabotage state policies or impose their own interpretations of the implementation process, leading to systematic deviation from the original intention of these policies. This situation is vividly captured in a popular Chinese saying: "From above there are imposed policies, and from below there are evading strategies" (*shang you zhengce, xia you duice*). As an illustration, an official in a township government recalled his experience in implementing the family-planning policies:

[In the family-planning area,] there were inspection teams from the family-planning agencies at the county, municipal, and provincial levels. When the provincial inspection team arrived to inspect, municipal, county, and township agencies would form alliances; when the municipal government team arrived to inspect, agencies at the county and township levels would form an alliance. When the provincial inspection team arrived in a county to inspect, it would not notify the local government. But local governments at different levels would be mobilized to deal with the inspection. Before the inspection team had even arrived, officials from the municipal government would notify their subordinate offices in advance: "Make sure that no problems arise during the inspection process." When the inspection team arrived at the county government, all township governments in the county received notification and were mobilized to respond. As soon as the inspection team left for a village, there would be phone calls to that township government and the village, with detailed information about the activities of the inspection team, including the license number of its vehicle, its whereabouts, travel routes, and so forth. Usually the inspection team arrived at the target village before eight o'clock in the morning. So, early in the morning the village head would send out village cadres to guard all the main roads leading to the village. As soon as they saw the inspection team arriving, they would notify people in the village and those babies that had been born in violation of the family-planning regulation would be moved out of the village.

Instances abound of strategic alliances among local governments in response to policies and inspections by the higher authorities, as frequently reported in the Chinese media and in the literature.

Stable organizational behavior is sustained by stable institutional foundations and it is reproduced through interactions and resource exchanges with their environments. Starting from this premise, I seek answers to this organizational phenomenon by developing an organizational analysis and theoretical explanation. The key arguments to be developed are as follows: In the Chinese bureaucracy, collusion among local governments has become an informal but highly institutionalized practice. Here "institutionalization" refers to the processes through which a specific organizational practice or form has been widely accepted in the organizational environment such that it is seen as appropriate, taken for granted, and hence legitimate. That is, such collusive behavior is a product of the institutional environment in which the local governments are situated; hence this behavior is justified and reinforced by the institutional logic of the Chinese bureaucracy. The institutional mechanisms in the organizational environment perpetuate and reinforce such organizational forms or practices (DiMaggio and Powell 1983, Meyer and Rowan 1977).

Indeed, the collusive phenomena described above share the characteristics of an institutionalized organizational practice: On the one hand, such collusive behavior has the effect of diverting or evading the original policies or directives, hence it is at odds with state policies and regulations. On the other hand, such behavior is by no means secretive, isolated behavior by individuals, groups, or agencies. More often than not, such behavior takes place in the open within the formal organizational structure; it is carried out through the formal authority of government agencies. Such behavior becomes common knowledge among subordinate and supervising agencies as well as among policy makers in Beijing. The goal of this chapter is to explicate the institutional logic and develop theoretical explanations for the organizational practice of collusion among local governments.

POLICYMAKING AND IMPLEMENTATION IN ORGANIZATIONS: AN ANALYTICAL FRAMEWORK

In the economic literature, collusion refers to behavior among large corporations in oligopolistic markets that aim to form secret (or tacit) agreements using noncompetitive strategies such as price fixing or market partitioning to gain benefits above those acquired from competitive prices. Such behavior harms social welfare, hinders market competition, and violates antitrust regulations; it is usually carried out in secret, informal, and hence collusive forms. In recent years, economic research has called attention to collusive behavior within organizations. For example, an important source of collusive behavior is the distribution of information within an organization. The presence of asymmetric information renders the owner of the corporation (the principal) ineffective in controlling the collusive behavior between managers (the supervisor) and workers (the agent). Tirole (1986, 1993) proposes a game theoretic model involving interactions among three actors (principal–supervisor–agent) to analyze collusive behavior between the agent and the supervisor in response to the principal in a hierarchical context; there is a growing literature in this area (Laffont and Rochet 1997). In Chapter 3, I also use the three-level bureaucracy model to set up the framework for control rights theory.

Drawing on Tirole's (1986) analytical concepts outlined above, I now provide a more precise delineation of the subject. The collusive phenomenon here refers to cooperative behavior between the lower-level local government (or agency) and its immediate supervising government (agency), often in the form of various coping strategies to deal with policies, regulations, and inspections by the higher authorities, which are inconsistent with the original intention of the policies. My analytical focus is on the relationship between the local government (the agent), its immediate supervising agency (the supervisor), and the higher-level government (the principal). Here, the locations of the local government, the immediate supervising government, and the high-level government are relative. In the implementation of policies from the central government, we can treat the provincial, municipal, and county governments as belonging to the category of "local governments"; but in instances of implementing directives from the provincial government, we should treat the municipal and county governments as the local governments. Similarly, in response to inspections by the county government, those below the county level, that is, township governments and village committees, become the "local governments." For the purpose of exposition, I will illustrate my arguments using the scenario in which local governments (the supervising and subordinate governments at the lower levels) collude to respond to the central government and its policies. But the theoretical model and the basic arguments developed here apply to collusive behavior among local governments (agencies) at other levels or in other settings as well.

There are both similarities and important differences between collusion among local governments and collusion among large corporations. In terms of similarities: First, in both government and business, such behavior involves nonmarket transactions, and they tend to be informal and hidden; second, the structures of information and the payoff among the principal, supervisor, and agent are similar in the collusion game among governments and among firms. It is not surprising, then, that similar mechanisms and environmental conditions cultivate parallel behavior in government and business.

But it is also important to highlight the key differences between the two. First of all, collusion in the business world takes place among independent firms, whereas collusive behavior among governments, as studied here, often involves interactions among agencies within the same hierarchical structure and often involves a direct, superior–subordinate authority relationship (e.g., between a county government and a subordinate township government, between the family-planning bureau at the county level and the family-planning office in the township government). Second, collusion among firms always faces the threat of government regulation and penalty; hence, it tends to be secretive. But collusion among local governments is widely accepted and legitimate, and it often operates openly within the formal government structure. Therefore, there are different enforcement mechanisms involved in these two areas.

Researchers on local government behaviors have studied this phenomenon extensively and have developed the concept of *biantong*, which refers to the adaptive use of informal devices or improvised strategies, often based on social relations, to carry out bureaucratic tasks, as a substitute for formal authority, official procedures, and rhetoric. For example, Sun and Guo (2000) find that in the process of tax collection in villages, local officials use informal social relations rather than formal authority to persuade villagers to pay their taxes. Ying Xing (2001) shows that local cadres adopt improvised strategies to deal with problems and conflicts at the local level, suspending or shelving formal procedures and directives from above. There is a growing English-language literature on selective implementation or the use of informal means (Chen 2017, Edin 2003, O'Brien and Li 1999). Whereas the earlier research emphasized the positive aspects of such improvisational behavior in carrying out government tasks or in problem-solving, this chapter focuses on more general patterns of collusion among local governments, which includes both (1) collusion between governments and individuals and groups (e.g., collusion between local officials and villagers in the area of family planning), and (2) collusion among government agencies.

The premise of the proposed organizational analysis is that an organization is an organism with bounded rationality that evolves continuously in interaction with its environment. A large number of studies in organization and management research have shown that changes in and the evolution of organizations do not always follow the blueprint of their rational design; instead, organizations are often constrained by processes and conditions in the larger environment (Scott and Davis 2007). Organizations must exchange resources with their environments in order to survive and prosper. As such, the latter impose constraints on, and hence shape, the behavior of organizations (Selznick 1949). Much of what an organization does reflects its efforts to cope with its environment. This recognition directs us to seek explanations for the behavior of organizations in their relationships with the environment. Moreover, the effectiveness of organizational design is always conditional on the specific context in which an organization is situated. For example, a hierarchical organization is likely to be effective in implementing administrative orders across levels, but such an organizational structure imposes serious constraints on its capacity to adapt to the local environment or to an environment that changes frequently. Those involved in the implementation process are not merely "organizational men" who mechanically follow orders from above; rather, they are socialized human beings with feelings, judgments, and interests. They bring their own cognitions, judgments, and interests to the implementation process. In brief, the bounded rationality of organizational behavior, the dependence of organizations on their environments, and the conditional nature of organizational design are the key themes in the proposed organizational analysis.

On this basis, March (1988) develops an important proposition in the organization literature: *Implementation is the continuation of organizational decision making.* That is, the implementation process will significantly affect and reshape the outcomes of the decisions made during early phases. This line of argument calls for an integration of decision making and decision implementation into one analytical framework. A decision made without full attention to the prospects of implementation is not effective decision making; in the same vein, there is a serious flaw in the design of research on organizational decision making that does not pay attention to the implementation processes.

ORGANIZATIONAL PARADOXES AND THE INSTITUTIONAL LOGIC OF COLLUSION

In this section, I develop my central argument that the collusive behavior described in the preceding discussion is an inherent and unintended consequence of organizational responses to the fundamental tension in governing China. I elaborate on this theme by developing an organizational analysis of three paradoxes in the Chinese bureaucracy and the role of collusion therein: (1) the paradox between uniformity in policy making and flexibility in implementation; (2) the paradox between the intensity of incentives and the displacement of goals; (3) the paradox between the impersonal bureaucracy and the patron–client relationships. Below I organize my discussion and illustrations around these three themes.

The Paradox between Uniformity in Policy Making and Flexibility in Implementation

The fundamental tensions in the Chinese bureaucracy, as outlined in Chapter 1, manifest themselves foremost in the relationship between the centralization of policymaking on the one hand and the diverse local conditions in policy implementation on the other. These tensions have been built into the patrimonial/party mode of domination in China's political architecture, and they often trigger various types of crises. In response, variable-coupling takes place over time between the central and local governments in the form of uniformity in policymaking and flexibility in implementation.

It is in this larger context that we can make sense of collusive behavior. It is useful to first describe the organizational environment in which local governments are situated. In the Chinese bureaucracy, governments or agencies at different levels all belong to the same bureaucratic system. In the Chinese bureaucracy higher authorities direct the work of their subordinate offices through policies or bureaucratic fiats; accordingly, a main component of the activities of local governments is to respond to and implement the policies and directives from above. A local government (e.g., a township government) and its immediate supervising government (e.g., the county government) have a direct administrative authority relationship, sending or receiving directives directly from or to each other. Other government agencies above the immediate authority link or those at lateral levels do not have direct administrative relationships. As such, a local government (or a government agency) at a particular level is mainly responsible to its immediate supervising government (agency).

In line with the principal–supervisor–agent framework, we can treat the higher authorities beyond this immediate superior–subordinate administrative link as the principal. From the perspective of organization–environment interactions, policies and regulations from above and demands by local constituencies and lateral government agencies can be regarded as the organizational environment in which a local government is situated and to which it must respond. Among the many possible environmental conditions, the most important one is the policies and regulations of the central government.

One characteristic of this organizational environment is the uniformity of state policies that local governments are required to implement within their respective jurisdictions. That is, the central government (through its ministries or agencies) develops policies or administrative fiats that are intended to be applied and implemented in all regions and localities or in the entire functional arena. For example, policies and regulations such as family planning, workplace safety, and environmental regulations are transmitted through a top-down process to different levels of the local governments or agencies, covering the different areas and localities in the entire administrative jurisdiction. Local governments add details to the policy targets, make plans and procedures, and mobilize organizational resources for implementation further downstream. Subsequently, supervising governments/agencies enforce and review the effectiveness of the implementation by collecting relevant data, receiving reports from subordinate agencies, and conducting periodic direct inspections. Studies have shown that local governments spend a large amount of time and energy dealing with the implementation of various policies and the subsequent inspections by the higher authorities (Zhao 2010).

Uniformity in policy making is by no means an incidental organizational practice. Rather, it is at the very core of the centralized authority in China. The very essence of the centralization of authority lies in the top-down decision-making process, whose content is necessarily uniform and disregards variations across localities and areas. What has been distinctive about the Chinese bureaucracy since the late 1990s is both the growing scope of policy areas and the greater extent of centralization of resources and decision-making authority, as compared with other national governments or as compared to the Chinese government during the early years of the post-Mao era. As the state expanded its authority and centralized resources in these areas, the so-called "top-level design" (*dingceng sheji*) in policy making has become increasingly prevalent and imposing.

Yet, an unavoidable consequence of uniformity in policymaking is that policies thus made do not necessarily fit each and every locality across administrative jurisdictions or across policy areas; as such, they engender difficulties, tensions, and challenges with which local officials must deal during the implementation process. For instance, the same state family-planning policy was applied to most regions in China, but because of local variations in kinship relations, government resources, and organizational capacities, the feasibility and challenges of meeting these policy targets varied greatly across local governments. These micro-variations imply that accompanying the uniformity of state policies comes the indispensable mechanism of *flexibility* in implementation. Here, flexibility refers to adaptive behavior that leads to a better fit between policy goals and local conditions or leads to deviations from intended policy goals due to conflicts of interest, political sabotage, or other circumstances. We can observe various types of flexibility in policy implementation in everyday life across localities and over time. Spatially, we find considerable variation across regions and across areas in the implementation of the same policy, and such differences are accepted by the supervising governments. Over time, these differences emerge as temporal variations in the effectiveness of policy implementation in the same locality. For example, when pressure for policy enforcement is high (e.g., the launch of a new anti-piracy campaign), various localities may become actively involved in implementing policy, producing a temporary situation in which there is high uniformity across localities. But once the pressure is lifted or diverted, local differences reemerge, which are recognized as legitimate by the higher authorities. Such flexibility is also reflected in differences between symbolic compliance and actual implementation: Symbolically, different localities may show a high level of uniformity in implementing state policies, but in actual implementation, considerable flexibility is present.

There are different kinds of flexibility in the implementation process. At the risk of oversimplification, I highlight three types. The most obvious is *flexibility by purposive design* – that is, the original policy making leaves room for flexible implementation. In the family-planning area, for example, there emerged considerable regional variations even in the official policy targets (Gu et al. 2007). A state policy may set the main parameters of the policy targets but allow the local governments to specify or adjust the details of implementation. Higher-level governments tend to either acquiesce to or explicitly encourage flexible local adaptation. This approach delegates the authority of interpretation and implementation to local governments and the authority of supervising to their immediate superior agencies. The rationale is straightforward: The immediate superior agencies have better information about their subordinate agencies and about the implementation processes, and they are in a better position to evaluate the implementation performance of these agencies. Thus, this institutional practice provides the main source of legitimacy for both the supervising and the subordinate governments to be flexible in adapting state policies to local conditions.

The second type of flexibility is what I label *behavioral flexibility*, characterized by making quiet behavioral adaptations while maintaining symbolic compliance. For example, local governments often make "resource transfers" across different policy areas or via different channels in order to get the job done. Such behavior may be in violation of the rules or regulations that dictate a specific designation of earmarked funds. I single out this type of flexibility because of its pervasiveness in the daily operations of local governments, whereby the local governments face multiple tasks and multiple goals that are themselves incongruent or even in conflict. Responding to these multiple, conflicting goals often gives rise to situations in which government behavior is seen as problematic in one policy area but reasonable and legitimate in view of another policy or regulation.

The third type is *flexibility by special interests*, which refers to situations where state policies are distorted during implementation such that some group can take advantage of the policies and benefit itself, and policy makers are unable to impose effective supervision to curb such behavior.

From a normative point of view, of the three ideal types of flexibility sketched above, the first is beneficial for general social welfare and is permitted and encouraged by policy makers. The second type is illicit from the point of view of policy makers/regulators in a specific policy area, but it is reasonable from the point of view of the local governments and their immediate supervising agencies that are involved in the implementation process; such behavior is generally beneficial to social welfare. The third type of flexibility is detrimental to social welfare and policy goals and is prohibited by governments at all levels.

Is it possible to develop an organizational design that distinguishes between these three types of flexibilities such that "good" flexibility is encouraged whereas "bad" flexibility is eliminated? This is unlikely in actual practice. We can illustrate this point in light of Williamson's "selective intervention" argument, which is formalized by Baker, Gibbons, and Murphy (2001). As Williamson (1985) argues, in an organizational context where both market and hierarchical mechanisms coexist, the principal cannot arbitrarily choose between market and hierarchical mechanisms to solve problems. This is because there are different incentives associated with the different governance mechanisms, such as hierarchies or markets. Once an organizational form or practice is institutionalized, it is likely to drive out other mechanisms that are incompatible with its own mechanism. Arbitrary substitution of alternative mechanisms will generate internal tensions and conflicts and will incur higher transaction costs.

This proposition can also be used to explain the dilemma of selective intervention in the choice of "good" flexibility versus "bad" flexibility. An organization with mechanisms for flexibility encourages employees to take initiatives and to be active in problem-solving and seeking local solutions. To accomplish this, such an organization must select and promote those employees who behave in this way and it must design incentives to encourage such behavior. Such practices are likely to become routinized for organizational retention. In contrast, temporary efforts in selective intervention to curtail "flexibility" are incompatible with the established behavioral patterns, shared norms, and incentive design. As a result, the strategy of selective intervention is unlikely to be effective. When the higher authorities acquiesce to the "flexible" response of their subordinate governments "here and now" in order to carry out the tasks imposed upon the subordinates, they are also unwittingly giving these subordinates a legitimate basis for the same flexibility "there and then" in the face of other pressing demands and challenges.

Another important source of legitimacy derives from the shared cognition that arises from cooperative behavior among officials in both supervising and subordinate governments. In the process of policy implementation, governments at different levels play the dual roles of "inspectors" and "inspectees" (that is, those being inspected). In one example (Ai 2008), when a county family-planning bureau was inspected by the regional and provincial bureaus, the officials in the county bureau colluded with the township governments and villages. But when they turned around to inspect these same township governments and villages for their work in the same area, the officials in the county government played the role of "inspectors." Often officials alternate between these two roles overnight. In this process, local officials acquire a dual identity, and they understand the rules of the game from both sides. Such experiences and identities provide a shared cognition among local officials and hence a strong basis of legitimacy for collusion. More interestingly, during this process the relationship between the supervising and subordinating offices also undergoes a subtle transformation – from a formal authority relationship to an informal, cooperative or collusive relationship. Accordingly, the hierarchical structure is weakened and patronized, while the boundaries between the formal and informal institutions become blurred.

Herein lies the organizational paradox between uniformity in policy making and flexibility in implementation: The more uniform the state policy and the greater the separation between policy making and implementation, the less the fit between the policy and local conditions, and therefore greater flexibility is needed in the implementation process. A related factor is that there is a huge transaction cost for the policy makers to directly inspect and evaluate the effectiveness of policy implementation. Often the cost is too high (relative to the benefits) for the policy makers to be directly and closely involved in enforcing policy implementation. Therefore, the very nature of policy uniformity foreshadows, intended or not, the presence of delegation, discretion, and flexibility in implementation. Indeed, we can see that the so-called "collusion" and "flexible implementation" may be the same type of behavior with different labels. When the higher authorities acquiesce to such behavior, their behavior is labeled flexible, even innovative, in adapting to local conditions. But when the higher authorities enforce their policies and do not tolerate such adaptive behavior, it is seen as deviant and thus will be penalized. I summarize the preceding discussion as follows: *The more centralized the top-down policy-making process is, the more uniform the policy is, and the more likely is it that it will be a poor fit to local conditions, therefore, the greater the extent and legitimacy of flexibility in the implementation process, and the more likely it is that there will be collusive behavior among local governments.*

Similarly, we can also see that when the channel of resource distribution is more centralized, or when the chain of command for implementing state policies is longer, then the local government will have a greater extent and more legitimacy of flexibility and the extent of collusion among local governments in the implementation process will be greater.

The Paradox between Intensity of Incentives and the Displacement of Organizational Goals

The preceding discussion highlights the role of flexibility in implementation as a legitimate basis for collusive behavior. In this section, I further argue that the increasing intensity of incentives in personnel management ironically provides an impetus for collusion within the bureaucracy. As noted above, an important component of government reform in recent years has been to increase the intensity of incentives for local officials by strengthening performance evaluations and providing more concrete task measurements (Zhou 2007). However, often such incentive mechanisms fail to produce the desired behavior; in fact, at times they induce behavior that runs counter to the intended organizational design. To put it succinctly, the incompatibility between the design of the incentives and the reality of the organizations gives rise to tensions and conflicts that exacerbate problems associated with interest articulation and collusive behavior. In this process, formal organizational goals are replaced by other goals that are pursued by local officials. I use the organizational paradox between the intensity of incentives and the displacement of goals to highlight this phenomenon.

"Goal displacement" has long been discussed in the organization literature. In his classic study of the labor and socialist parties in Europe in the 1920s, Michels (1968) observes that in organizational processes political parties often deviate from their original goals and pursue other goals that are different from or even opposite to their original goals. He uses the concept of "goal displacement" to describe this phenomenon. Collusion among local governments discussed here is likely to be associated with goal displacement. That is, often local responses to state policies replace policy goals with other goals that are pursued by those who are active in the implementation process. As the example quoted at the beginning of this chapter shows, in the family-planning area, when local governments responded to an inspection of policy implementation by the higher authorities, they were concerned less about ensuring actual implementation of the policies and more about concealing any problems from the inspection team. Similarly, when safety-related accidents occurred, local governments worked to cover up the extent of or even the existence of such accidents rather than to investigate their causes and to find solutions.

To a large extent, I argue, such bureaucratic behavior is an unintended consequence of the incentive mechanisms in the Chinese bureaucracy. My proposition here is that the incentive design within the Chinese bureaucracy has induced a strategic alliance among local governments for collusive behavior and this leads to goal displacement. Since the 1990s, the Chinese government has adopted a series of administrative reforms, an important component of which aims to regulate the behavior of officials, to provide incentives to induce appropriate behavior, and to deter distortion or ineffectiveness in the implementation process. These incentive designs have the following characteristics: First, many policies have specific, measurable targets and performance evaluations. For example, one county government decomposed implementation of the family-planning policy into a 1,000-point plan, ranging from meeting the fertility rate target (200 points), to the chief executive officer's direct involvement in the family-planning area (130 points), to upward reporting of information and work summaries (10 points), and so forth. These measures directed the attention of local officials to those issues and areas intended by the policy makers. Second, the incentive design has adopted a so-called joint responsibility principle (*liandai zeren zhidu*): Once a problem is found, not only the official who is directly responsible is to be penalized but so too are the chief executive officer and the supervising officials. Third, the intensity of incentives has increased greatly. For example, the so-called "one item veto" rule (*yipiao foujue*) in the family-planning area dictates that once there is a serious problem in one area (e.g., the fertility rate does not meet the policy target), all other accomplishments by the local government will be negated and the chief executive officials will be penalized regardless of their performance in other areas. Obviously, such an incentive design aims to set policy priorities and enforce implementation by increasing the costs of deviation from policy intentions (incentive intensity), measurement accuracy (concrete policy targets), and a clear specification of responsibility (the joint responsibility principle).

Yet, often these measures have had unintended consequences during the actual implementation process. The premise of an effective incentive design is that those who design such a mechanism have a deep understanding of the relationship between the incentive mechanisms and organizational behavior. A poor incentive design induces behavior that is inconsistent with the organizational goals. Kerr (1975) puts it succinctly in his well-known statement on "the folly of rewarding A, while hoping for B" (see also Gibbons 1998). In recent years, there have been extensive studies of incentives and motivations in social-science research. Milgrom and Roberts (1992) summarize a set of incentive principles in an economic analysis that sheds light on the observed bureaucratic behavior.

The "incentive-intensity" principle states that the design of incentive intensity should take into consideration the relationship between an employee's effort and his output. For example, if the output level is less elastic to an employee's effort (due to, say, task interdependence on other parts of the organization, or unrealistic policy targets), increasing the incentive intensity will induce the employee to distort his or her performance record to "meet" the policy targets. Another principle of incentive design states that incentive intensity should be proportional to the accuracy of performance measurement. If an official's performance is difficult to measure accurately and objectively, increasing the incentive intensity will only induce him/her to strengthen his/her ties with those supervising officials who conduct subjective evaluations. The same logic can also be extended to explain collusive behavior among local governments. In this regard, higher authorities often work for "administrative achievements" (*zhengji*) to achieve career advancement and they often impose policy targets without due consideration of the costs and challenges in the implementation process. An official at the residential management office of a municipal government made the following observation:

In the past, a policy would undergo a certain process of experimentation and evaluation in selected localities before it was formally adopted. But now our superiors are anxious to have an "administrative achievement." They will often propose a new project and push for broad adoption even before the experiment has been completed. This creates a great disparity between the proposed policy and local circumstances. ... We [local officials] have to face many challenges in our daily work, and the most challenging are those derived from the unrealistic, unachievable goals that our superiors impose on us. Superiors today just pat their foreheads and make decisions arbitrarily. Sometimes they ask that we give them the moon within three days! They don't care whether we are able to do it or not. They give us an order, but they don't give us a chance to reason with them. All that they are concerned about is the outcome, and not the process by which we get it done.

Facing unrealistic policy targets and strong incentive pressures, local officials develop coping strategies in the form of collusive behavior to "manufacture" records and statistics to meet policy targets or to transfer resources from one policy area to another to accomplish the impending policy tasks. Such transfers of resources are in violation of government regulations, thus inducing further collusive behavior in order to provide a cover-up. It is not surprising then that intensive incentives often exacerbate organizational behavior that runs counter to official goals, leading to the phenomenon of goal displacement. At the height of the implementation of the family-planning policy some years ago, a township official observed:

The family-planning area is governed by the "one item veto" rule. If there are problems in this area, governments at the township, district, and municipal levels will all be affected. But if we have done our work too well, that's not good, either. In a township, there are only two full-time staff members in charge of family planning; we are short of staff and we have to hire another some twenty temporary staff members to implement the policies and to deal with emergencies. These extra hands are not paid from the government budget. Rather, we pay them from the fines we collect from those who have violated the policy. If our work were really good and there were no violations, we would not be able to impose fines and hence we would not be able to afford to hire these extra hands. Therefore, there is always some natural point of equilibrium. We will find two or three violations each year, and the imposed fine of about RMB 200,000 to RMB 300,000 will support the extra hands we have hired to implement the family-planning policy.

At the same time, the "joint responsibility" policy induces a strategic alliance of shared interests among local officials. Again, take as an example the family-planning arena. According to this policy, once a serious problem is revealed, the official in charge and the chief executive official, as well as those in the supervising agency, will be penalized. This incentive mechanism, intended to induce local officials to play an active role in the enforcement of policy implementation, also inadvertently induces collusive behavior among those officials. This trend has accelerated along with the centralization of resources in the central government, as local governments often have only limited resources to respond to the many tasks and crises they face. Often resources intended for the implementation of one policy will dwindle quickly as they move through the various levels of the government, and few resources will be left for the local officials. In the month of the Beijing Olympic games in 2008, for example, the township government where I conducted my fieldwork had to receive dozens of inspection teams and also had to accommodate the daily presence of more than one dozen members of work teams that were sent by the county, municipal, and provincial governments. Facing hard budget constraints, and in response to the frequent inspections by the higher authorities, local governments often have to resort to collusion to deal with these inspections. The immediate supervising agencies, which have better information about the challenges and the unrealistic demands that a policy imposes upon subordinate governments, acquiesce to such behavior.

The preceding discussion highlights the organizational paradox whereby, *when incentive mechanisms are inconsistent with the organizational goals, and the incentive mechanism is intensified, the phenomenon of goal displacement becomes more salient, and collusive behavior among local governments is more serious.*

The Paradox between the Impersonal Bureaucracy and the Patron–Client Relationships

A puzzle about the Chinese bureaucracy is that along with the increasing bureaucratic formalization due to the multiplicity of rules and regulations and the increasing personnel requirements in terms of education and professionalization, we observe a trend of increasingly informal relations and personal ties among bureaucrats that permeate across authority lines and offices. A salient characteristic of bureaucratic organizations is their impersonality; that is, officials within a bureaucratic structure tend to follow rules and to discard personal emotion. A long-standing proposition in organization research is that, along with the formalization process, organizational activities tend to be routinized and to operate on the basis of formal rules and procedures(Cyert and March 1963). In this sense, a trend toward formalization should curb or constrain the extent and effectiveness of collusive behavior among local governments. In real life, however, internal government processes and inter-agency relationships in China operate, to a considerable extent, through informal, social networks; officials in different government agencies spend a great amount of time and energy cultivating informal and particularistic ties with their superiors and with colleagues in other agencies or other organizations. We observe a paradoxical phenomenon, whereby, on the one hand, formal rules and regulations are developed and continuously put into effect; on the other hand, more informal, particularistic ties in both scope and intensity are extended into and permeate work activities within and across government agencies.

How do we make sense of the coexistence of an impersonal bureaucracy and patron–client relationships that are characteristic of the personalization of administrative ties in the Chinese bureaucracy? As outlined in Chapter 1, the institutional logic of the Chinese bureaucracy has cultivated informal social relations among bureaucrats within and across agencies. In China's organizational environment, formalization processes present great uncertainties and risks to local bureaucrats who care about their career advancement. The personalization of administrative ties is a main coping strategy by which such bureaucrats can respond to these environmental uncertainties. The formalization process in the Chinese bureaucracy ironically provides an impetus for the cultivation of informal ties. And such informal but stable relationships provide an important institutional basis for collusive behavior.

Students of organizations have long observed that members of an organization not only have formal relationships on the basis of authority positions but also cultivate informal relationships that may or may not coincide with the formal structure. Informal relations are characterized by particularism, that is, interactions among the members vary significantly depending on their social relations. Social relations outside of the organization (e.g., among friends, classmates, or former colleagues) provide important bases for informal relations within the organization. This is what sociologist Fei Xiaotong (1992[1948]) calls "differential modes of association" – the traditional Chinese model of social relations – extended to the organizational context. Therefore, both formal and informal institutions coexist in a Chinese organization. At times, these two institutions may complement each other: Informal relations may help improve interpersonal contacts and reduce the stress of the formal structures, and hence increase productivity. But these two may also be in tension with each other: Informal institutions may cultivate informal authorities that are at odds with the formal authority, thus undermining the effectiveness of the formal institution. The reasons for informal relations vary with organizations and their environments, and the roles of informal relations also vary across organizations.

In the Chinese bureaucracy, along with the formalization process, bureaucrats at different levels increasingly face specific policy targets issued from above, intensified incentive mechanisms, and competition with other bureaucrats for promotion. The prospects for career advancement depend heavily on their on-the-job performance and achievements (Zhou, 2005; see also Chapter 8). At the same time, the salience of impersonal bureaucratic institutions increases the risks and the uncertainties of policy implementation and of their performance evaluations. For example, in the past when there was a lack of specific policy targets, an official's performance appraisal critically depended on the subjective evaluation of the official's superiors, and one could gain advantages through lobbying. Today, however, when policy targets are clearly specified (e.g., GDP growth level to be achieved, the environmental regulations to be enforced, and so forth), there will be dire consequences for an official's career advancement if he or she does not meet these specific policy targets. In response to such risks, local officials develop various coping strategies: First, they will need to develop networks to expand their capacity to mobilize resources to achieve the policy targets; second, they will need to cultivate ties as a safety-net in case serious problems arise in their work activities. These circumstances place a high value on cooperation and interdependence among officials and hence accelerate the demand for strong social network ties along vertical lines of authority as well as laterally across agencies to soften the rigidity of the formal boundaries. The personalization of administrative ties is a manifestation of these coping strategies. In the township government where I did my fieldwork, during important holidays (e.g., Mid-Autumn Festival or Spring Festival), officials in different offices spent much time preparing and sending presents to officials in their supervising offices. This is imperative, as they put it, for these are the very officials who will come and inspect their work in the future. If one does not treat them well, they will find fault during the next round of inspections.

Collusive behavior is usually rooted in informal social relations. Unlike collusion among firms, collusion within the Chinese bureaucracy has stable bases of legitimacy, as we have seen in the preceding discussion. Therefore, the prevalence of informal social relations is caused less by the need for secrecy than by the need for resource mobilization across the boundaries of agencies and organizations. Let us consider the case of "illicit resource transfers" (*zijin nuoyong*), which is a prevalent practice in local governments. As is widely reported in the Chinese media and research, local governments often adopt strategies to transfer resources across agencies, between policy arenas, or across governments and other organizations in response to emerging problems or crises. Such resource transfers are illicit because they violate the regulation that ties a particular government fund to a particular area or for a specific purpose. For example, Wu (2007) found that when a township government could not fulfill the policy target for agricultural taxes, the local officials bribed the agency in charge of taxation so that the extra taxes collected by other township governments were "transferred" into the account under the name of this particular township government to meet its policy target (see also Tian and Zhao 2008). In another example, in the process of requisitioning farmland for public projects, when the compensation standards did not meet the expectations of the affected villagers and no agreement could be reached, local cadres found excuses to increase the compensation (e.g., by reporting the area of the land to be larger than it really was) to reach an amount of compensation that was acceptable to both sides. In other words, resources were transferred across different categories so as to carry out the tasks assigned from above.

The extent of collusive behavior is contingent on several factors. First, the availability of resources is an important institutional condition for the extent of collusive behavior. In a sense, the extent of informal cooperation among local governments (or agencies) is proportional to their dependency on extrabudgetary resources. In agencies where resources are abundant, there will be a lower demand or less pressure to cultivate informal ties for external resources. Second, whether or not such resource transfers are "illicit" is largely arbitrary depending on the regulations made by different government agencies. That is, if the authority of local governments in resource allocations were to be increased, as has occurred during various "decentralization" periods, then there would be no "illicit" resource transfer phenomenon, as such transfers across policy areas or agencies would be, by definition, normal and rational. In other words, the problem of so-called "illicit resource transfers" is a consequence of the centralization of authority.

If "illicit resource transfers" are an effective means for local governments to mobilize resources, informal social ties are important vehicles for such mobilization. In this light, it is not difficult to understand why local officials spend an enormous amount of time and energy cultivating and maintaining social relations. Furthermore, there is a reciprocal relationship between informal social networks and collusive behavior: The implementation process generates a demand for informal ties and social relations, facilitating the need to cultivate social networks; in return, the prevalence of social networks reduces the costs of collusive behavior, and as a result it increases the returns to such behavior. Thus we observe a vicious circle: On the one hand, in order to avoid collusive behavior, the higher authorities centralize power, intensify incentive mechanisms, and promote bureaucratic formalization. On the other hand, such endeavors in fact induce and exacerbate collusive behavior. I summarize the preceding discussion as follows: *In the formalization of the Chinese bureaucracy, the greater the extent of centralization of authority, the higher the uncertainty in policy implementation, the stronger the impetus for informal ties among administrative relations, and the greater the tendency for collusion among local governments.*

THE "INSPECTION AND APPRAISAL" GAME: TWO EMPIRICAL STUDIES

In this section, I draw on two case studies on the practice of "inspection and appraisal" (*jiancha yanshou*) in the Chinese bureaucracy to illustrate the theoretical arguments developed above.

The Research Setting: Bureaucratic Power and the Practice of "Inspection and Appraisal"

Let me first introduce the research context. To ensure effective implementation of state policies in the Chinese bureaucracy, as a routine practice the higher authorities frequently send out inspection teams to lower-level governments to conduct reviews and inspections. A large proportion of such inspections are casual, ad hoc, and inconsequential. But the category "inspection and appraisal" is of particular significance because this type of inspection is formal, institutionalized, and carefully scripted; local officials are evaluated and as a result are subject to rewards or penalties. To use the language of the "control rights" theory developed in Chapter 3, this is the phase when the policy outcome of the subcontract between the principal and supervisor-as-subcontractor is delivered and evaluated for acceptance.

Such inspections mainly take place at fixed time intervals, such as mid-year and end-of-year reviews, with clearly specified goals or criteria for appraisal, and they involve elaborate procedures. Some inspections are comprehensive, such as the annual review of the overall performance of a local government; others center on a specific policy or an administrative fiat in a targeted area, such as family planning or environmental protection. Oftentimes, inspections are conducted across bureaucratic levels and they take place at the very ground level where the specific policies meet the street-level bureaucrats and those who are directly affected by the policies. For example, inspections of family-planning policy implementation in the rural areas take place within villages, when inspection teams from county, prefectural, and provincial levels visit families in selected villages to inspect policy implementation and the accuracy of the official records filed by the local government office.

In Chapter 3, I argue that collusive behavior among local officials is especially salient when the principal inspects policy outcomes. An empirical study of the inspection phase fits nicely with this chapter's theme of collusion among local governments: Inspections serve the purpose of enforcing compliance by local officials with the administrative fiats from above. The inspection process involves intensive interactions between the supervising agencies and the subordinate agencies, often across several administrative levels. Inspections from above are one of the most important items on the agenda of local bureaucrats, and in response local bureaucracies engage in intensive mobilization (Zhao 2010). They also induce intense preparatory interactions among local officials. The actual inspection process, the local coping strategies, and the final outcome provide a glimpse into the Chinese bureaucracy in action, especially into those interactions that involve collusive behavior.

The empirical evidence to be presented below is drawn from two case studies based on our research team's participatory observations of the inspection processes in two distinct areas of state policy implementation. The first one is in the family-planning area. In 2007, one researcher from our team followed several government-inspection processes in D County of southern China. In the second case, in 2008 one researcher from our team conducted participatory observations of inspections in a municipal environmental protection bureau (MEPB). In the family-planning area, we observed three inspection episodes in the same county from three bureaucratic levels – the county, prefectural, and provincial levels. In the environmental regulation area, we observed two inspection episodes in the same prefectural jurisdiction by teams from the Ministry of Environmental Protection (MEP) and the provincial level. Each inspection episode lasted between three to fifteen days. In both cases, our researchers were involved in participatory observations prior to, during, and after the inspection process. Therefore, we have rich information not only about how these inspection processes unfolded but also about how these bureaucracies prepared for the inspection and how they responded to the aftermath of the inspections.[1]

Information Control as the Contested Terrain: "Sudden Attacks" and Response Strategies

One way to characterize the "inspection and appraisal" practice is that this is an inspection game, with the inspector on the one side and those being inspected on the other side. Among the many aspects of the inspection game, we first focus on the issue of *information control*. Here information refers to those items that are relevant to the specific goals or targets designated for a specific policy or program. For example, in the family-planning area, the actual fertility rate and the accuracy of the report on fertility statistics, among other items, are scrutinized. In the environmental regulation area, the reported pollution data or data on water treatment at specific manufacturing sites are evaluated in an effort

---

[1] Unless otherwise indicated, all the quotes below are drawn from our fieldnotes based on participatory observations.

to ensure that information is reported truthfully to the higher authorities and that a specific policy target is met.

The role of information is central in formal organizations and in organizational analysis (March 1988, Milgrom and Roberts 1992, Simon 1947). In the inspection game between the inspectors and the inspected, information is strategic, asymmetric, and ambiguous. Information is strategic in that there is an incentive for both parties, especially those being inspected, to use information strategically to their advantage. Information is also asymmetric in that one side, the side being inspected, has more information about the actual state of implementation than the side of the inspectors. Finally, much information regarding the state of implementation is ambiguous, that is, the same piece of information is subject to multiple interpretations (March 1994). This is the case even when the tasks and evaluation criteria are tangible and measurable, as we will see below.

It is not surprising, then, that the control of information is a contested terrain in the inspection game. On the one hand, the inspector seeks true information regarding the implementation of a particular project or policy; on the other hand, that which is being inspected seeks to make strategic use of information to serve its own interests. The interplay between the two sides provides us with a port of entry to look into the exercise of bureaucratic interactions.

On appearance, the principal seems to be highly effective during the inspection process. For example, the inspection team, or the supervising agency behind it, decides *at will* on where, when, and how to conduct an inspection within its jurisdiction. In some cases, the inspections are routine-based, with advance notice and with the content and location well specified. In other cases, inspections are conducted with only partial information provided to the local government. The local office may be informed of the date of inspection, but the specific location (e.g., which village) where the inspection will take place is not provided in advance. The most extreme form is what local officials call a "sudden attack" strategy, in which the inspection team arrives to inspect a specific site without giving prior notice so as to minimize the local officials' attempts to manipulate or falsify information. The higher authorities may also decide upon the composition of the inspection teams and introduce cross-jurisdiction mutual inspections by teams led by outside officials from other counties (or regions), with the stipulation that those governments whose jurisdiction ranks at the bottom of the performance appraisal order will be severely penalized. The rationale is that the cross-inspections will introduce lateral competition and will provide a strong incentive for outside inspectors to uncover problems during the inspection process so that their own jurisdictions will not be placed at the bottom of the ranking order.

However, our observations show that local collusion is equally effective in devising various coping strategies to compromise any inspection effort. Below, I provide some details on the specific ways in which information is strategically used and how such practices inform us of the bureaucratic process and the larger social context in which government behavior is embedded.

Let us begin with the "sudden attack" strategy by the inspection team. As a typical practice, during the 2007 family-planning provincial inspection, the inspection team arrived at D County in the early morning and did not provide the local officials with any information about when or where the inspection would be conducted. After breakfast, the inspection team made a phone call to the headquarters at the provincial government to receive instructions about the exact location of the villages to be inspected. The inspection team members then got into their vehicles and drove to the inspection site, without any advance notice to the local officials. Upon arrival, the inspection team blocked the entire village so that the inspectors could visit each and every household and could check for the presence of children, especially newborns, against the official fertility records reported by the local government. Violation of the designated fertility rate and false statistical reports were to be penalized. The purpose of these measures was to ensure that local-government officials would not have prior information about the inspection sites so as to be able make special preparations to cover up problems or to sabotage the inspection process.

But our participatory observations show that local officials usually gained an upper hand by undertaking highly coordinated responses to the tactics employed by the inspection teams. Let us take a look at the different response strategies by the local government.

First of all, local officials worked with their subordinate cadres to adopt a wide range of guerrilla warfare tactics, such as surveillance, disruption, and skirmishes, to obtain critical information about the inspection team, its whereabouts, or the destination of its inspection; in so doing, they were able to compromise the inspection process. For example, shortly after the inspection team arrived at the county government, information about the membership of the team, the license numbers of their vehicles, and other related information was gathered and transmitted to all township governments whose villages were the likely inspection targets. Every move by the inspection team was under the watchful eyes of local officials. As soon as the inspection team's vehicles left for their unannounced destinations, they were followed by designated local officials, who watched the team's every move and provided minute-by-minute updates on the team's whereabouts to those towns and villages on the path of the team's movement. In one instance, the inspection vehicles stopped briefly at the roadside to ask for directions to the village to be inspected. Local officials who were following the team quickly learned where the team was headed and they immediately notified, via cellphone, the officials in the township where the village was located. This was followed by mobilization for a quick response. As a result, the effectiveness of the "sudden attack" was seriously compromised.

Second, even when the inspection team arrived at an inspection site, there was no guarantee that what they saw was accurate. It is a common practice for local officials to hide or to manipulate information in order to meet the goals and targets. In one instance, an inspector arrived at a household and inquired whether the wife had regularly received a phys-ical checkup in the township hospital, as required by the family-planning regulation. The inspector then double-checked the answer against the official record in the village office. However, as our informant noted: "All the documents in the village office were hastily made up to fool the inspectors, using official stationery, doctors' signatures, explanations, the official seal, and the contact information of the local hospital. The only accurate information in the record was the name of the woman who was alleged to have had a physical checkup" (Ai 2008, pp. 10–11). In another example: One family-planning requirement was that there should be a clinic in the village to provide villagers with birth-control devices. But in the particular village under inspection, there was no clinic at all. On the eve of the inspection, when local officials learned that this village was the likely inspection target, they rushed equipment to the village to set up a makeshift clinic. The clinic included made-up records about the distribu-tion of birth-control devices so that it appeared as if the clinic had always been in full operation.

In the environmental regulation area, we observed similar patterns. On the eve of the Ministry's inspection, the municipal bureau officials went to a local electricity company that was subject to inspection to make sure that the data were ready for inspection. In fact, these officials were colluding with the company to quickly make up data so as to show that the company followed the required procedures for the treatment of pollutant materials. As one official at the treatment site coached: "Nowadays the ability of the Ministry's inspection team has greatly improved. If you present fake data like this linear line, they take one look and they immediately know that these data are false. Such a graph might have fooled the inspector a few years ago, but not anymore. You need to learn from [another company]; it has graphs that go up and down, and are not always stable, so they appear to be real, not artificially made up." This was a mutual learning process between the two sides. For example, to gain accurate information about the levels of pollution, during the earlier inspections the inspectors would use energy consumption to measure potential environmental hazards. Local officials learned from this for their subsequent inspections. They would give detailed instructions to the local firms about how to prepare receipts and other documents regarding expenses for electricity purchases so that the estimated environmental hazards would be minimized. The inspection process was like a cat-and-mouse game, as the higher authorities developed new ways to seek unfiltered information, and local officials engaged in collusion to come up with corresponding strategies to defeat the purposes of the higher authorities.

Third, even when evidence of policy violations was discovered during the inspection process, there might be mysterious incidents or skirmishes to disrupt the inspections and to cause the negative evidence to suddenly disappear in the confusion. In one instance, an inspector found an unreported newborn. Before she could check the baby's information against the official record, the local cadres "accompanying" the inspector on the inspection tour forcefully took away the newborn and his parent and put them in a vehicle waiting nearby and drove away. All this took place within a matter of a few minutes; as a result, the inspector was left without any physical evidence of a policy violation. In fact, the local officials explicitly adopted a strategy of "resolving any problem here and now" and at the very time when a problem first appeared, they would use all means at their disposal – persuasion, bribery, and diversion of attention, among others. Obviously, such behavior cannot be successful without collusion among the local officials and the villagers.

Finally, in the larger scheme of things, even the choice of the very inspection site can be subject to manipulation. In the province of our research on family-planning inspections, the bureaucratic regulation stipulated that those counties that were evaluated at the bottom of the rankings by their municipal or prefectural governments would be subject to closer scrutiny during the provincial-level inspections. To avoid embarrassment and negative effects on their career mobility, prefectural government officials deliberately selected D County, which was a county that had a record of good performance, and put it at "the bottom of the ranking order" so as to direct the provincial inspection team to this county. In so doing, the inspection process would likely find evidence of successful compliance. As the head of the county bureau commented: "This is the rule of the game. For the prefectural government, it is important to protect its image and its administrative achievements, so it does not want to report to the provincial government the name of a worse-performing county with the most serious problems. All counties and prefectures do the same thing – they don't want to expose those ugly spots to the higher authorities" (Ai 2008, p. 16). In the area of environmental regulation, similar strategies were adopted to divert the inspectors' attention. In one instance, the bureau head went to the provincial bureau and asked its supervising agencies to direct the Ministry's inspection team to other prefectural areas, thus sparing their region from an official inspection. During the 2008 inspection, the central government inspection team selected four sites for review and inspection. However, the MEPB deliberately arranged the sequence of the four site visits such that attention would be directed away from the most problematic site. As one local official said to the head of the problematic company: "We will try our best to make your site the last stop. If they [the inspectors] run out of time, they will not come to inspect your facility at all."

Clearly, by manipulating both the content and the location of the inspection, local officials are able to weaken and compromise the very purpose of the inspection and to gain an upper hand in the inspection game. These observations raise further questions: Why are the organizational designs and the incentive mechanisms not effective in soliciting truthful information about performance and inducing appropriate behavior? With this question in mind, we now consider other mechanisms underlying the bureaucratic practice of inspection and appraisal.

"Softening" the Bureaucratic Grid: The Role of Informal Institutions

Collusive behavior is based on social relations and informal institutions. This is in sharp contrast to the Weberian bureaucracy, where a main source of bureaucratic power is derived from rules and regulations as the basis for formal authority and the execution of commands. We found that social relations permeate every corner of the Chinese bureaucracy and are woven into every step of the inspection process.

For example, even though the inspection team sought to bypass the local officials during the inspection process, in most cases it needed the cooperation of the targeted village or company and local officials. The villagers, sanctioned by local officials behind the scenes, would disrupt the inspection process or even block the entry of the inspectors. As a result, the inspection team, upon arriving at its destination, was typically accompanied by local officials on its inspection tour. This opened doors to carefully constructed interactions and the cultivation of informal relations between the local officials and the inspection team. The choice of which local officials would "accompany" the inspection team was a careful decision, as revealed by the following instance:

Two days before the provincial inspection team arrived in the county, a confidential report had arrived with detailed information about the composition of the forthcoming inspection team and the license numbers of its vehicles. The head of the team was an official from the neighboring city, who happened to have close connections with the local family-planning bureau. ... An official in the county office also realized that another member of the team was his former classmate. (Ai 2008)

Therefore, the staff members who "accompanied" the inspection team were carefully chosen to activate the latent social connections in the inspection process. Even without previous social ties, effective interpersonal relationships could develop rapidly. Our researcher observed that during the inspection tours the local officials often developed rapid friendships with the inspectors through informal conversations, such as chatting about hobbies and leisure activities. Intimate social relations then spilled over to smooth negotiations when problems were discovered during the inspection process. In one instance, a local cadre got along with the inspector so well on the inspection tour that she thrust a red bag of cash into the hand of the inspector and whispered: "I am in charge of this village and responsible for what happens here. If you find problems, please go easy on me." And the inspector responded: "Oh, why didn't you tell me earlier? I know now." It is not surprising, then, that when policy violations were discovered, local officials could negotiate with the inspectors in an informal manner and soften the impersonal bureaucratic rules.

Social relations not only reflect reciprocal, particularistic interpersonal ties but they are also ingrained in the deeper cultural expectations and the logic of appropriateness. During the prefectural family-planning inspection, the head of the inspection team had a strong, impersonal disposition and tried to maintain an arms-length relationship with those local officials whose work was being inspected. She refused to attend the banquet prepared by the local officials, declined their courtesy calls, and insisted that local cadres stay away from the inspection process. She even threatened to call off the entire inspection process if the local officials were to "accompany" the inspectors. Her attitude was seen as "cold and unreasonable," and it was met with strong resentment, not only by the local officials but also by the other members of the inspection team. It is obvious that there was a strong sense of how inspectors should respond to social relations (the hospitality of the host, and the cultivation of inter-personal ties based on alumnae, former colleagues, or place of origin). Her actions violated the logic of appropriateness based on social relations and cultural expectations, and hence produced strong resentment. In the end, during the final phase of the fact-finding evaluation, the "cold" team head had to compromise and soften her interpretation of the findings in the face of pressures from all sides.

Why do we observe a pervasive presence of social relations in bureau-cratic practices? Social relations play an important role in the manage-ment of uncertainty in the Chinese bureaucracy. As discussed earlier, along with the formalization process in the Chinese bureaucracy, bureau-crats at different levels face increased policy targets from above, intensi-fied incentive mechanisms, and competition with other bureaucrats for promotion. The salience of impersonal bureaucratic institutions increases the risks and uncertainties of policy implementation and the evaluation of their performance. In response to such risks, local officials develop strong social relations to expand their capacity to mobilize resources in order to achieve their policy targets; they also have to cultivate social relations as a safety net in case serious problems should arise in their work. For example, in the environmental regulation area, statistics on pollution depend on other measures – such as population size, commercial activities (e.g., number of restaurants) – that are collected by other government agencies. The MEPB must maintain good relations with these other agencies so as to make sure that its efforts are successful in fulfilling the designated tasks. In one instance (see Chapter 7), the statistics collected by the urban development bureau were inconsistent with those prepared by the MEPB. Several officials in the MEPB spent time entertaining the head of the urban development bureau to persuade him to revise the statistics provided by his bureau and to resolve the inconsistency.

As can be seen, the strengthening of impersonal rules and incentive mechanisms has accelerated the uncertainties and risks in bureaucratic careers, which ironically increase the demand for social network ties and the need for cooperation and interdependence among officials along vertical authority lines as well as among lateral agencies. The erosive power of social relations successfully softens or, on some occasions, even melts down the iron grid of the bureaucratic rules and procedures.

Shared Experiences, Shared Meanings, and Institutionalized Practices

Collusive behavior is built on stable organizational bases that give meaning to the actions taken by the different parties in the collusion. Shared experiences may also cultivate segmented norms and loyalty, providing the institutional basis for collusion. Indeed, one of the recurrent themes in the organization literature is that bureaucratic structures tend to produce segmented interests and turf wars across bureaus, offices, and other organizational boundaries (Wilson 1989). This is not surprising given that members of an organizational unit (e.g., a bureau or an office) tend to have similar experiences, face similar tasks, endure long hours of working together, and hence develop solidarity with one another. They also face similar bureaucratic pressures imposed from above, to which they must respond by adopting similar coping strategies. As a result, boundaries of these workunits tend to induce and enforce institution-based collective responses to bureaucratic power imposed from above.

Consider the environmental protection bureau and the family-planning bureau where we conducted our fieldwork. The staff members in both bureaus have worked with one another on a daily basis for a long period of time (usually several years). As independent government agencies in the local government, the two bureaus are self-contained, conducting their daily work within their organizational boundaries. Staff members share similar work experiences in carrying out tasks and in responding to repeated inspections from above. Furthermore, their performance evaluations are closely tied to the overall appraisal of the bureau as a whole. As a result, a subculture and ideology emerge within these bureaus and among the immediate supervising and subordinating agencies. For example, in our fieldwork we observed intensive interactions between the municipal environmental protection bureau and its subordinate offices at the county level: These officials frequently went on inspection tours together, frequently had lunch and dinner together, and often sat together at various meetings. As a result, they knew each other very well, including information about one another's hobbies and family lives. In their working relationships, they treated each other as "brother officers" and they shared information and coping strategies to respond to inspections from above.

Another important source of segmented identity is the shared cognition and mentality that arise from the cooperative behavior among officials in both supervising and subordinate governments. Government officials at different levels play the dual roles of "inspectors" and "being inspected." For example, when the family-planning bureau in the county government receives inspections from the prefectural and provincial bureaus, officials in the county bureau are the recipients of the inspection; as such, they collude with the township governments and village cadres to respond to the inspection from above. But when they turn around to inspect these same township governments and the village cadres in their jurisdiction, they play the role of "inspectors." Because of their strategic location, these officials have richer, more accurate information about the actual implementation processes at the lower levels, and they are actively involved in cover-ups and false responses to inspections from above. However, as inspectors they also make sure that the implementation processes at the lower levels are on track and on target so as to accomplish the required tasks.

These two roles can often change overnight. Our observations of a county bureau meeting illustrate this point well. After inspections by the provincial and municipal governments were completed, the county bureau began its own end-of-year inspection. The bureau head held a preparatory meeting for all staff members and announced different measures for the inspection process. An experienced inspector was invited to give a presentation about how to uncover hidden problems during the inspection process. The bureau head emphasized: "We must take our inspection seriously. The previous inspections (from above) were from the outside; now it is our own evaluation. This is real and no falsification or cover-up will be allowed." As one staff member commented: "It really is funny that, the day before, he [the bureau head] was coaching us on how to respond to the inspectors from the higher authorities and how to produce fake data; now he turns around and tells us to treat the inspection seriously and honestly." Here, we observe a clear sense of in-group versus out-group mentality. Facing inspections from above, bureaucratic offices at different levels form strategic alliances of in-group responses so as to minimize potential damage in the implementation process. Such collusion is institution-based; hence it is stable, effective, and enforceable. Within the in-group, however, the authorities make considerable efforts to get things done and minimize the risks of inspections and other enforcement mechanisms.

Through these role-playing processes, then, local officials acquire a dual identity, and they come to understand the rules of the game from both sides. Such experiences and identities provide a shared cognition and a shared identity among local officials and hence a strong basis of legitimacy for collusion.

SUMMARY

In this chapter, I develop an organizational analysis and explanation of the prevalent phenomenon of collusion among local governments, which offers glimpses into the implementation game after local officials choose the "quasi-exit" option from bureaucratic bargaining, as discussed in the last chapter. The collusive phenomenon cannot be attributed to the quality or the ability of local officials or those involved in the implementation process. Rather, the production and reproduction of collusion among local governments largely result from the organizational design and the institutional environment of the Chinese bureaucracy, and collusion becomes an integral part of the institutional logic of governance in China. This is a consequence of and a response to the fundamental tension in the increasing distance between policymaking and policy implementation. As decision-making authority and resources are increasingly centralized upward toward the central authorities, top-down decision making and subsequent resource allocations will depend on correspondingly longer administrative links and different levels of the bureaucracy to *flexibly* implement policy in order to adapt it to local conditions, thereby providing both the organizational basis and the institutional environment for collusive behavior. In brief, collusion among local governments is the very cost of and the remedy for the centralization of authority and resources.

Collusion takes place on the stable basis of authority relationships among supervising–subordinating agencies, and it is reinforced by formal government institutions. When the immediate supervising government demands that its subordinate governments participate in collusion (e.g., by providing inflated statistics to create the semblance of achievements in governance, or to cover up bad decisions), it is impossible for the subordinate governments to refuse to participate. Similarly, when the subordinate agencies plead for help through collusion, the supervising government has an incentive to participate, partly due to the penalties associated with the "shared responsibility" principle in the performance evaluation, partly because of the informal social ties that permeate across the boundaries of bureaucratic offices, and partly because the immediate supervising agency is better informed about, hence is more sympathetic to, the challenges that lower-level governments face in implementing policies. Finally, and more importantly, in the Chinese bureaucracy it is often difficult to distinguish between collusive behavior and reasonable flexibility in the actual process of policy implementation, with the reasonable flexibility having broad legitimacy.

It is not difficult, then, to understand why collusion has been an ongoing organizational phenomenon in China despite repeated efforts by the central government to combat it. Although shared interests among officials are important, shared interests are not a necessary precondition for collusion. The interests involved in collusion may vary on different occasions and evolve over time, and collusive behavior may vary across different government agencies, different policy areas, and different officials. Even if the participants do not share common interests, it is difficult and often impossible for them to avoid collusion. The institutional logic of the Chinese bureaucracy, as embodied in the organizational paradoxes discussed above, perpetuates and reinforces such behavior.

Finally, the collusion phenomenon is an organizational response to the fundamental tension in China's governance. Much so-called "collusive behavior" reflects efforts by local officials to get the job done through *flexible* implementation of state policies. Given the diverse economic, historical, and institutional conditions across Chinese localities, such behavior can be reinterpreted as an effective adaptive strategy under the bureaucratic protection of their immediate supervising agencies. Seen in this light, the collusion phenomena point to the coexistence of a symbolically strong state and effective governance at the local levels. On the one hand, we witness a symbolic state, where all major decisions have to be made by a centralized authority and must be reflected by uniformity in policymaking; on the other hand, collusive behavior in the implementation processes allows for effective local adaptation as an adjustment mechanism to address problems that plague centralized decision-making processes. In this sense, bureaucratic collusion may unwittingly serve as a corrective and a countervailing force to the centralization of authority in China.

7

"Muddling Through" in the Chinese Bureaucracy

This chapter continues my inquiry into the role of the Chinese bureaucracy in China's governance by examining local bureaucratic behavior in policy-implementation processes. The previous chapter focused on a class of phenomena in bureaucratic collusion, this chapter examines another class of behavioral patterns characterized by "muddling through" in policy implementation – adopting ad hoc, improvised strategies; exhibiting a course of action that focuses on short-term, incremental gains; and sequential adjustments in strategy as conditions change, leading to patterns of shifting courses of action over time. The theme of this chapter is that bureaucratic behavior is governed by multiple bureaucratic logics that often generate inconsistent, or even conflicting, demands on local officials in their work environment, leading to a course of action characteristic of muddling through.

The proposed behavioral model of muddling through puts in perspective the rational incentive design in the Chinese bureaucracy and its limitations. As already noted, recent literature on the Chinese bureaucracy pays considerable attention to the role of the incentive design in the Chinese bureaucracy to align the interests of local officials with the goals of the central authority (Li and Zhou 2005, Oi 1992, Walder 1995a, Zhou 2007). But what is often observed is collusive behavior among local officials and selective implementation of state policies, as discussed in the last chapter and in the larger literature. Many empirical studies of the Chinese government portray local bureaucrats responding to state policies and incentives in haphazard ways and adopting improvised strategies that deviate considerably from the intentions of the higher-level policies (Ai 2011, Ouyang 2011, Wu 2007).

These contradictory images of the Chinese bureaucracy raise important questions: How do we explain the distinct behavioral patterns of the Chinese bureaucracy that are both highly sensitive to policies and administrative directives from the higher authorities and, at the same time, are often collusive and deviant during the implementation process?

In this chapter, I propose an alternative model that is based on what I term "muddling-through" behavior because of its resemblance to Lindblom's classic model of public administrators. I use this model to explain the multiple processes that shape behavioral patterns among Chinese officials at the local levels. I then apply this model to interpret the observed behavior of a municipal environmental protection bureau (MEPB) over a five-year period. The proposed model shows that what appears to be contradictory behavior over short time periods within local governments is in fact consistent with, and shaped by, the multiple logics that underlie the behavior of local governments.

A BEHAVIORAL MODEL OF "MUDDLING THROUGH" IN THE CHINESE BUREAUCRACY

To develop a behavioral model of "muddling through" in the Chinese bureaucracy, I begin with Lindblom's insight on the choice behavior of public administrators (Lindblom 1959, Lindblom 1979). In Lindblom's writings, public officials are seen to have limited capacities to gather and process information and they recognize that there will be uncertain consequences associated with their choices. As a result, in practice public officials do not make choices based on what is sometimes referred to as "rational decision making" or according to a "rational comprehensive method." Instead, officials adopt strategies characterized by incrementalism – what Lindblom refers to as "successive limited comparisons." In this process, which is distinguished by serial searches (i.e., sequential rather than comprehensive searches for solutions to problems) and repeated attacks on the same problems, attention is directed to simple incremental evaluations and feasible responses to short-term pressures. As a result, important alternatives may be neglected because of limited attention and limited search capabilities, and goals are constantly readjusted in response to changing conditions and new information. These behavioral characteristics are in sharp contrast to the image of a rational decision maker who takes consistent, anticipatory, and goal-directed actions to meet well-articulated objectives based on complete information.

Lindblom's portrait of muddling through processes provides the basis for my proposed model. Similar to the public administrators in Lindblom's model, Chinese bureaucrats face multiple pressures, high uncertainty about policy consequences, and limited attention and information gathering and processing capabilities. These factors impose significant constraints on the way local officials respond to the incentive designs developed by the central government. Unlike the policy makers in Lindblom's model, however, local officials at the intermediate level of a Chinese government are more preoccupied with the implementation and enforcement of policies imposed by the higher authority. Their behavior represents reactive responses to multiple and sometimes conflicting pressures imposed from the top, and they rely on incremental changes as strategies to cope with the unintended consequences of their actions and changes in the rules imposed by higher levels of government. This decision-making strategy is analogous to an acrobat walking on a wire; she continuously makes adjustments or compensatory gestures in different directions in order to keep her balance and to advance toward the goal post. The process may be successful but more often than not it exhibits a path involving fluctuating, wave-like twists and turns.

I characterize the proposed model as a "behavioral model," in the tradition of Cyert and March (1963), in that I explain how an organization or its members *actually* behave, and I explicate the mechanisms and processes that generate the observed behavioral patterns. I draw key insights from the behavioral theory of the firm – attention allocation, firms as political coalitions – to develop my argument and explanation. As demonstrated below, the behavioral patterns of muddling through are not always efficient or optimal, but the proposed model offers an explanation as to *why* such decisions and behaviors are widespread and persist in the Chinese bureaucracy.

Haphazard and improvised as they may appear, such behavior and coping strategies are not random or disjointed. Rather, they are cultivated and reproduced by the *bureaucratic logics* – stable, patterned interactions induced by the institutional arrangements – that govern the behavior of government officials. Furthermore, these bureaucratic logics are part of the larger, institutional logic of governance in China. They shape government behavior in performing organizational tasks, such as agenda setting, attention allocation, and resource mobilization. These bureaucratic logics are often incongruent, and they may generate conflicting pressures on local officials. An understanding of these multiple logics, their interactions, and their effects on local governments provides a basis for explaining the observed behavioral patterns. At the risk of oversimplification, below I highlight three distinct logics that govern the behavior of local officials.

Three Bureaucratic Logics of Government Behavior

The logic of meeting targets. The logic of meeting targets refers to the imperative in the Chinese bureaucracy for officials to effectively respond to directives and to meet specific goals set by their supervising agencies. Although the mode of governance may vary depending on the allocation of control rights (Chapter 3), bureaucrats may act either in the form of an employment relationship, or act as subcontractor, but they are always in a subordinate position in the mode of party-state domination, as discussed in Chapter 2.

As a result, to a large extent the Chinese bureaucracy has been organized to ensure the effective implementation of top-down policies: The authority structure rests on the principle of upward accountability, with personnel and career-advancement decisions firmly in the hands of higher authorities. Reviews, inspections, and performance evaluations of subnational leaders and organizations are common and intensive to ensure effective policy implementation. Not surprisingly, for government offices and chief officials in those offices, the most immediate, paramount goal is to satisfactorily carry out the tasks and meet the targets set by the supervising agencies. Those who fail to meet their assigned targets are seen as incompetent, and they are subject to stalled career advancement or even demotion.

Under these circumstances, we would expect the behavior of local officials to be extremely sensitive to the targets and directives imposed by higher authorities. Oftentimes, the Chinese bureaucracy is mobilized by political mechanisms to foster the implementation of policies and directives set by higher authorities. It is not surprising, then, that the importance of meeting targets is a central, defining feature of this bureaucracy.

This does not mean, however, that behavior driven by the logic of meeting targets is necessarily consistent with the intentions of the original policy. Increasing top-down pressure is proportional to the extent of tight-coupling that exacerbates the fundamental tension toward centralization and the loss of local initiative. Not surprisingly, as discussed in Chapter 6 and the large and growing literature, the logic of meeting targets often induces coping behavior (both legitimate and illicit), such as selective implementation, collusive behavior to distort or fabricate records, which will lead to a decoupling of symbolic compliance from substantive compliance and the pursuit of short-term gains at the expense of long-term benefits. In addition, pressure to meet targets may cause officials to adopt measures and accounting rules that are inconsistent with other bureaucratic logics.

The logic of coalition building. Formal organizations have long been characterized as political coalitions (March 1962). The very design of a public bureaucracy induces not only competition but also cooperative behavior because there is often a high degree of interdependence in the task environments, that is, to carry out its tasks, a bureau must cooperate and coordinate with other bureaus and reconcile conflicting demands. For example, the MEPB, as shown in the case study in Chapter 3 and in this chapter, must carry out tasks such as reducing the level of pollution released to municipal surface waters, but it cannot carry out this work on its own. Funds for the construction of municipal wastewater treatment plants must be provided by the urban construction bureau and subsidies for industrial wastewater treatment must be allocated by the municipal finance bureau. To calculate the levels of pollution reduction, the MEPB may also need GDP and population-growth statistics from the local office of the bureau of statistics.

In addition, the MEPB must work with the subordinate county environmental protection bureaus (CEPBs), which are responsible for enforcing environmental regulations in their respective jurisdictions. These bureaus are also under pressure from their own principals, the municipal and county governments, to meet local economic growth goals, which typically means that they do not exert undue pressure on local firms to cut pollution. As a result, the bureaucratic logic of coalition building dictates that the MEPB carefully maintains a balance in its relationships with these offices. It must form strategic alliances to respond to crises, to engage in mutually beneficial agreements, to maintain smooth working relations with the CEPBs to ensure future cooperation, and to be on good terms with county government officials because the latter have ultimate authority in terms of implementing and enforcing environmental regulations in their jurisdictions.

The logic of incentive provision. Motivating subordinates is a central concern of officials in government offices, just as it is for managers of firms. In the Chinese context, the central government provides the framework for incentives at lower levels, and that framework is then implemented at the lower levels in the administrative hierarchy. The higher authorities evaluate performance based on explicit criteria to induce behavior that is in line with their goals. The logic of incentive provision is the idea of rewarding performance while discounting random factors beyond an employee's control (Gibbons 1998, Kerr 1975, Milgrom and Roberts 1992). In the government context, performance evaluations must therefore account for the specific conditions under which officials' efforts are exerted and results are realized. When agencies are located in different jurisdictions with distinctive circumstances, the link between efforts and outcomes often becomes ambiguous.

The role of incentives in the Chinese bureaucracy must be understood in a broader context in which there are multiple bureaucratic logics that are often in tension with one another. For example, the logic of meeting targets is typically of singular importance in China, and pressure to meet targets may cause a municipal bureau to knowingly allow its subordinate bureaus to distort performance records in order to satisfy the target requirements. In this context, symbolic compliance is decoupled from the process of actually meeting targets. The final results are at odds with the incentive provision logic since the subordinate bureau's symbolic compliance (as opposed to its effort and performance) may be rewarded. In other instances, the logic of coalition building may impose constraints on the effective provision of incentives. This does not mean that officials do not care about rewarding behavior based on performance. They do care about this, but their ability to provide incentives is often constrained and compromised by other competing logics, such as the need to maintain coalitions.

Muddling through in the Chinese Bureaucracy: Empirical Implications

What are the behavioral patterns induced by these multiple, competing bureaucratic logics? As discussed below, tensions among the bureaucratic logics and the developed coping strategies have shaped the key behavioral patterns in the Chinese bureaucracy.

First, behavior in the face of competing bureaucratic logics tends to be *reactive* rather than proactive, and it is characterized by improvised strategies in response to multiple directives and targets set at the higher administrative levels. This reactive behavior is largely shaped by the prevailing bureaucratic logic of meeting targets, which dictates that local officials act in response to directives from the top. Some tasks are part of a long-term plan, such as the designated goals in a five-year plan, and are regulated by bureaucratic milestones such as annual reviews. Frequently, however, tasks are imposed with an arbitrary exercise of power by multiple principals and the tasks arrive at these agencies in an unpredictable manner. As a result, the behavior of local-level bureaucrats is characterized by reactive responses to multiple directives or to unexpected consequences resulting from the implementation of these directives.

Second, constant readjustment is an important strategy for coping with the conflicting pressures generated by the multiple bureaucratic logics. The key mechanism here is the *allocation of attention*, and the related distribution of resources across different areas and at different times. The organization literature has long recognized that attention is a scarce resource. Because of limited attention, an organization may exhibit behavior that is at odds with the rational model of decision making, and it may exhibit an inconsistent trajectory, as shown in the strategy of "putting out fires" (Allison 1971, Cyert and March 1963, Radner and Rothschild 1975). Organizations also develop explicit strategies for attention management. In the Chinese bureaucracy, bureaucratic milestones, such as annual reviews and on-site inspections, serve as mechanisms for local governments to mobilize attention in response to predictable reviews and inspections.

Third, bureaucratic behavior in the context of Chinese local governments tends to focus on short-term solutions rather than long-term goals. Because an intermediate government office has to respond to multiple tasks and is constrained by multiple bureaucratic logics, typically it is unable to take action in accordance with its own long-term goals. It is even questionable whether an intermediate government bureau has independent goals of its own beyond those prescribed by, or reformulated according to, directives from the higher authorities. This does not mean that local officials do not pursue their own interests and agendas; rather, they do so in ad hoc ways using improvised strategies in response to the challenges in their task environments and the unintended consequences of their efforts to implement policies.

To sum up, my argument is that bureaucratic behavior in response to such multiple pressures yields a course of action characterized by *muddling through* – a focus on short-term goals, constant adjustments, improvised coping strategies in response to pressures from the task environment, and tensions in the face of competing bureaucratic logics. Instead of a steady course of action as dictated by a single bureaucratic logic, or intended by the provision of clear incentives, we expect to find bureaucratic behavior that varies with the interplay of the multiple bureaucratic logics that are identified above.

The kinds and extent of the multiple pressures facing an agency or a policy-implementation process vary from case to case. To sharpen the analytical power of the model, I now highlight the institutional conditions that affect muddling-through behavior. An immediate implication from the preceding discussion is that behavioral patterns vary with the extent of *autonomy* that a bureau has in managing its task environment. As previously mentioned, the reactive response to tasks imposed from above is a key feature of the muddling through by Chinese officials. The extent of autonomy is distributed unevenly among different government offices. For areas in which tasks are simpler, more routine, or more predictable, a bureau can manage its task environment through routines and a division of labor. Under these circumstances, the logic of meeting targets causes less tensions with other bureaucratic logics such as coalition building and incentive provision. By cultivating patronage relationships and extra-budgetary resources, a government office may create greater autonomy and have an enhanced ability to exercise discretion. In general, we expect behavior characterized by muddling through to be inversely related to the relative autonomy of the government agency in managing its task environment.

By similar reasoning, behavioral patterns of local Chinese agencies are also sensitive to the extent of interdependence among agencies. Different government organizations are located variously in a web of interorganizational relationships, and the specific tasks assigned to an organization dictates its links with other organizations even where there are no formal connections. In those areas where there is a high interdependence, the bureaucratic logic of political coalitions becomes especially important. A special-purpose organization, as an ideal type, may have only a single task or be under a single principal, and it would act differently than an organization that faces multiple tasks and multiple principals. As noted, an environmental-protection agency cannot carry out its tasks without coordinating with other agencies. Therefore, we expect that behavior that is characteristic of muddling through to be positively associated with the extent of interdependence among organizations in the task environment.

As is observed in the context of bureaucratic bargaining (Chapter 5), time is a critical dimension for understanding processes and rhythms of behavior characteristic of muddling through. Patterns of attention allocation over time may vary with the pressures exerted at different points in the implementation process. For example, the logic of meeting targets may exert strong pressures at the beginning of a policy-implementation process, but success of getting things done at an early stage may lessen the pressure as time passes. Conversely, failure to meet targets during the early stages of policy implementation may generate increasing pressures at later stages, thereby moving the need to meet targets to center stage and pushing aside other agenda items.

Organizations are governed by multiple bureaucratic milestones, such as annual budget setting and annual evaluations. These cyclic events may regulate attention allocation and implementation processes. In a typical organizational setting, multiple tasks and demands are dealt with by distributing attention across different offices using structural arrangements. But in the Chinese bureaucracy, there is a tendency to temporarily direct resources, attention, and personnel to a particular area or task in response to mobilization efforts from the top, often at the expense of overlooking issues in other areas. As a result, great attention to a task during the early phase of policy implementation may lead to over-achievement, and in response task-achievement efforts are slowed down during later phases of policy implementation. In contrast, a slow start may trigger enormous pressures to catch up during later phases, leading to a significant increase in effort. Therefore, we expect behavior characteristic of muddling through to be sensitive to bureaucratic timetables that dictate the allocation of attention over time, thereby generating different rhythms within the policy-implementation process.

MUDDLING THROUGH IN ENVIRONMENTAL REGULATION: A CASE STUDY

Context: The Five-Year Plan Policy Cycle

Let us now return to the case study of the MEPB, first introduced in Chapter 3, to illustrate the analytical concepts and theoretical arguments developed in the proposed model. In this chapter, I analyze the MEPB's implementation of environmental-protection requirements designated in China's Eleventh Five-Year Plan during the 2006–2010 period. Focusing on the implementation process during a multi-year period allows us to show how tensions among the multiple bureaucratic logics play out over time and how those tensions lead to bureaucratic behavior that is characteristic of muddling through.

As noted in Chapter 3, between 2008 and 2011 our research team conducted field research using the participant observation approach in an MEPB in W Province of northern China. For the first two years (2006–2007) before our researcher entered the field, we collected

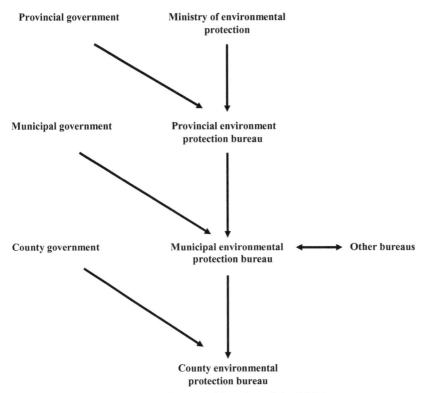

FIGURE 7.1. Structural location of the MEPB

retrospective data. As Figure 7.1 (reproduced from Figure 3.2) shows, the Ministry of Environmental Protection (MEP) was the highest authority in the functional line for environmental protection. Within W Province, the provincial EPB (PEPB) was the highest authority for environmental protection and the supervisory agency for the sixteen MEPBs in the province. Each MEPB in turn supervised the county EPBs (CEPBs) within its jurisdiction. The MEPB in the case study had twelve CEPBs under its administrative authority.[1] In addition to the authority relationship in the environmental protection functional line, each EPB was subject to the authority of the territorial government in its jurisdiction. For example, the MEPB was under the authority of its municipal government, and each CEPB was under the authority of its county government. In addition, the MEPB also had to

---

[1] To protect the anonymity of the research site, technical changes were made in the presentation of the descriptive information, such as the number of MEPBs and CEPBs as well as the designated reduction goals in COD and SO_2 for the MEPB.

cooperate with other municipal bureaus and county governments to implement the environmental regulations. Within its functional line, the EPB had
the challenge of providing incentives to motivate its subordinates, the
CEPBs, to take action consistent with the MEPB goals.

Recall the inspection and evaluation processes for the MEPB office
outlined in the case study reported in Chapter 3. Performance of the EPBs
at all levels is evaluated annually by their supervising agencies. Typically,
the higher-level authorities (e.g., the MEP and the PEPB) send inspection
teams to review the records compiled by their subordinate EPBs regarding
their claimed enforcement efforts and outcomes (e.g., the closing of
pollution sources) and the levels of pollution before and after these
efforts. Inspection teams may also conduct their own on-site inspections
to verify these claims.[2] On these bases, an inspection team decides which
of the claimed accomplishments are officially accepted and it places an
official stamp of certification on the final version of the documentation.

During the time frame of our participant observation fieldwork, the
MEPB's central task was to achieve the goals promulgated by the central
government for the Eleventh Five-Year Plan. The main tasks in pollution
reduction were measured by two policy targets: chemical oxygen demand
(COD) of wastewater releases, and sulfur dioxide (SO_2) in air emissions.
For the MEPB, the designated targets for its jurisdiction were specific: the
reduction of COD by twelve percent and reduction of SO_2 by eight
percent during the 2006–2010 period. The outcome of each annual
inspection was added to the level of cumulative reduction counted in
meeting the designated targets in the five-year plan. The MEPB decomposed its aggregate goals into specific targets for each CEPB within
its jurisdiction.

Figures 7.2 and 7.3 show the percentage of *cumulative* accomplishments toward achieving the designated five-year goal (100 percent) in
COD and SO_2 releases, respectively, among all CEPBs over the five-year
period.[3] These figures reflect the achievements officially accepted by the
PEPB and the MEP. In the figures, county EPBs are arranged based on
high to low levels of cumulative achievements. As indicated, differences in

---

[2] There may be other unannounced inspections throughout the year conducted by the
higher authorities, the results of which also become the bases for the annual
performance evaluations.
[3] Note that three CEPBs were given no task quota for the reduction of SO_2 due to the targets
of economic growth set for these jurisdictions. Hence, they are not represented in
Figure 7.3.

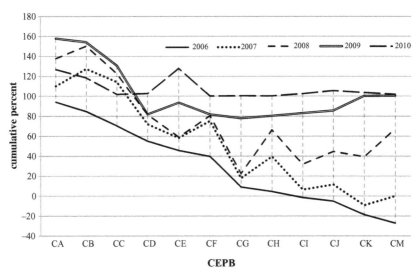

FIGURE 7.2. Cumulative percentages of accomplishment of COD reductions among County Environmental Protection Bureaus (CEPBs), 2006–2010

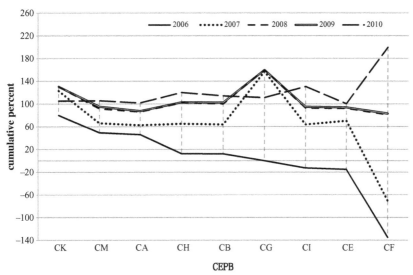

FIGURE 7.3. Cumulative percentages of accomplishment of SO_2 reductions among CEPBs, 2006–2010

performance evaluations among the CEPBs narrowed over the years, with some CEPBs having particularly large upward shifts in later years.

Taken at face value, the patterns and trends in the two figures give the impression of a steady, well-managed improvement toward fulfilling the designated goals during the policy cycle. However, the figures do not represent the actual accomplishments of the CEPBs. Instead, they reflect the results of a process in which the MEPB redistributed certified credit for accomplishments among the CEPBs based on the various pressures generated by the three bureaucratic logics described herein. For example, Figure 7.2 shows that the CM County EPB made what appears to be a spectacular jump from a position where it had a minus twenty percent achievement in 2006 and a zero percent achievement in 2007 to attaining the five-year target within only three years. However, this is not what actually occurred; it is the result of adjustments made by the MEPB for CM county in the official documents. Significantly, PEPB and MEP staff knowingly accepted the manipulated records in Figures 7.2 and 7.3, thereby implicitly allowing the adjustments in credit allocations made by the MEPB.

As a result, Figures 7.2 and 7.3 show the actual allocation of credit reflecting the accomplishments of the CEPBs that were adjusted in response to pressures generated by multiple bureaucratic logics. Indeed, behind the appearance of a steady process of goal attainment in Figures 7.2 and 7.3 there was a circuitous journey of muddling through toward reaching the goals of the five-year plan. Below I discuss the events, processes, and responses that generated the results shown in these two figures.

An analysis of the actual and adjusted CEPB performance results shows that a well-defined rhythm existed over the five-year policy cycle. The first year of inspection and evaluation yielded an uneven set of officially accepted outcomes that shaped the MEPB's behavior in later years. The mid-term review, which took place at the end of 2008, reflected the MEPB's response to notable changes in the PEPB certification procedures. The MEPB's efforts during the last two years were geared toward ensuring that its own aggregate five-year plan targets were met. As the discussion below makes clear, it is difficult to make sense of bureaucratic behavior in a single year without considering the entire five-year policy cycle. Below, I chronicle key processes and events during the 2006–2010 period based on our participant observation fieldwork.

2006–2007: Creating an Uneven Playing Field

I treat the first two years of the five-year period as the first phase of the five-year policy-implementation cycle. This marked a trial-and-error environmental-regulatory period – a long neglected policy area that by

2006 was garnering increased attention and was under considerable scrutiny. Detailed targets for SO_2 and COD reductions were announced in the Eleventh Five-Year Plan, but no operating procedures had yet been established to implement the targets.

Because of the existence of well-defined metrics, performance evaluations in the field of environmental regulation are not as elusive as they are in some other areas. Since 2005, China's environmental-protection regulations have focused on reducing SO_2 and COD releases, with the performance of all EPBs being evaluated based on these two indicators. Concrete measures for reduction are based on well-defined monitoring protocols, and enforcement outcomes can be tracked over time. Given that measurable pollution-reduction targets exist, it might appear that the MEPBs and PEPBs would design internal incentives for their agents and that the tournament model of competition would describe agency behavior, but this is not the case.

The actual events departed significantly from what the tournament model would predict. Instead of the MEPB (the supervisor-as-subcontractor in this context) carrying out straightforward performance evaluations based on the accomplishment of the CEPBs (the agents) in meeting the pollution-reduction goals, evaluations by the MEPB reflected complex readjustments. Adjustments were made for three main reasons, none of which were taken into consideration during the inspection and evaluation processes. First, the ability of the CEPBs to meet the designated policy goals depended on matters beyond the area of environmental regulation, such as population growth and industrialization. Consequently, the numerical COD and SO_2 pollution-reduction goals for each CEPB were moving targets that were adjusted over time. The MEPB anticipated that the MEP and PEPB would allow it to reallocate CEPB credits for reducing pollution provided the aggregate reduction over all CEPBs indicated that the MEPB had met its own reduction targets. Second, the extent of possible reductions varied, depending on the availability of municipal wastewater treatment projects within a CEPB's jurisdiction and the capacities of industrial waste sources to cut pollution. Third, the certification criteria used by the MEP and PEPB inspection teams varied significantly over time, as shown in Chapter 3, thereby creating uncertainties in the proportion of the accomplishments claimed by the MEPB and the CEPBs that would be officially accepted.

With the above background in mind, consider the variations in the CEPBs' officially accepted performance results for 2006 (see Figures 7.2 and 7.3). Some CEPBs achieved more than fifty percent of their reduction goals during the first year, whereas others had negative reductions (i.e., their pollution levels were worse than in 2005). One might infer that the drastic variations across these CEPBs were evidence of the effectiveness of a tournament competition, whereby all CEPBs were rank-ordered according to their performance evaluations. However, based on conversations with MEPB officials, nothing could be farther from the truth. By the end of 2006, the MEP and PEPB had not developed clear guidelines and criteria by which the CEPBs claimed accomplishments were to be evaluated, and thus a large proportion of the claims made by the local offices were accepted. Due to the lack of well-defined review criteria, these variations in claimed accomplishments reflected neither the efforts nor the achievements at the county levels. Rather, to a great extent they reflected the different extents of distortion efforts by the individual CEPBs. As an MEPB official put it:

They [the MEP and PEPB] conducted reviews and made acceptance decisions in arbitrary, inconsistent ways. [Pollution reductions claimed by] some counties were as much as fifteen percent, whereas others actually increased pollution. This is unbelievable! The key problem is that we [the MEPB] have no say in any of this.[4]

The CEPBs that carefully prepared for the inspection process and dared to inflate their achievements were much better off than others because a large proportion of the claimed achievements were accepted by the inspection teams from the PEPB and MEP in 2006. The officially accepted CEPB reductions were not generated by the MEPB; rather, they resulted from inspections conducted by the MEP and PEPB. In fact, the MEPB, which had more accurate information about the efforts and achievements of the CEPBs, had no say in the certification process and the ranking of the CEPBs. Even worse, the shared interests between the MEPB and the CEPBs in the same jurisdiction of achieving their designated goals led to collusion between them in the process of meeting their shared goal of official acceptance for meeting the targets. The PEPB's concerns about such collusion was one reason the MEPB was not given a voice in the inspection process, but collusion nevertheless occurred.

The conflicting pressures faced by the MEPB from multiple bureaucratic logics were evident. For the MEPB, the bureaucratic logic of rewarding effort and performance took a back seat to that of meeting targets. Because inflated claims were accepted, real efforts were not properly rewarded. The MEPB's main concern at this stage was to ensure

---

[4] Quotations and descriptions of the case study are drawn from our fieldnotes.

eventual completion of the designated five-year plan pollution cuts. Therefore, despite their bitter internal complaints about the unfair certification outcomes, the MEPB officials accepted the results without raising any questions. At that point, the MEPB's priority was to encourage the inspection teams to accept as much as possible of the claimed achievements by the CEPBs; it turned a blind eye to the inflated statistics filed by some CEPBs.

A series of unexpected events in the next year sheds light on how the MEPB responded to tensions generated by the multiple bureaucratic logics: meeting policy targets, maintaining political coalitions with the CEPBs, and administering incentive provisions that linked rewards to the CEPBs' actual efforts and performance.

By 2007, the MEPB and all the CEPBs had learned from their experience during the previous year and made full preparations to claim greater pollution reductions than what they had actually achieved. In the annual review process conducted by the PEPB, the MEPB (in aggregate) easily surpassed its annual targets. But, according to the PEPB evaluation, quite a few CEPBs within the MEPB jurisdiction did not meet their individual annual targets – five percent reduction from the previous year for COD, and seven percent reduction for SO_2 from the previous year. Now that the annual aggregate pollution-reduction goals were met at the MEPB level, the logic of meeting the targets receded in importance, and the MEPB worked on building coalitions with the CEPBs. It aimed to do this by reallocating the certified achievement quotas among the CEPBs and thereby leveling the uneven playing field created by the certifications in 2006. The MEPB planned to lower the 2007 achievement levels of the CEPBs that had performed well in 2006 and to lift the achievement level for the CEPBs that had performed poorly. Instead of following the logic of a tournament competition, the MEPB improvised a strategy based on an adjustment of the claimed reductions to ensure that a relatively large number of CEPBs met their annual targets for 2007. In short, as pressures from the logic of meeting the MEPB's aggregate targets eased, pressures generated from other logics – especially the logic of building and maintaining political coalitions – increased.

However, before the MEPB could formally adopt and publicize its adjusted performance evaluations, a series of unexpected events took place. Toward the end of 2007, shortly after the PEPB's certification of the COD and SO_2 reductions, the MEP unexpectedly tightened its inspection procedures and rejected a large proportion of the claims made by the PEPB in that year. As a result, the PEPB revised and lowered the performance levels of all MEPBs by making proportional reductions in their previously certified levels. Based on these new certifi-cations, the MEPB's claimed achievement level was drastically reduced. Instead of surpassing its annual targets, the MEPB now fell short of meeting its COD target. Not surprisingly, the logic of meeting the targets returned to center stage, forcing the MEPB to abandon its earlier attempt to strengthen its political coalitions with the CEPBs by leveling the playing field among them. Instead, the MEPB adopted the PEPB's strategy of proportional reductions as a basis for lowering the accom-plishments of all CEPBs in the official certifications. As a result, the general pattern of uneven accomplishment in 2006 was maintained at the end of 2007.

As Figure 7.3 shows, almost all CEPBs were certified for reaching more than sixty percent of their five-year target SO_2 reductions by the end of 2007, and two CEPBs (CK and CG) had already more than satisfied their five-year goals. In contrast, most CEPBs were still struggling to make substantial COD reductions by the end of 2007 (Figure 7.2). In terms of the official certification records, a clear rank-order of the CEPBs existed for pollution reduction. However, because the inflated accomplishments of many CEPBs had been accepted, the link between the rank-order and actual performance was elusive at best.

Three things can be learned from the events in 2007, when the MEPB responded to the multiple bureaucratic logics and the unexpected changes. First, the rank-order of subordinate CEPBs created by the MEP and PEPB reviews had little to do with the actual performance levels, and the acceptance of distorted CEPB claims by the PEPB created an uneven playing field among the CEPBs. Second, the logic of political coalitions became salient as soon as pressures to meet the targets lessened, as was shown by the MEPB's initial attempt in 2007 to readjust the performance evaluations such that a large number of CEPBs met their annual targets regardless of their actual performance. However, as soon as the PEPB unexpectedly changed its certification results, the threat of failure to meet its aggregate targets led the MEPB to abandon its planned effort to build coalitions. Third, contrary to what the tournament compe-tition model would predict, the logic of incentive provision was not at all evident in the bureaucratic responses at all levels of the hierarchy. Collectively, these observations reflect behavior that is characteristic of muddling through. Instead of taking anticipatory, consistent actions, as events unfolded the MEPB improvised new strategies and made adjust-ments to alleviate tensions among the competing bureaucratic logics.

2008: The Mid-term Evaluation

In 2008, a mid-term review of the five-year plan was conducted. The official goal for that year was to surpass sixty percent of the pollution-reduction goals set by the five-year plan as well as to meet the annual targets – five percent and seven percent cuts in COD and SO_2, respectively, from the previous year. The mid-term review was notable for two reasons. First, in response to shortcomings in its own loose certification procedures in the previous years, in 2008 the MEP issued stringent new rules for the certification process. The tightening of the MEP's acceptance criteria triggered new adjustments by the MEPBs and CEPBs. Second, the provincial and municipal governments included environmental measures in the mid-term reviews of their subordinate, territorial governments. Thus, for the first time, measures of pollution reduction were formally included as part of the criteria to evaluate county governments. This meant that the MEPB's evaluation of the CEPBs' performance would have important consequences for county governments within the jurisdiction.

Thus, in preparation for the mid-term review, MEPB officials juggled the attention it gave to the three bureaucratic logics: meeting targets, building coalitions, and providing incentives. The immediate, top-priority task was to meet the designated targets for the mid-term review. At the same time, MEPB officials had to maintain its political coalitions with the counties (particularly the county governments) so that future cooperation could be solicited. Because county government performance evaluations depended in part on the MEPB's evaluations of CEPB performance, the MEPB had to ensure that none of the CEPB performance outcomes were notably low. In addition, the MEPB wanted to ensure that there were some incentives to motivate CEPB performance. Such incentives for the CEPBs were necessary to balance the uneven certified (but often distorted) performance results of the previous two years. The three bureaucratic logics were in tension with one another. To ensure the effectiveness of incentives that rewarded effort, the officially certified achievements had to be modified to account for the manipulated results submitted by the CEPBs. Similarly, to maintain the political coalitions, adjustments had to be made in the allocation of quotas so that all CEPBs would meet their targets; this would avoid jeopardizing the performance evaluations of county government leaders. However, in adjusting the certified results to ensure that all counties met their targets, compromises had to be made in the incentive design of rewarding effort and performance. For the MEPB, dealing with these conflicting logics was not only a delicate balancing act but also an imperative for survival.

By the third year of the policy-implementation cycle, the MEPB was on track to meet its aggregate targets for the five-year plan. The goal of satisfying sixty percent of the targets by the third year had already been met at the MEPB level, so MEPB officials were less preoccupied than they were in 2007 with the logic of meeting targets. In contrast, the occasion of the mid-term review could adversely affect a larger number of stakeholders, particularly the county government officials. As a result, the bureaucratic logic of building political coalitions became a central concern.

Officials at the MEPB clearly recognized the serious pollution-reduction challenges facing some CEPBs, and they thus adopted multifaceted strategies to rescue those CEPBs. By making a series of internal adjustments, the MEPB was able to balance the performance evaluations among the CEPBs, while still meeting the aggregate target levels for the MEPB. Consider, for example, the adjustments made for the COD results. With a large wastewater treatment facility put into operation in that year, the MEPB could now claim a significant amount of COD reduction within its jurisdiction. Instead of allocating the COD reduction according to the actual proportion of wastewater from the various counties being treated, the MEPB allocated a larger volume of the treated wastewater to counties CK and CM, which, at the end of 2007, were seriously lagging. This adjustment significantly boosted the performance results for these two counties in 2008. Another county (CC) received a minimum allocation from the new wastewater treatment facility because it was already doing well in meeting its COD target. As shown in Figure 7.2, after these adjustments, the majority of counties had achieved the target of sixty percent COD reduction of the 2005 COD levels, which was the targeted goal in the five-year plan. The certified performance of the three very low-scoring CEPBs (CI, CK, CM) increased significantly. To varying degrees, these types of adjustments, which were intended to make all counties look reasonably successful, continued for the remainder of the five-year period. By adopting this strategy, the MEPB managed to avoid being in a position whereby particular county leaders would be harshly penalized for poor performance.

Our field observations verified that the logic of building coalitions played a major role in the MEPB's certification adjustment procedures. The MEPBs were under tremendous pressures from county officials because their career advancements were at stake. As one official in charge of making these adjustments noted:

Our bureau head told me that many county party secretaries or county administrative heads had come to him [for special consideration], explaining that they had special situations. For example, someone would have faced an end-of-term evaluation that may affect where he would go next. In the mid-term personnel adjustments, he could be promoted to be head or vice head of a county administration. He would say, if you do not issue a report card with a good performance evaluation, my promotion will be denied.

The irony is that the increased pressures imposed from above (in the form of the provincial government's 2008 procedures for evaluation of the performance of territorial governments) were translated into additional pressures to obtain protection from below (i.e., pressures on the MEPB that were placed by county officials). In recent years, China's higher authorities adopted the "one item veto" rule (*yipiao foujue*) in the environmental protection area: If a local government did not meet the designated environmental-protection targets, its performance in all other areas would be offset and the evaluation by the top officials would be seriously compromised. The severe penalties imposed on a failure to meet one's targets makes the logic of political coalitions more noteworthy. As one MEPB official commented:

I have to balance among the CEPBs before we submit the materials to the statistics bureau. We cannot do what the PEPB did [referring to the uneven CEPB performance results created by imposing strict evaluation criteria]. There are three or four CEPBs that are hopeless and cannot meet their quotas no matter what we do. But the "one item veto" practice is too harsh; it is difficult for us to take that step. [Recently, one CEPB behaved very irresponsibly.] Our bureau head was furious and wanted to impose a serious penalty. But after he calmed down, he became soft-hearted and asked us to help that CEPB find a way out.

The granting of incentives to reward efforts also affected the MEPB's manipulation of the county reduction quota allocations and achievement claims, especially after the MEPB had taken care of meeting targets and maintaining its coalitions with the counties. In a conversation between two MEPB officials about making adjustments among the CEPBs, one official inquired whether they should help the two counties that had negative performance evaluations. The other official, who was in charge, was against it:

This is not about offering a helping hand. Now our priority is not only about whom to help but also to make clear the seriousness of the situation. If we make adjustments [to lessen the pressure], some CEPBs will take a look and say wow, they already had twenty percent reduction and there is no problem with meeting the target. Then they will not make any more efforts; they will do nothing but wait. We cannot let them think that this is so easy.

As is evident from the above discussion, the bureaucratic logic of incentive provision oftentimes gives way to pressures from the logics of meeting targets and building coalitions.

2009–2010: The End Game

In 2009, implementation of the five-year plan entered its fourth year, and the MEPB officials felt meeting the designated final goals was within reach. The evaluations of the CEPBs no longer had serious implications for the county governments within the municipality. Thus, the logic of meeting targets retreated from center stage and other bureaucratic logics became salient.

For example, once the MEPB made sure it could meet the aggregate five-year targets for its jurisdiction, it initiated efforts to ensure that all its subordinate CEPBs met their individual five-year targets. Toward the end of 2009, the MEPB moved on its own to accept the additional claimed reductions by the CEPBs that had been rejected by the PEPB; in other words, the MEPB increased some of the CEPB accomplishments above the levels recognized by the PEPB. In addition, the MEPB made some adjustments to the quotas assigned to each CEPB to ensure that all CEPBs would successfully meet their respective five-year plan targets. As an MEPB officer commented: "We have to figure out ways for them to meet these quotas. If not, they will be in big trouble. . . . The 'one item veto' rule cannot be activated lightly. It creates huge pressures, and it cannot be used under normal circumstances." With respect to several counties that could not meet the five-year plan quotas through their own efforts, the MEPB made further adjustments by reallocating the task accomplishments among the CEPBs. In the end, all of the CEPBs met the official five-year targets.

Once the designated pollution-reduction goals were attained and all the CEPBs and county government leaders were well-protected from the danger of serious penalties imposed by the higher authorities, the logic of incentive design became salient. As one official observed in the middle of the rank-ordering of CEPB performance:

This time [2009], we can conduct evaluations based on real performance. The way we allocate reduction targets among these CEPBs should, on the one hand, reflect the relative contributions among the CEPBs, and, on the other hand, make sure that they all have met their targets. Overall performance across years should also be taken into consideration. Even when you are doing well in this year, if your overall cumulative reduction is poor, we will not give you a high spot in the rank-order.

But near the end of the policy cycle, MEPB officials were keenly sensitive to the tensions among the multiple bureaucratic logics, and they were careful not to make the performance differences among the CEPBs too pronounced. As one official in charge put it:

If we make the differences in the environmental scores among the CEPBs too large, the overall ranking of these counties will be affected. We don't want to have the environmental scores decide the ranking of these county governments. ... So, we need both to create a ranking order [based on these scores] and to avoid creating tensions because of environmental protection issues. We don't want to direct all these tensions to our bureau.

In 2010, the final year of the five-year plan, all quotas for the CEPBs had been fulfilled. In that sense, it was an uneventful ending. In April 2011, the head of the MEPB declared that the bureau had exceeded meeting the five-year pollution-reduction targets for the municipality – 108 percent for COD and 159 percent for SO_2. But he added a somber observation:

[The reason] some CEPBs did not fail is not because they did their job, but because we [the MEPB] made internal balancing adjustments on the premise that our bureau had achieved overall good performance; and we took into consideration the contributions of the counties. We should make it clear that these achievements are somewhat inflated. ... Pollution reduction is a serious indicator in the evaluation of local governments. Failure in this area will lead to removal of the chief officials from their present positions. During this five-year plan period, we did not let any CEPB fail to meet its goals. This is not to say that all counties did their job equally well. We balanced the performances in our municipal jurisdiction. So the achievements of some of the counties were not real. Such adjustments were possible due to the overall [aggregate] achievement at the MEPB level.

Beyond the MEPB: Performance Evaluations at the Provincial Level

Our fieldwork allowed for close observations of the coping strategies adopted by the MEPB officials to conduct the performance evaluations, the reasoning behind their decisions, and how these coping strategies varied over time in response to tensions among the three bureaucratic logics. The following question naturally arises: To what extent might the case-study findings be applicable to other bureaucratic levels and to other sectors? The trajectories and episodes we observed are clearly specific to the context in which the events unfolded. However, I submit that the general patterns of muddling-through behavior based on competing

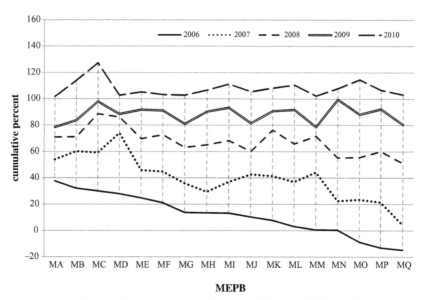

FIGURE 7.4. Cumulative percentages of accomplishment of COD reductions among MEPBs, 2006–2010

bureaucratic logics are prevalent in other contexts as well. In looking at the PEPB's performance evaluations of the MEPBs within its jurisdiction and we found strikingly similar patterns.

Figures 7.4 and 7.5 show the officially accepted performance results for the cumulative reductions in COD and SO_2 of all MEPBs in W Province over the five-year plan period. For simplicity, the metropolitan cities are arranged on the basis of their general performance, beginning with the best performing MEPBs. As shown in the figures, variatios in the performance evaluations among the MEPBs narrowed over the years. By the mid-term evaluation of 2008, most MEPBs had met the sixty-percent-reduction target set by PEPB for that year, and some MEPBs had notably larger shifts upward in later years. These patterns are similar to those observed for the MEPB's evaluation of the CEPBs during the same years (cf. Figures 7.2 and 7.3).

Unlike our case study at the MEPB level, we do not have detailed information about the actual behavior and considerations that went into the performance evaluations at the provincial level. We only had glimpses into the inter-MEPB relationships during the pollution-reduction certification process based on occasional conversations among MEPB officials at our case study research site. The evidence suggests that similar adjustment processes and mechanisms found in the case study of the MEPB

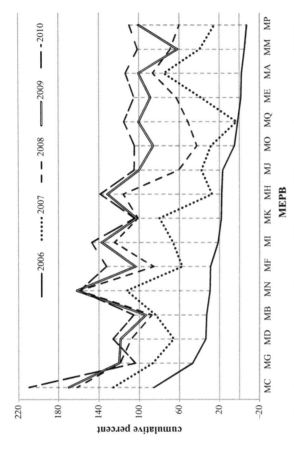

FIGURE 7.5. Cumulative percentages of accomplishment of SO_2 reductions among MEPBs, 2006–2010

were at work at the provincial level as well. For example, in 2007, the PEPB asked the MEPB at our research site to postpone until the following year one-third of its COD quota so as to keep a balance of the reductions attained among the MEPBs in the province. The MEPB officials in our case study understood such strategies well. As one MEPB official commented:

This year [2008], the PEPB imposed very restrictive evaluations on the MEPBs so that it can have some flexibility in adjusting the MEPBs' performance level after the MEP evaluation.

Accordingly, he instructed his subordinate officials to prepare to bargain over the performance evaluation results. After the PEPB's semi-annual review in 2008, a MEPB official observed that the PEPB would adopt a strategy of decreasing the performance evaluations of those MEPBs that had performed well and increasing the evaluations of those that had not performed so well. "This is like the [Chinese] game of 'breaking hands.' Once you move over the middle line too much, you will be pushed back to a balanced position." The outcome is consistent with this view. In that review process, the PEPB certified less than one-seventh of the accomplishments claimed by the MEPB in our case study.

One driving force behind the constant readjustment at the provincial level, like that at the MEPB level, was the pressure to maintain political coalitions by ensuring that all MEPBs accomplish their designated goals; this would avoid application of the one item veto rule to municipal officials during their performance reviews. The MEPB officials understood this rationale and acted in the same way to protect the CEPB officials within their own jurisdictions.

In summary, although we only have glimpses of the processes at the provincial level, these anecdotes, together with the patterns observed in Figures 7.4 and 7.5, suggest that similar mechanisms and processes are at work at different levels of the Chinese bureaucracy. This outcome is not surprising given the extent of isomorphism in organizational structures, authority relationships, and task environments in the Chinese bureaucracy, especially in those contexts where notable tensions exist among the bureaucratic logics.

SUMMARY

In this chapter, I develop a behavioral model of muddling through to make sense of the behavior of local officials during the policy-implementation processes. Instead of a rational organizational design and provision of incentives, what we observed is a process of haphazard responses to multiple, conflicting goals by short-term, inconsistent behavior. My central argument is that in the face of the pressures generated by competing bureaucratic logics, local bureaucrats adopt improvised strategies, make constant readjustments, and focus on short-term gains rather than exhibiting a course of consistent, anticipatory actions. My explanations of the alternative mechanisms and processes that induce distinct behavioral patterns in the Chinese bureaucracy are markedly different from those based on rational incentive designs. The proposed model and the empirical implications are illustrated by the case study of a municipal government agency's policy implementation over a five-year plan period. These observed behavioral patterns are induced by competing pressures and mobilization of attention by multiple, and often conflicting, bureaucratic logics.

This chapter takes another look at the micro-processes of local bureaucracies that fit into the larger institutional logic of governance discussed in the previous chapters. As discussed in Chapter 2, the Chinese bureaucracy is located in a subordinate role in the mode of party-state domination in China, acquiring its legitimacy from the delegation of power from above. This is a stable basis for the logic of meeting targets. However, the bureaucracies exhibit distinct behavior in response to their work environment, including the formation of political coalitions to get things done and their response to the provision of incentives. The muddling through behavior is also part of the interactions between the formal rules and the informal practices that generate variable-coupling between policy making and policy implementation, with tight-coupling and loose-coupling taking place at different points in time. These considerable variations cannot be accounted for by the "top-level design" or by the rational incentive provision. Rather, they result from the local officials' haphazard response to the high uncertainty and pressures from these multiple logics and their ensuring attention to competition, agenda setting, and changes in priorities to meet multiple targets.

The micro-behavior of the Chinese bureaucracy, as captured by the proposed muddling through model and our case study, has broad implications for understanding the institutional logic of governance in China. Many Chinese agencies, including territorial governments, face multiple principals and respond to multiple, conflicting pressures. They are under pressure to meet targets from the higher authorities; they operate in a task environment that is interdependent with other bureaus or offices; and they are in charge of providing incentives to their subordinate bureaus and employees. We would expect such governmental organizations to exhibit behavioral patterns that are similar to those discussed in this chapter. These findings suggest that we should pay close attention not only to the official rhetoric of the performance evaluations and outcomes but also to the actual processes used to carry out the evaluations. What appears as steady improvements in performance evaluations may turn out to be, as in our case study, outcomes that are manipulated in a muddling-through process in response to tensions from the competing goals of meeting targets, maintaining coalitions, and rewarding good performance.

The findings highlight the importance of examining bureaucratic behavior in the multi-year context of the policy-implementation processes because behavior associated with muddling through is characterized by sequential adjustments. The specific acts in our case study at a certain point in time can only be interpreted meaningfully when placed in the context of the entire five-year plan period. In many ways, the observed patterns of behavior in muddling through help us to make sense of the larger picture of governance practice in China.

8

Inverted Soft Budget Constraints and Resource Extraction

In this chapter, I examine another salient phenomenon associated with local government behavior; that is, local governments engage in extensive extractions of resources from below – firms, subordinate agencies, or residents within their jurisdictions – in order to obtain extra-budgetary resources. Such extra-budgetary resource-seeking activities often take the form of imposing various taxes and fees or using political pressures or incentives to induce local firms to sponsor government-initiated projects. This type of behavior is especially salient at, and associated with, lower-level government administrations (e.g., governments at the township or county levels), where resources are scarce and where governments come into direct contact with ordinary citizens and all kinds of enterprises. Over the years, such behavior that seeks extra-budgetary resources from below has been remarkably persistent, extensive, and widespread, despite the central government's repeated efforts to curb it.

I develop an organizational analysis of extra-budgetary resource seeking by local governments. I begin my discussion with the following observation: There are many interesting parallels between the kinds of organizational behavior described above and the "soft budget constraint" (SBC) syndrome described by Kornai (1979, 1986). In his study of Soviet-type command economies, Kornai observes the lack of hard budget constraints on socialist firms. That is, in a central planning system, socialist firms seek to maximize output, and they break through existing budget constraints with no regard to efficiency considerations. The firm can always lobby its supervising agency to obtain an inflow of extra-budgetary funds to cover any losses incurred during the production process. Because of the paternalistic nature of government-firm relationships based on state ownership, the government cannot credibly commit to the promise of hardening the budget constraints, resulting in the widespread SBC syndrome in the socialist economy. Similar SBC phenomena are observed in firms and governments in market economies (Dewatripont and Maskin 1995, Kornai, Maskin and Roland 2003).

In China's command economy, government agencies also suffered from the SBC syndrome. Local governments had incentives to disregard the existing budget constraints and to lobby their superiors for extra-budgetary resources to expand both in size and administrative capacity. Because of paternalistic relationships, the superiors could not credibly harden their budget constraints, thereby generating SBC behavior in government administrations.

In the course of the Chinese economic reforms, the central government initiated a series of administrative reforms that aimed to harden the budgetary constraints and to impose constraints on bureaucratic expansion. But these efforts have not achieved their intended results, as we have observed an expansion-contraction-expansion cycle in which the drive for bureaucratic expansion is repeatedly regaining momentum (Qian and Roland 1998). In the meantime, along with the hardening of the government's budget from above, a new trend has emerged, whereby local governments today look downward to extract extra-budgetary resources from producers (firms), subordinate agencies, or residents under their administrative control. Such behavior existed prior to the reform era, but it has become much more prevalent and widespread, in both scale and scope, since the 1990s.

Such downward extra-budgetary resource-seeking behavior and expectations and impulses to disregard existing budget constraints demonstrate the characteristics of the SBC syndrome as described by Kornai. However, unlike traditional SBC behavior in which firms/local governments turn *upward* to seek extra-budgetary resources from their superior administrative agencies, the behavior described here demonstrates that local governments reach *downward* to extract extra-budgetary resources from firms and residents within their jurisdictions. In other words, this extra-budgetary resource-seeking behavior resembles the traditional SBC syndrome, but the targets toward which this behavior is directed are in the opposite direction. I thus label this kind of government behavior an "inverted soft budget constraint" (ISBC) phenomenon; see Figure 8.1 for a contrast between the traditional SBC and the inverted SBC.

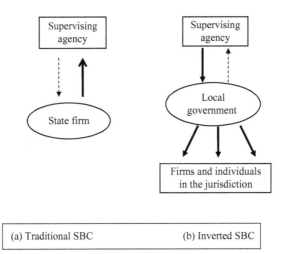

FIGURE 8.1. Comparison of Kornai's soft budget constraint (SBC) and inverted SBC models

Before I develop the ISBC model in the next section, let me first describe some common forms of the ISBC phenomenon, as revealed in government behavior.

First, the most salient form of ISBC behavior is, as mentioned above, the many *ad hoc* taxes and fees imposed by various administrative agencies, which convert resources from outside the government into (formal or informal) budgetary capacities at the disposal of government officials. To this category we should also add a considerable proportion of fines or other penalties imposed by local governments. This is because, under mounting pressures from the central government, local governments today try to avoid any direct violation of the rules and regulations that forbid the imposition of new taxes and fees; instead, they change the form of resource extraction from tax and fee collection to that of imposing fines or other administrative charges, outside of regulations or laws.

Second, local government officials use political pressures or positive incentives to direct local firms or other organizations within their administrative spheres of influence to "sponsor" government-initiated projects. As a result, the government can pursue projects beyond its budget constraints through the inflow of resources from the business sector. Usually, such sponsorship affects only a small group of firms and often these activities are not explicitly associated with a specific government agency; therefore, this form of resource extraction does not attract much attention. But the scale and extent of such resource transfers from the non-government sector into government-initiated projects are considerable and deserve careful scrutiny.

Third, local governments also adopt strategies characteristic of so-called "fishing projects," in which the local government offers a small portion of "matching" funds as "bait" to attract firms or other organizations to contribute to or to mobilize a much larger proportion of resources to carry out certain types of projects that are desired by government officials. For example, as part of a rural development project initiated by a local government, the government offers to provide cement used for road pavement projects to any village that is willing to build cement roads. However, the cost of the cement is less than twenty percent of the total cost of such road construction projects; the much larger share of the costs associated with road construction must be covered by lower-level governments and villages that are induced (oftentimes forced) to participate in the projects; see the road construction project case study in Chapter 9.

The preceding discussions show that (1) local government behavior is not constrained by on-the-book budgetary resources, and local governments can go beyond the budget constraints by extracting and mobilizing resources from below; (2) government behavior and goal setting are built on the expectation that an ISBC exists. The concept and model of the ISBC proposed here covers not only extra taxes and fees, which have received a great deal of attention as well as complaints in the media and in academic discussions, but also other apparently legitimate strategies, such as political pressures and positive incentives that local governments adopt to extract resources and expand their administrative capacities. Although the specific motives, forms, and channels of such extractions may vary with the occasion, such behavior shares the characteristics, and underlying mechanisms and consequences, of soft budget constraints. It is in this sense that such behavior can and should be understood and analyzed within the same theoretical model as the SBC. Indeed, only when we put such apparently disparate but substantively identical behavior into the same analytical framework can we understand the profound significance of the ISBC phenomenon.

There are also significant differences between the traditional SBC syndrome and the ISBC phenomenon. In the former, the central actor is the socialist firm, which actively lobbies for extra-budgetary resources from the supervising agencies. The analytical focus in the traditional SBC model is the relationship between the firm and the supervising agency. In the ISBC model, however, the local government is the central player and hence the center of the analytical focus. Here, we need to evaluate the local government's *downward* relationships with local firms and residents as well as its *upward* interactions with the supervising agency. The underlying mechanisms differ in these two models. In the former, firms need to *lobby* and persuade the supervising agencies to extend resources, whereas in the latter the local government has administrative power to *impose* its will upon local firms or residents. We therefore need to go beyond the traditional SBC model to understand the ISBC phenomenon.

A MODEL OF INVERTED SOFT BUDGET CONSTRAINTS

In this section, I introduce a model of the ISBC phenomenon based on organizational analysis by paying particular attention to the behavioral consequences of the organizational contexts and incentives for government officials (Cyert and March 1963).

My analysis begins with observations of the micro-behavior of government officials. The traditional SBC syndrome is associated with firm behavior, and the ISBC phenomenon is associated with the behavior of governmental officials. Our questions are: What are the mechanisms that generate downward-directed governmental extra-budgetary resource-seeking activities? Why are such activities persistent and widespread, despite repeated efforts by the central government to curb them?

Stable behavioral patterns must be induced and maintained by stable incentives offered to organizations. Thus, my first task is to explain the incentive mechanisms in the Chinese bureaucracy that induce the extraction of extra-budgetary resources from below. To further explain how these incentives emerge and are perpetuated in governments, a related task is to conduct a macro-analysis of the institutional sources of such behavior. My central argument is that ISBC-driven behavior is rooted in incentive mechanisms and authority relationships within the Chinese bureaucracy. At the micro-level, the incentive mechanisms induce government officials to pursue the goals of short-term achievements, leading to investment in resource-intensive "administrative achievement projects" (*zhengji gongcheng*) that are beyond their existing budget capacities.[1] At the macro-level,

---

[1] "Administrative achievement projects" is a term coined in the Chinese media and academic writings to refer to government-initiated projects that aim to showcase the "achievements" of the chief officials and to serve as a signaling device to the supervising agency, often at the expense of long-term development in that area.

FIGURE 8.2. The analytical scheme of the inverted SBC model

the rules and administrative commands do not impose any effective constraints on such micro-behavior; in contrast, the macro-political processes
often acquiesce to or even encourage such behavior. My analyses below are
organized around (1) the micro-incentive mechanisms, (2) the macro-
institutional conditions, and their roles in the generation and perpetuation
of the ISBC phenomenon. Drawing on the scheme of macro-micro links in
Coleman (1994), I present my conceptual framework in Figure 8.2.

Incentive Mechanisms and Micro-Behavior

A central characteristic of the ISBC phenomenon is that government
officials pursue goals and initiate projects (e.g., investments in infrastructure or other public projects) with little regard to the existing budgetary
constraints. In other words, the kinds of goals and projects that local
officials pursue often far exceed their budgetary capacities or the
resources that are at their official disposal. Such endeavors inevitably lead
local governments to expend great efforts to extract resources from
outside of the government in order to accomplish these goals. At the
micro-level, our question is: What are the motivations and incentives for
local government officials to pursue goals and projects that are beyond
their budgetary constraints?

It is well established in organization studies that the goals of an
organization are not always congruent with the goals of its members; in
fact, the two may be in serious conflict. A fundamental task in organizational design is to align the interests of the employees with the goals
pursued by the organization. For example, the design of distributing
company shares to employees has the effect of providing incentives for
employees to take actions that are consistent with the interests of the
organization. Conversely, when incentives are designed without a keen
awareness of the interests and expectations of the recipient parties, such
incentives cannot induce the desired behavior. Moreover, an organization

usually has multiple goals and these goals themselves may be in conflict. As a result, when one designs an incentive mechanism to induce behavior that is consistent with one goal, such behavior may be in conflict with the other goals of the organization.

These considerations shed light on the behavior of government officials. A bureaucracy consists of officials who are concerned about their own career advancement (promotion along the administrative hierarchy) or with the protection of their vested interests (holding on to their current position). This is not difficult to understand: In the Chinese bureaucracy, an official's administrative position is closely associated with his/her salary, status, other latent benefits, as well as with a sense of achievement. One's administrative position is the crystallization of the key interests associated with a government official.

Based on this premise, I put forth the following proposition: *A government official cares most about his/her achievement in his/her current administrative position because this is the most critical factor for career advancement; moreover, the pursuit of short-term achievements is the most important incentive for disregarding existing budget constraints.* Below, I elaborate and substantiate this proposition; specifically, I examine how such bureaucratic behavior is induced by incentives in the performance-evaluation system and by related recent government policies.

My discussion begins with a recognition that, after a series of administrative reforms in the Chinese governments, in order to advance their careers government officials today must demonstrate tangible achievements in their job performance. Government agencies at all levels have developed elaborate indicator systems to evaluate an official's performance associated with his/her position. These indicator systems have both established quantifiable measures of performance and have greatly increased the intensity of such incentives.

What are the effects of these incentive mechanisms on an official's behavior? We can analyze this scenario in light of the "principal–agent" model (Jensen and Meckling 1976). In this scenario, we treat the supervising agency as the "principal" and the local government official as the "agent." There is a serious information asymmetry problem in this principal–agent relationship regarding the performance evaluation. Specifically, the agent has far more information than the principal regarding his/her own efforts, difficulties, and achievements. Given this information asymmetry, there is an incentive for an official at a lower level to take actions, such as signaling devices, to inform the principal in the supervising agency about his/her ability and achievements so as to achieve a favorable performance evaluation for his/her career advancement.

In this light, we observe a dual process: First, the promotion mechanism directs an official's attention to those activities that can be quantified and measured; second, there are also incentives for the official to focus on those measurable outcomes to signal his/her ability and accomplishments in order to alleviate the information asymmetry problems in the principal–agent relationship.

The incentive mechanisms outlined above have several implications. First, such incentives direct an official's attention to short-term accomplishments, often at the expense of the benefits of long-term development. This is a natural consequence of the tournament system in the Chinese bureaucracy. As in a tournament competition in sports, the "tournament" model of promotion in organizations has the following rules: The candidates start to compete at the lower levels for promotion, progressively moving to the next higher level. If one loses in a round of competition, the person is out of the promotion game and is no longer eligible to participate in the next round of competition for promotion (Lazear and Rosen 1981, Rosenbaum 1984). Economist Li-an Zhou has extended this model to the Chinese context (Zhou 2007, 2017). The tournament model has several characteristics: (1) The game adopts relative performance criteria to select the winner among the competitors; (2) in this system, early success is critical, because it sends strong signals about one's ability and facilitates the possibility of moving into a more favorable fast-track for promotion. In contrast, when an official's pace of career advancement stalls, there are long-term, negative effects for his or her career development.

It is not surprising, then, that the rules of the tournament model and the incentives therein induce and reinforce an official's pursuit of short-term achievements: The official must resolutely focus on the goal of promotion to the next higher position, which is indispensable in order to further climb the bureaucratic ladders for career development. If the official fails to receive a promotion within an expected (short) period of time, he/she will be forever denied future promotion opportunities. Here the length of a "short term" varies with the different administrative positions. Along with the increasing mobility among government officials, tenure in a position has been considerably shortened. For example, in my fieldwork study between 2004 and 2015, I found that, on average, the heads of the township government in a county in northern China remained in their positions for only about three years. An official must mobilize considerable resources beyond the budget constraints within such a short period of time in order to send positive signals to his/her supervisors.

Second, under this incentive system, officials tend to adopt *resource-intensive projects* as a signaling device. By "resource-intensive projects," I mean those projects that are large in scale and demanding in resource input. As suggested by the signaling theory in economics (Spence 1974), to resolve the information asymmetries in performance evaluations in organizations, one needs reliable signals that are able to distinguish abilities (or performance) among officials. "Resource-intensive projects" as effective signaling devices match these requirements quite well. First, most local governments face severe resource scarcities; the ability of officials to initiate and accomplish resource-intensive projects therefore serves as a credible signal to differentiate the abilities of various officials. Second, the capacity to mobilize resources effectively and to get things done (rather than depending on one's superiors for more resources) are critical to local development and are recognized and appreciated by superiors in higher-level agencies. Third, "resource-intensive" projects are tangible and attract a great deal of attention, thereby reducing any arbitrariness in performance evaluations. Not surprisingly, once a type of "administrative achievement project" is recognized and adopted by the superior administrations (such as the growth rate or the volume of foreign investment), it quickly becomes widely adopted by officials across the local governments and induces similar behavior in different administrative jurisdictions.

Third, the incentive mechanisms also intensify competition among officials across government agencies. As noted, the tournament model adopts "relative evaluation criteria" in the promotion competition, which encourages lateral competition among officials to get ahead. In this light, the performance evaluation system not only provides incentives to encourage officials to seek extra-budgetary resources, it also intensifies competition among officials across different agencies, different work-units, or different regions, thereby infusing new momentum into behavior that generates the ISBC phenomenon.

To sum up, the extra-budgetary resource-seeking activities observed in local governments are in part a consequence of the incentive mechanisms. A government must have capacities to mobilize resources to accomplish measurable goals and to showcase administrative achievements. For example, to meet the family-planning goals, the government needs considerable human resources at its disposal to monitor fertility behavior and to respond to unexpected crises. Similarly, to attract foreign investment and to promote local development, the government must invest heavily in local infrastructure. Faced with the hardening budget constraints from above, local governments must find alternative ways to finance their projects. The specific behavioral means by which local governments overcome the existing budget constraints include the imposition of extra taxes and fees, pressures for firm sponsorship, or "fishing projects."

The preceding discussion portrays two different images of local governments. On the one hand, local governments play a leading role in local development within their jurisdictions. As such, their behavior can be seen as having a positive effect on the economic and social welfare of their respective jurisdictions. The other image that emerges from the preceding discussion, however, is that local government officials compete with their peers to seek new development targets and new projects to signal their own accomplishments. In so doing, they engage in projects far beyond their budget constraints and they pursue short-term goals at the expense of long-term development, thereby generating and perpetuating the ISBC phenomenon.

Macro-Institutional Conditions and ISBC Activities

As outlined in Chapter 2, the Chinese bureaucracy is an "upward responsibility system." That is, the main task of the subordinate agencies is to implement the administrative fiats promulgated from above. In this sense, the prevalence of the ISBC phenomenon suggests that such behavior at the micro-level is cultivated by macro-level conditions and that the supervising agencies do little to rein in local government extra-budgetary resource seeking from below. Turning our attention to the macro-level, I propose that *the micro-behavior of government officials and the incentive mechanisms discussed above are sustained and reproduced by macro-institutional conditions.* We consider three macro-institutional conditions below.

(1) *Top-down institutional constraints.* Historically, local governments in the Chinese bureaucracy were under an "incomplete budget" (He 1998), whereby local government functions and local officials were funded only partially by top-down budgetary allocations. Local governments were expected to make up for the remainder of the budget through extra-budgetary resources in the form of additional fees and local taxes. This practice has continued in the People's Republic as local governments are encouraged to achieve policy targets that are set beyond their existing capacities. After the taxation reform of the mid-1990s, many local governments (counties and townships) faced budget shortfall in operation

budget and salary expense. ISBC became especially prevalent during this period, in part in response to budgetary crises but more a reflection of the fundamental tensions in governance (Zhou 2012).

First, government behavior associated with the ISBC phenomenon has deep, legitimate roots in the Chinese political system. Similar behavior has been advocated or encouraged by governments at different levels or often by the central government. In the history of the PRC, with tools of campaign-style mobilization, the top leaders often impose unrealistic goals and policy targets upon local officials. The famous slogan associated with socialist construction during the Mao era, "if there are favorable conditions, we will launch the project; but even if there are no favorable conditions, we will create such conditions and launch the project anyway," aptly describes the historical model and the behavioral tendency to break through any existing (budgetary) constraints. Some ISBC-driven behavior may also benefit local development and residents. For example, government-advocated education projects and public-facility projects may be beneficial to the residents in a particular area. Therefore, ISBC-inspired government behavior tends to gain legitimacy and social expectations even among residents at the grass-roots levels.

Second, the supervising agencies also motivate local officials to engage in ISBC-driven behavior. Chinese bureaucracies at different administrative levels are situated in similar institutional environments. That is, officials in the supervising agencies also face incentive mechanisms that are similar to those faced by officials in lower-level governments; hence, they tend to pursue similar goals and to show similar behavioral patterns. This implies that our discussion about incentives and officials' behavior at the local levels also applies to officials in the supervising agencies. Indeed, we often observe that whenever a new head of a higher-level government comes to power, he/she is likely to launch a series of new "administrative achievement projects." More often than not, these projects cannot be carried out within the existing budgetary constraints and therefore they require the infusion of extra-budgetary resources. These new projects generate new demands on, and provide incentives for, the supervising agencies to further extract resources from below – to encourage lower-level governments to increase investments, to increase the scale of production, or to take new initiatives. Officials at the lower levels cannot meet these demands within their own budget constraints and thus have to reach further downward to extract resources in a similar fashion, generating chain effects across different administrative levels. In this context, supervising agencies must tolerate or even encourage local government extra-budgetary resource-seeking behavior from below, thereby perpetuating the ISBC phenomenon.

(2) *Upward accountability.* Local firms and residents are the targets and victims of ISBC behavior, and their bottom-up resistance should impose constraints on such government behavior. Unfortunately, the institutional conditions are such that there is a serious asymmetry in the organizational capacities between the local government on the one hand and the local firms/residents on the other; thus, bottom-up resistance is likely to be limited and ineffective. This is not difficult to understand. Local governments exercise administrative power in their interactions with firms and residents within their jurisdictions. Although the government withdraws from a firm's internal operations, it can significantly affect a firm in many other ways, from regulations on resource supplies, employment, work safety, environmental protection, to regulations on sanitary conditions. Therefore, it is difficult for a firm to openly oppose officials' demands for resources. Moreover, because of the lack of autonomous associations among firms and other business entities, they cannot act together to effectively negotiate with local governments. Instead, individual firms pursue the strategy of passive resistance (noncooperation, providing false information to evade taxes and fee collections), or of forging close ties with officials to seek political protection (Wank 1999). Such particularistic relationships further undermine the collective basis of developing bottom-up institutional constraints upon ISBC behavior.

It is worth pointing out that the relationships between local governments and local firms are not a one-way channel of downward resource extraction. In many instances, the two sides cultivate mutually beneficial exchange relationships. Local governments have monopoly power over important resources (e.g., land use), and they are in a unique position to interpret and implement state policies. Therefore, local firms can take strategic actions to meet officials' demands in exchange for mutually beneficial relationships. Such reciprocal relationships are the stable foundation upon which local governments continuously obtain extra-budgetary resources from below.

(3) *The failure of the "position responsibility system."* In recent years, the organizational reforms of the Chinese bureaucracy have led to a series of new measures aimed to impose constraints on government officials. For example, the position responsibility system (*gangwei zerenzhi*) requires the establishment of a close link between administrative power, responsibility, and the benefits associated with an administrative position. In an

ideal scenario, for example, the head of a county government is given full authority to establish priorities for local development; but he/she is held accountable for these decisions. That is, the official will benefit or will suffer from his/her decisions in terms of career advancement.

But in the ISBC model developed here, we can easily see the inevitable separation of administrative power, responsibilities, and benefits in real life for a specific government official. As noted, usually the head of a territorially based government or the chief official in a government bureau stays in his/her position for only about three years. Consider the dynamics of career mobility in which an official moves from his existing position to a new position as the head of a county government. The administrative power associated with this position allows the official to pursue "achievement projects" beyond the existing budgetary constraints, thereby sending signals about short-term performance and reaping private benefits for career advancement. The prospect of future promotion means that the official will no longer be in his/her current position to bear the consequences when the problems associated with the ISBC-driven behavior emerge in the future. Even for those who do not have a prospect for upward mobility, engaging in ISBC behavior can satisfy demands from supervising agencies, thus protecting the officials' own vested interests in her current position. In terms of bureaucratic career dynamics, the relations among administrative power, responsibilities, and the benefits associated with a position inevitably become attenuated.

SUMMARY

In this chapter, I draw on insights from Kornai's arguments on soft budget constraints to propose an ISBC model that sheds light on this class of bureaucratic behavior. As Kornai points out, the traditional SBCs distort the price mechanisms in the allocation of resources, leading to overproduction and incurring efficiency losses. The ISBC phenomenon in the Chinese context shares similar consequences: The expansion of investment and development beyond the budget constraints implies that the government appropriates a large proportion of its resources from nongovernment sources, thereby weakening the price mechanisms in resource allocations. Moreover, unlike the traditional SBCs in which a firm has to lobby the supervising agencies for extra-budgetary resources, the local government can impose its will through administrative fiats upon those who are unorganized and cannot engage in effective resistance.

As a result, compared to the traditional SBC syndrome, ISBC-driven behavior tends to have fewer constraints, to involve larger scales, and to have broader impacts.

Another implication of ISBC behavior is that it induces unintended consequences in government behavior. Because budget constraints are not effective, local governments develop behavioral patterns based on their expectations of extra-budgetary resources. To meet these expectations and the demands of the supervising agencies, the local government must maintain a mobilizational structure in its internal organization, with duplicated roles, redundant offices, and flexible boundaries among organizational agencies, so that it can mobilize organizational capacities to extract resources from below when the occasion arises. Moreover, unlike in the traditional SBC setting where only a few top managers in a firm are involved in lobbying the supervising agencies, in the ISBC scenario the targets of resource extraction – individuals and firms – are highly dispersed; the local government often maintains a considerable bureaucratic size, manpower, and administrative capacity to carry out the resource extractions. Ironically, then, the ISBCs provide incentives and momentum for bureaucratic expansion.

The ISBC phenomenon has profound impacts on state–society relationships in China. In the shift from traditional SBCs to the ISBCs, the supervising agencies are no longer under constant pressures from subordinate agencies (firms) for extra-budgetary resources; instead, they can even benefit from local government ISBC behavior, thus contributing to their administrative achievements. However, ISBC-related behavior does have political consequences. For example, higher-level governments must respond to the pressures or political conflicts generated by local government behavior in downward resource extraction (e.g., petitions, complaints, or social protests). Under the traditional SBCs, we observe tensions and conflicts among agencies within the government. In the ISBC model, in contrast, tensions and conflicts arise between state and society. As ISBC-driven behavior becomes widespread across administrative levels and regions, we are likely to observe an increase in collective actions based on "unorganized interests," with significant impacts on the course of political and social changes in China (Zhou 1993), a theme I will pursue in Chapter 11.

This chapter leads us to other related questions: What are the processes in which ISBC behavior takes place? What are the patterns of interaction among state policies (macro-level conditions), local government behavior (the role of incentives), and bottom-up responses by local citizens? These questions will be further examined in the following three chapters. This chapter provides a bridge between the examination of government behavior in the previous chapters to the theme of interactions among the state, local bureaucrats, and social groups in the next section.

THE LOGIC OF GOVERNANCE AND CHINESE SOCIETY

9

The Road to Collective Debt: Bureaucrats
Meet Villagers

"Roads, more roads and always roads," wrote the prefect of Loiret in
September 1867, "this sums up the political economy of the countryside."
Eugen Weber (1976, p. 195)

This chapter begins Part III by examining the second theme of this book –
the interactions between state and society, mediated by the local governments at the county and township levels. The three chapters to follow
look at different episodes at the grass-roots level: (1) public goods provision for a road pavement project in two villages, (2) village elections in a
township, and (3) collective action based on unorganized interests on the
national scene. These episodes allow us to take a close look at patterns of
interactions among state policies, local governments, and villagers, and to
make sense of the underlying institutional logic of governance at the
grass-roots level. I begin with the road pavement public project in an
agricultural township in northern China in the mid-2000s.

PAVED ROADS COMING TO VILLAGES: GOVERNMENT
IN ACTION

In the summer of 2004 when I first arrived at FS Township, an agricultural town in northern China, the road conditions in the rural areas were
in a miserable condition. The dirt-paved road in FS Township was
rugged, with ditches and ridges all over the place, scarred by heavy usage
and lack of maintenance. During the rainy season, the road would turn

into muddy streams, and motor vehicles were often stuck in the mud and could not get out, let alone a cart pulled by a mule.

These were the road conditions off the main highway, within and across villages, or between villages and commercial centers in this township. By the early twenty-first century, highways of different grades – built with funds from national, provincial, or local governments – were traversing this area, across or near the main centers of government or economic activities. But the villages scattered throughout this region were left on their own after decades of inattention to secondary roads and a viable road network. Only those villages that happened to be close to the highway, or where there was a highway running through the village, benefited from the economic prosperity brought about by access to transportation. In contrast, the distance between the village and the closest commercial center seemed insurmountable for those villages that were situated away from a highway. During the harvest season, it was difficult for large vehicles to reach the village; the produce – grapes, apples, and other fruits – had to be first transported in small vehicles to the side of the main roads. If arbitrageurs managed to get their trucks into the village, the price offered for their produce was notably lower than the price in the villages that were just one or two kilometers away from the main road.

Against this background and as part of a national program launched by the Ministry of Transportation in Beijing, in early 2004 the provincial government initiated the "Paved Road to Every Village" project (PREV) in this region. The goal of the PREV project was to build cement-paved roads to link the center of every village to the main road so as to expand transportation capacities in the rural areas and to facilitate the integration of isolated villages into regional economic centers. At long last, government efforts to provide public goods had reached this underdeveloped area.

The significance of road construction reaches far beyond these rural localities. Historically, road construction was closely related to rural development, the rise of national markets, and nation building. In his study of the transformation of rural France between 1870 and 1914, historian Eugen Weber (1976, p. 206) likens road building to nation building:

So, roads and rail lines that were secondary in name but primary in fact brought the isolated patches of the countryside out of their autarky – cultural as well as economic – into the market economy and the modern world ... the conjunction of secondary lines and of the roads built to serve them resulted in a crash program of national integration of unparalleled scope and effectiveness ... economic and technological conditions offered the possibility for radical cultural change. Before culture altered significantly, material circumstances had to alter; and the role of road and rail in this transformation was basic.

In the early twenty-first century on the eve of the PREV project, rural China had already undergone more than half a century of nation building and integration in the People's Republic. Thus, road construction in rural China did not take on the kind of critical role in nation building as it did in nineteenth-century France. Nevertheless, the PREV project provided an occasion for state policies, government bureaucracies, and villages to interact extensively to provide public goods. Furthermore, this was an occasion of utmost interest to all parties involved: In a region where financial capital was scarce and local governments and village collectives survived on meager resources and were heavily in debt, the PREV project provided an opportune occasion for local bureaucrats and village cadres to have access to, and to mobilize for, financial resources. Therefore, the PREV episodes provide an appropriate occasion for our study of public goods provision in rural China.

In this chapter, I report on selected episodes in the implementation of the PREV project in FS Township and their aftermath, which I tracked for five years since the inception of the project. As the stories in this study show, implementation at the local levels of this well-intended effort to provide public goods incurred a huge amount of collective debt, led to tremendous strains on the social fabric of rural life, and undermined the basis for collective governance. The main purpose of this study is to reexamine the role of state and local social institutions in public policies and their unintended consequences for rural governance.

Two literatures on the provision of public goods are relevant here: One is related to the role of the state and its bureaucratic organizations in economic development and the other is related to the role of social institutions in local problem solving and "informal accountability." Ever since the intellectual movement to "bring the state back in" of the 1980s, social scientists have highlighted the role of the state in institutional changes and societal transformations. Within this framework, research in political science, sociology, and economics has developed a large literature on the role of bureaucracies in economic development and societal transformation (Acemoglu and Robinson 2012, Evans 1995, Migdal, Kohli and Shue 1994, Wade 1990). Evans and Rauch (1999) demonstrate that the Weberian bureaucratic forms of the state "significantly enhance prospects for economic growth" (p. 748). Nowhere is this role better exemplified than in the Chinese state and Chinese local governments. As China scholars have argued, the state and local governments have been the leading force propelling economic growth and institutional transformation in the post-Mao era (Cai and Treisman 2006, Landry 2008, Naughton 1996, Oi 1999, Qian and Weingast 1997, Walder 1995a, Whiting 2000).

On the other side of the debate, scholars have emphasized the pitfalls of the interventionist state. Collusion between bureaucratic agencies and interest groups in rent seeking has long been discussed in the public choice literature (Bates 1981, Buchanan, Tollison and Tullock 1980, Mueller 2003, Tullock 1967). Such problems associated with the planned economy are well recognized in research on state socialist societies (Kornai 1986), and it is not only market-centered advocates who offer such critiques. Political scientist James Scott (1998) has assembled wide-ranging historical episodes to critique those state programs that were intended for public goods provision but led to disastrous consequences. Though the intellectual connections are not always made, these arguments are parallel to and supported by the large literature in organization research that has documented bureaucratic turf wars, collusion, and goal displacement (Cyert and March 1963, Lipsky 1980, Pressman and Wildavsky 1984, Wilson 1989).

In the field of China studies, the role of local bureaucrats in the implementation of state policies has often been questioned. On the one hand, the elaborate bureaucratic evaluation system is seen as providing strong incentives for local bureaucrats to follow directives from above in order to be promoted; on the other hand, local officials are seen as being asked to take initiatives to carry out unfunded policy mandates. The Chinese state and its local governments are often seen as predatory, captured, or acting like brokers in the midst of societal transformation and they are entrenched in the bureaucratic logic (Edin 2003, Huang 2003, O'Brien and Li 1999, Oi 1989, Shirk 1993, Shue 1988, Zhou 2010a). The PREV episodes provide us with an opportunity to take a close look at two issues in economic development and local governance – the political process in action and the role of the Chinese bureaucracy in the provision of public goods.

In contrast to formal institutions such as government bureaucracies, informal social institutions – village kinships, network ties, and communal trust – play an important role in resource mobilization, local problem solving, and rural governance (Duara 1988, Huang 1990, Ostrom 1990, Peng 2004, Putnam 1993, Tsai 2007). The key insight here is that local institutions provide norms, expectations, and sanctioning mechanisms to discourage free-rider problems and to provide a basis for collective action in public goods provision. In this sense, formal and informal institutions complement and facilitate one another in the public sphere.

Two interrelated themes run through the episodes reported in this chapter: First, these are political stories – the implementation of state policies through bureaucratic agencies, especially interactions among state policies, government agencies, and village cadres. Second, at the same time, these are also social stories – how social institutions and network ties within and across villages are involved in resource mobilization, problem solving, and responding to crises. These two processes reflect two distinct institutional logics: the bureaucratic logic that dictates the local bureaucrats' behavior to implement state policies and the logic of social institutions for resource mobilization and local problem solving. These episodes inform us of how these two logics interacted and, in the process, transformed each other, thus leaving their marks on rural governance. As we see below, implementation of the PREV project and the subsequent response to its aftermath involved intensive interactions among local agents on the basis of social institutions. Therefore, these episodes provide an occasion for us to look into those social processes and mechanisms involved in resource mobilization through which the social fabric of rural institutions was sorely tested, renewed, and transformed.

In the remainder of this chapter, I first delve into the episodes and microprocesses to understand the issues, mechanisms, and dynamics involved in local implementation of the PREV project. I then move on to the macro-level and consider their broad implications for understanding the role of the state, government bureaucracy, and social institutions in economic development and governance.

THE ROAD LEADING TO COLLECTIVE DEBT: A TALE OF TWO VILLAGES

The Empirical Setting

Located in a mountainous terrain of northern China, FS Township is an agricultural town comprised of twenty-seven villages, where peasants grow corn, grapes for wine-making, and other fruits. With a per capita annual income of less than RMB 3,000 in the mid-2000s, the standard of living in this area is slightly above average for rural China; but it is certainly an underdeveloped rural area compared with its counterparts in the coastal regions or even in the economically prosperous neighboring areas. There are considerable variations in cropping/labor activities across the villages in this township: Those villages near the town center have a large nonfarm labor force, whereas the majority of villagers in the deep mountainous area have left home to seek jobs in urban areas as migrant workers. These variations have implications for the role of village governance structures. In those villages where a large number of families have already given up their land or migrated, village elections are marginal to their lives, but in other villages where the majority of the villagers depend on their crops for survival, village cadres, and thus village elections, play a significant role in their lives.

The PREV Project from the Local Point of View

The PREV project arrived in FS Township in 2004. Like many public projects, when one first read of its high-minded principles and public rhetoric in official documents and the media, as exemplified in official speeches, stories, and statistics, it appeared that the PREV project would indeed be beneficial. Of course, no public projects are without constraints. In the case of the PREV project, from the very beginning the authorities recognized that the financial constraints – insufficient funds for the project – would be a serious problem. "Through extensive studies and thorough evaluations," declares an official announcement, "the provincial government decided to fund the PREV project from three sources: (1) direct funds from the provincial bureau of transportation; (2) matching funds subsidized by government budgets at lower levels; (3) additional social funds raised" (*Hebei Daily*, August 12, 2004). This sounded like a great plan that would mobilize resources from multiple channels to ensure success of a project that would benefit those who were least able to afford them.

As it was pushed through the various bureaucratic levels – provincial, municipal, county – and finally reached FS Township, the PREV project took on a tangible, concrete form: For every kilometer of designated road construction, the government would provide a fund of RMB 70,000 in the form of cement to be used for road pavement, which was to be purchased at the county government-owned cement factory and to be charged at an above-market price.[1] However, the average cost of

---

[1] At the time, the market price was RMB 270 per ton, whereas the official price charged for the PREV project was RMB 350 per ton, a thirty percent price increase.

constructing a paved road in this region – even after taking into consideration the free labor from the villagers and the cheap, low-quality materials – was estimated to be about RMB 240,000 per kilometer. This means that for every kilometer of road built as part of the PREV project, the villages had to self-finance at least RMB 170,000 or, more likely, to incur such an amount of collective debt. This was a colossal figure for a region where the per capita annual income was less than RMB 3,000, and almost all villages already had collective debts in the hundreds of thousands or even in the millions of Chinese yuan. Furthermore, this cost estimate is considered conservative because road construction may involve the use of additional land, which requires compensation for both use of the land and for the crops planted on it.

Not surprisingly, many villages gave a cold shoulder to the PREV project. This did not mean that the villagers did not care about having a better road; in fact, they longed for one. But they did not have much faith in the government's initiative. Such feelings of resentment actually ran very deep. Witnessing the numerous government-initiated projects in the past – promoted by the higher authorities and implemented by the local governments, but ultimately failing miserably in the end – villagers were deeply suspicious of both the intention and the feasibility of government policies and projects. Many vividly recalled that local governments had earlier fervently promoted township–village enterprises, but in the end such enterprises left the villages heavily in debt and with dwindling collective assets.

The county government clearly foresaw the challenges and unpopularity of the PREV project. One township official observed:

Now the municipal government is promoting the PREV project. The chief executive officer of the county government launched the PREV project in person. At the preparatory meeting, he declared, "First, this is a political task, we must resolutely get it done; second, it cannot result in any problems or petitions; third, villagers cannot be forced to share the costs."[2]

However, as we will see below, the township officials pushed hard for this project, with full recognition that it would not be beneficial, certainly not in the short run, for the villages, and that they [the township officials] would have to persuade or force some villages to take on the task.

[2] Unless otherwise noted, all quotations in the text are drawn from interviews and conversations during my fieldwork.

Embracing the Opportunity or Avoiding the Trap?

In the early summer of 2004, two villages – Uphill Village and Downhill Village – were chosen by the township government to be the recipients of the PREV project. The two villages are adjacent to each other – it is only a fifteen-minute walk from one village center to the other. Both villages grow similar crops – grapes for wine-making, corn, and other fruits – and their fields lie side by side or, in some places, they even crisscross each other. Local legend weaves these two villages together in colorful episodes about Chinese ancient civilization.

But the similarities end there. In many other respects these two villages cannot be more different. For a long time, Uphill Village acted as a leader in many innovations, whereas Downhill Village was merely a follower. Uphill Village was the first to begin to grow grapevines on a large scale, to greatly expand collective irrigation facilities to cover almost all of the fields of the village, to actively participate in the SLCP program,[3] and to rebuild its temple to become a local attraction. In all of these, Downhill Village followed suit, to a lesser extent, on a smaller scale, and, in some instances, many years later.

One does not have to look far to find the reasons for these differences – they coincided with, and indeed can be attributed to, the contrasting governance structures in the two villages. For the past twenty years, Uphill Village had one stable center of authority, with only one person, Mr. Kang, serving as both party secretary and village committee chair, together with essentially the same group of village cadres. In contrast, there had been frequent changes of village leaders in Downhill Village, not because of contentious politics but, even worse, because few were interested in these positions.

On the eve of the PREV project, collective assets in the two villages were markedly different. To be sure, like almost all villages in this region, both villages faced collective debts. This was largely the legacy of predatory state policies and irresponsible government micro-management that unwittingly had resulted in disastrous consequences for these villages. But in terms of tangible collective assets, Uphill Village

---

[3] The Sloping Land Conservation Program (SLCP, *tuigeng huanlin*), an ambitious ecological conservation program initiated by the central government, committed 337 billion yuan (US$ 40 billion) over eight years to subsidize peasants in selected regions of the country in exchange for conversion of their cultivated fields to grow trees and wild grasses. The first phase of the program in FS Township began in 2002.

was in an envious position. It had two motor-pumped wells that irrigated more than 2,000 mu[4] of grapevines, both of which were leased to private management in return for a total of RMB 20,000 per year – a stable source of revenue for the village collective. Even amid the decollectivization process, Mr. Kang was able to carve out a piece of village-owned land, about 260 mu, that was then leased to the villagers. The leasing fee, again, provided a recurrent source of revenue to the village collective. In addition, by 2004 nearly 2,000 mu of the land was participating in the government SLCP program, which brought in RMB 300,000 each year to the families of the village. The spacious village courtyard consisted of two rows of rooms – one row for an elementary school, and another row to house the village committee and an exhibition room that proudly showed off the political achievements and economic prosperity of the village, a rare scene of a collective stronghold on display in this region.

Now contrast Downhill Village. With a weak, high-turnover governance body, collective assets were minimal. By 2004, no village land was participating in the SLCP program, "because," as Mr. Long, who became the village party secretary in 2003, put it, "the former village head had felt it was too much trouble." The village courtyard was dirt-covered, rugged, and the rooms were shabby and unattended. By 2004, the village had only 500 mu of irrigated land, the lease fee for two aging motor-pumped wells was about RMB 10,000 per year, and the lease fee had already been spent in advance by the former village head. Mr. Long recalled:

When I became party secretary last year [2003], the village accountant told me that there was not a cent left in the collective account. During the Chinese New Year, there is a tradition in our region to hang "Chinese posters" [*duilian*) on the gates of every house. The village collective did not even have money to buy red paper for the posters for the gates in the village center, so I had to borrow fifteen sheets of red paper.

Thus, it comes as no surprise that the two villages had very different dispositions toward the PREV project. In fact, the same leader–follower pattern re-emerged: Uphill Village head, Mr. Kang, jumped at the opportunity, whereas the head of Downhill Village dragged his feet and was grudgingly pushed into accepting this project by the township government. Here begins the tale of the two villages, as we will see below, with markedly different experiences, dramas, and consequences.

---

[4] 1 mu ≈ .165 acre.

Our story begins one morning in early June 2004, when I tagged along with two township officials to pay a visit to Mr. Long's home in Downhill Village. The purpose of the visit was to persuade Mr. Long to take part in the PREV project. Several days earlier, when township party secretary Jin demanded that Downhill Village participate in the PREV project, Mr. Long had refused to commit his village's participation. In the ensuing confrontation, Mr. Long's resignation as village party secretary was demanded and submitted. But it was difficult to find another person willing to take on the position of village party secretary. So the two township officials were sent to the village to persuade Mr. Long to continue on in his job as party secretary and to accept the PREV project.

In his mid-fifties, Mr. Long looked older than his age, his dark face browned by years of sun, with deep lines carved in his cheeks and curving beside his mouth. In the past, he had intermittently been involved in village governance and in the previous year he had become village party secretary. Mr. Long and his wife lived in an old, shabby adobe house with a dirt-paved courtyard that was crowded with piles of firewood and debris and was carpeted with thick layers of dust. Inside, the two small, low-ceiling rooms were plain, and barely furnished. Piled high in the corner of the living room, there were several grain bags covered with patches. Following the local tradition, the couple had spent all of their savings to build a new brick house in the village for their son's marriage, whereas they would most likely remain in this old house for the remainder of their lives.

Sitting on improvised stools consisting of stacks of bricks, the two township officials began their difficult conversation. They were fully aware of the unpopularity of the PREV project and the consequences for the village from participating in the project. That is, any village that undertook this project would surely incur a considerable amount of collective debt. Instead of trying to convince Mr. Long of the merits of the project, the two officials first tried to express their sympathy:

We understand the pressures that you as party secretary have to shoulder. From above, the township officials pressure you; among your peers the village head undermines you; from below the villagers complain about you; and at home your spouse drags you backward.

Then, they attempted to plead their case:

Let's not talk about the principles of being a party member [you should follow the party line]. Now that we, your two brothers, have come here to help you address this problem, you have to let us save face, right?

They tried to persuade Mr. Long by painting a rosy picture for his personal gain. They talked about the prospects of other collective projects – raising fish in the pond, growing grass to raise cows – that would not only contribute to the village's economic prosperity but also would personally benefit the village cadres. "A long tenure in office will surely make one rich," one of the officials cited an old Chinese proverb and concluded emphatically.

After several hours of conversation, with no better alternatives and perhaps allured by the elusive but tempting picture about the future, Mr. Long grudgingly agreed to stay on as village party secretary and undertake the project.

Mr. Long's great reluctance was in sharp contrast to the enthusiasm of Mr. Kang in Uphill Village. In his early forties, Mr. Kang was medium-built, with a straight back and paced steps that were traces of his military service many years earlier. With his piercing eyes and loud voice radiant with energy and confidence, Mr. Kang was full of ideas, imagination, and infinite hope, and he was eager to talk to whomever cared to listen about his ambitious plans for his village. Two decades in the role of village head had prepared him with all the familiar political rhetoric and the official script that he could rely on to step on the stage to perform whenever such an occasion arose. In addition, his attitude toward the PREV project could not be more different from that of Mr. Long. He embraced the opportunity as soon as he heard about the project and he insisted that Uphill Village take part. In fact, Kang was so enthusiastic that the county government held an on-site demonstration meeting in the village, attended by cadres from all over the county, including the chief executive officer of the county as well as the head of the county's transportation bureau. This was a rare achievement and recognition for the village.

To my question "Are you worried about how to pay for the project?" Mr. Kang did not answer directly, but responded as follows:

We cadres have to take a long-term view about this. We cannot wait to begin the project when all resources are finally in place. This is like building a house in the village. If you wait until you have saved 50,000 yuan before you begin, you will never build your house. When you have over 10,000 yuan, it is time to begin. You make do by borrowing from here and there, you incur debts of about 30,000 to 40,000 yuan, and you have your house built. Then you spend the next three or four years to pay back the debt.

Either excitedly or grudgingly (depending on the case), by the summer of 2004 both villages were about to undertake their road construction projects. Before we track the actors and their experiences with the PREV project during the next few months and years, let us readjust our analytical lens to look at the research questions emerging from the depictions thus far. Considering the scarcity of resources in this region and the heavy collective debts the villages had already accumulated, how did the villages intend to make up for the huge gap in order to finance the project? What mechanisms were involved to mobilize resources, and what was the response?

"We Just Cheat and Lie, Again, and Again": Mobilizing for Collective Debt

The next time I saw Mr. Long, one month later, it was at the beginning of the road construction project. Amid the roaring of trucks and crowds of villagers busy working on the road, Mr. Long invited me into his village office. He was eager to pour out his anxieties and complaints:

> We have a huge gap in financing the road construction.... We asked the villagers to contribute. They all said this was a good project, but no one was willing to contribute. [Is it because they do not want to contribute, or because they cannot afford to contribute? I asked.] Mainly because they cannot afford it. This is the most financially demanding period of time for farming activities. We collected contributions of only RMB 300.... We have to continue to cheat and lie – for sand and for macadam.... As long as we put sand and macadam in the pavement, there is not much they [the suppliers] can do the following year when we cannot pay off the debt.... For example, the guys on a transportation team asked me for RMB 5,000 to fill their gas tanks. I told them that we didn't even have RMB 5 for them. "Brothers, if you want the job, just go ahead and get the job done, and pay for the gas yourself." They had no other choice but to complete the job.

As Mr. Long's above account suggests, there were mainly two ways to fill the gap to finance the road project: donations and debt-financing. Let us trace the two villages' efforts to mobilize resources.

Both villages took the first step to get some start-up funds ready for the project. Since government funds for the PREV project came only in the form of cement, both villages needed some initial funds to get the project started. In Downhill Village, Mr. Long requested advance payment from the lease of the village irrigation facility (RMB 16,000), and he received a donation of RMB 5,000 from a source outside of the village. In addition, he received approval to sell some collectively owned trees for another RMB 5,000. In total, on the eve of undertaking the PREV project Mr. Long had about RMB 30,000 in hand. Uphill Village did a much better job. The village party committee required that each villager donate

RMB 100 to the project. This request was well received by the villagers, who collectively came up with RMB 60,000. Mr. Kang traveled everywhere his village ties might lead and he managed to receive donations from several who were working in the city but had family ties in the village. In total, Uphill Village raised donations in the amount of RMB 220,000 for the project. In addition, villagers in both villages volunteered their free labor to assist in the construction.

Despite the impressiveness of the initial mobilization in this poor region, it was still a far cry from filling the financial gap for the project. By the time the projects were completed, Uphill Village had built 4.5 kilometers of paved road and Downhill Village had built about 1.5 kilometers. After spending the donations, within only several months the former had incurred a debt of about RMB 630,000, and the latter had incurred a debt of about RMB 200,000 – both were astronomical figures for a village in this region, accumulated in only several months.[5]

This means that the remainder of the gap had to be debt-financed – borrowing from various sources and incurring debts to be repaid in the future. Before they would begin to worry about whether and how the villages would be able to repay such debts, the village heads first had to deal with the following question: How would it be possible for the two villages to debt-finance at such a large scale in the first place?

To appreciate how daunting this would be, some background is in order. In this region, and nationwide, a large proportion of villages were already in heavy debt (Oi and Zhao 2007). A major source of the collective debt stemmed from earlier state policies that encouraged villages to set up collective enterprises (TVEs) by borrowing from government banks (or local credit unions). Another source of their collective debt was due to the agricultural taxes that a village owed the government or owed some well-to-do villagers from whom the village collective had borrowed money to pay its agricultural taxes. As the TVEs collapsed in succession and the peasants resisted the taxes and fees over the years, the collective debt was piling up and accumulating interest, with no solution

---

[5] The amount of collective debt given to us by the village heads varied from time to time, partly depending on what items were included in their calculations. For example, the labor provided by the villagers for the PREV project was free but it could be calculated in monetary terms to impress an outsider or to plea for help. Also, the expenses for various items could be renegotiated informally at a later time. Certain items – such as compensation for land use – could be added to the road project or they could be paid for from a different source (i.e., the SLCP program), and hence they would be excluded from the calculation.

in sight. As a result, the village collectives became notorious for their inability to repay the debt to the government, to the banks, and to their own villagers. Against this background, it appeared to be an insurmountable challenge for the village collectives to ask for additional credit to debt-finance the PREV project.

It turned out this was not the case. One word that I heard frequently during this period is the Chinese word *"she,"* a special term used in economic transactions, meaning "to first take the goods and to make payments later." Both villages adopted this strategy. This is analogous to a debt-financing strategy for economic development or public projects. But, unlike typical debt-financing whereby one incurs debts from a single source or from a limited number of sources (i.e., borrowing from a bank, or from the issuance of bonds) with a well-specified payback schedule, both villages had to incur debts to a large number of parties, with no clearly specified payback schedule. This is because road construction involves a variety of materials and technical work: It requires equipment to pave the road and to press the bases; it requires oil/gas for the equipment, which is often separate from the leasing of the equipment. It requires materials such as sand, macadam, and cement as well as a construction team to lay down the cement surface, and vehicles to provide for the transport of the materials. It also requires cash to prepare daily food for those who work on the project. To make things worse, it was often the case for both villages that there was more than one supplier for each type of material. For example, for the transportation of sand, oftentimes more than a dozen different owners of small vehicles were hired. This meant that the village had to incur debts to all those various parties that provided the materials, equipment, transportation, and construction work. As a result, upon the completion of the project each village had taken in several dozen creditors. How was it possible, then, that such a mobilization of resources was accomplished within such a short period of time?

The main mechanism by which to obtain credit was *informal social relations*. Much of the *"she"* was based on informal social ties and communal trust, which was the source of the basic materials and transportation to pave the road. Social relations also allowed the villages to reach out to other localities and to mobilize donations from those well-to-do persons who lived and worked in the urban areas but had family ties in the village. However, the use of social networks here is drastically different from the typical social ties that are characterized in the literature as time-tested, reciprocal, and mutually beneficial social/economic exchanges. Rather, the village cadres knocked on every door that their social ties could reach. For example, Mr. Kang reached out to a senior manager of an oil company, hundreds of miles away, through an indirect tie in the village, which landed him 10 drums of gasoline at a market value of RMB 25,000, and no returns were expected. As for strong ties, they were exploited to the fullest possible extent. As Mr. Long recounted sometime later:

At that time, what I really was thinking about was how to cheat and lie. Everywhere we went we asked for a delay in payment. I dared to take as much as they dared to lend us ... At that time, we needed gas to operate the equipment. I went to a gas station run by a relative of my mother-in-law. I asked for 2 drums of gas and a delay in payment. Later, when we ran out of gas, I could not do the same thing at that same gas station, so I just went to another station. When you cheat and lie, you can only cheat and lie to your relatives or friends; they trust you. You cannot cheat and lie to strangers.

This account is borne out by actual expenditures. If we look at the sources of the debt-financing, one particular pattern clearly stands out. Among those various parties that contributed to the road construction, those who were most distant or who had no social ties invariably demanded immediate cash payment. In contrast, most debts were incurred to those parties that the village cadres knew well or with whom they had strong ties, either directly or indirectly. Table 9.1 depicts Uphill

TABLE 9.1. *Sources of debts/cash payment for material, equipment, and labor (Uphill Village)*

Items	Sources	Relationship	% cash paid upon completion
Cement	Government	Bureaucratic	0
Macadam	Local owners	Strong	0
Sand	Local (indirect ties)	Strong	0
Equipment for road pressing	County transportation bureau	No	100%
Equipment for road flattening	Military base	No	100%
Transportation	Local villagers	Strong	0
Road pavement	Local construction team	Strong	0

Village's main expenditures for road construction and how they were paid or debt financed.

As one can see, most materials in Uphill Village were debt-financed. The two items that were paid for in full came from those parties with whom the village had no social relations, hence no "*she*" was allowed. The pattern for Downhill Village was similar. Where there were differences for specific items, these differences followed the same principles. For example, when the village employed a county construction team to which the village had no social ties for road pavement, Mr. Long had to make more than one-half of the payment before the team would begin to work on the project. When an outside company transported the cement, because of the lack of social ties, the company insisted on an upfront cash payment and the village had to oblige.

The second source of resource mobilization came from the active involvement of the township government. After all, road construction was a project organized by the township government and could be considered part of the township's administrative achievement. The township government also sent township officials to the two villages to facilitate resource mobilization and to make sure that the project remained on track and on pace with the government plan. From the very beginning, Mr. Jin, the township party secretary, was pushing hard for this project. He led a group of township officials to visit a military base stationed in the area. As the atmosphere warmed through binge drinking and friendships were established, Jin asked for, and was granted, the right to rent the heavy equipment owned by the military base as well as the right to use the military personnel to operate the equipment. He also asked (unsuccessfully) that the local bank provide loans for this project and he pressured (successfully) the suppliers of the raw materials – sand and macadam – to let these two villages "*she*" their materials, throwing the weight of the township government behind these deals.

The township government was careful not to commit its own financial resources to the PREV project. But on several occasions Mr. Jin did go out of his way to mobilize resources for Mr. Kang because in terms of both ambition and activism, he and Mr. Kang were good matches. During an early phase of the project, Jin, on behalf of the township government, even directly provided funds in the amount of RMB 10,000 to Uphill Village – a rare, generous move from a financially stricken township government that in general would grab, rather than give, as many financial resources as it could. In another case, the head of the county bureau of transportation promised RMB 50,000 to Uphill Village. With this pledge in hand and in the face of pressing expenses, Mr. Kang took out a short-term, high-interest loan from a source rumored to be associated with an underground society. The bureau head later retracted his pledge and Mr. Kang was left with this short-term loan, with interest accumulating rapidly. Mr. Jin came to his rescue at this critical moment and instructed the irrigation office, a well-financed office in the township government, to make a loan to Mr. Kang so that he could immediately pay back the high-interest loan to the supposed underground society.

We may also ask the same question on the "supplier" side: Why were these suppliers willing to take such risks and to offer credit to these debt-laden villages? These "*she*" transactions were intertwined with dense social relations, as economic sociologists (Granovetter 1985, Zelizer 1994) have shown in other contexts. The head of a local construction team put it this way: "I have known Mr. Kang for many years. When he asked me for help, I certainly had to lend a hand." Of course, one important factor was the expectation that the loan would eventually be repaid. Again, social institutions played an important role in smoothing these transactions. The suppliers had intimate knowledge about these villages in terms of the mobilizational capacities of Mr. Kang and Mr. Long as well as in terms of the villages' available collective assets that could be used as collateral. Another reason was that in this underdeveloped area there were few opportunities for alternative uses of these facilities or materials; the PREV project provided valuable opportunities that the suppliers did not want to miss. This was clearly illustrated in the case of the transportation team for Downhill Village described above. Even though the request for prepayment of gas went unmet, the team still decided to take part in the project because its vehicles would otherwise remain idle. Moreover, there were enforcement mechanisms at its disposal to ensure that the debt would be repaid. Not long after the completion of the project, the transportation team, led by a bullish leader, blocked the main road of Downhill Village with large vehicles as he demanded, and ultimately received, payment. In another instance, as we saw before, the high-interest short-term loan was paid back promptly in anticipation of effective enforcement by the underground society.

But what happened to the other creditors who were not as bullish and who were bound by dense social relations in the local community? As often taught in public finance, debt-financing is common in the provision of public goods as long as there is an assurance that the debt will be repaid in some predictable way. The most astonishing aspect of the episodes that I observed is that no one involved in these deals had the faintest idea, let alone a clear plan, about how to repay these debts. There were no legal or formal requirements to guarantee that the two villages would pay back their debts. Lawsuits or other legal actions rarely took place in this region. Indeed, if history was any guide, for many years both villages had already amassed collective debts in the amount of tens of thousands of yuan. Even among those who had incurred these huge debts, no one had a clear idea about how to pay them off. In the middle of the PREV project, I asked Mr. Jin how the villages would pay off their debts. He responded:

I have no idea. But even with these gaps we have to launch the project. If we were to keep waiting [until we knew how to repay the debt], there would never be a good time to complete the project. To mobilize resources, we utilize all channels to borrow – debt-financing, fundraising, and loans.

I witnessed a scene in which a township official in charge of implementing the PREV project openly coached Mr. Long: "Don't tell them [the suppliers of the materials] that you do not have the money. Just say that they will get paid when the project is completed. After all, lying and cheating are not punished by the death penalty." Then, without a pause, he added his own little lie:

The officials in the municipal and county governments have already made it clear that they will not let those who take an initiative [to commence the PREV project] be penalized. They know that the villages cannot afford such projects, so they will provide subsidies in the future.

When I asked this official what would happen to these debts down the road, with a wry smile, he responded: "We can only wait and see. We just jumpstart the project; no one knows how the debts will be paid off in the future."

Indeed, amid such pleading, bargaining, and promises, one got the sense that everyone played his or her part in this game and acted recklessly, as if there was no tomorrow; hence, no one cared about the consequences of incurring such huge debts. Or, maybe, unconsciously they knew better – that somehow down the road something would eventually work out.

DEALING WITH THE AFTERMATH: SOCIAL INSTITUTIONS FOR
PROBLEM SOLVING AND RESPONDING TO CRISES

With the cement-paved road completed, solidified, and opened for transportation, and with the dissipation of the initial excitement about the project, pressures from the debts began to mount, as waves of creditors rushed to the villages seeking repayment. Looking back, the first round of debt-financing seemed so easy; now came the second, much more challenging, round of mobilization of resources to deal with the aftermath of the PREV project. Both villages embarked on the long journey of taking many years to pay off their debts. Turning now to the aftermath of the PREV project, as these episodes continued to unfold, we asked the same set of questions: What were the available channels and mechanisms for resource mobilization to pay off the debts?

"The Cart Will Find Its Way around the Hill When It Gets There": Struggling to Pay off the Debts

This is another Chinese expression that I heard frequently from the village cadres who struggled in the face of the mounting debt pressures due to the road construction project. Let us begin with some glimpses into their experience of living in debt. While the village heads stood tall in the midst of the PREV project – directing, coordinating, and mobilizing for the road construction – they were desperate to dig a hole and hide underground as soon as the road was completed, as their suppliers turned from playing the role of needed facilitators to the role of demanding creditors. Pressures were especially high as the Chinese New Year holiday season approached. In this region, it is a tradition for all parties to settle their debts before the Chinese New Year. It is also a legitimate occasion to openly and actively demand a settlement of debts. On the eve of the Chinese New Year in 2005, all creditors converged on these two villages. They stayed all day and all night at the homes of the party secretaries, pleading for payment; some would even stay in their homes for many days on end. As a custom in this region, the host family had to treat the creditors as guests, provide accommodations, and prepare food and even cigarettes for them. Mr. Long recalled:

On the eve of the Chinese New Year, the creditors came to our house and slept on the floor. Sometimes more than ten parties would arrive within one day. One creditor even brought his own creditor to stay at our house. For those few days, we could barely breathe because of the heavy cigarette smoke in our house.

The pressure took its toll, especially on Mr. Kang. Although the debts were owed collectively, the responsibility was largely personal, as most deals had been struck on the basis of interpersonal relationships. Several months after completion of the project, Mr. Kang had lost weight and his complexion had become dark. It was as if he had undergone a change of personality; he became dispirited and reticent, no longer eager to share with others his ambitions for the future of the village. There were many stories swirling in conversations in FS Township about Kang's situation and even about his mental health. At the time, creditors demanding payment would incessantly call Kang's cell phone. On one occasion, Kang got so mad that that he simply threw away his phone. Sometime later, when I inquired about his debt situation, he said:

As the Chinese New Year approached last year, the village office and my own house became crowded with creditors, who stayed day and night. We party committee members went to seek help from Party Secretary Jin, but to no avail. We then went behind his back to seek help from the head of the county administration. But the assistant to the head of the county administration stopped us and we did not have a chance to see him directly. So, three days before the Chinese New Year, the three of us [village party committee members] had to flee our homes to hide from the creditors. We only returned to our homes after ten o'clock at night on the eve of the Chinese New Year. Some creditors returned the following day.

In what ways did the two villages respond to and manage these looming crises? Let us first take a look at Downhill Village. In the midst of the road construction in the summer of 2004, Mr. Long requested and received the SLCP quota for his village, a total of 750 *mu*, which infused extra outside resources into the village. This was a significant gesture of support from the township government to reward those villages that were participating in the PREV project. The SLCP policy stipulated that the special-purpose fund be used only for its designated purpose and the transfer of these resources to other areas was strictly prohibited. Although the fund's ultimate destination was to reach village families whose land had participated in the SLCP program, all the resources (in cash) had to pass through the hands of the village head, thus providing him with an opportunity to divert some of the funds in response to the debt crisis. The township government acquiesced to such a practice. By the end of 2004, Mr. Long had retained fifty percent of the SLCP funds that flowed into his village, about RMB 50,000, under the pretense of deducting the villagers' debts to the village collective, which represented their agricultural taxes that had become due in previous years.[6] Mr. Long

---

[6] Since the late 1990s, many village families had refused to pay their agricultural taxes. As a common practice in this region, the amount they owed in taxes was recorded as their debts to the village collective, under the assumption that the village collective would pay the agricultural taxes on their behalf. In fact, the village collective was in debt to the township government in a similar manner.

was lucky that there was relatively low resistance among those in his village. When some families refused to accept the deduction, Mr. Long mobilized the village cadres to persuade them. He preempted the threat of petitions on the part of some villagers by announcing over loudspeakers that he would stand up to any interventions by the authorities: "I am not afraid that you might report me to the authorities. I am doing this for the benefit of all villagers." In subsequent years, Mr. Long continued to deduct the SLCP funds, in a reduced proportion – forty percent in 2005, and thirty percent in 2006. Even after Mr. Long stepped down as party secretary in 2006, the new party secretary followed the same course of action to pay off the debt.

By the end of 2008, four years after completion of the PREV project, only about RMB 25,000 remained unpaid from the PREV project in Downhill Village, and the entire debt was expected to be paid off within several years. "Finally, next year there will be some revenue left for us to plan for new projects," Mr. Jun, who succeeded Mr. Long as village head in 2006, said to me with relief. For Downhill Village, then, the collective debt was dealt with largely through the "illicit" transfer of resources provided by the central government for a different policy target in another area. Nevertheless, it was the relatively small size of the collective debt that made it manageable, even with the village's limited mobilizational capacities.

Compared with Downhill Village, Mr. Kang and his Uphill Village embarked on a much longer and more arduous odyssey, with long-lasting consequences. Upon completion of the road project, as part of his initial effort Mr. Kang likewise sought to put his hands on some of the SLCP funds that were infused into the village annually. Uphill Village had nearly 2,000 mu of land that benefited from the SLCP program, with an inflow to the households in the village of RMB 300,000 each year. Mr. Kang's plan was to deduct part of those funds and to transfer them to pay off the road debt. As soon as Kang had devised this plan, an anonymous call was made from his village to the higher authorities at the provincial level to complain about the illicit transfer of funds. The township government soon received an inquiry from the higher authorities; as a result, township party secretary Jin had to stop Kang's attempt so as to avoid further complications. Thus, Uphill Village was unable to raise any additional funds within the village to ease its debt burden and Kang was fully exposed to a flood of creditors as the 2005 Chinese New Year approached.

Among the many village cadres whom I came to know in FS Township, Mr. Kang stood out in several ways, one of which was his outward thinking. Whenever asked about the future of his village collective, he had always talked, at times fantasized, about potential resources from outside. It was no exception in 2005. A search for outside opportunities came to his mind instinctively. In October 2005, one year after completion of the road, Kang sent a letter to the chief executive official of the county government, pleading for financial support. In his wishful thinking, if the county government could provide him with RMB 200,000, his debt burden would be largely resolved. But even some RMB 20,000 or RMB 30,000 would be of great help, he told me. The letter was sent to the address of the county government but he never received a response. It was obvious that Kang was going to be left on his own to deal with the aftermath of the PREV project. He tried moving both heaven and earth, as we shall see below.

As the second Chinese New Year approached in early 2006, Kang became restless. This time he had learned from his earlier mistakes and he devised other ways to legitimately claim part of the SLCP funds from the villagers. Following Downhill Village's example, Kang justified resource transfers under the pretense of settling old debts that the villagers owed the village collective. Toward the end of 2005, Kang went through an elaborate process of seeking approval at the villagers' meeting, with signatures from all households approving that this would be an entirely "voluntary" agreement among the villagers to pay back their debts to the village collective, mostly through deductions from the SLCP funds. In addition, he also persuaded the villagers to give RMB 5 per *mu* of land to the village collective as a "management fee," which amounted to RMB 10,000 per year. But with the villager-owed debts dwindling fast – only about RMB 20,000 remained by early 2006 – it became apparent that this well of resources would soon dry up and would not be a viable source of payment for the remainder of the debt.

The township government offered a helping hand here and there when doing so would not harm its own financial well-being. In 2006, a brick maker was looking for a manufacturing site in this township. Mr. Jin used his authority to persuade the investor to set up his site in Uphill Village. The investor thereupon infused RMB 50,000 into the village collective in exchange for a twenty-year lease of a large piece of desolate land. According to Mr. Kang, Mr. Jin was supportive throughout this process and he let this project operate under the name of the township government, thus facilitating the processing of the application permits and the other government authorizations. The township government helped in other ways as well. By designating Uphill Village as one of the "model villages" in the government-sponsored "ecological village" program, doors were opened for the infusion of RMB 15,000 in 2006.

By 2006, two years after completion of the PREV project, outside funds dribbled in only occasionally and unpredictably. Helpless and desperate, Kang turned inward to the remaining collective assets for a solution. For a long time, Kang had his eyes set on the two motor-pumped wells. In Uphill Village, as already noted, management and operation of irrigation were leased to two private individuals. The leasing fee – RMB 10,000 per well per year – was an important, stable source of income for the collective. But the two wells were already leased out for ten years, with two more years still left on the lease. Desperate for cash to pay off the debt, in 2006 Kang renewed the lease of one well for another ten years before the current lease had expired, gaining RMB 100,000. For the second well, Kang arranged to have it leased for twelve years to the head of the construction team as payment for the road-pavement debt of RMB 100,000. In other words, both irrigation facilities were already mortgaged out for ten years into the future. A regular source of revenue would no longer be available to the village collective for the next decade!

Still, this was far from enough. The next year, 2007, Kang set his sight on the two rows of houses in the village center. As it turned out, the row of rooms housing the village committee was already mortgaged to a local bank as collateral for previously unpaid loans. But this did not stop Kang. Unable to sell that row, he moved the elementary school to the row of rooms for collateral, and relocated the village committee offices to an old house that had been abandoned many years earlier. This maneuver allowed Kang to sell, for RMB 100,000, the row of rooms that had previously housed the elementary school. In the same year, renewal of the lease on the village's collective land for another five years collected another RMB 75,000.

Let us now conduct an accounting check on both villages. For Downhill Village, debts incurred from the PREV project were being paid off largely by villagers drawn from a single source – the SLCP fund. Because the SLCP fund was an unexpected infusion of resources from the government, the burden on the village collective was manageable and the collective assets, small in scale in the first place, remained largely intact: The village center's courtyard was rented out for twenty years – for seasonal use of the ground to dry grain – to cover a debt of RMB 3,000. The village offices were put up as collateral for the unpaid loans, but given the progress made in repaying the debt, it was unlikely that these offices would change hands.

The picture for Uphill Village was bleaker. Figure 9.1 shows the various sources of revenue over the years, as described above. The amount of these items added together would come close to paying off the debt for the entire

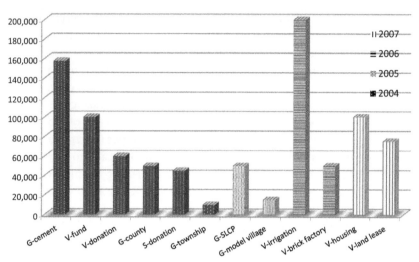

FIGURE 9.1. Debt payment schedule in Uphill Village

road. But not all these funds were used to pay off the debt for the road; other business of the collective had to be taken care of as well, such as the interest on previous loans, renovations for the relocated village offices, and so forth. In the course of paying off its debts, the assets of the collective were almost entirely exhausted: The two motor-pumped wells – the main source of revenue for the collective – were mortgaged for at least a decade into the future. The collective land was leased again for another five years, with the lease fees spent on payment of the debt. The row of collective-owned rooms was sold off. A large piece of land was leased to the brick maker for the next twenty years. The debts that the villagers owed to the village had almost all dried up, making them no longer a potential source of resources to draw upon in times of need. All the income from these projects was drained into paying off the huge debt for the PREV project. By 2008, a staggering RMB 300,000 remained unpaid from the PREV project, according to Mr. Kang.

What we have revealed in the tale of the two villages are two distinct attitudes toward government-promoted public projects, with drastically different experiences and consequences for the collective assets. One village was laden with heavy collective debt and its collective assets were hollowed, whereas the collective assets in the other village remained relatively intact. The distinct responses of the two villages toward the PREV project, and the aftermath of the project, cast a long shadow on collective governance in these two villages.

Mr. Kang suffered not only from those tangible losses – the depletion of the collective assets and a burden of collective debts – but also the intangible weakening of his mobilizational capacities. His capacity to engage in any other collective project in the near future had been seriously undermined. Moreover, his judgment was questioned and his reputation as an innovative and able leader was seriously tarnished. As the village head in another village commented: "Mr. Kang dares to take risks. Sometimes he becomes reckless and makes big mistakes. The village collective cannot afford the consequences of such missteps." Villagers became reluctant to participate in collective projects and resisted Kang's efforts to mobilize resources to pay off the debts. One instance illustrates this well. In 2006, the most difficult year in terms of debt pressures, Kang tried to lure outside investment into the village on the site of an old, abandoned temple. Upon hearing of this attempt, the villagers mobilized themselves and, virtually overnight, donated RMB 200,000 to rebuild the temple. The spontaneity of their efforts to rebuild the temple was in sharp contrast to their rather passive attitude to the tremendous pressure from the collective debt and it represented an implicit rejection of Mr. Kang's efforts to meddle with the temple site to pay off the collective debt.

Relationships between village cadres and the township government also evolved over time, and the PREV project marked a critical turning point. Upon completion of the PREV project, those who actively supported government advocacy were well received and those who did not comply were pushed aside. Mr. Long was removed from his position as village head in 2006. In contrast, Mr. Kang was selected as a "model party secretary" by the township government and he was showered with praise. But such relationships were fragile and could easily change with the turnover of officials in the township government. After Mr. Jin left the township government in 2007, the new township head saw the PREV episode in an entirely different light, as he told Mr. Kang:

If I had been township head then, I would not have encouraged you to undertake this project. You don't want to be the last one, but you should not always want to be the first one either. For your own benefit, don't compete to be the "model cadre" every time.

Indeed, the new township leaders began treating Kang as a marginal player and a liability that they wanted to cut loose.

Before we leave the details of these episodes behind and turn to their implications in a broader context, the following question should be addressed: To what extent are these episodes accidental, isolated, or idiosyncratic to this particular location and time? My assessment is that the episodes discussed here were by no means isolated cases that happened to have taken place in this locality. Similar instances were reported in other areas as well. As late as 2008, a delegate to the National People's Congress from a different province complained:

> Presently, there is a serious problem of insufficient funds for the PREV project in the underdeveloped areas.... In the underdeveloped areas, per capita income is low and it is impossible for local villages to have sufficient resources to pay for the PREV project by drawing from the local government budget and by self-financing by the villagers. The lack of funds will affect the quality and progress of road pavement in the rural areas, increase the amount of new collective debts, engender social tensions, and undermine social stability.[7]

As one can see, these complaints echo the episodes reported in FS Township four years earlier. In other words, similar bureaucratic behavior was observed across different localities and different administrative jurisdictions located hundreds of miles apart.

Especially alarming is the fact that the pattern of government behavior to promote the PREV project and its aftermath also echoes other disastrous government-promoted programs in this region and elsewhere in the not-too-distant past. In my fieldwork during this period, village cadres and villagers frequently recalled stories about how the township government had earlier encouraged the villages to start up successive TVEs, financed by collective assets or by borrowing from banks. Eventually, none of these TVEs survived, and huge collective debts piled up in the process. In the midst of the PREV project, a village cadre likened the current government push for the PREV project to the TVE episodes of the 1980s:

> At that time [the 1980s], the TVE project was similar to the present PREV project; they were both political tasks that you had to carry out as long as you were a village cadre. One day we would start a cobblestone manufacturing site with an investment of some RMB 200,000; and the next day we would open up a brick-making factory, with an investment of some RMB 300,000. In its heyday, there were seven or eight enterprises in our village. None of them were profitable and eventually they all closed down. All these ventures were promoted by the township government as part of its advocacy for rural enterprises.

Moreover, the consequences could have been on a larger scale and could have been much worse. During the 2004 round, the government

---

[7] www.gov.cn/2008lh/content_921913.htm. Last checked on April 8, 2022.

mercifully limited the imposed task – the length of road construction that was allocated to each township – because it too had to chip in part of the funds for the project. Also, as we have observed, the burden of the incurred collective debt from the PREV project was greatly alleviated or effectively dealt with by the "illicit" transfer of resources from another government program – the SLCP – in the rural areas. This observation raises counterfactual questions: What would have happened if the SLCP program had not been in place at the time or if it was on a smaller scale (as it was scheduled to be scaled back during its second phase starting in 2010)? One distinct possibility, as often occurred in the past, is that the PREV project would have been imposed upon more villages and there would have been an even more serious impact, such that the collective debts would hang over these villages for a much longer period of time, the collective assets would have been depleted to a greater extent, and public trust would have eroded even further.

SEEING LIKE A STATE AND ITS PERILS

In his *Seeing Like a State*, Scott offers an indictment of the grand schemes of the state that, intended to improve human conditions, lead to disastrous consequences. Scott (1998, pp. 4–5) writes:

The most tragic episodes of state-initiated social engineering originate in a pernicious combination of four elements. All four are necessary for a full-fledged disaster. The first element is the administrative ordering of nature and society.... The second element is what I called a high-modernist ideology.... The third element is an authoritarian state that is willing and able to use the full weight of its coercive power to bring these high-modernist designs into being.... A fourth element is closely linked to the third: a prostrate civil society that lacks the capacity to resist these plans.

In many respects, this fits well with what we have learned from the episodes during the PREV project. Here we observed an active role of state and government policies, with both a "high-modernist ideology" and organizational capacities to impose and enforce an ambition for the "administrative ordering of nature and society," and a weak society – villages and local communities – unable to resist the state imposition or to protect their interests.

Moreover, these pursuits in social engineering do not take place in a vacuum; rather, to take effect, they interact with local social institutions. There are two intertwining themes running through the episodes discussed in this chapter. The first is the story of the political – the processes of state policy implementation and the role of state bureaucracies; the second is the story of the social – the role of social institutions and social relations in resource mobilization, problem solving, and responding to crises. It is obvious that these two processes were intertwined throughout these episodes. We need to consider the interactions between these two themes and, broadly, between the government bureaucracies and social institutions in the larger societal context to understand the role of the bureaucratic state in economic development and societal transformation. An assessment of the role of the state and its bureaucracy in socioeconomic life would be incomplete and biased if we were to ignore the role of social institutions, which may intensify, redirect, or buffer the impacts of state intrusion.

How do we make sense of the role of the state and government bureaucracies in the PREV episodes? The active role of state and government policies in economic development and institutional changes has been widely recognized in the social science literature (Evans, Rueschemeyer and Skocpol 1985). What we observed in the PREV episodes was a bureaucratic state in action, in which the paramount task of the local bureaucracy was to implement administrative fiats from above.

But for whom and to what end was this efficient and effective bureaucratic state? Here, we need to consider Merton's critique of bureaucracy (Merton 1968a), especially the effect of the bureaucratic structure to induce corresponding bureaucratic behavior. Unlike the image of the Weberian bureaucracy where bureaucrats follow rules and procedures, and strive for efficiency, in the Mertonian bureaucracy, the behavior of officials is governed by the bureaucratic logic reflected in the organizational design of incentives and authority relationships. In the Chinese context, a key component of the bureaucratic logic is that upward accountability, incentive designs, and task environments induce Mertonian bureaucrats to be extremely sensitive to the directives from their immediate supervisors and to focus on short-term "administrative achievements," often at the expense of long-term economic development (Sun and Guo 2000, Wu 2007, Ying 2001, Zhang 2018, Zhao 2010, Zhou 2006). Instead of treating such behavior as accidental, we need to address the following questions: What motivates the behavior of local officials? What are the implications of their behavior for long-term rural development?

One important behavioral consequence is the shift in the role of government officials from ideologically zealous revolutionary cadres to methodical bureaucrats who often single-mindedly strive to get the job done at any cost. This is especially the case during episodes of heightened mobilization when different parts of the bureaucracy become tightly coupled for selective policy implementation. The PREV episode is such a case. Evidence abounds from the PREV episodes whereby the local bureaucrats implemented these policies with the aim of accomplishing "administrative achievements" for their own career advancement rather than for any long-term prospects of local development. I followed township government cadres on numerous trips to observe their efforts to mobilize for the project and to respond to various problems and crises. Throughout all these processes, I found little evidence that local officials cared about the burden of public debt upon the villages. Rather, their primary goal was simple – *get the job done so as to meet the demands of their superiors*. To accomplish this, local officials pushed through the project using all means at their disposal, showing little concern about the consequences for the villages.

The episodes in FS Township raise issues about the perils of state policies that aim at social engineering and about the role of the state, state policies, and government bureaucracies in China's transformation. To be sure, the PREV project was far from those disasters of social engineering described in Scott (1998) or some other episodes in China (Friedman, Pickowicz and Selden 1991, Yang 1996). Even in Uphill and Downhill villages, the benefits of road construction were evident. Motor vehicles and motorcycles could smoothly ride in and out of the village, and merchants could drive all the way to the village center to purchase and transport produce, thus allowing better prices for the villagers.

These merits notwithstanding, there are serious pitfalls that are less tangible but have long-lasting impacts. First, there may be better, alternative ways of using these resources. Resources put into the PREV projects are resources taken away from other projects. Political pressures forced local officials to transfer resources from those areas in which there may have been a more urgent need to those areas where the higher authorities demanded outcomes. In another township in the same region, the government head decided to transfer the irrigation budget of RMB 200,000 to the PREV project because the latter was a political task that had to be completed, even though irrigation facilities were sorely needed in this township. Second, the implementation of such policies has important implications for the basis of rural governance. Failures of government-sponsored public projects undermine the basis of public trust. Over time, a chasm is created between the villages and the government, and suspicion and distrust loom large. As shown in the above episodes, through these interactions the relationship between the township government and the village cadres evolved. The burden of collective debts and the ensuing crises led to strains and confrontations between the township government and the village cadres. Third, the PREV project greatly undermined the basis of collective authority, as we have seen in the case of Uphill Village. Moreover, active government intervention may have discouraged the rise of an autonomous public sphere for self-governance, undermining institutions of informal accountability in the provision of public goods. Therefore, irresponsible government programs inflicted pain on these villages not once, not twice, but several times – by pushing villages into huge collective debt and bringing bruises and pains to the village collective, by eroding the social fabric of public trust and social relations, and by undermining the basis of rural governance.

Thus far, our discussions have focused on the implications of how government policies and public projects were imposed and implemented and what their impacts were on collective governance. We now turn to the second theme – tales of the social, regarding how social institutions are mobilized for resources and problem solving.

As we have seen, these episodes provide valuable information about the role of social institutions in problem solving and in responding to crises. Social institutions and network ties based on kinship and the village collective played a critical role in mobilizing resources for debt-financing the project, as clearly evidenced by the episodes reported above. But these relations were by no means instrumental in the sense of "reciprocal" exchanges or mutual benefits; instead, to a great extent these relations were exploited. Payments to those with strong social relations tended to be postponed again and again. In this context, social relations were used to buffer or alleviate such pressures. One interpretation is that such delays amounted to taking advantage of the social relations; therefore, such irresponsible borrowing or cheating and lying, as it was bluntly called, undermined the social fabric of trust and social relations in the rural areas.

Unless, of course, we can entertain an alternative interpretation, that is, to be in debt to another party is itself a social relation. Consider Mr. Kang in Uphill Village. As soon as he recovered from the initial pressure of the debt, Mr. Kang tried to make the best of the terrible situation. In his usual, self-important way, he fondly recounted the various strategies he devised to fend off the creditors. "I turned these pressures into initiatives," he said proudly:

One guy to whom we owed a debt was a person in our village who had previously sold us macadam. I told him: "If you wait for me to pay off your debt, it will take many years. If you can help us get a project from outside, I can pay back your debt immediately." Now this creditor is actively helping us introduce an iron-mining project in the village. If it is successful, we can pay off his debt.

During the first year, Kang also learned lessons from the wave of creditors on the eve of the Chinese New Year. As the next Chinese New Year approached, Kang gathered the party committee members and, with gifts in hand, they visited the main creditors ahead of time, explaining their financial situations and making vague promises about future payments. In so doing, the creditors softened the debt pressures. Kang quoted a local idiom: "When you are rich, money can help you smooth relations; when you are poor, words can help you smooth relations." Through such interactions, were social relations exploited, hence undermined, or were they renewed, reinforced, and transformed? This critical question remains to be answered.

In any case, from these episodes we can clearly see the intertwining of the political and the social in the provision of public goods. In particular, the logic of social institutions played a critical role to make it possible for political tasks to be carried out, to deal with the aftermath of poor policy making and implementation, and to absorb the disastrous consequences of this process. It would be difficult to imagine that the villages, hence the township could have carried out the PREV project without the effective role of social mechanisms in mobilizing resources through debt-financing. In other words, the stories of the political would not have played out in the ways that we have observed without the active participation of the social mechanisms throughout this entire process. In this light, in order to assess the role of government bureaucracies in economic development and societal change we need to place them in the larger social context and in their interactions with the social institutions.

SUMMARY

The story of the road pavement project reveals many parallels with the issues discussed in the previous chapters. State policies such as the road pavement project were made by the higher levels; but these top-down policies were negotiated quietly and implemented selectively as they moved down the hierarchical levels. Similar to the behavior of the MEPB officials in the environmental protection area (Chapters 3 and 7), we witnessed here efforts by local governments to get things done and to accomplish administrative achievements.

Moreover, these efforts ultimately met with the logic of rural China, at the intersection of state and society, which led to new governance dynamics in China. The road construction episode in this chapter shows the critical role of grass-roots society – the logic of rural China in this case – in local problem solving and alleviating the kind of policy blunders that fall within local boundaries. Our understanding of the institutional logic of governance would be incomplete and defective if we did not pay attention to the other side of the fundamental tension – the side of local governance where the state and its bureaucracy meet social institutions and local residents.

It may take many years for us to understand the PREV episodes and the unfolding of their consequences. But it is clear that these micro-processes have important implications for understanding the role of public policies aimed at the provision of public goods, the bases of collective governance, and the evolution of social institutions. To reflect on the significance of these episodes and events, let us revisit the role of road construction in rural France. From a long-distance historical lens, Eugen Weber (1976, p. 220) could afford to observe admiringly:

If, as Maurice Bedel would have it, the roads "have forged the profound sensibility of France and, above all, its patriotic feelings," then it is in the latter part of the nineteenth century with macadam and steel rails that these feelings were hammered out.

Considering the episodes reported in this chapter, one wonders – has the road construction in FS Township, with macadam, sand, and cement, in some way added a psychological distance between the village and those well-intended state policies? Moreover, in recent years, there has been an increasing trend of infusing resources into the rural areas through earmarked funds and government projects, and the governments have played a salient role in this process, inducing new changes in rural governance. After years of neglecting and marginalizing the rural areas during the decollectivization era, villages began to experience a new era of reintegration into the national political and economic systems through the infusion of resources and through public projects promoted by government policies. As a more resourceful, assertive state and its bureaucratic apparatus re-entered the rural areas and took on a more active role in rural development and transformation, what lessons have we learned from the episodes in the PREV project?

10

Multiple Logics of Village Elections

Stipulated by the provisional "Organic Law of Village Committees" promulgated in 1987, village elections are an institutional practice by which, every three years, villagers elect or reelect members of the village committee – the governing body of their village. Both in form and in practice, village elections are an institution associated with a set of clearly specified rules, procedures, and expectations regarding both the election process and the functioning of the elected village committee. During the two decades between the 1990s and 2000s, village elections evolved through intensive interactions among multiple actors, involving state policies, local governments, and villagers. There have been a large number of studies on this topic (He 2007, Manion 2006, O'Brien and Li 2000, O'Brien and Han 2009, Perry and Goldman 2007, Shi 1999). The emergence of village elections in rural China presents a fascinating case for understanding how different institutions work and change in relation to one another, especially how over time state policies and the evolving role of local governments interact with villagers in the process of rural governance.

In this chapter, I examine the interaction among state policies, local governments, and villagers in the evolution of village elections in FS Township, over four election events between 2000 and 2008. I emphasize the interplay of multiple institutional logics, their behavioral implications for interactions among social groups, and the ensuing processes of change. By focusing my empirical analysis on one agricultural town, my goal is to take a microscopic look into the processes of governance in China.

ON THE STAGE OF VILLAGE ELECTIONS: SCENES FROM FIELD OBSERVATIONS

Village elections are an *emergent* institution in that the principles of village elections – the one-person-one-vote direct election procedure, the open forum for the selection of candidates, and the subsequent form of self-governance – mark a major departure from the traditional gentry-based mode of village governance (Fei 1992[1948], Hsiao 1960) or the top-down organizational apparatus during Mao's collective era (Friedman, Pickowicz and Selden 1991, Parish and Whyte 1978, Shue 1988). Village elections acquire particular significance in that, decorated as "grass-roots democracy," the formal voting procedures come close to familiar democratic practices in other societies – a practice that was largely alien to both the rule-makers in Beijing and the practitioners in the Chinese villages. In this light, the institutions of village elections introduced a new logic of governance in rural China that has evolved along with the interactions among the multiple players in the process.

Willow Village

Tucked away in the corner of a mountainous area, more than fifteen kilometers away from the town center, Willow Village appeared remote and unimportant to those in the township government, where its name and affairs seldom surfaced in casual conversations or serious discussions. All of this suddenly changed in the early days of the election season in 2006 when, in the preliminary election, the then village committee – the party secretary, the village head, and the accountant – all faced serious challenges. Mr. Wang, the party secretary who also stood for election to the village committee, narrowly made it to the second round; his partner, the village head, failed to win enough votes to advance. This shocked the township government for several reasons. First, in recent years the collective authority in this village had been in relatively good standing. Several years earlier, an outside investment project infused the village with significant financial resources in exchange for use of village land. The exchange enabled the village to pay off a collective debt of RMB 120,000 and even to maintain a surplus of RMB 40,000 in the collective account – an enviable financial situation for most village governments in this region. Second, since there had been no signs of trouble before, such unexpected results suggested considerable, behind-the-scenes organizing efforts beyond the control of the village government. The township government panicked. The unexpected election of new faces on the village committee meant that the township officials would have to deal with strangers.

During our long ride to the village, Mr. Chen, the head of the township government work team, was worried and dispirited about the dreaded second round of formal elections. He informed his team members that Mr. Wang had called him the previous night and had told him that the young challenger in his village had been working hard in recent days, mobilizing his kinship network and handing out promises. To make matters worse, Mr. Wang had few kinship ties upon which to rely; his was an outside family that had moved into the village, albeit many years ago. Almost resigned to a certain defeat by Mr. Wang and the other incumbents, Mr. Chen bitterly complained about the villagers: "They don't care about cadre performance. In the end, they only vote along kinship lines."

When we arrived in the courtyard of the village government, the election committee, comprised mostly of the current village committee members, was already busy working – hanging up banners, posting prescribed election slogans, and setting up a voting booth. In his late fifties, Mr. Wang was quiet, soft-spoken, and unpresumptuous, unlike some of his peers with whom I had become familiar during my fieldwork. I had learned much about Mr. Wang on our ride to the village. He was a veteran village cadre, and he had worked as village (brigade) cadre since the collective era. According to Mr. Chen, Mr. Wang had done an excellent job in this position and he significantly improved the well-being of the villagers.

When the voting started, the air in the crowded village courtyard turned tense. In a corner away from the crowd, Mr. Wang stood alone, awkward and resigned. I walked over to him and he eagerly struck up a conversation, complaining in a low voice that he expected to fail in the election and that the villagers did not appreciate what he had done for the village because they were only loyal to their next of kin. His bitter remarks echoed what Mr. Chen had said earlier, or was it the other way around?

The voting lasted several hours. Slowly the crowd dispersed, voices quieted, and the courtyard emptied. At around two o'clock in the afternoon, the number of ballots cast well exceeded the legal requirement of at least 50 percent of the eligible voters, so the voting booths were closed and the ballot counting began. Members of the election committee, the township government work team, and several "concerned villagers" from the challenger's side were present to count the ballots and to oversee the process. The names on each ballot were simultaneously broadcast through the loudspeakers to the entire village.

In the final result Mr. Wang received the most votes – 150 out of the total 251 valid ballots. His partner, the village accountant, received 149 votes, the second largest number of votes, and the challenger received 133 votes. The three candidates who won the most votes – the two incumbents and the one contender – were elected to the next village committee. As the outright winner of the election, Mr. Wang was selected to head the village committee – a pleasant surprise to him, to those on the township government work team, and especially to Mr. Chen, the head of the work team. "After all, the eyes of the masses are discerning," noted Mr. Chen, quoting a well-known expression related to Chinese politics, with a relieved smile.

Boulevard Village

Boulevard Village is one of four adjacent villages that constitute the center of the township. For many years, Boulevard Village was a headache for the township government. In 2003, the township government had dismissed the former village party secretary from his position for abuse of power. However, with the backing of a strong kinship base, he refused to hand over the seal that signified his authority. Worried about his influence, the township government dared not hold a meeting of village party members to elect a new party secretary. As a result, the party branch was paralyzed and the township government had to rely on cooperation from Mr. Liu, the elected head of the village committee. Tensions between those who supported the former party secretary and those who backed the village head persisted for many years and from time to time erupted into open confrontations.

Village elections offered the chance for an open, legitimate contest, and both sides actively mobilized their votes. On the eve of the election, Mr. Liu appeared to be the front-runner. Resentful of this expected outcome, the other side – the supporters of the old party secretary – made a desperate last-ditch effort to disrupt the preliminary election: Several villagers stormed into the voting site, tore apart the ballot boxes, and threw away the ballots that had already been collected in the boxes, thus temporarily halting the voting process. But the election committee, backed by the township government, quickly printed new ballots and restarted the voting process. The first round of the election concluded with no further incidents, and all members of the incumbent village committee were voted in to stand for the second, final election.

The formal election proceeded uneventfully. Perhaps in response to the disruptions during the first-round election, a larger-than-usual crowd amassed at the voting site. As more and more villagers entered the village courtyard, the single-file line of those waiting in front of the voting booth grew longer, twisting and wrapping around the courtyard, as villagers chatted and laughed. By the end of the election process, Mr. Liu had received 91 percent of the votes, a number he often proudly cited on subsequent occasions.

The high turnout and overwhelming outcome solidified Mr. Liu's position and forced his opponents to retreat. Several weeks after the village election, the party branch election was formally held, and a new party secretary was elected. Everything soon calmed down and there were no more confrontations. In Boulevard Village, it appears that the village election has finally brought closure to a contentious past, ending a chapter – indeed an era – of open conflicts.

Bao Village

To the township government, Bao Village has been a long-running nightmare. Mr. Ren, the current village head, was elected to office three years earlier after he had mobilized his fellow villagers to overthrow the previous party secretary and his team. Incessant, intensive fighting engulfed kinship groups within the village and strained the village's relationship with the township government. Mr. Ren was despised because, as some government officials alleged, he repeatedly bypassed the township government and petitioned the higher authorities (*shangfang*) directly. In a much talked about episode, a county government bureau promised to provide RMB 40,000 to develop a project in the village, but it never followed through. When Mr. Ren found out that the bureau had falsely reported this promise to the media as an accomplishment, he immediately filed a complaint with the county government and insisted that the bureau fulfill its promise. Grudgingly, the bureau finally complied under pressure. Mr. Ren was noncooperative in other ways as well. Three years earlier, during the previous election, he announced over loudspeakers that if elected, he would lead Bao Village to resist the collection of government taxes and fees. Many township government officials saw him as a thug.

Meanwhile, the township government was tactfully building its case to discredit him. Government aid to the village was withheld, funds from

government programs were not allocated, and outside investment opportunities were diverted to other villages. Even when government funds that
were specifically designated for Bao Village were transmitted, the township government was reluctant to make them available to Mr. Ren's
village committee. All of this was done under the pretense that village
governance was so erratic that no one could be sure that the funds would
be used appropriately. But the real motive behind these efforts was to
cultivate grievances against the current village committee so that Mr. Ren
and his team would be voted out of office in the election.

At the time of the election, I asked Mr. Jin, the township party secretary, if he anticipated that the village head of Bao village would be voted
out. He confidently responded, "Of course," and he added: "The villagers
should know what is in their best interest. With such a village head, no
outside opportunities will land in this village." To facilitate the desired
outcome of the election, the township government hastily appointed a
new village party secretary and nominated him as a candidate to challenge
Mr. Ren. Anticipating potential confrontations and disruptions, the
township government cautiously postponed the election in Bao Village
until after the other villages in the township had completed their elections.

The preliminary election in Bao Village was held on a cold morning,
just before the last snowfall of the season. The village courtyard was
crowded with villagers wrapped up in bulky winter clothes. The atmosphere was tense: An unusually large number of the township government
work team members were deployed, clearly marked police cars were
parked in the village courtyard, uniformed local police officers were
present to deter altercations, and a videotaping crew had been hired to
record the whole process. As the election proceedings commenced, confrontations broke out. First, loud, bitter voices were heard from the
crowd; then, two or three men emerged at the front of the crowd, where
Mr. Ren was presiding over the meeting. They pointed fingers at him and
demanded that he explain to the entire village why he had not secured the
kind of government aid that other villages had received. The shouts and
near-physical gestures were so fierce that the township government officials had to step in from time to time to calm both sides. As the shouting
was heard in waves, with one voice after another, Mr. Ren quietly advised
his supporters: "Don't pay attention to what is going on here, go and cast
your votes." An interesting scene ensued. At the center of the courtyard
the shouting continued, but on the other side, the voting line snaked
around the noisy crowd. Within a few hours, the township government
received an unequivocal message: Mr. Ren received the most votes (189

out of 341) in the preliminary election. His successful reelection in the formal election followed several weeks later. Soon thereafter, his challenger – the township-appointed village party secretary – resigned from his position, packed his belongings, and left the village.

* * *

After the conclusion of the village elections, Mr. Jin, the party secretary of the township government, declared the election season had been a great success. There were good reasons for self-congratulations – all villages except one had carried out elections and the new village governments were up and running. A tough job had been completed. With only a few exceptions, most elected village cadres were the same familiar faces that the township government had either already worked with or was willing to work with. Moreover, through the election process, several difficult cases – such as the governance crisis in Boulevard Village – were resolved to the satisfaction of the township government. Finally, and most importantly, there were no major incidents to threaten "social stability" and no petitions beyond the township boundaries.

As an outside observer, I too saw the elections as a success story, but for different reasons. In most cases, the procedures were meticulously implemented. On most occasions, official instructions were followed closely: beginning with the formation of the village election committee and moving through the voter certification, the two rounds of voting, and the process of counting, registering, and sealing the ballots. One particular scene stuck in my memory. Election time was approaching on a chilly morning in Willow Village courtyard, but the villagers were still in their houses or scattered in small gatherings far away. Facing an almost empty courtyard, the current village head – who had failed in the preliminary election a few days earlier – bravely began to read the script that the government had prepared for this special occasion:

Dear voter comrades:

On behalf of the village election committee, I now preside over today's election meeting. Starting on [insert date/month], formal candidates for the village committee in our village have been engaged [insert date/month]. Today, [insert date/month], in the village committee election, through broad communication and mobilization and the full participation of the voters, we are holding our election meeting to elect a new village committee.

To ensure the smooth progress of the election, I now announce the basic procedures ... for today's election.

The announcement, lingering in the cold sky, was broadcast over loudspeakers. Drawn by these pleading calls, villagers gradually converged in the village center, filling the courtyard with greetings, chatting, and laughter. As I listened and watched, I felt the solemn power of the formal procedures that was sustaining the institution of Chinese village elections.

Although these formal procedures were often ceremonial, the progress made over time was real and substantial. At the voting site in one village, a township cadre pointed to a nearby corner and told me: "I was here during the village election a few years ago. At that time, the villagers sat there, and they were given the ballots. Then someone walked among them and said, 'Let me fill out the ballot for you.' And he collected many ballots from these villagers and did just that. No one cared." But this time, right behind us, an empty room with doors on two sides was used for voting booths. Inside, three desks were set up far apart. Voters went through the checkpoint, where their voter certification cards were inspected, after which they headed into the room through one door, walked alone to one of the desks, filled out their ballots, and exited from the other door, casting their ballots on the way out.

How do we make sense of these different scenes of village elections? How have village elections evolved over time? In which direction? These are the issues I will address in the remainder of this chapter.

MULTIPLE LOGICS IN INSTITUTIONAL CHANGE

I begin with a sketch of the theoretical arguments that highlight the multiple logics in institutional change that shape the evolution of village elections in China. The premise of the proposed model is that institutional changes involve multifaceted processes and mechanisms and that these underlying mechanisms and their effects on institutional change must be understood in relation to one another. I further argue that these institutional logics take effect through their interactions with one another. Moreover, a focus on the institutional logics provides an analytical link between the macro-institutional configuration and the micro-behavior of those actors in a particular field. At the micro-level, institutions are patterned behaviors that involve both material and symbolic practices (Friedland and Alford 1991, Thornton and Ocasio 2008). Institutional changes take place through the behavior of those actors who have stakes and who are involved, willingly or unwillingly, in the change process. Hence, patterns of behavior at the micro-level shed light on the interplay of institutional logics in the change process. To provide a satisfactory account of institutional change, then, it is critical to understand why these actors behave in certain ways and how their behaviors interact with one another. Institutional logics entail concrete, observable behavioral consequences; by specifying the institutional logic in a particular field, we are able to account for and predict those behaviors, making institutional analyses tractable and analyzable at the empirical level.

The focus on the interplay among institutional logics also points to the need to pay particular attention to the endogenous processes in which the timing and patterns of interactions evolve and shape the subsequent path and trajectory of institutional change. The actual behaviors associated with these logics evolved over time, subject to interactions among these forces. One needs to move toward a "process-oriented" approach to institutional change in light of multiple mechanisms through their interactions with one another.

The proposed theoretical model thus directs our attention to the following analytical tasks: First, we need to identify the distinct institutional logics and their behavioral consequences in the process of change. Second, we need to examine the properties of the endogenous processes, such as the timing and changes in the patterns of interactions among these logics over time, as revealed in the behavior of the actors at the micro-level. Only in the concrete historical setting and through substantial institutional analyses can we demonstrate how these changes take place and the specific trajectory they take. Below, I turn to the first task of identifying and analyzing the multiple institutional logics involved in village elections.

Specifying the Institutional Logics in Village Elections

To gain a port of entry into the village election processes, let us turn to the common scenes in village election events in rural China. At every election site – usually in the courtyard of the village center – we would observe crowds of villagers who had come to cast their votes. Their mobilization and behavior constitute the very election process under study. Looking closely, we also find members of the work team from the township government standing in strategic positions, guarding the ballot booths, helping illiterate voters fill out their ballots, and directing voting traffic. Moreover, invisible but felt everywhere is the presence of the state and state policies. Indeed, every step in the election process – from the announcement of the election proceedings, voter registration, voting procedures, to the slogans posted at the election site – closely follow the directives from the central government. Emerging from these noisy and at times chaotic scenes, then, are three distinct groups of actors – the *villagers-as-voters*, the officials from the *township government*, and the pervasive presence of *the state and state policies*. As argued before, the behavior of these groups is governed by the distinct logics of the institutions that have shaped the evolution of village elections; hence, they are the analytical focus here. I now discuss these underlying institutional logics, paying particular attention to the behavioral consequences that are entailed.

The State Logic

That the state plays a central role in the emergence of village elections as an institution is well recognized. Village elections were initiated and promoted through a top-down process in legislation and enforcement, in which the central government was the major driving force. In every election cycle, the central government issued directives that set up the major parameters for the village elections, which led to further elaboration of the rules and procedures in the implementation process through governments at the provincial, municipal, county, and township levels. Indeed, if we place our analytical focus *narrowly* on state policies in the area of village elections (i.e., the series of administrative fiats on the organization of village elections), one may even find a consistent and active voice advocating democratic practices.

Such an analytical focus, however, would be too narrow and misleading. It is here that we need to attend to the state logic – the institutional arrangements of the central government and the policymaking processes that dictate the behavior and policies of the central authorities in Beijing. The Chinese state, like its counterparts in other societal contexts, is by no means monolithic. Instead, it is fragmented with multiple agencies, multiple and inconsistent goals, and competing interests (Lampton 1987, Lieberthal and Lampton 1992, Wilson 1989). This recognition points to several salient characteristics of the state logic. First, state policies toward village elections stem from a process of policymaking that involves competing interests among government agencies. Research shows that officials from the Ministry of Civil Affairs, the main agency in charge of village elections, are active in promoting village elections, whereas the Communist Party's Organization Department is deeply concerned about the detrimental effects of the village elections on the authority of the party in rural China (He 2007, Shi 1999). As a result, there are inevitable institutional contradictions in state policies toward village elections.

For example, the core principle of the village committee, "self-governance under the leadership of the Communist Party," reveals a profound contradiction in terms. That is, village elections and self-governance must fit into the party-state framework (O'Brien and Li 2000).

Another important aspect of the state logic is that, beyond the immediate village election arena, there are other spheres of state governance that impose incongruent demands and goals upon those who are implementing, or who are recipients of, state policies at the local levels. For example, state efforts to extract resources in the rural areas require effective bureaucratic mobilization and intervention into the villages, which are at odds with the principle of village self-governance in the institution of village elections. Therefore, recognition of the state logic leads us to take a broader view to examine how multiple goals and interests of government agencies and state policies in other areas exert inconsistent, even conflicting, effects on village elections.

The behavioral consequences of the state logic in the evolution of village elections need to be understood in this light. First, state policies toward village elections evolve amidst multiple, inconsistent, and often competing, goals. To focus narrowly on only one particular policy advocate (e.g., the official rhetoric), in only the immediate policy area (e.g., the village election area), and at only one point in time, would overlook the fundamental characteristics of the state logic and their effects on the behavior of those involved in the village elections. For those who participate in the village elections, the various policies induced by the state logic, at an aggregate level, are characteristic of the inconsistencies and shifts between spurts of advocacy, indifference, or even containment. I summarize this line of argument as follows: *The state logic dictates that state promotion of village elections is a function of multiple, conflicting goals and interests among agencies and groups. As a result, at the aggregate level, state policies toward village elections are inconsistent and shifting over time.*

Second, state policies also evolve in response to tensions and crises emerging from the election process. An important implication of the state logic is the presence of temporal political coalitions among multiple agencies or interests in the state apparatus (Shirk 1993). The maintenance of such coalitions depends on a key mechanism – feedback from the practice of village elections. Positive feedback – the reduction of political tensions and crises in the rural areas, the effectiveness of political control, and positive appraisals from the international community – would help maintain and strengthen the political coalition in this area and encourage further promotion of village elections, whereas negative feedback – increasing contention in the rural areas and the undermining of political control, among others – would weaken the political coalition and induce policy shifts in different directions. Thus: *State policies evolve in response to feedback from the implementation process. Positive feedback encourages the state to develop more elaborate policies and to strengthen enforcement, and vice versa.*

In summary, the state logic introduces both exogenous and endogenous factors to village elections: The presence of inconsistent even conflicting policies introduce the possibility of exogenous shocks outside of the immediate village election arena, whereas the feedback loop implies an endogenous process that can be best understood by looking into the interplay among state policies and other parties involved in the process of change over time. In this light, an explication of the state logic requires that we sharpen our analytical focus in two respects: First, we need to broaden our analysis of the state and state policies beyond the immediate area of village elections and attend to other policy areas and government agencies whose goals and policies may indirectly affect village elections. Second, we need to look closely into the ways in which the multitude of goals and interests reflected in policymaking interacts with the local governments and the villagers, to which we now turn.

The Bureaucratic Logic

State policies are implemented through the local governments. Although there is only a nominal role for local governments in the "Organic Law," local governments are nevertheless one of the key players, oftentimes the decisive player, in this process. The township government is the main organizer of the village elections in its jurisdiction: It decides on when, where, and how the village elections are to be carried out, and it sends its work teams into the villages to directly organize the elections, safeguarding the procedural rules. Empirical studies reveal a variety of government behaviors over time and across localities, ranging from imposition, manipulation, and indifference, to the active safeguarding of procedural fairness (Edin 2003, O'Brien and Li 1999, Perry and Goldman 2007). How do we make sense of the varieties of bureaucratic behavior in this area?

Varied as it may be, I submit, local cadre behavior follows a stable bureaucratic logic. Organizational behavior is induced by the incentive mechanisms in organizations and the environment to which they must adapt (Scott and Davis 2007). Local bureaucrats face a task environment consisting of multiple policies and administrative fiats to which they must respond or with which they must cope in their daily work. As I argue in Chapter 6, among the multiple goals that local officials face in their daily work, getting things done is the most important because of the dominance of the political logic. The centralization of authority in the Chinese bureaucracy implies that local bureaucrats heavily depend on their supervising agencies for evaluations, promotions, and other favorable career moves. The primary concerns of the chief bureaucrats in the township government are to implement the top-down policies such that there is no negative consequence for their own career advancement. Therefore, a key component of the bureaucratic logic is that: *Upward accountability and incentive designs in the Chinese bureaucracy are such that local bureaucrats are sensitive to the demands from above and the tasks imposed by their supervising administration.*

Yet, by the bureaucratic logic, we cannot derive the implication that local officials will follow and implement state policies *in the area of village elections*. Recall that the state logic implies that policies from the central government involve multiple tasks and multiple goals that are often incongruent, even in conflict, among themselves. Even if we confine our attention to only the area of village elections, we can easily see that local governments face multiple, conflicting goals. First, the act of carrying out a village election is itself a challenging task, since conflicts within a village may stall the election process, as has frequently occurred in the past; second, local officials also aim to facilitate the election or reelection of their favorite candidates so as to ensure smooth cooperation in the future; third, local officials are required to maintain "social stability" – a coded term meaning the avoidance of resistance, petitions, or open protests in the election process. These goals are inconsistent among themselves: An effort to promote favorite candidates may lead to villager resentment and protests that threaten the goal of "social stability." Moreover, if we look beyond the village elections, it is obvious that the implementation of village elections is but one of the many demands – such as family planning, public projects, or collective debt crises, among others – with which local bureaucrats have to cope.

Small wonder that local officials must weigh, balance, and prioritize among the multiple, inconsistent goals and tasks in their task environment. The bureaucratic logic dictates that officials will choose a course of action that can best promote their career advancement or at least that will best minimize the risks to their career advancement. These considerations give us the following proposition: *Local officials' disposition toward village elections is shaped by the relative costs and benefits associated with the implementation of a wide range of policies in their task environment.*

This proposition, mundane as it may be, has important implications. It directs our attention to the broader task environment of the local government to evaluate the payoffs associated with the choices that local officials face. To a great extent the role of local bureaucrats in village elections is contingent on the relationship between the township governments and the village cadres, which is dictated by the task environment surrounding the local bureaucrats. Local officials carry out a wide range of tasks imposed by state policies, such as the extraction of resources (e.g., collecting the agricultural tax), and the implementation of other state policies (e.g., family planning regulations), which require the effective cooperation of the village cadres. But the very principle of self-governance is likely to lead to the election of those village heads who may not be cooperative. Local officials have to cope with such tensions in their task environments. These considerations suggest that: *The closer the interdependence, dictated by the task environment, between the local government and the village cadres, the stronger the incentive for the township government to intervene in village elections, and vice versa.*

To sum up, although the bureaucratic logic is stable, specific bureaucratic behaviors vary significantly in response to changing task environments and incentives in the Chinese bureaucracy. The state logic involving multiple goals and tasks implies that local government officials must prioritize and give selective attention to various tasks in order to cope with environmental complexities. This recognition calls for a close look into the specific task environment that local bureaucrats confront to make sense of the changes in bureaucratic behavior patterns over time.

The Rural Logic

The institutional practice of village election dictates a particular role of villagers-as-voters – the one-person-one-vote, direct participation of every adult villager. However, villager behavior and participation in the public arena are not necessarily in accordance with the contemporary image of citizenship. Fundamentally, rural life is *not* organized around autonomous individuals. Rather, the logic of rural life organizes villagers into webs of social relations. One way to characterize the rural logic is what Fei (1992[1948]) calls "differential modes of association," which generate concomitant social circles with varying social distances on the basis of social institutions, such as family, extended family, neighborhood, and kinship ties. As China scholars have shown, such culturally embedded authority was historically significant in the organization of rural governance and interactions with the state (Duara 1988, Lin 1995, Yan1996). Despite socialist transformation, as Friedman, Pickowicz, and Selden (1991) show, these rural institutions survived the encroaching state during the collectivization era, being renewed and reinforced by everyday practice, through mutual assistance in daily life, in farming activities, and on social occasions such as weddings, funerals, and temple worship.

Land reform in post-Mao rural China reinforced the rural logic. In the era of decollectivization, rural land was allocated to the peasant family, which has reinforced the family, not individuals, as a decision-making unit. Indeed, the size of the allotted land, contingent on the number of adult laborers and the size of the family at the time, has provided the single most important basis on which economic, political, and social relations are established and reinforced. In many ways, state agricultural taxation has been largely based on the size of the land allocated to the family; similarly, contributions to collective village projects are usually calculated based on the size of the land allocated to the family. Economically, the family develops its division of labor among multiple tasks – farming, childrearing, off-farm work, and so forth. Social relations are reinforced through family-based mutual assistance in farming and on other social occasions such as weddings and funerals. Not surprisingly, patterns of social relations, cooperation as well as tensions, largely reflect the logic of rural life organized around family, kinship, and neighborhood.

Scholars have shown that local institutions may facilitate the provision of public goods, problem solving, or economic development in villages (Peng 2004, Tsai 2007). But the rural logic is a two-edged weapon, which may also generate fragmented and contending interests within a village. As a distinct organizing mechanism, the rural logic may be in tension with the formal institution of village elections. For example, family-based proxy votes have been widespread in elections. By the rural logic in which the family is the decision-making unit, such a practice is seen as reasonable and legitimate. As many young villagers now work as migrant workers far away from their home villages, their families want to have their voices represented in the election process. As a result, proxy voting practices have been a constant source of contention in the implementation of the one-person-one-vote procedures.

What are the behavioral consequences of the rural logic in village elections? The role of the rural logic is not static; it has evolved along with the emergence of the institution of village elections. In the early days of decollectivization, the rural logic was largely confined to the social and economic areas of village life – mutual assistance in daily social exchanges and farming activities – and it was not extended to village elections. But as village elections became more important in the villagers' lives, the rural logic provided the basis on which the villagers were mobilized. As a result, the rural logic has become more active and effective, as villagers have learned to better mobilize resources, coordinate activities, and organize interests. These considerations can be summarized as follows: *Over time, the rural logic becomes more active and salient in village election processes, in terms of increasingly autonomous voting participation and in terms of extending from the social and economic arenas into the political arena.*

The prevalence of the rural logic also amplifies village-bound variations in kinships, neighborhoods, and other social relations. In those villages where kinship organizations are less prevalent, the rural logic may be built on other corporate bases. For example, the collective legacy of the Mao era may facilitate the position of a strong village party secretary; or historical legacies and the revival of kinship institutions may generate leadership on a mixed basis combining political authority and kinship institutions. Therefore, *the rural logic is likely to exacerbate and perpetuate diversity in both the practice and effectiveness of village elections across villages.*

In brief, the rural logic reflects and draws on particularistic social relations and institutions in a village and, to a great extent, it evolves independent of, and often at odds with, the state logic or the bureaucratic logic outlined above. Hence, the rural logic implies a strong historical continuity that is stubbornly resistant to external intervention. It takes part in the evolution of village elections as a distinctive, independent organizing mechanism.

The recognition of these three logics and their interplay highlight some important implications for understanding village elections as an emergent institution and suggests that it would be inadequate and misleading to consider only one mechanism, without carefully attending to the interactions among these multiple logics and their behavioral consequences. Now I return to the research site of FS Township and take a more systematic look at the changes in the village elections over time, between 2000 and 2008, and illustrate how the multiple logics operated and interacted with one another to generate the observed patterns.

VILLAGE ELECTIONS IN FS TOWNSHIP: CHANGES OVER TIME

The Context and Overall Patterns

What are the markers that we should use to track and assess the extent of institutional change in village elections? Researchers have examined different aspects of this institution, from voter turnout rate and procedural fairness to competitiveness and the function of the elected village committees. I will focus on the following aspects: first, *the extent of participation.* Democratic elections involve the participation of ordinary citizens; hence, the voter turnout rate is an important measure of the effectiveness of electoral politics. Second, *competitiveness among the candidates.* Here the main concern is about the threat of government manipulation whereby a candidate is put forth without serious contention. The more competition that exists among the candidates, the more likely is it that the elections are free from manipulation.[1]

Third, a key issue in village elections is *the relationship between the two lines of authority – the village head and the party secretary.* Although nominally elected by the party members in the village and approved by the township government, village party secretaries are in effect appointed and controlled by the township government. In contrast, members of the village committee, including the village head, are elected by popular vote in village election. Therefore, the village head and the party secretary represent two lines of authority with distinct bases of legitimacy: The former is based on bottom-up popular support, and the latter is based on top-down government imposition. Historically, villages during the socialist collective era (the "production brigade" as they were then called) were organized into a people's commune. It was conventional then that the village party secretary wielded power, with the village head (the head of the production brigade) playing the role of second fiddle. This practice continued into the post-Mao decollectivization era. Therefore, one important indicator of the effectiveness of village elections is the extent to which the relationship between the two lines of authority has evolved. In the late 2000s, in response to tensions between the party secretary (*cunzhishu*) and the elected village head (*cunzhuren*), the central

---

[1] Admittedly, the meaning of competition is elusive. In some villages, the lack of competition may reflect government meddling or kinship-based mobilization; in others, it may be due to a high consensus among the villagers regarding the candidate. In either case, however, variations in this indicator over time are suggestive about the overall trend of change.

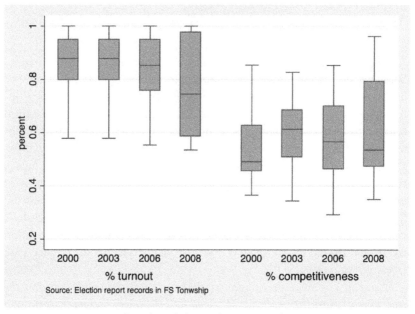

FIGURE 10.1. Boxplot of share of turnout and competitiveness

government has advocated the so-called "one-shoulder" (*yijiantiao*)
policy; that is, occupancy of both positions by the same person. This
policy has important consequences for village elections, as we will illustrate below.

My analysis focuses on elections *after* the amendment of the "Organic
Law" in 1998, when the formalization and enforcement of village elections were greatly strengthened.[2] Figure 10.1 shows changes in the turnout rate and competitiveness across the four elections cycles between
2000 and 2008.[3] Here, "percent turnout" is measured as the percentage
of eligible voters in a village who actually cast their votes in an election;
"percent competitiveness" is measured as the percentage of votes that the
elected village head received out of the total number of eligible voters. The
higher the percentage, the lower the competitiveness. As we can see, over
time the level of participation has changed considerably. In the early days

---

[2] In FS Township, both local cadres and villagers view the passage of the amended "Organic
Law" in 1998 as the beginning of the *real* election era, because elections before that time
were largely symbolic and decidedly controlled by the township government.

[3] Data for the figures in this study come from the archives of village election records between
2000 and 2008, compiled by FS Township government.

when the local government exerted strong control, the turnout rate was high and variation was low across villages. Across the first three election cycles, the mean rate of participation was over eighty percent. But there were significant changes in the last two cycles, especially in 2008, with noticeably greater variations in participation across villages. The trend of competitiveness shows a similar trend of increasing variation over the years. In the early phase of 2000, the elected village head received a lower percentage of votes than in the later years, with lower variations across villages, indicating a more homogeneous but lower level of popular support for those candidates who were promoted by the township government. In contrast, by 2008 the level of competitiveness was considerably higher than in the previous years, with much larger variations across villages. Clearly, there are significant changes in both the turnout rate and competitiveness over the four election cycles.

Let us now take a look at the relationship between the two lines of authority across village elections. Figure 10.2 shows, across the four election cycles, the proportion of the three types of elected village head: (1) the "one-shoulder" position, where one person "shoulders" both the party secretary and the village head positions; (2) being elected as village head only – often an indication of a popular leader independent of

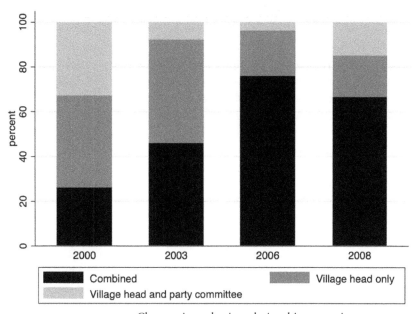

FIGURE 10.2. Changes in authority relationships over time

the party secretary; (3) being a village head and, at the same time, also serving as a member of the village party committee. Again, we find significant variations over time, indicating important dynamics of change in the relationship between the two lines of authority. I will provide substantive interpretations of these patterns below.

Tracking changes along these markers over time, we observe the evolution of village elections as an emergent institution: Over the years, village elections have become more substantive and meaningful, mirroring the increasingly intensive competitiveness, diversity, and non-linear paths of change among these villages. I now turn to discuss, in chronological order, how the consideration of multiple institutional logics helps us to account for the observed patterns of change in village elections, and the implications for studying the processes of institutional change in general.

2000: The Manipulated Election

The first election cycle after adoption of the amended "Organic Law" took place in 2000. By 2000, rural China had experienced two decades of decollectivization, which returned farming decisions to the peasant households. However, the Communist Party's political dominance was still unrivaled; local governments played an active role in implementing state policies – collecting agricultural taxes, enforcing family planning regulations, and engaging in various public projects. Village cadres, led by the party secretary, forged close ties with the township government. At the same time, the rural logic, long suppressed during the collective era (Friedman, Pickowicz and Selden 1991) became active in the economic and social arenas by coordinating farming and social events, but it had not yet been extended to the political arena.

What was the role of the state in village elections at this juncture? The state logic outlined above suggests that state policies reflect multiple and conflicting goals and interests. This was indeed the case. If we only look at state policies in the area of village elections, we would get the impression of strong policy advocacy for village self-governance: Building on the momentum of the recent passage of the amended "Organic Law," the proponents of village elections in the central government (especially those in the Ministry of Civil Affairs) actively mobilized for enforcement of the "Organic Law," with detailed procedures and regulations developed and elaborated upon through various levels of the local governments. The main message was loud and clear: Village elections should follow the formal procedures prescribed in the "Organic Law," and village affairs should be managed by self-governance through the elected village committee. But this was not the only voice. There were other, even louder, "voices" from other parts of the central government, in the form of other policies and bureaucratic fiats that ran counter to the very principle of village self-governance. This was also the period when the state exerted strong efforts to extract resources from the rural areas through taxation and other fees, and state policies in other areas such as family planning also pushed local governments deep into village affairs.

On the ground, then, local bureaucrats faced a task environment characterized by multiple and conflicting goals. In addition to the task of village elections, local governments faced more urgent pressures from above – to actively collect agricultural taxes, to enforce family planning, and to carry out other public projects – all of which required effective cooperation from the village cadres. These tasks entailed competing goals: Whereas village elections aimed at promoting autonomous village leaders to manage village affairs, other government tasks demanded more compliance from village leaders in the implementation of state policies.

How did the township government respond to these inconsistent demands in its task environment? The bureaucratic logic dictates that local officials prioritize and weigh among the multiple tasks in accordance with their prospects for career advancement or avoidance of severe penalties that might stall their careers. This was not a difficult choice for local bureaucrats. Above all, effective control of village affairs, and hence control of village elections, was critical for township governments, because the fiscal policy of the time dictated that the collection of agricultural taxes and fees would be the main source of the local government budget. During this early phase of village elections, as noted above, the legacy of the collective era still exerted a strong influence. Within the village, the party secretary was the center of authority, and the elected village committee, together with the village head, played at best the role of second fiddle. Moreover, long suppressed during the collectivization era, the kinship-based rural logic was not yet activated in the political sphere of electoral competition. All in all, there was little cost but great benefit for the township government to intervene in the election process and to shape its outcome.

Thus, the township government made all-out efforts to intervene and shape the outcomes of the village elections. In almost all cases, the township government handpicked the key candidates for the village committee and the township government work team actively promoted these candidates during the village election meetings. In the immediate aftermath of the collective era, villagers were generally receptive to government advocacy.

What emerged from this episode was a pattern of village election processes and outcomes that represented a strong continuity with the past, with the party secretary still at the center of authority and the village elections largely a symbolic gesture. This was clearly reflected in the election patterns. On the one hand, as Panel 1 in Figure 10.1 shows, there was a high turnout rate (over eighty percent) with small variance across villages and a highly homogenous pattern resulting from the strong grip of the township government over the election process. On the other hand, the elected village head received a low number of votes, reflecting passive involvement and a low level of popular support among the villagers.

As a legacy of the collective era, it was conventional practice at the time that the position of party secretary and that of village head were separate and would be occupied by two separate persons. The first panel of Figure 10.2 shows that, of the twenty-seven villages, the share of villages where one person held the "one shoulder" position was small. Party secretaries in ten villages did not even participate in the village election. Party secretaries did participate in the elections in the other seventeen villages, but in most cases their presence as candidates was merely a token to make up the requirement of multiple candidates for each position. Only seven party secretaries (mostly in small villages where there was a tradition of one person taking the positions of both party secretary and village head) were elected to be the head of the village committee. Those party secretaries who were not elected to be the village head did not lose the elections; rather, the candidates for village heads were handpicked by the township government and by the party secretaries in these villages. A close look at the election records shows that in some villages, the party secretaries received a higher number of votes during the preliminary election but they persuaded the villagers to vote for their handpicked candidates for village head during the second round. This interpretation is consistent with the fact that nine village heads were also members of the party committee under the leadership of the party secretary, a common practice in the collective era.

To put these patterns in the larger context, the election cycle of 2000 was characterized by a continuation of the traditional patterns of party dominance embodied in the active role of local governments, with the state logic characterized by multiple and competing goals and interests, and minimal involvement of the rural logic. These institutional conditions created the task environment and set the parameters of the costs and benefits for the local bureaucrats to prioritize and balance their multiple tasks. Under these circumstances, the bureaucratic logic led to an active role of the township government in the village election processes and in manipulating the election outcomes. In hindsight, however, the manipulated elections had two important, unintended consequences: First, the fact that the village elections showed a strong institutional continuity provided positive feedback, and much-needed reassurance, to the central government for the maintenance of a political coalition to continue the promotion of village elections. Second, symbolic as these election events were at the time, the rules and procedures of the elections, along with the expectations and opportunities, were being practiced and institutionalized, providing a stable and recurrent occasion for future interactions among these multiple logics.

2003: The Contentious Election

By 2003, rural China had entered a period of contention and resistance. State efforts to extract resources had induced an active role for local governments and village cadres and, at the same time, they fermented tensions between local authorities and villagers. Nationwide, both the abuse of power and open protests against local authorities were on the rise. In FS Township, a sharp increase in agricultural taxes and fees in the late 1990s led to widespread popular protests in the villages. By the early 2000s, the township government was unable to collect agricultural taxes in one-third of the villages, and it collected only some of the taxes in another one-third of the villages.

Not surprisingly, the 2003 election echoed the larger, contentious context. As villagers protested against taxation and the abuse of power by local authorities, village elections became one of the very few legitimate opportunities through which they could voice their grievances and seek leaders who could represent their interests. On the one hand, these efforts led to an extension of the rural logic to the political arena, triggering active mobilization among families and kinships in the village elections. On the other hand, rising contention created tremendous challenges for the township government to carry out state policies. Given the demanding tasks of tax collection imposed from above, coupled with the increasing resistance from below, the township government made even greater efforts to ensure the desirable outcomes of the village elections. In this context, it was inevitable local bureaucrats and villagers were on a collision course and there would be serious crashes between the two.

As the above case of Bao Village shows, the party secretary's bullying behavior in the village triggered a popular protest led by villager Mr. Ren. Through a series of petitions and open confrontations, the township government was forced to remove the village party secretary, toppling both the party committee and the village committee. In the ensuing village election of 2003, Ren challenged the township government manipulation and ran his own campaign for village committee. He defiantly announced over loudspeakers that, if elected, he would lead the villagers to resist the government tax collection. Thus, he was elected to head an entirely new village committee.

This instance was not an isolated case. Such tensions and confrontations were present in other villages as well. As we see in Figure 10.1, although the turnout rate in 2003 was similar to that in 2000, there was a significant increase in popular support for the village head. To interpret this pattern, note that, as shown in Panel 2 of Figure 10.2, the percentage of stand-alone village heads increased significantly in 2003, as did the percentage of "one-shoulder" roles, because the township government made an effort to take control in some villages. Of the twenty-seven villages in FS Township, fifteen (fifty-six percent) of the village heads were replaced. The outcomes were heterogeneous: Some reflected successful government manipulation, but a much larger proportion resulted from challengers, as exemplified by Mr. Ren, running in defiance of government meddling. Compared with the previous episodes, the year 2003 marked a significant change in village elections – from a ceremonial occasion to a substantial and contentious event, and a change in the villagers – from passive to active participants.

In this episode we saw the active involvement of local bureaucrats, village cadres, and villagers. Let us now make sense of such behavior by considering the interplay of the multiple logics involved. As alluded to before, the active involvement of the local bureaucrats was dictated by the bureaucratic logic in that the heavy tasks dictated by state policies reinforced the interdependence of the township government and the village cadres, thereby providing an incentive for local governments to actively seek and promote their favorite candidates in the village elections. At the same time, tensions in the rural areas activated the rural logic in defiance of the local governments, and the village elections provided an opportunity for the villagers to legitimately mobilize and to voice their grievances. In this process, the rural logic gained momentum, partly due to the fact that the occasion of a routinized election provided an enlarged public space for political action and partly because repeated participation in the elections increased the villagers' awareness of their collective voices. Activation of the rural logic also increased the cost of government manipulation, as open protests and petitions seriously challenged the ability of the local authorities to govern.

Ironically, both the township government and the discontented villagers found support from the state – or dissonant voices in the state. Local officials derived their authority from the intrusive state to intervene in village affairs, whereas rebellious villagers often evoked the rules and procedures in the "Organic Law" and related state policies to challenge the meddling attempts by the township government (O'Brien and Li 2006). As one official recalled: "These villagers often know more about the election regulations than we cadres know. They can challenge us if we are not careful about what we say or do." The state logic, with its multiple goals and voices, fueled conflicts among villagers, village cadres, and local governments, unwittingly fostering a governance crisis in the rural areas.

One significant consequence of the 2003 election cycle was the rising tensions between the two authority lines in the village – the village committee and the village party committee. As a large number of independent village heads were elected into office, relationships between the village head and the village party secretary faced considerable strains, casting a long shadow on rural governance even after the village elections were over. These tensions, echoing ongoing contention and protests in the rural areas, sowed the seeds for future changes in rural China.

2006: Safeguarding Procedural Fairness

By 2006, major changes had taken place in the rural areas that significantly altered the institutional context of village elections. In particular, the succession of top leaders in the central government – the new leadership under Hu Jintao as general secretary of the Communist Party and Wen Jiabao as premier – led to a series of policy reorientations, including the abolition of the agricultural taxes and other fees in the rural areas. These policy changes had several important consequences: (1) Tensions in the rural areas, especially between local governments and villagers, were greatly reduced; (2) the interdependence of the township government and the village cadres was significantly weakened. Although these policy changes were made with no consideration at all of the village elections, their impacts on the village elections were felt immediately, as we see below.

One important policy change in 2006 was promotion of the "one-shoulder" policy – advocacy of one person occupying the positions of both party secretary and village head. This was largely an improvised response of the central authorities to tensions and conflicts between the two lines of authority in village governance during the previous years, but it had important consequences. Because the village elections were no longer controlled by the township government, compliance with the "one-shoulder" policy meant that the voice of the person popularly elected as the village head was now given more weight in the choice of the party secretary. In other words, the choice of the party secretary was now linked to one's popular vote in the village elections. This rendered more legitimacy to the village elections and also posed a threat to those party secretaries who could not win the popular vote in the village elections. More importantly, this policy constrained the township government's authority to select the village party secretary.

These institutional conditions led to significant changes in the task environment of the local government, hence in its ensuing bureaucratic behavior. Abolition of the agricultural taxes and fees meant that the township government no longer had to rely on the village cadres to carry out the most challenging tasks in the villages; in fact, there were few tasks that involved interactions between the township government and the village cadres. Moreover, the emphasis on "social stability" by the new leadership became a priority among the multiple tasks that dictated bureaucratic behavior, further discouraging the local government from intervening in village affairs and thus possibly avoiding the triggering of confrontations and protests.

At the same time, the active rural logic greatly increased the cost of government manipulation. Through repeated village elections, by 2006 villagers came to recognize that village elections did matter and elected village cadres played an important role in decision-making, and that village elections were a viable channel to voice their complaints and to challenge those cadres who had lost their trust. As a result, there was active mobilization among the villagers in the election processes, and the rural logic became increasingly effective and assertive. As one village head put it: "If I want, I can easily get reelected. I have been helping folks in the village for all these years. In the last three years, I was involved in the funerals for several dozen families. Each family has at least twenty-some kinship members, and they can be easily brought to vote for me."

Under these changing institutional conditions, the bureaucratic logic induced the township government to make a significant change in prioritizing its tasks and to shift from active intervention to the role of safeguarding procedural integrity. Procedural fairness was used as a weapon for maintaining "social stability." The township government adopted a wide range of tactics – the presence of police cars, uniformed policemen, video-taping, work team arrangements, and so forth – to intimidate and deter the potential disruption of the election proceedings and to ensure smooth completion of the election process. Along with this shift, the township government adopted a new disposition toward the village elections. First, there was an emphasis on procedural fairness. It is interesting to note that the township officials came to use procedural fairness as a deterrence weapon to ensure that the village elections were successfully carried out and to deter those protestors from interrupting the election proceedings. This was done even at the expense of their preferred candidates. Second, although the township government still tried to promote their own candidates, they were refrained from directly intervening or overtly manipulating the results. In fact, a frequently used open statement made by the government work teams at the village election meetings was as follows: "We are here to ensure procedural fairness; we do not care about who gets elected. You voters make that choice." In the few cases where the government tried to manipulate the results, none were successful. In one village the villagers reelected the village head despite various efforts by the township government to discredit him. In another village, villagers insisted that the township government address the problems in the village before they would participate in the election.

One important consequence of the 2006 election was a shift in the authority relationship between the village head and the party secretary. As the rural logic became more salient, we observed a larger variation in both the turnout rate and popular support across villages, as shown in the pattern observed in Figure 10.1. Moreover, as Panel 3 in Figure 10.2 shows, a large number of elected village heads also assumed the party secretary position. Eight (thirty percent) of the party heads came from the candidates who were elected to be village heads, not from the party heads. Among the newly elected village heads, eighty percent of them eventually (i.e., within their three-year duration as village head) assumed the position of party secretary in their respective villages. In other words, the new "one-shoulder" policy significantly shifted the center of authority from a top-down appointment to a bottom-up election, from the party secretary position to the village head position. These patterns occurred in tandem with the broader shift in the role of the township government from manipulating outcomes to safeguarding procedures, and with a more assertive role of the rural logic in the election process. These major changes were induced by the interplay among the multiple logics as well as by significant changes in state policies that were not immediately related to village elections.

2008: The Year of Readjustment

The next election cycle, due in the spring of 2009, occurred a few months early, in late December 2008. The general trend of government withdrawal from village affairs had continued since 2006. The township government was charged with the new tasks of developing commercial centers and other nonagricultural sectors in the township. At a township government meeting in 2007, the message of the township party secretary to the village heads was loud and clear: "Now that the state will no longer ask for anything from your village, we [the township government] do not have many tasks for you to do. All you have to do is to manage your village affairs well and maintain social stability." This was clearly indicative of the further weakening of the interdependence between the township government and the village cadres.

This is not to say that the township government was merely a bystander in village elections. After all, it still had responsibility to see to it that the village elections were carried out smoothly, and local officials still had to work with the elected village cadres on a range of issues: land development, the infusion of government resources into the village, and social stability. Furthermore, the township government still faced high uncertainty from the village elections – potential disruptions of the election process, the selection of unfavorable village heads, or confrontation and conflicts that might spill over to open petitions and protests. The higher authorities continued to advocate the "one-shoulder" policy of combining the position of party secretary and village head into one person, with a policy target of eighty percent. Thus, the township officials made considerable efforts to work behind the scenes and, as usual, they organized work teams for the election.

Against this larger context, several important changes characterized the 2008 village election cycle in FS Township. First, unlike during the previous election cycles when there was a high frequency of grievous villagers trying to disrupt the village elections in order to have their voices heard, in 2008 almost all the villages experienced smooth election processes without major disruptions. One government official characterized this new situation as "order-based competition" (*youxu jingzheng*). In the early days, village elections were seen as being manipulated by the local government; hence, grievous villagers wanted to disrupt this process to draw attention to their cause. By 2008 villagers accepted the elections as a legitimate occasion to compete and challenge the village authorities through formal procedures. On this account, both the local government and the villagers came to embrace the institution of village election.

Second, as seen in Figure 10.1, we have also witnessed marked variations in the turnout rate and in the competitiveness across villages. In some villages, the candidates were not controversial, and there was a high turnout rate and a smooth election process. In others the election was intense and contentious, over the selection of the candidates and the implementation of the formal election procedures. During my field observations, I also found considerable variations – often the same procedure was implemented in widely different ways even in two neighboring villages. Interestingly, the extent to which the election procedures were implemented followed a predictable pattern: The more competitive the election was, the more strictly the procedures were implemented. In one village where there were threats of disruption on the part of the challenger, the township government and the incumbent village committee made sure that the election procedures were followed to the letter. For example, it was required that all absentee ballots went through a formal process of proxy vote registration. Additionally, information about the registered proxy vote representation was posted on a wall for public review. In contrast, in another village not far away but where there were no threats of disputes, the formal procedures were largely ignored. Proxy voting was carried out unchecked, with one person carrying seven or eight proxy votes, well beyond the official limit of no more than two proxy votes, and without the required proxy vote registration. To a large extent, such variations reflect the diverse paths of governance across villages, indicative of the dual trends of the declining influence of the township government and the increasing assertiveness of the rural logic.

Finally, we also observed tensions between the party secretary and the village head positions, as shown in Panel 4 of Figure 10.2, where there is a drop in the percentage of "one-shoulder" positions in the 2008 election. On the one hand, the "one-shoulder" policy still exerted strong pressures on those party secretaries who could not win the popular vote in the village elections. In one village, the party secretary stood for village election but did not receive enough votes to move beyond the preliminary round of the election. As a result, he quit his position as party secretary. On the other hand, tensions between the township government and the elected village heads also loomed large. Whereas ninety percent of the new village heads eventually took over the position of party secretary in 2006, fewer than twenty percent did so in the 2008 election. The field research shows that this pattern largely resulted from the fact that the increasing dominance of the rural logic had led to the election of those village heads who were unacceptable to the township government, reflecting the tensions between the township government on the one hand and the more autonomous village head on the other. As a result, the actual percentage of "one-shoulder" positions (sixty-seven percent) was well below the eighty percent policy target.

Making Sense of the Patterns and Trajectories

Over the last two decades, especially since 2000, village elections in this small corner of rural China have undergone years of government manipulation, popular contention, a significant turn toward procedural fairness in 2006, and finally arriving at the phase of so-called "order-based competition" in 2008. One characteristic of this process of change is that, over time, the township government gradually loosened its grip on the election processes and, at the same time, there was a corresponding increase in the salience of the rural logic moving to the foreground on the election stage. These two trends were both propelled by and fed back into state policies, which underwent a series of adjustments during this period. Attention to the context and the interplay of the multiple logics helps us to make sense of the observed patterns. During the early years when traditional government control was strong, the stable institutional conditions produced a pattern characteristic of local government domination, as reflected in the more homogeneous behavior among the villages and the low variation in both participation and competitiveness. However, over time, changes in state policies (e.g., abolition of the agricultural taxes) and activation of the rural logic significantly changed the task environment as well as the costs and benefits associated with local government intervention, leading to new patterns of interactions among the institutional logics. As a result, variations across villages became more pronounced, generating greater divergence in both participation and competitiveness across villages.

The process of institutional change is by no means linear, nor does it always evolve in the same direction. As noted above, a key indicator is the relationship between the two lines of authority – village head versus party secretary – in a village. During the early years when the party secretary wielded power in village governance, the percentage of "one-shoulder" positions was low. This pattern changed significantly in 2006, when there was a significant shift of authority from the position of party head to the position of village head, but it leveled off in the 2008 election. Over time, the share of change in the village head also decreased, as more elected village heads came to office and were subsequently reelected. In particular, those instances of an "authority shift" – that is, a candidate was first elected as village head, but then took over the job of party secretary – are especially informative because they were directly related to the shifts in authority from the party to the elected village head. The pattern shows that this shift was the most pronounced in 2006, when eighty percent (five out of six) of the newly elected village heads assumed the position of party head; in contrast in 2008 the situation was reversed, with only seventeen percent (one out of six) of the newly elected village heads being given the position of party head. The stagnation in the implementation of the "one-shoulder" policy in the 2008 election reflects the fact that the more assertive rural logic was leading to the election of new village heads who were seen as suspect by the township officials. As a result, the township government insisted on appointing those whom it trusted as party secretary, even at the expense of not meeting the "one-shoulder" policy target, an indication of the increasing tensions between the bureaucratic logic and the rural logic.

Village elections are not flawless nor do they fit nicely into the ideal model of democracy, however that is defined. There are still bribes, slanders, and occasionally physical confrontations in the election processes. The local government has been and continues to be actively involved in the election, guarding the procedures but also imposing its will whenever the circumstances allow. These flaws and variations notwithstanding, village elections as an emergent institution have evolved to become a widely accepted institutional practice, associated with specific rules and procedures as well as specific expectations and participation. Moreover, as the 2008 elections show, new tensions and problems emerged over time in the process of change, triggering a further interplay of the multiple logics in the evolution of village elections as an emergent institution.

SUMMARY

In this chapter, I have focused on village elections as an emerging institution to develop a model that places the multiple institutional logics in the processes of institutional change. I illustrate the research issues and theoretical arguments in a case study of village elections in an agricultural town in northern China. I take advantage of the case study methodology to gain a deeper understanding of the involved dynamic processes and actors so as to see the evolution of the village elections in FS Township as a microcosm of institutional change in China.

As Mahoney and Thelen (2009, p. 3) write: "If theorizing is going to reach its potential, however, institutional analysis must go beyond classification to develop causal propositions that locate the sources of institutional change – sources that are not simply exogenous shocks or environmental shifts." I hope the case study in this chapter can shed light on, and speak to, larger issues about the sources and processes of change in the institutional logic of governance in China. Like Chapter 9 on road construction, this chapter again demonstrates the dynamics of the interplay between local governments and the logic of grassroots society in China's governance. I now take stock of what we have learned from this episode about the multiple processes involved in governing China.

First, at the core of my argument is an insistence that we take into consideration the multiple logics underlying the state, the local bureaucracy, and the villagers, and that we understand their roles in relation to one another. As we have shown, the effectiveness of the three institutional logics in village elections are interrelated. For those in the central government to maintain a political coalition to promote village elections, positive feedback from the implementation process based on interactions between the bureaucratic logic and the rural logic is required. Similarly, we cannot account for the changes in the behavior of local bureaucrats without paying attention to their interactions with the state logic, which establishes the parameters of the costs and benefits associated with their tasks, and the activation of the rural logic, which changes the costs of government meddling in the village elections. Therefore, instead of "isolating" or "teasing out" one mechanism or another, it is critical to take seriously the interplay among these multiple processes and mechanisms.

Second, the proposed model highlights the patterns of interactions at the micro-level by focusing on the behavioral consequences of the institutional logics. Consider the bureaucratic logic and its behavioral implications. During the four election cycles described above, the role of the township government changed most dramatically, largely as a response to the changes in the task environment and they can be explained by the bureaucratic logic. By theorizing about the links between the institutional logics and their behavioral implications, we are able to make sense of the observed changes in bureaucratic behavior.

Third, a focus on the interplay among multiple logics also calls attention to the endogenous processes of change. For example, an analysis of the state logic alone does not provide an explanation as to why and how state policies and dispositions toward village elections evolved over time. The feedback from the election events at the local level, that induced state policies to evolve in certain ways (e.g., adoption of the "one-shoulder" policy), in turn affected the behavior of local bureaucrats and villagers during the next round of interactions. As a result, the patterns of inter-actions among these institutional logics evolved considerably over time.

Finally, let me note that, in the Xi Jinping's era, the role of the party secretary and the party committee has been greatly strengthened. Along with this general trend, village elections have receded from center stage in rural governance, a reversal of the general trend depicted during the past two decades. Again, it is those changes in state policies in unrelated areas that provided the most important impetus for changes in village elections. This is a somber reminder that we need to pay attention to broader contexts in which these institutional logics are situated and sustained to understand the sources of institutional change.

I I

Unorganized Interests and Collective Action

> We shall know that a new era has begun not when a new elite holds power
> or a new constitution appears, but when ordinary people begin contending
> for their interests in new ways.
>
> Charles Tilly (1986, p. 9)

In this chapter, I examine the relationship between the institutional logic of
governance and patterns of popular contention and resistance in contemporary China. As Tilly (1986) points out, forms of contention provide important
information not only about how the society has been governed but also on
the extent of changes in the underlying logic of governance. Indeed, the
fundamental tension between the centralization of authority and effective,
local governance evolves and is often intensified in response to grass-roots
inputs from the society. Different forms of collective resistance have been
widespread in China, and they have even become more visible and on a
larger scale in the post-Mao era (Cai 2010, Chen 2009, Chen 2012, Zhou
and Ai 2016). A closer look at collective action from the bottom-up provides
clues about how China is governed and the response by the resistance.

I focus on a particular class of collective action based on unorganized
interests. The popular uprisings in China and Eastern Europe in 1989 are
recent examples of the "power of the powerless" in the state socialist
societies. But the current literature on collective action, which emphasizes
organizing capacity, resource mobilization, and interest articulation, is
not prepared to account for such events under state socialism. In typical
socialist states, society consists of unorganized interests that contrast
with the organizational apparatus of the state. China, for example, saw
minimal autonomous organizing efforts prior to the outbreak of the 1989

pro-democracy movement. The lack of strategic maneuvering and the prevalence of conflicts among student leaders illustrate the unorganized nature of the movement. Nonetheless, within a short time, millions of people across the nation poured into the streets. The participants cut across the boundaries of work units, localities, and social groups. The 1989 pro-democracy movement, although the most spectacular, was by no means an isolated event. Instances abound of mass mobilizations initiated by the Chinese state that eventually went beyond state control and became a challenge to the state.

How can we explain collective action based on unorganized interests in the state socialist context? My central theme is that the formation and outbreak of collective action are rooted in the particular institutional structure of the state–society relationship. I argue that collective action in China is less a process of purposive and rational organizing than an aggregation of large numbers of spontaneous individual behaviors produced by the particular state–society relationship. Although individuals are unorganized, their actions in pursuit of their own self-interests tend to convey similar claims, share similar patterns, and point to the state, that is, they "converge" into collective action. We need to understand collective action in light of the institutional logic of governance; conversely, making sense of the former also helps us better understand the latter.

THE CHINESE BODY POLITIC AND THE LOGIC OF COLLECTIVE ACTION

Marx (1963[1852]) argued that French peasants of the nineteenth century shared the same economic situation and had the same political demands among themselves. But the lack of communication and organic links among the peasants led to isolated and unorganized interests; peasants formed "a class of itself" but not "a class for itself." More than a century later, Chinese citizens are far more organically integrated into the national system and more interrelated with each other than were the French peasants. In terms of self-organization, however, the Chinese are no better than the French peasants. From the metropolis to the rural area, social life in China has been organized by a state bureaucratic system (Parish and Whyte 1978, Whyte and Parish 1984). Accompanying the state organizational apparatus are political sanctions such as political labeling, monitoring, and campaigns that systematically repress and deter opposition to the state (White 1989). Thus, the state has effectively monopolized the resources for social mobilization and denied the legitimacy of any organized interests outside of its control.

At the same time, "the positive incentives offered for compliance" (Walder 1986, p. 6) in the so-called "workunit-ownership system" *(danwei suoyouzhi)* tie workers to their workplaces, peasants to their villages, and individuals to their "work units." Work units function not only as the state apparatus of political control but also as redistributing agencies in which rewards and opportunities are linked to the political attitudes and loyalty of individuals. One consequence of this institutional structure is the prevalence of a clientelist system for individuals to pursue their interests by cultivating social ties and political loyalty with those of higher status and power (Walder 1987, p. 47). In contrast to "civil society," in which autonomous groups are formed and interests are articulated through the political process, the counterpart in China can best be labeled "subordinate society." The populace constitutes society, but it does not constitute an organized political force countervailing the state.

To students of collective action, particularly those who take a "resource mobilization" approach, the Chinese polity appears to present formidable obstacles to collective action opposing the state. If the success of collective action depends on the strategy adopted, the extent to which interests are organized (Gamson 1968), or on a social movement "industry" (Zald and McCarthy 1987), China is a puzzle. The absence of organized interests makes it impossible to identify stable interest groups or to find some systematic distribution of rewards or sanctions that would motivate individuals to join in collective action. The state has kept the cost of organized resistance high and positive incentives based on work units have eroded the basis for social mobilization by encouraging individuals to pursue personal interests through particularism rather than through collective action. As Walder (1986, p. 19) argues, the Chinese state has an "extraordinary ability to prevent organized political activities even from reaching the stage of collective action."

However, to understand mass mobilization in China the logic of collective action cannot be uncritically accepted from a literature that has been largely built on non-state socialist (mainly Western) experience. Two assumptions in various theories of collective action seem particularly problematic in this regard: (1) that there is a separation between the public realm and the private realm; and (2) that individual activities in the private realm involve market-like transactions.

Olson (1965) argues that when individuals calculate the costs and benefits of participating in collective action, they compare the option of participation with the opportunity cost incurred by deferring the pursuit of individual interests without collective action. This assumption is spelled out by Hirschman (1982), who holds that the separation of the private and public realms leads to cycles of involvement in collective action. On the one hand, when individuals find that their self-interests can be satisfied by engaging in activities in the private arena, they are unlikely to participate in collective action. On the other hand, frustrations and dissatisfactions over issues in the public realm often lead to changes in individuals' preferences that push them to collective action. The private sphere thus offers an exit from public life and hence from collective action.

The presence of a market economy also reduces the probability of collective action. The basic feature of market transactions is an equilibrium between supply and demand among individuals engaged in market activities. Individuals enter the private arena with divergent demands and preferences. Given the individuals' rational calculations, transactions tend to produce a market-like solution to their self-interests. In terms of political analysis, this is a process through which individuals' pursuit of their self-interests will compensate for each other so that collective action is impossible or unnecessary.

Both of the above assumptions fail miserably in the Chinese context. The boundary between the public and private arenas, if it exists at all, does not prevent state intervention into the individual's everyday life. "The penetration of the state into all realms of life did not extend a public sphere so much as negate it, for without attachment to the party or one of its subsidiary organizations no particular individual could make claims with any general validity" (Stark 1989, p. 22). Moreover, students of comparative politics have noted "the importance of the nonmarket economy in shaping a pattern of social and political relationships unlike those that have been elucidated for capitalist states" (Perry 1989, p. 581) and the role of the state in forging particular forms of mass mobilization (White 1989). These considerations point to a link between the institutional structure of state socialism and collective action based on unorganized interests.

THE INSTITUTIONAL LOGIC OF COLLECTIVE ACTION

Organized or unorganized, people everywhere pursue their interests and resist what they perceive as injustices. To explore the causal link between individual behavior and the collective outcome, researchers classify such behavior as purposive action versus spontaneous response, organized interests versus unorganized interests, and everyday forms of resistance versus open protests. Collective outcomes are explained in terms of their purposiveness, leadership, organizational resources, and the circumstances surrounding them.

At a deeper level, however, the institutional arrangements shape the stable patterns in the state–society relationship, the interconnectedness among social groups, and the channels and directions of political input. In this respect, research on the formation of nation-states and collective action provides important insights. A main theme in these studies is the close association between the expansion of the nation-state on the one hand and the increasing scale of interest articulation, organizing capacity, and social mobilization on the other. Tilly (1986) argues that the rise of a capitalist economy and the modern state in the nineteenth century produced the "proletarianization" of society, engendered widespread discontent, and transformed local conflicts and revolts to the national level. Skocpol (1979) emphasizes the link between crises and the dynamics of social mobilization. She argues that social mobilization often occurs when the state experiences crises and cannot effectively control political resources. This creates new opportunities for bottom-up mobilization. Birnbaum (1988) directly links the types of regimes with variations in collective action and empirically examines this causal model in different polities. Although his studies are confined to Western Europe and North America, his findings strongly suggest that collective action cannot be fully understood without incorporating the state into the theoretical models (Tarrow 1989).

The institutional arrangements circumscribe both the solution space and channels of political input. Apparently similar political and social phenomena may have quite different implications in different institutional contexts. For example, Birnbaum (1988) finds that trade unions in the United Kingdom and the United States prefer to reach agreement directly with employers in a contractual setting because the institutional structure does not provide for state intervention. In France, in contrast, collective agreements do not exist, and recourse to the state and the courts is often necessary. In the same vein, it is important to understand the political significance of local grievances in the workplace and conflicts among social groups by examining how they are interconnected and where they are channeled in the Chinese institutional setting.

The nature of collective action is defined by the institutional logic of organizing, which specifies the legitimacy of forms of political participation. The state claims a monopoly of the public goods and denies the legitimacy of interests at the individual level. An important consequence is that any behavior outside of state control is seen as a challenge to the state. As Havel (1985) observes: "Anything which leads people to over-step their predetermined rules is regarded by the system as an attack upon itself. And in this respect, it is correct: Every instance of such transgression is a genuine denial of the system" (p. 30). When such behavior appears in large numbers, it constitutes collective defiance against the state.

Tilly (1986) emphasizes the importance of the existing repertoires that constrain the types of collective action and the availability of opportunities. Changes in the repertoires of collective action are often the result of the evolving state–society relationship. As Dyson (1980) points out, the state "represents not only a particular manner of arranging political and administrative affairs and regulating relationships of authority but also a cultural phenomenon that binds people together in terms of a common mode of interpreting the world" (p. 19). An examination of the particular state–society relationship can help us understand how the repertoires of collective action are maintained and shared among individuals across local and organizational boundaries.

I use the dichotomy between a market economy and state socialism as ideal types and choose this comparative framework for the purpose of theoretical exposition. One fundamental difference between the two is that in the capitalist market economy, organized interests outside of the state exist and are legitimate. In the Chinese context, in contrast, if interests are organized, they are based on the state organizational apparatus and hence they are not autonomous; if interests are independent of the state, they are often unorganized. The state monopoly of the public sphere reduces the private space in which individuals can pursue their self-interest through market-like transactions. Consequently, individual behavior, even in pursuit of self-interest, is unlikely to lead to a market-like solution. That is, although unorganized, the demands and behavior of individuals are nonetheless structured by the institutional constraints that connect individuals, social groups, and the state.

INSTITUTIONAL ARRANGEMENTS AND COLLECTIVE ACTION IN CHINA

In studying the popular uprisings in France and England during the transition to a capitalist economy between the eighteenth and the nineteenth centuries, Rudé (1981) observes:

This was still a period when popular attachment and antipathy tended to focus not so much on causes and institutions as on individual heroes and villains. As the crowd had its heroes, like Wilkes, Lord George Gordon, Marat, or the semi-mythical Rebecca, so it had its clearly identifiable villains in the shape of the individual employer, merchant, forestaller, baker, landlord, or official; and such men became the natural targets of its vengeance when wages were cut, prices were high, the harvest failed, or traditional rights were threatened. (pp. 240–41)

Piven and Cloward's (1977) account of the "poor people's movement" in the United States after World War II reveals a similar picture:

People experience deprivation and oppression within a concrete setting, not as the end product of large and abstract processes, and it is the concrete experience that molds their discontent into specific grievances against specific targets. Workers experience that factory, the speeding rhythm of the assembly line, the foreman, the spies and the guards, the owner and the paycheck. They do not experience monopoly capitalism. (p. 20)

Obviously, a market economy presents particular obstacles to collective action because it produces a complex stratification system and a structure of fragmented grievances and discontents. The presence of private spheres and market transactions also provides a wide range of alternatives for pursuing self-interest without resorting to collective action. Within this market context, the collective action literature emphasizes the ways in which incentives, resources, and organizations affect individuals' choices between private and public spheres and between market and political solutions. In recent years, students of collective action have pointed to the importance of "the critical mass" – a group of individuals that takes the initiative in pursuit of public goods (Oliver 1980, Oliver, Marwell and Teixeira 1985). The roles of leadership, cumulative involvement, and the prospects for success then alter the incentives of the latent group and attract the participation of more people (Chong 1991, Granovetter 1978) .

In contrast, I argue that it is the very institutional arrangements of state socialism that prevent organized interests and facilitates collective action based on unorganized interests. Central to my argument is the proposition that the institutional structure of state socialism reduces the barriers to collective action by producing "large numbers" of individuals with similar behavioral patterns and demands that cut across the boundaries of organizations and social groups. The creation and reproduction of these "large numbers" of individuals provide the basis for social mobilization on a broad scale.

My second proposition is that the institutional structure of state socialism provides a direct link between the workplace and the state and influences the direction of local demands. Once the opportunity is given, large numbers of discontented individuals in workplaces tend to converge toward the state in the same direction. Even conflicts between social groups and workplaces tend to be directed toward the central government for solutions. These instances of discontent may not be based on common interests, nor are they necessarily consistent with each other. But they often take a "collective" form because of their similar patterns and targets.

Finally, the opportunity for collective action is embedded in the state–society relationship. The use of political campaigns and mass mobilizations by the state to deal with its bureaucratic and economic problems enables individuals to articulate their interests through their responses to state policies. State policy shifts lead them to "act together" and to converge in collective action challenging the state.

The "Large Numbers" Phenomenon

By incorporating all citizens into its webs of organizational control, the state can effectively extract resources to fulfill the leadership's ambitions of economic development and political control. Two important consequences for the state–society relationship follow. First, the state eliminates the traditional intermediate strata between the state and society and it directly links each citizen with the state, thus reducing all social groups to a similar structural position subordinate to the state and its bureaucratic organizations. Although private enterprises are not under the administrative control of the state, they nonetheless are subject to direct state intervention or indirect interference, as numerous instances of government-enterprise relationships have shown (Wank 1999).

Second, state policies tend to penetrate the boundaries of social groups and organizations and affect all individuals simultaneously. Mass mobilization and resource transfers across sectors subject different social groups to the same state policy vibration, that is, individuals and groups tend to be mobilized simultaneously through their vertical links with the state. The induced spontaneous individual behavior across workplaces and localities at the same time leads to collective action. In brief, the institutional links impose a structure and an organization on these otherwise unorganized interests. For example, the Great Leap Forward Campaign in 1958 was initiated by the state to increase steel production. To achieve its goals, the state mobilized not only workers in the steel industry but also intellectuals, workers in other industries, and even peasants in the campaign. As a result, the ensuing disaster spread throughout the countryside and to other sectors, affecting all social groups in a similar way. In a centralized polity, state policies designated for a specific area tend to affect individuals in other areas as well. The 1987 anti-bourgeois liberalization campaign was launched by the state to deal with liberalization in the "ideological and political areas." However, peasants and workers were also placed under political pressures, and they responded by withholding their market activities (*Renmin Ribao* October 10, 1987). As a result, even without a conscious articulation of interests, individuals and social groups tend to exhibit a spontaneous articulation of behavior in response to state policies.

In the Chinese context, the similarity of the links between social groups and the state exerts a much stronger effect on individual behavior than do local within-group conditions. The institutional structure constrains individuals' choice-sets and opportunities and thus narrows the directions and types of claims generated in society. Moreover, this similarity in structural dependency and vulnerability to the rhythms of state policies implies that social groups in China not only live in a similar political and economic environment but also tend to share similar life experiences. It is not surprising, then, that these macro-political conditions produce similar behavioral patterns among individuals across the boundaries of workplaces and localities. Like bees that always swarm, similar individual behavior in China presents itself in large numbers.

This is in sharp contrast to the formation of interest groups in other institutional contexts. Studies of the rise of professionalism in the United States and Western Europe, for instance, have demonstrated that the formation of interest groups is often driven by competition in the labor market. Interest groups strive to establish their own identities and boundaries and to differentiate themselves from each other (Freidson 1986, Larson 1977). Consequently, the boundaries of social groups, occupations, and organizations lead to different paces of change and different rhythms to absorb external shocks.

The "large numbers" phenomenon is reinforced by the state organizational apparatus in the workplace (*danwei*). The bureaucratic apparatus is effective in preventing the formation of autonomous organized interests and perhaps also diffuses many potential protests at the local level. However, the workplace does not prevent the penetration of the state into its boundaries, nor does it lessen the tension between the state and social groups. On the contrary, the bureaucratic apparatus in the workplace facilitates the "large numbers" phenomenon by (1) directly linking local grievances to national politics, and (2) creating similar bureaucratic problems and breeding a similar dissatisfaction across organizations. This leads me to the institutional arrangements in the workplace, especially the role of local bureaucrats in linking local conflicts and the central state.

As discussed in Chapter 2, bureaucrats at the local level acquire their authority and legitimation from the state and they act as state agents, interpreting and implementing state policies. In addition to its supervising agencies, the government often sends work teams directly to local enterprises or villages to inspect and implement state policies. In this context, the ability of local bureaucrats to solve local problems is constrained by the state. Through its bureaucratic apparatus, the central government controlled not only workers' wage levels, but also the internal managerial and incentive structures. Laba's (1986) observations of the Polish workplace fit the Chinese context as well: "The political controls of the Leninist state are so direct, so unmasked, that they generate a critique of state power within the workplace" (p. 66).

Bureaucrats are not merely state agents; they also have their own interests, and they tend to exhibit similar behavioral patterns across different workplaces and localities, a tendency that is reinforced by an institutional arrangement that grants bureaucrats monopolistic power at the local levels. Thus, bureaucratic problems, which are pervasive, also exhibit the "large numbers" phenomenon and cut across organizational boundaries (Harding 1981, Lampton 1987). The dual identity of local bureaucrats as state agents and as a class suggests a link between the workplace and the state. Although grievances and discontent tend to be engendered in the workplace, they are often attributed to constraints imposed by the central government. Conflicts with bureaucrats in the workplace are unlikely to be solved at the local levels because local bureaucrats have a monopoly on power and, normatively, they are state agents. Consequently, once the opportunity is presented, these instances of discontent tend to go beyond the boundaries of the workplace and they are directed toward the state. This argument is consistent with the political history of the People's Republic of China during which anti-bureaucratism has been an effective weapon used by the state to mobilize people across organizations and localities (Whyte 1980). The collective defiance during the Hundred Flowers period and the 1986–87 student demonstrations were triggered by widespread bureaucratic problems at the local levels.

Different, even conflicting, interests among localities or social groups in China are embodied less in lateral competition than in their similar vertical demands made on the state. Perry (1985) documents numerous instances of collective violence and feuds in rural villages that clearly show that the state and its local governments treat these local conflicts as a threat to The political authority. The absence of institutional arrangements allowing different social groups to settle their own disputes means that these competing interests cannot be dealt with in a market-like transaction. Rather, the state must intervene to provide political solutions. Thus, divergent local interests and conflicts, at a higher level of analysis, share similar behavioral patterns that either directly make political demands or indirectly generate political pressures on the state.

Group conflict during the Cultural Revolution provides an illuminating example. Although the episode is complicated, it is clear that the conflicts among social groups during this period were constructed by the top leaders (White 1989). As a result, the disputes were ultimately referred to the center for solutions and thus created political pressures on the top leaders. Because the top leaders failed to reconcile the conflicting demands, these demands represented a challenge to the leadership's authority. This was evidenced by the repeated but unsuccessful appeals for alliance by the Maoist leaders. The political pressures resulting from group conflicts changed the course of the Cultural Revolution (Walder 2019, Wang 1995).

Opportunities for Collective Action

Collective action depends on opportunities. In the context of unorganized interests and state political control in China, why do "large numbers" of discontented individuals emerge across localities and organizational boundaries?

The asymmetry between a strong state and a weak society under state socialism suggests that opportunities for collective action are more often provided by the state and state policy shifts than they are created by conscious organizing efforts on the part of society. Ironically, institutional arrangements in China have intermittently provided such opportunities. Collective action has often grown out of political campaigns initiated and organized by the state or has stemmed from cleavages created by the relaxation of state political control.

The Chinese political process is characterized by frequent policy shifts that alternate between bureaucratic implementation and political campaigns, as discussed in Chapter 4. This phenomenon can be partly attributed to the organizational failures of state socialism. State dominance over society depends on a huge bureaucratic apparatus. The state's monopoly of power is duplicated at the lower levels of the bureaucratic system. State policies are transmitted through documents, and only local bureaucrats have access to these documents and the authority to interpret them (Oksenberg 1974). Thus, local bureaucrats can manipulate state policies to serve their own interests. Consequently, two types of organizational failures emerge: (1) systematic bureaucratic deviations in implementing state policies; and (2) the accumulation of incompetent bureaucrats, which reduces state capacity (Lampton 1987, Whyte 1980). Moreover, the bureaucratic system cannot adequately deal with these organizational failures because the structure of upward accountability creates close ties and personal loyalties between local bureaucrats and their immediate supervisors. As a result, the state often adopts alternative modes of mobilization, usually political campaigns, to remedy bureaucratic problems.

Arendt (1951) observes that mass mobilizations are a core characteristic of a totalitarian movement. As discussed in Chapter 4, political campaigns serve the purposes of the leadership by mobilizing resources to achieve the state's ambitious political and economic goals or to respond to crises in other areas. Mass mobilization has been adopted to deal with economic shortages, to enhance economic development, or to support factional struggles within the leadership (Feng 2011). In the economic arena, for example, the Great Leap Forward Campaign of 1958 mobilized human resources from other sectors to increase steel production. In the political arena, the most dramatic example is the Cultural Revolution when Mao Zedong mobilized millions of students, workers, and peasants to attack his opponents and the bureaucratic organizations. The response of individuals and social groups to state policy shifts provides clues to the outbreak of collective action in China. The positive incentive for compliance in China encourages and even forces individuals to take part in state-initiated campaigns and to respond to shifts in state policy (Burns 1988). The politics of life chances are highly significant in state socialism (Whyte 1985, Walder 1986). Shifts in state policy either affect individuals' lives directly or they indirectly signal impending dangers or opportunities, with severe consequences for those who fail to adapt to these dramatic changes. As a result, individuals must be keenly aware of these signals and respond accordingly. However, individuals' responses to shifts in state policy do not suggest adherence to the political line set by the state. Participating in state-initiated political campaigns provides an opportunity for individuals and groups to pursue their own agendas and exploit new opportunities (Harding 1981, Shirk 1982). State-initiated political campaigns provide opportunities for unorganized groups and individuals to act together.

So far, my discussion has been confined to what I call *institutionalized collective action* whereby the collective action is initiated by the state and the participants follow the rules of the game and employ legitimate institutional channels. Moreover, individuals take part in these campaigns more as spontaneous and adaptive responses to state policies rather than as self-conscious organizing efforts. The sources of shifts in state policy may vary – factional conflicts in the Cultural Revolution, bureaucratic problems during the Hundred Flowers period, or mobilization for economic development in the 1980s – but as long as these opportunities are offered, individuals' behavior tends to go beyond state-prescribed boundaries and to take the form of collective action.

Another type of collective action, *non-institutionalized collective action,* refers to protests and displays of open defiance that are not initiated by the state – they bypass legitimate institutional channels to directly challenge the state. This type of collective action was especially salient in the post-Mao era (Cai 2010, Chen 2009). Unlike collective action in the pre-reform era, social protests in the post-Mao era were not initiated by the state. For instance, the student demonstrations in 1986–87 and the pro-democracy movement of 1989 both defied warnings and threats of repressive measures by the top leaders. The participants made explicit demands on the state and in both cases there were open confrontations with government officials, police, and/or the army. In many respects, the social protests of the post-Mao era resemble collective actions in other social contexts.

The emergence of open protest is rooted in the new opportunity structure created by the recent economic reforms in China. In the economic reforms after 1978, the state relaxed its policy of political control and introduced market mechanisms for the allocation of resources (Nee 1989). The reforms facilitated lateral communications across localities and group boundaries, and some freedom of expression was tolerated. These reform measures created two conditions that facilitated collective action: (1) The relaxation of political control lowered the fear of repression and hence reduced the expected costs of participating in collective action; and (2) political and economic resources were decentralized and, indirectly, were made available for the mobilization of collective action.

However, the discontinuity between the Mao era and the reform era should not be overdrawn. The institutional arrangements that created the "large numbers" phenomenon have not fundamentally changed. The state remains at the center, initiating reform through a top-down process. The basic characteristic of the decentralization process is that power is "granted" to local authorities by the state, and thus it can also be withdrawn by the state. This is evidenced in the recentralization of financial resources in the mid-1990s and the reassertion of the party-state in the Xi Jinping era. Not surprisingly, although the state monopoly has been eroded considerably, conditions for the "large numbers" phenomenon still exist and, more importantly, political pressures generated by the reform process are still directed toward the state. Thus, in many ways non-institutionalized collective action resembles institutionalized collective action.

TWO CASE STUDIES

To illustrate my arguments, I examine two cases of collective action in some detail.

Institutionalized Collective Action: The Hundred Flowers Period

By 1957, after a period of economic reconstruction, nationalization, and collectivization that began in 1949, the Chinese Communist Party had consolidated its territorial control and had carried out the nation-building process. At the same time, the bureaucratic system had greatly expanded and administrative problems loomed large (Harding 1981, pp. 87–115). In addition, popular revolts in Hungary and Poland during this period challenged the legitimacy of the state socialist political order. Incidents of conflict between the populace and bureaucrats at the local levels were also reported (Mao 1977b [1957]).

In this context, the Chinese Communist Party adopted a "rectification campaign" to correct its bureaucratic problems. Mao identified subjectivism, bureaucratism, and sectarianism as major problems within the party. In February 1957, Mao declared "let a hundred flowers bloom and a hundred schools of thought contend" and that "long-term coexistence and mutual inspection" were the long-term state policies for the handling of contradictions among the people, thus signaling the beginning of the Hundred Flowers period (Mao 1977b [1957]). Mao also advocated open criticism of the problems in the Communist Party.

At first, intellectuals were reluctant to respond for fear of repression. On April 30, Mao invited leaders of the democratic parties[1] and intellectuals not affiliated with any political parties to discuss the Communist Party's rectification, and he welcomed their criticisms. From May 6 to June 3, the

---

[1] In Chinese practice, all political parties outside of the Communist Party are labeled "democratic parties."

Communist Party's United Front Department organized a series of meetings to gather criticisms from non-Communist Party members, most of whom were intellectuals. Encouraged by the leadership's attitude, many individuals openly criticized problems in the Communist Party. Within a few weeks, criticism from different sectors, workplaces, and localities began to flow.[2]

Several characteristics of this episode are worth noting. First, the criticisms were clearly individual spontaneous responses to state advocacy. Except for some gatherings of senior members of the democratic parties in Beijing encouraged by the Communist Party, there is no evidence that the criticisms were coordinated or organized by autonomous interest groups. Numerous accounts of this period indicate that most participants acted on the basis of appeals from the top leaders. For instance, some university students were later purged simply because they criticized the heads of the Communist Party branches in their departments or at the university. In an interview, a professor who was purged during this period recalled that, at the invitation of the party secretary of his department, he wrote an article supporting the Communist Party's "Hundred Flowers" policy and warning that subjectivism, bureaucratism, and sectarianism, if not corrected, would lead to a national disaster. As he put it: "Those were the same words the top leaders used when they advocated the rectification campaign." Second, not only intellectuals but other social groups, such as managers, doctors, civil servants, and religious groups, responded with complaints and demands (MacFarquhar 1960). Official published materials provide examples of nonparty members criticizing the Communist Party's monopoly of power, doctors complaining of bureaucratic coverups of medical malpractice (*Guangming Ribao* May 3, 1957), students questioning the procedures for electing student representatives (*Guangming Ribao* May 26, 1957), and writers demanding creative freedom (*Wenxue Yanjiu* (5)1957). Open criticisms by peasants and workers were less frequent and their expressions of discontent took other forms. According to a report by the official media, thirteen workers' strikes or "trouble-making" incidents occurred in one year alone in Guangdong province. In the countryside, over 10,000

[2] My discussion relies mainly on *Xinhua Banyuetan* (Apr.–Aug. 1957), an official news-collection series that assembled information on the background, participation, and state responses during this period. The best source available in English is MacFarquhar (1960), which collects a sample of criticisms from this period. In 1979, after the Communist Party rehabilitated those purged during this period, many individuals recounted their experiences in their workplaces during this period.

households withdrew from the cooperatives in Guangdong province during the same period (New China News Agency May 14, 1957 as quoted in MacFarquhar 1960, p. 234).

A common characteristic of these incidents is that critics across different workplaces and localities raised similar criticisms. The centralized political system produced large numbers of similar bureaucratic problems across localities and large numbers of individuals faced similar experiences and dissatisfactions. These criticisms, while differing in specifics, all demanded that the Communist Party correct local bureaucratic problems and relax its political controls over society. There was a clearly perceived link between local bureaucratic problems and the central authority. As two students at a teachers' college in Shenyang put it: "The main source of the bureaucratic problems lies in the central government. If we don't eliminate these problems at their roots, they will emerge again" (*Shenyang Ribao* June 10, 1957).

The collective nature of these spontaneous and large-scale criticisms exceeded the state's expectations. On May 15, 1957, less than three months after he declared the Hundred Flowers policy, Mao Zedong charged that such criticisms represented a concerted effort by counter-revolutionaries to overthrow the Communist Party (Mao 1977a). On June 8, the Party launched its Anti-Rightist Campaign. Those who had earlier criticized the Communist Party were labeled as "rightists," and "conflicts" between rightists and the state were declared to be "contradictions between the people and the enemies" rather than "contradictions among the people." Within several months, about 550,000 "rightists" were purged nationwide.

This episode is an example of institutionalized collective action, that is, the state mobilized the masses to deal with the bureaucratic problems. However, even though the participants clearly were unorganized and followed the stated rules of the game, their remarkably similar criticisms and demands, and the political pressures put on the state, followed the pattern of collective action. Consequently, they were seen as a challenge to the state and were severely repressed.

Non-institutionalized Collective Action: Student Demonstrations in 1986–1987

Near the end of 1986, China was full of frustrations, expectations, and excitement. The frustrations stemmed from the difficulties in carrying out the economic reforms. In 1986, China entered its eighth year of economic reforms. During the initial three years, China had experienced the most rapid agricultural growth in its history. Encouraged by this economic miracle, the state extended the reforms to the industrial sector in the urban areas in 1984. It soon became clear that the political system was the biggest obstacle to urban reform. Bureaucratic interference and corruption were leading to economic stagnation and engendering mass grievances.

Nevertheless, expectations were high. In an effort to overcome these difficulties, the top leadership advocated political reforms. On June 28 and September 13, 1986, Deng Xiaoping instructed the Politburo to consider political reforms in order to enlist mass support for the economic reforms and to overcome bureaucratism (Committee 1986). Inspired by these signals, in the summer of 1986 heated discussions occurred among intellectuals on the problems of the current political system and prospects for political reforms. Articles, debates, and proposals appeared in newspapers, professional journals, and public forums.[3]

While talk of political reforms was in the air, university students could wait no longer. The apparent willingness of the state to consider political reforms released long-suppressed tensions in society. On December 5, 1986, students at China University of Science and Technology in Anhui province took to the streets to protest invalid election procedures in a local election and to demand political reforms and democratic procedures. The government realized the potentially explosive nature of this event and on December 8, 1986, an editorial in *Renmin Ribao* warned that political reforms must proceed according to the Communist Party's blueprint. But it was too late. That same month, student demonstrations took place in Shanghai, Beijing, Nanjing, Wuhan, Hangzhou, Shenzhen, and other large cities. In many places, students confronted police and local officials in defiance of the government's chilly warning.[4]

Eyewitness accounts and media reports noted the spontaneity of participation and the lack of organization and clear goals. For example, students at Fudan University mobilized after a group of students from a nearby university marched to Fudan and asked Fudan students to join them. One student organizer at Fudan recalled: "We [classmates] were all excited about what was happening. Someone posted an announcement

[3] Many publications on political reforms appeared during this period. Interested readers can refer to articles in *Renmin Ribao, Guangming Ribao, Jiefang Ribao,* and *Xinhua Yuebao* in mid-1986 for details.

[4] My discussion here is based primarily on published eyewitness accounts, news reports in Chinese journals in Hong Kong, and interviews in the summer of 1987 with student participants at a Chinese university.

that there would be a demonstration the following day. We discussed it during lunch and decided we would prepare banners and join the demonstration." Within a few days, students from major universities in Shanghai were participating in the demonstrations. The unorganized nature of the protests was also reflected in the lack of sustained mobilization or coherent demands (Wasserstrom 1991). On December 18, just a few days after the first outbreak, students returned to their classrooms in spite of some student organizers' calls for a boycott of classes (Schell 1988, p. 230).

Although demonstrations in different areas were triggered by different local incidents, they all converged on the same issues. In Anhui province, student demonstrations broke out to protest the violation of election procedures when a local party office tried to impose its candidates on the students. In Shanghai, demonstrations were triggered by the abuse of students by police in a public place (Ninetith [Jiushi niandai] February. 1987, pp. 74–76). In Shenzhen, demonstrations protested high tuition (Schell 1988). Even in Shanghai, different demands were made during the course of the demonstrations. For instance, the initial demands at Fudan University included complaints about dormitory conditions and food quality, among others (Schell 1988, Wasserstrom 1991). Diverse as these complaints were, the student demonstrations quickly converged on a demand for the central government to speed up the political reforms and to correct bureaucratic problems.

The general atmosphere of political reforms created by the top leaders had provided a basis for the mobilization of students in different campuses and localities. These demonstrations actually supported the top leaders' reform efforts. As one student explained: "We were responding to the call last July by Deng Xiaoping for political reforms. We are impatient that in spite of all the newspaper articles advocating mass participation, nothing concrete has yet been done to allow us a say in government affairs" (Schell 1988, p. 213). Nonetheless, the party leadership saw the student demonstrations as a challenge to party rule and interpreted them as "riots" inspired by "bad elements." In response, the government took strong political measures to suppress the demonstrations. General Secretary Hu Yaobang was forced to resign; three famous intellectuals who advocated political reforms were purged; the president and a vice president of China Science and Technology University, where the student demonstrations had begun, were replaced and the university administration was reorganized. In the meantime, a nationwide Anti-Bourgeois Liberalization Campaign was launched. The Communist Party organized mass criticisms of Western liberalization. Within a month, major party newspapers were publishing numerous editorials and commentaries to promote this campaign *(Xinhua Yuebao* January 1987).

Although they occurred thirty years apart, these two instances of collective action share some similarities. In both cases, participants were motivated by shifts in state policy rather than by their own organizing efforts. Political control and fragmented interests based on formal organizations did not prevent collective action across these boundaries. On the contrary, bureaucratic problems at the local levels were the immediate cause of the collective action. But these criticisms and protests quickly moved from local issues to the center and began to threaten the state.

The puzzles of the 1989 pro-democracy movement can be understood in a similar manner. The wide participation in the movement cannot be accounted for by either common interests or organizational efforts. On the eve of the 1989 protests, Chinese society was highly differentiated; inequality generated tensions among social groups (Davis and Vogel 1990). Even university students were divided (Zhao 2001). Just a year earlier, the president of Peking University had lamented that students had lost their enthusiasm and had become apathetic (*Zhongguo Qingnianbao* April 4, 1988). Although there were a few informal dissident groups among the students at Peking University on the eve of the 1989 events and the members of these groups were actively involved in the social protests, there is no evidence that these groups initiated, or were capable of mobilizing and organizing, such large-scale open confrontations. In fact, the original student representatives of the Independent Student Alliance of Beijing Universities, established during the protests, included no members of these dissident groups (Shen 1990). Nonetheless, the institutional structure created interconnections among individuals and social groups. Individuals from various social groups and organizations, victims of the reforms, such as workers and cadres in state-owned enterprises, as well as beneficiaries of the reforms, such as private entrepreneurs, joined in the demonstrations. Although participants may not have shared a common interest, they shared a common enemy. The central state and its policies engendered widespread discontent among students, workers, cadres, and other social groups. Though demands varied across social groups (Strand 1990), it was the position of the central state as the cause of, and the solution to, the social problems that were the basis for the articulation of protest among these participants.

In the preceding discussion, I have focused on the causal link with the institutional structure of state socialism. However, micro-conditions such as organizing capacity, leadership, incentives, personal networks, and existing repertoires of collective action also played important roles. There is evidence of mobilization across universities during the 1986–87 and 1989 student demonstrations (Zhao 2001). Informal channels of communication were available through personal networks, travelers, hearsay, and, in more recent years, foreign broadcasts. The mobilization of student protests was also based on existing repertoires of collective action, such as patriotic symbols, big-character posters *(dazibao)*, and work units. These symbols and forms can be traced to the May Fourth movement of 1921 and the Cultural Revolution. Furthermore, the 1989 pro-democracy movement clearly reflected the profound social changes that had occurred during the ten years of economic reforms that had undermined the capacity of the state. Whether the reform process can continue and whether it will lead to fundamental changes in the patterns of collective action remain to be seen.

COLLECTIVE INACTION AS A FORM OF COLLECTIVE ACTION

Thus far, I have considered collective action in the form of open defiant behavior. However, collective action under state socialism also includes noncompliance, apathy, and pessimism among the populace (Mason, Nelson and Szklarski 1991, Townsend and Womack 1986). Certainly, these forms of resistance are not unique to state socialist society; they have been documented in many other social contexts (Colburn 1989, Scott 1985). But I argue that due to the institutional structure of state socialism, noncompliance and apathy assume a collective character and have a special political significance. I label this phenomenon *collective inaction*.

Collective inaction may take different forms: a lack of enthusiasm for participating in state-initiated political campaigns, absenteeism or inefficiency in the workplace, evasion of public duties, or the emergence of subcultures opposing the official ideology. Some of this behavior is more visible than others and may well be seen as "action" rather than "inaction," such as the looting of crops or the slaughter of animals. But a common characteristic is that it is individual-based and takes the form of escape from state control rather than open confrontation. This type of behavior has minimal symbolic visibility. "When they are practiced widely by members of an entire class against elites or the state, they may have aggregated consequences out of all proportion to their banality when considered singly" (Scott 1989, p. 5).

In a market economy, problems resulting from noncompliance and inefficiency at the workplace do not assume a collective character beyond the local boundary and a set of complicated economic layers absorbs their impact. For instance, inefficiency in the American automobile industry has been suggested as a major source of its competitive disadvantage. However, the cost of inefficiency in the workplace is shared by company owners, consumers, and, indirectly, the state, through declines in tax revenue. Furthermore, the adverse impact of inefficiency at the national level may be partly alleviated by the success of other industries. Even when discontent spans social groups, it tends to be directed at multiple targets with multiple demands.

The case of state socialism is the opposite. In the institutional structure of state socialism, the state monopoly over the public sphere means that noncompliance directly challenges state authority, affects the state's extraction of resources, and threatens state capacity to govern. Collective inaction emerges when state policies shift toward political repression and tighter control. During periods of repression, open protests are severely punished, so individuals protect themselves by resorting to invisible forms of resistance rather than open defiance. Collectively, these forms of resistance put enormous political pressures on the state, challenging its legitimacy and constraining its capacity to implement policies. In this light, the "large numbers" of noncompliant behavior resemble collective action.

Although it is difficult to document instances of collective inaction, several studies shed light on this phenomenon. Skinner and Winkler (1969), in a study of state agricultural policies during the 1950s and 1960s, find that peasants' indifference toward state policies and their collective resistance inhibited the state's capacity to implement its policies and forced the state to abandon old policies and to take a different direction. Lee (1998) finds this type of phenomena in labor relations in the post-Mao era. Zweig (1989), in an examination of peasant resistance over collective land in the 1960s and 1970s, reaches similar conclusions. Townsend and Womack (1986, pp. 265–69) also recognize this type of behavior as a distinctive type of interest articulation. Perhaps the most spectacular example is the change in agricultural productivity that occurred during the reforms. The collectivization of agriculture before 1979 deprived peasants of their land and the policy met with tacit resistance, such as free-riding, low productivity, and evasion of farm duties. The pervasiveness of the resistance constituted collective inaction and its cost was clearly reflected in a stagnation of agricultural production. During the 1971 through 1978 period, when the peasants were still under the commune system, the annual growth rate of the gross value of agricultural output was 4.3 percent (Perkins 1988). During the reform era, after collectivization was abandoned and private households were allowed to lease the land, the growth rate jumped to 7.5 percent during the 1980 through 1982 period, and to 13.0 percent from 1982 to 1986. As Perkins (1988) notes, "the growth of such key inputs as mechanical and electric power and chemical fertilizer all increased at rates no higher and in most cases lower in the 1979–85 period as contrasted to the 1965–78 period" (p. 612). Clearly, these high growth rates in agriculture are attributable mainly to human factors, "particularly the release of energies connected with private household output" (p. 612). It is evident that collective inaction in agriculture before the reform era had a devastating effect on the capacity of the state to extract resources.

In some instances, collective inaction directly affected state policy. For example, in 1987, when the Communist Party launched the anti-bourgeois liberalization campaign to suppress the student demonstrations, individuals sensed the impending political repression and policy shifts. Peasants cut down the trees they were growing and slaughtered the pigs they were raising out of fear that they would be confiscated by the state. Enterprises withheld production and investment because of the possibility that the autonomy granted to them by the government might be revoked (*Chengming* March 1987, pp. 19–21). Although similar responses may occur in a market economy, the difference is that the Chinese were responding to political uncertainty rather than to market uncertainty. and their behavior was translated directly into political pressure. A speech by then Acting General Secretary Zhao Ziyang represented an effort to change the course of the political campaign:

If the current [reform] policy is interpreted as the result of bourgeois liberalization, it will create great uncertainty among the people. If production is unattended, commercial activities disrupted, forests destroyed and pigs killed, who can shoulder all these responsibilities? (*Renmin Ribao* October 10, 1987)

Clearly, collective action in the Chinese context manifests itself not only through open resistance and demonstrations but also in more subtle forms of noncompliant behavior that fall outside the conventional scope of collective action. Unlike other social contexts, however, in China these forms of resistance share the characteristics of collective action. In a sense, collective inaction is an invisible "sit-in" in the Chinese political context. Its message is loud and clear, even without symbolic actions.

In a capitalist market context, as Hirschman (1982) notes, the dichotomy between the public and private arenas allows individuals to shift between public and private realms and between collective action and the pursuit of self-interest. In state socialism, however, shifts of individual involvement are more likely to be between collective action and collective inaction. Whether individuals strive for the public good or pursue their own self-interest, their behavior assumes a collective character and challenges the state monopoly.

COLLECTIVE ACTION IN A COMPARATIVE PERSPECTIVE

I have examined collective action in China by contrasting state–society relationships in a capitalist market economy with China's state socialist redistributive system. The Chinese experience is not an isolated case; collective actions based on unorganized interests have also occurred in market economies. The student protests in France in the 1960s and 1986 emerged spontaneously rather than through careful organization (McMillan 1992, Wilsford 1988). What conditions foster these similar types of collective action in different social contexts?

According to Hirschman (1982), one cause of this phenomenon is market failures that shrink the private realm where individuals can pursue their self-interest and alter their preferences, thereby pushing individuals into the public arena. In a study of the poor people's movement during the Great Depression, Piven and Cloward (1977) make similar arguments. Under these circumstances, collective action may occur with or without conscious organizing efforts. The maintenance and expansion of collective action, however, depends heavily on leadership, organizations, and the evolving political process (McAdam 1982).

Another factor contributing to collective action is the increasing concentration of power that accompanied the rise of the nation-state and redefined the boundaries of the public and private realms. "As capitalism advanced, as national states became more powerful and centralized, local affairs and nearby patrons mattered less to the fates of ordinary people" (Tilly 1986, pp. 395–96). These evolving state–society relationships led to fundamental changes in the forms and channels of political input from society. Wilsford (1988) attributes the student protests in France to the dominance of the state apparatus there: "For the French state, by dealing high-handedly with its opponents, cuts them off from normal avenues of political negotiation. In doing so, it forces its opponents to exit normal politics" (p. 152). The student demonstrations of the 1960s in the United States were interconnected in a similar manner; they were largely a collective response to the federal government's foreign policy.

The emergence of new social movements in Western Europe also illustrates this point. In contrast to the traditional organizational base of social movements, scholars have observed the emergence of social movements since the 1970s that arise from a diffuse and fluid social base and that cut across group boundaries and traditional political arenas (Dalton and Kuechler 1990). This pattern of social mobilization is mainly the result of the rise of the welfare state in industrialized societies that has blurred and widened the boundaries of the political (Maier 1987).

In contrast, the centralized authority in China places individuals under the control of the state. The lack of organized interests limits the effectiveness of leadership, personal networks, communications, and mobilization. Furthermore, the track record of the state's repressive measures against collective action makes the cost of participation high. Why does collective action occur under these adverse conditions?

An institutional perspective sheds light on this puzzle. Although unorganized, collective action in China is systematically structured by the particular type of state–society relationship. The socialist state and its institutions have fostered interconnections among otherwise unorganized interests by generating "large numbers" of discontented people, by linking local discontent with national politics, and by a mobilization policy that periodically incorporates social groups into the political process. Thus, collective action is unwittingly "organized" by the socialist state.

Consider the role of formal organizations. It has been argued that factories, communes, and universities are part of the state organizational apparatus whereby the socialist state exercises control through political pressures and positive incentives. During the student demonstrations in the 1980s, university authorities discouraged students from participating. The government also threatened workers through party branches at the workplace. However, workplaces and universities are places where personal ties and social networks are formed. When opportunities open up, they provide a channel for social mobilization, as evidenced by the 1989 pro-democracy movement. In this light, the workplace is a social space where individuals share similar interests and similar experiences, and they interact. It is also a political space where discontent against the state and local bureaucrats is bred. In time, it becomes an organizational basis for mobilization of its members in pursuit of their interests.

Moreover, in the instances of collective action that I consider, participation was either mobilized by the state directly or induced by state policy. During the Hundred Flowers period, for instance, the state took great pains to motivate individuals to participate in the anti-bureaucratism campaign. The student demonstrations and student attacks on bureaucratic organizations in 1986–87 were also prompted by the call for political reforms by the top leaders. In such an institutional setting, individuals may start with diverse targets and demands, but they tend to converge in a common direction owing to the centralized polity and opportunity structure. Regardless of the participants' motivations, the large amount of criticism directed toward the state and also the open protests are causally defined as collective action. Even rural tree-cutting and pig-killing within the private realm take a "collective" form to challenge the state and its policies.

Political practices also generate and maintain repertoires of collective action. Several scholars have noted similarities between the student protests of the 1980s and other social movements in Chinese history (Strand 1990, Wasserstrom 1991). The student protests of the 1980s repeatedly invoked the imagery of the May Fourth movement of 1921, whose patriotic symbols legitimized participation. Students also drew on memories of the Cultural Revolution, which provided forms of organization and mobilization. For instance, big-character posters were displayed on campuses; student organizers in Beijing sent representatives to other cities to mobilize fellow students; workers joined by displaying the banners of their work units. All these actions were remarkably similar to actions adopted during the Cultural Revolution. Interestingly, both sources of the actions were created and maintained by the socialist state. The centralized political system creates a cultural context in which the repertoires of collective action are maintained and shared by individuals across organizations and social groups.

Outbreaks of collective action are triggered by shifts in several important parameters. Political controls are relaxed, individuals are encouraged to participate in the political process, lateral communication networks are activated, and cleavages open up owing to factional conflicts at the top. During such episodes, individuals are encouraged by the state to "speak out." Thus, the populace becomes aware of widespread discontent, which in turn promotes further participation in this process. More important, such a political process must persist long enough to affect individuals' incentives and perceptions of risk. Because the simultaneous emergence of such conditions is rare, collective action in China is infrequent. Obviously, the collective actions discussed here differ in many respects from the collective actions in other social contexts. Because they are less "purposive," they can be termed "aggregates" of individual behavior or "crowd behavior." However, the transformation of individual behavior into collective action discussed here is too systematic, structurally embedded, and politically significant to be treated merely as a circumstantial outcome. The large number of individual responses is rooted in the nature of the state–society relationship and it is reproduced in everyday activities. These responses are part of the political process, both as product and as input. They should be treated as "collective" because they are perceived and responded to as such by the state, and because they affect the political process as collective actions.

Although I have focused on China, the issues and mechanisms involved are more general and are rooted in the patterns of state–society relationships typical of state socialism. In developing these ideas, I have benefited from studies of the Soviet Union and Eastern European politics where the "large numbers" phenomenon has also been observed. Griffiths (1971) finds a "parallel articulation of behavior" cutting across formal groups in the Soviet Union. Bunce (1992) uses the concept of "homogenization" to characterize the basis for spontaneous interest articulation in the Eastern European countries. The direct link between the state and the workplace has been most evident in the Soviet and in Eastern European contexts (Laba 1986). Political campaigns and mass mobilizations have occurred frequently in the Soviet Union (Viola 1987). Studies of mass resistance – instances of "collective inaction" – and its political effects on state policies have also emerged in recent years (Scott 1989).

Hankiss (1989) examines the mobilization process in Hungary and finds that shifts in state policy toward openness created the opportunity for the society to mobilize and challenge the state. Even in Poland before the birth of Solidarity in the 1980s, workers' uprisings exemplified collective action based on unorganized interests. For instance, workers' strikes in 1976 occurred in more than 100 factories throughout the nation on the day the Polish government announced its price reform program. Bernhard (1987) shows that these strikes were immediate responses to state policy rather than carefully organized efforts. There were noticeable differences in the participants' demands across sectors and regions. The unorganized nature of the strikes is also indicated by their short duration: They lasted one day, ending when the government withdrew its price reform policy. The basic features of the institutional arrangements and state–society relations discussed here have direct implications for understanding collective action in other state socialist societies.

SUMMARY

This chapter examines the link between the institutional logic of governance and the patterns of collective action and popular resistance in contemporary China, characterized by collective action or inaction based on unorganized interests. The distinctive institutional logic of governance in China, especially the encompassing role of the state in all walks of life and its bureaucratic reach, has organized citizens of all walks of life and channeled them into collective action.

In the previous chapters, I emphasize the historical comparison between the party-state today and the bureaucratic monarchy in history. This chapter introduces a comparative lens with other societies where state–society relationships and the role of the bureaucracy are similarly configured. Clearly, under state socialism, society is *organizationally* weak compared to the state apparatus. Political demands in such a context are not generated by the formation and shifting of interest groups typical of a liberal representative polity. Nor are these demands embodied in different organizations striving to obtain state licensing for privileged access to resources typical of a corporatist system. However, collective action in a society of unorganized interests plays a critical role in the political process. The impact of collective action is revealed in its timing. Collective action based on unorganized interests is largely a response to the state and to state policies. It tends to occur when the state shifts policy. This is when the state is "weak" owing to leadership changes, fragile coalitions, or a lack of confidence in its new orientation. This type of collective action resembles social mobilization prompted by the breakdown of the state (Skocpol 1979).

Returning to the theme of this book, collective action based on unorganized interests has intensified the fundamental tensions and eroded the legitimacy of the party-state; it also underlies the dynamics of the reform cycles in China and other socialist states. Similar to campaign-style mobilization, collective action based on unorganized interests plays an important role in inducing shifts in the modes of governance. Moreover, collective action has disrupted state policies, weakened the state organizational apparatus, limited the state's capacity to implement policies, and undermined its ability to govern. Ultimately, the collective resistance of the populace forced the socialist states of China and Eastern Europe to undertake the reforms of the 1980s that led to the popular uprisings in 1989.

12

Conclusion: The Logic of Governance and the Future of China

> While it is true that Western tradition has supplied much of the basis for the world civilization now emerging, it remains to be seen whether China will participate in that world culture in the same sense that Algeria or India or Japan or Nigeria will; China may yet throw out a powerful challenge to the Western principles upon which the emerging international culture is based.
>
> G. William Skinner (1964, p. 518)

In this concluding chapter, let us reflect on the questions raised at the beginning of the introductory chapter in the quotations by Samuel Huntington, Philip Kuhn, and David Landes: Why has Chinese civilization survived its two thousand years of history and not suffered the same demise that was experienced by many other ancient civilizations? Why has China's centralized authority survived for such a long time over such large territories with significant cultural and economic diversity? Why has Chinese society experienced long years of stagnation in modern history but witnessed an outburst of vitality and spectacular economic development during the last four decades? All these questions are interrelated and lead to the theme of this book, that is, the institutional logic of governance in China.

This book began with the proposition that, both in history and in contemporary society, there has been a fundamental tension in governing China, namely, the tension between the centralization of authority and effective, local governance. In response, distinctive institutions and practices arose and evolved over time. The preceding chapters have examined different aspects of these institutional arrangements and mechanisms, including the locus of the bureaucracy in the mode of domination, the

shifting modes of governance in the government, and state–society interactions mediated by the Chinese bureaucracy. Below, I first summarize
the main contributions of this book and then turn to their implications for
understanding the past, present, and future of China's governance.

THE INSTITUTIONAL LOGIC OF GOVERNANCE IN CHINA: WHAT
HAVE WE LEARNED?

The title of this book suggests an ambitious theme. In this journey, I have
proposed and elaborated on a series of theoretical concepts and arguments, some drawn from classical and contemporary social sciences,
especially organization research, and some drawn from empirical observations to capture and explicate the mechanisms and practices in Chinese
governance. In so doing, I aim to develop what Merton (1968b) calls
"theories of middle range" that focus on specific mechanisms and relationships based on empirical observations, connecting macro-historical
contexts, institutional processes, and micro-behavior. What has been
developed here can be seen as a "tool kit" – a set of the theoretical ideas
and analytical concepts, and the mechanisms therein – that can be assembled and applied to analyze or interpret empirical observations of governance practice in China.

These proposed ideas and mechanisms are interrelated. Central to such
a theoretical enterprise is the relationship between the Chinese state and the
bureaucracy. In contrast to the overarching image of authoritarianism and
its variants (Landry 2008, Lieberthal 1992, Nathan 2003), I draw on
Weber's comparative institutional analysis to develop a new theoretical
interpretation of the mode of party-state domination in contemporary
China and the role of this bureaucracy therein (Chapter 2). The
Weberian lens delineates the distinctive bases of legitimacy and the corresponding authority types of the party-state and the bureaucracy, highlight-
ing both the interdependence and tensions between the two, placing this
relationship at the center of the logic of governance in China. Such a
framework also provides a historical and comparative perspective to trace
the historical origins as well as the distinctive features of the Chinese
bureaucracy as opposed to a Weberian bureaucracy that is based on
legal–rational legitimation.

The fundamental relationship between the state and the bureaucracy
remains stable, but the allocation of decision rights in different dimensions across different levels of the hierarchy may vary, giving rise to
different modes of governance in the Chinese bureaucracy. This key

insight is captured and elaborated upon in the "control rights" theory and the related analytical concepts presented in Chapter 3. Drawing on incomplete contract theory in economics, the proposed theoretical model seeks to shed light on the dynamics of governance processes. That is, we can make sense of the shifts across the different modes of governance – tight coupling, loose coupling, subcontracting, and federalism – in light of the allocation of control rights along several dimensions across different levels of the hierarchy, thus leading us to further explore the processes and mechanisms, and the conditions that give rise to these shifts. The proposed control rights theory provides a unified theoretical framework to account for the different modes of governance and their relationships with one another as well as the underlining mechanisms and the scope of the conditions within which these mechanisms take effect. The shifts among modes of governance may at times take place in drastic, violent ways in the form of campaign-style mobilization and at other times in more routine forms of bureaucratic interactions and bargaining.

For example, the subcontracting mode is a salient mode of governance in China (Zhou 2014, 2017). But the allocation of control rights at different levels of the hierarchy may vary depending on the circumstances, leading to changes in the authority relationships as well as different modes of governance in the bureaucracy. Strong top-down pressures to achieve policy targets (the fertility rate or an environmental regulation target) may lead to a shift of decision rights in the provision of incentives to the higher-level authority, inducing a tight-coupling mode of governance. In contrast, the relaxation of control rights during inspections may result in a subcontracting mode of governance, or even produce a shift to a loose-coupling system. During the evolution of governance practices in China, there have been continuous adjustments in the interactions between the central and local governments. The allocation of decision rights may also change because of internal negotiations between the supervising and subordinate agencies so as to adapt to differing circumstances (Chapter 5).

We can illustrate these issues using the episodes of implementation of the five-year plan in the area of environmental regulation, as illustrated in Chapter 7. During such a multi-year policy implementation process, the relationships between higher authorities and subordinate bureaus (MEP – PEPB – MEPB – CEPB) were not static; rather, they evolved with changes in the top-down pressures, the specific circumstances encountered in the implementation process (i.e., resource availability), and the relationships among the different offices. Although the principal held the decision rights in goal setting during the first year of the five-year plan, lax inspection efforts in effect transferred actual authority to the hands of the MEPB. But this authority shifted upward in subsequent years as a result of the adoption of more elaborate rules and the enforcement of stringent inspection and evaluation measures. However, such a centralization process was not permanent; it also evolved along with the different stages of the implementation process and varied with changing pressures of task accomplishment. In the later years of the five-year plan, when the MEPB ensured its satisfactory fulfilment of the expected tasks, top-down implementation pressures were greatly alleviated, and the MEPB enjoyed much greater discretion in the allocation of tasks and the provision of incentives among its subordinate offices (Chapters 3, 7).

We observed similar behavioral patterns in village elections, but the processes took place in a broader social context rather than being confined to the bureaucratic organization. Although government policy allowed village self-governance during the early years of the village elections, the actual power of policy implementation was in the hands of local governments. Along with changes in the task environment of the local governments and the active participation of the rural logic of governance, in later years village elections were gradually transformed into the institutional practice of village self-governance (Chapter 10).

The conceptualization and theorization of these mechanisms help us make sense of the interactions between the central and local governments as well as the interactions between the state and society. As shown in previous chapters, the arbitrary power of the top leaders and the alternation between campaign-style mobilization and bureaucratic routines play important roles in mediating the interactions between central and local governments. In particular, the use of campaign-style mobilization from time to time – to disrupt bureaucratic routines and to induce a tightly coupled system for policy implementation – provides an important mechanism to shift across modes of governance (Chapter 4). Moreover, collusive behavior among local governments (Chapter 6) and response strategies in the interactions among the multiple logics allow local officials to bridge the gap between top-down policies and local circumstances, providing room for flexible adaptation during the policy implementation stage (Chapters 7, 8). In a broader context, the logic of rural society and unorganized collective action provide important bottom-up inputs into the political process and help shape the pace and direction of changes in the governance practice (Chapters 9–11).

It is in this larger, institutional framework and in relation to one another that we can make sense of the specific mechanisms and governance practices, such as provision of incentives, collusive behavior among local officials, and patterns of bureaucratic bargaining, of the interactions between the bureaucracy and society, and of the cycles of centralization and decentralization in China's governance.

A larger picture emerges from the patterns of governance in China. These patterned practices are not always characterized by a high centralization of power, nor are they always a stable subcontracting system; rather, they reflect a process of variable-coupling between the state (the emperor) and bureaucratic (local) power: First, the central authority dominates bureaucratic power, which historically has been sustained by a set of Confucian cultural institutions, traditional rituals and ceremonies, the civil-examination institution, and the institution of bureaucratic upward accountability. In contemporary society, this is institutionalized by the party-state organization. Second, the exercise of substantive authority varies over time between the central and local governments and across the levels of the bureaucratic hierarchy, inducing different modes of governance, from tight-coupling and subcontracting to loose-coupling or even some form of federalism in certain areas and during certain periods of time. In other words, the modes of governance in China shift with the different interactions between the top-down arbitrary power and the bureaucratic power, between negotiations across levels of the bureaucratic hierarchy, and between top-down policy imposition and bottom-up societal responses.

Based on the discussions reported in this book, we are in a position to address the question that Skinner (1964) anticipated more than half a century ago, as quoted at the beginning of this chapter: What are the distinct ways in which China has been governed? How have these distinct features shaped the kinds and directions of change in China's future?

FROM FUNDAMENTAL TENSIONS TO TENSIONS BETWEEN THE STATE AND THE BUREAUCRACY

Although my focus is contemporary China, as we have seen throughout this book, today's institutions and practices have been shaped by a long process of responses to past challenges and crises. Therefore, I begin with a macro-historical perspective to discuss the implications of what we have learned in this book.

The fundamental tension between the centralization of authority and effective, local governance is manifested in the tensions between the Chinese state and the subordinate bureaucracy. Two types of power coexist in this relationship: the arbitrary power of the ruler and the bureaucratic power based on routine. Historically, the arbitrary power of the state rested with the emperor and the bureaucratic power rested with officials at various levels of the governments. In contemporary China, these two types of power remain intact, with the former resting with the top leader(s) of the party-state, and the latter held by officials in the government hierarchy. The relationship between the two has been ingrained in their respective bases of legitimation and corresponding institutions, making them both interdependent and in tension while they make continuous adjustments over time, generating a distinct historical path of state-making in China as compared with paths of state-making in other parts of the world (Burbank and Cooper 2010, Tilly 1990).

As Levenson (1965) points out, historically tensions between the emperor and the bureaucracy infused vitality into the bureaucratic monarchy. Governance in China has been realized amidst tensions and mutual constraints between these two powers. Because bureaucratic power came from and was legitimized by top-down delegation, the arbitrary power of the state could intervene and disrupt bureaucratic processes at any level, during any step of the process, and at any point in time. The exercise of arbitrary power was sustained by the institutional arrangements of upward accountability and personnel management, and it was reinforced from time to time by political campaigns, such as those in the soulstealer episode during the Qing dynasty, during the Cultural Revolution of the Mao era, or during the anti-corruption campaign in the recent Xi Jinping era.

Conversely, the power of the state was also constrained in the governance process. Past research has emphasized the role of political culture, especially the Confucian doctrine that was imposed upon the emperor. From the lens of organizational analysis, these constraints had a stable institutional basis. Given the extraordinary scale and the long chain of command, the power of the state had to be exercised through the delegation of power to officials at different levels, which led to – not by design but by the imperative of scale and complexity – a patterned practice of acquiescence and even encouragement of local flexibility to implement top-down policies. Local officials for self-protection and to get things done have thus developed a set of informal institutions and patronage ties to respond to the top-down arbitrary power, intensifying the interactions and tensions between ruler and bureaucrat.

Distinct institutional arrangements and mechanisms of governance emerged and evolved in the state-making process in response to the tensions between the deployment of bureaucratic machines to implement state policies and, at the same time, to tame deviant behavioral tendencies at local levels. To a great extent the long history of Chinese civilization has been characterized by flexible, loosely coupled institutional practices. But such flexibility and adaptability have come with costs, *a trade-off between efficiency and stability.*

This defining characteristic of the empire has long been recognized in the social science literature. At the beginning of the twentieth century, Weber pointed out that the centralization of authority in the Chinese empire, especially the civil examination–based bureaucracy, contributed to the stability of the empire, but this was gained at the expense of the rationalization of the economic and administrative institutions. As Weber (1968) puts it, "We may recall that, in the Warring States, the very stratum of state prebendaries who blocked administrative rationalization in the world empire were once its most powerful promoters. Then, the stimulus was gone. Just as competition for markets compelled the rationalization of private enterprise, so competition for political power compelled the rationalization of state economy and economic policy both in the Occident and in the China of the Warring States. ... The impulse toward rationalization which existed while the Warring States were in competition was no longer contained in the world empire" (pp. 61–62). Weber's view is also echoed in the literature on Chinese history. Levenson (1965) writes: "In the Ch'ing period, for example, we see the emperor forced to choose between two of an autocrat's objectives, political safety and administrative efficiency" (Vol. 2, p. 59). And the emperor more often than not chose the former over the latter. In his study of the taxation system in the Ming dynasty, historian Ray Huang (1974) reaches a similar conclusion: "In traditional China the major concern was always governmental stability, which was well served by the Ming fiscal system" (p. 321). "Hung-wu [the founding emperor], being a cautious man, preferred to create a centralized fiscal authority with extensive rather than intensive coverage. His main concern was to prevent any sub-system arising within this monolithic structure, rather than to refine and improve on its operations. From the beginning, therefore, the fiscal administration was characterized by simplicity and even crudity" (p. 314). In other words, the trade-off between efficiency and stability reflects the fundamental tension between the centralization of authority (stability) and effective, local governance (efficiency).

We can also see the trade-off between efficiency and stability in the institutional arrangements of the Chinese state. First, during its long history Chinese society was ruled by a minimalist state, with a limited size and narrow scope of governance (Huang 2008, Skinner and Baker 1977). As Ray Huang observed, in Imperial China, the government did not have the tools of currency and did not encourage economic activities in those areas that it could not control. In many instances, its policy amounted to suppressing those advanced arenas in the economy so as to make them in sync with those backward arenas (Huang 2001, p. 200). Second, the emphasis on centralization over efficiency was especially pronounced in the personnel management system. Officials were dispatched and frequently rotated across different localities to avoid alliances with local interests, at the expense of long-term economic and social development. The lack of reliable institutional constraints led to a reliance on the officials' moral character and political loyalty. Over time, their so-called moral character and political loyalty deteriorated into personal loyalty, often at the expense of ability. Third, there was stubborn resistance to the rule of law in institution building because such institutional arrangements would set limits on the arbitrary power of the higher authorities as well as on the flexibility in policy implementation at the local level. Zelin's (1984) study of fiscal reform in the Qing dynasty shows that the fiscal reforms increased the effectiveness of local governance and lessened upward pressures on the higher authorities. But, at the same time, local autonomy threatened top-down power and undermined the supreme power of the emperor. This effort to rationalize the bureaucracy came to an end when the Hongli emperor assumed the throne.

Despite recognition of the internal forces for change and the endogenous mechanisms in Chinese history (Cohen 2010), it is also clear that here and there the empire attempted to repair broken institutions in order to survive, but the fundamental mode of domination did not change during the two thousand years from the Qin dynasty (221 BC) to the fall of Qing dynasty in the early twentieth century. Significant institutional changes required new governance mechanisms and a new mode of domination based on a new basis of legitimacy. The prospects for such changes presented major threats to the emperor's interests as well as to the interests of the bureaucratic class. Unlike the intensive international competition that gave rise to the formation of modern states in Europe, the logic of the Chinese empire survived for a long time because, until the modern era, it did not face, or could insulate itself from, credible threats or competition from the outside world. But by the late nineteenth century the empire could no longer survive as the door to the outside world was forced to open. Thereafter, China entered a new era in the search for an alternative mode of domination and embarked on a new path of state building and nation building.

INSTITUTIONAL LOGIC IN CONTEMPORARY CHINA:
CONTINUITY AND CHANGE

As I argue in Chapter 2 and elaborate upon in subsequent chapters, there has been a strong continuity between the mode of domination in the bureaucratic monarchy in history and the mode of party-state domination today. As a result, neither the fundamental tension nor the key institutional logic of governance and the patterned practices in bureaucratic behavior have changed.

Nevertheless, major changes have indeed taken place since 1949 under the authoritarian rule by the party-state. One key aspect of such change has been the tremendous expansion of the organizing capacity of the Leninist Communist Party, which has significantly reconfigured the relationship among the Chinese state, the bureaucracy, and Chinese society, leading to an intensification of both interactions and tensions. Making sense of these aspects of continuity and change is essential to gain a better understanding of the institutional logic of governance in China today and the potential direction of change in the future.

First, *the rhythm of shutting down and opening up*. Historically, China experienced a series of events and episodes shifting between opening and shut modes, both globally and domestically (Skinner 1971). During the long stretch of Chinese history, China was by and large insulated from influences from the outside world. Major institutional changes in state-making took place in modern history due to the forced opening up from outside, resulting in the inflow of ideas, practices, and institutions and an internal pursuit to catch up with the industrial world.

Modern China came into being through a long, arduous process of opening up and a break away from the shadow of the closeness and inwardness of the old empire. This trend began in the late Qing dynasty, went through the transitory Republican era, and entered the era of the People's Republic as a nation state in the world community. After its founding in 1949, the People's Republic of China was heavily influenced by the Soviet model of state socialism and a planned economy. Under the rule of the Chinese Communist Party, the party-state exerted strong political control and sought to develop economically with a series of large-scale political, economic, and social movements.

The making of the contemporary Chinese state took place in the larger, "cold war" international environment, which was characterized by confrontation, closeness, and mutual exclusion between the two ideological blocs. Between the 1950s and the 1970s of the Mao era, China entered another episode of closeness. It is only since the late 1970s as China entered the so-called "reform and opening up" era that China began to actively participate in international interactions and global activities. As a result of these drastic changes both domestically and internationally, the institutional logic of governance has evolved in interacting with broader, international environments, adapting as well as competing in the face of challenges significantly different from those it faced in the past. All these have shaped China's trajectory of change and will surely have a lasting impact on the future of China.

Second, *the organizational basis of the Chinese state*. Compared with the traditional Chinese empire, there has been a *qualitative* transformation in the organizational capacities of the Chinese state since 1949. A mode of party-state domination has been built on a distinct Leninist party-type of organization, with strong organizational links between the ruling party and the bureaucratic apparatus and with a personnel system that emphasizes discipline and loyalty. The charismatic authority's pursuit of political control and "miracles" to achieve economic development led to a strengthening of bureaucratic organizations as instruments of mobilization, with the tight-coupling organizational system and planned economy complementing each other. Many salient aspects of the Chinese bureaucracy discussed in the preceding chapters – intensive top-down pressures for meeting policy targets, political-following instead of rule-following, great capacities for mobilization, extensive and intensive interactions between the bureaucracy and the populace (Cai 2008, Lee and Zhang 2013) – all bear distinct marks of a Leninist party-state.

In this larger context, the Chinese bureaucracy can be described as a two-edged sword: On the one hand, it provides a strong organizational basis for the top leader's ambitions, response to crises, and mobilization to achieve policy targets, as demonstrated in the early years of the nationalization, collectivization, and Great Leap Forward campaigns. It also played a significant role in leading the rapid economic growth since the 1980s. On the other hand, the problems of bureaucratic-information transmission and processing or provision of incentives in the bureaucratic process contributed to some major blunders in contemporary China, such as the great famine of 1959–1962. In response, alternative, informal institutions, strategies, and flexible behaviors became widespread. These informal mechanisms alleviated the rigidity of the bureaucracy; at the same time, they weakened the legitimacy and effectiveness of the formal institutions and became a threat to the centralized authority.

Such tensions have induced a shift to upward recentralization, which has been greatly accelerated during the Xi Jinping era since the mid-2010s.

Third, *values and ideologies*. The official ideology in contemporary China appeared to have made a major break with the political culture of traditional China. Under Mao Zedong, the ruling party abandoned the traditional mode of domination, together with its basis of legitimation on traditional institutions. Instead, it embraced Marxist doctrine as the basis of the official ideology. Along with the tight control in culture, education, and other areas of propaganda, Marxist historical materialism offered command of the historical law, which served as the basis of legitimation for the charismatic authority of the top leaders. Corresponding to the rise of the charismatic authority was a suppression of autonomous public space. In Chinese history, despite the powerful Confucian ideology associated with the civil examination institution, there were diverse popular religions and cultural beliefs in grassroots society (Feuchtwang 2001, Tan 1986). In contemporary China, in contrast, the tight control by the party organization and the frequent political campaigns have greatly suppressed nonofficial, autonomous space, extending and strengthening the uniformity, exclusiveness, and monopoly of the official ideology.

But the disastrous consequences of the Cultural Revolution, the political turmoil, and the economic underdevelopment of the Mao era cast deep doubts on the "miracle"-based charismatic authority, fermenting a deep crisis in the official ideology. During the reform era, broadened interactions with the outside world, from trade, technology, education, and culture to personnel flows, led to major changes in the values, expectations, and pluralistic developments in Chinese society, cultivating an increasingly pluralistic civil society. To appreciate these changes, one need only take a look at the diverse views expressed on the Chinese Internet before the crackdown of the mid-2010s (Yang 2009, Zhou 2020a).

As a result, two major shifts in governance have taken place in the post-Mao era. First, economic development has become the main basis of legitimacy for the ruling party-state (Zhao, Gong and Hu 2012). Cheung (2008) and Xu (2011) attribute the success of such economic growth to competition among Chinese local governments, or to "regional decentralized authoritarianism," which released tremendous energy for economic development. As a result, the pendulum between stability and efficiency was temporarily tilted toward the "efficiency" side. Second, with the crisis of charismatic authority and the erosion of the ideological basis of persuasion, the party-state increasingly resorted to organizational discipline, the provision of incentives, or political coercion to ensure compliance. To do this required organizing capacities and political mechanisms to control and stifle dissenting voices and to mobilize economic resources for positive compliance. The very trade-off between efficiency and stability is revealed in the tensions between these two trends.

In view of the macro-history of China, the decentralization-induced economic development of the past four decades appears to be a tentative, new experiment that departs significantly from the established track of state building in Chinese history. As we can see, pressures and tensions resulting from the new experiences, the vested interests in existing institutions, and path dependency have all been mobilized to pull China back to the old track, under the rule of an all-encompassing centralized authority. During the last decade or so, the pendulum has been moving in the reverse direction, toward a reemphasis on stability over efficiency.

Indeed, we are witnessing China today at another historical turning point, a great reversal of the course of reform and the opening up of the past four decades. What is the relevance of this book at this historical juncture? The reader may notice that some episodes discussed in this book, such as public goods provision in rural areas, village elections, policy implementation in family planning or environmental protection areas, all have undergone significant changes in recent years, along with major shifts in macro-political environments and state policies. Nevertheless, I do believe that the kinds of issues, processes and mechanisms, and the larger patterns of state–society relationships discussed in this book remain relevant and significant, and they will continue to shape the future of China. I hope that this book will give testimony to the power of social science analysis that goes beyond a particular time and space.

GOVERNANCE IN CHINA: FUTURE CHALLENGES AND DIRECTIONS

Looking to the future of China, let us take another look at the trajectories of change in the post-Mao era, which have been shaped by the distinctive institutions and practices of governance discussed in this book. In the early years of the post-Mao era, the Chinese state was actively involved in leading economic development and its performance-based legitimation rested on an expansion of the market economy and the growth of the private sector. But since the mid-1990s, the Chinese state has gradually moved toward recentralization, and bureaucratic power has expanded and entrenched to all corners of society. This trend has accelerated in the recent decade.

The role of local governments and their bureaucratic institutions has been especially salient in this process, with a significance far exceeding the view of "local governments as the headquarters of local firms" (Walder 1995a), thus deserving another closer look. To a great extent, local governments in China today do not play the role of merely regulator, coordinator, or patron of local firms and other economic entities; rather, they become increasingly a main economic actor on their own, competing with other nonstate economic organizations for resources and opportunities. In other words, local governments as "revenue maximizers" have often become direct or potential competitors with other nonstate firms in local economic development. Local governments make use of their administrative control of factor resources (capital, land, labor market mobility) to contribute to economic activities. Such bureaucratic power-centered economic activities are unprecedented historically, especially in those areas that provide the largest source of government revenue. This generates a different type of competition, not among economic actors in the marketplace but among local officials in the political arena. Bureaucratic power grows with the centralization of power toward the state: State ambitions, bureaucratic power, and performance incentive designs reinforce one another, leading to the grand trend of the bureaucratization of society after China entered the twenty-first century.

In hindsight, we can see how the institutional logic of governance foreshadowed the distinct trajectory of state building in contemporary China as well as the path of changes in the post-Mao era (Nathan 2003, Pei 2006). Several themes loom large over the course of China's institutional transformation characterized by progress, frustrations, setbacks, and reversal. Take, for example, institution building in the rule of law, which is claimed to be one of the central goals of institutional transformation by the party-state and which was once actively pursued by those open-minded top leaders. But little substantive progress has been made over the years, despite tremendous development in the economic arenas.

From the discussion developed in this book, the reason behind this paralysis is not difficult to fathom. At the core of the legal system is the fundamental principle of equality before the law and judgment and evaluation by the same set of rules and procedures. This logic is especially challenging to the centralized authority in two ways. First, the effective operation of the legal system requires a series of reforms in legislation, prosecution, law enforcement, and so forth, with a new, independent judiciary and the implementation of stable, impersonal legal rules. Such institutions are incompatible with the system of the party-state, and they impose constraints on the arbitrary power of the top leaders and on the campaign-style mobilization in response to threats and crises. Second, an independent judicial system also imposes constraints on the problem-solving capacity and flexible adaptation of local governments. In actual political processes, we often observe behavior by local governments in urban affairs, in policy implementation, among others, that follows the top-down arbitrary power and is at odds with the established rules and procedures. Such behavior has strengthened the capacity of local officials to get things done but, at the same time, it has undermined the basis for the rule of law.

The same logic can be extended to account for the stagnation in the rationalization of the government bureaucracy. In a Weberian bureaucracy, the rules of behavior for officials are characterized by impersonal relations, leading to a tendency toward an "iron cage" of bureaucratic rigidity (Weber 1978). As such, bureaucratic rationality defies the arbitrary power of the higher authorities and, at the same time, constrains the flexibility in policy implementation, accelerating tensions between the centralization of authority and effective, local governance. In the Western context, Karl Mannheim (1936) observes the fundamental tendency of all bureaucratic thought to turn all problems of politics into problems of administration. In the Chinese bureaucracy, we observe the opposite characteristic. The effective mechanism of campaign-style mobilization turns administrative matters into political matters, so that political mechanisms can replace bureaucratic routines to mobilize attention and resources effectively. In policy-implementation settings, we often hear declarations from higher authorities to their subordinates: "This is a political task. Get it done at all costs." In campaign-style mobilization, local governments use all their resources and manpower to get things done, as we saw in the episodes of village elections and environmental regulation in the previous chapters. In this process, the rational foundation of the bureaucratic organizations, such as rules and procedures, is disrupted and undermined time and again.

In this broad context, we can also make sense of the difficulties in the development of professionalization in Chinese society. The centralization of authority in China has facilitated the enforcement of universal standards (such as the weights and measures since the Qin dynasty), but they are in tension with the professional logic of contemporary society, in which professional processes and the associated professional organizations and professional self-governance have become key institutions. For example, the professionalization process in the medical arena has shaped doctor-patient, doctor-nurse, doctor-hospital relationships. Professional relationships in legal, educational, managerial, and many other areas play a key role in integrating different walks of life. Professionalization in these areas is made possible through professional training, knowledge cumulation and diffusion, professional associations and journals, and related institutions. These processes have their own realms of autonomy and self-governance, which are at odds with the centralization of authority. Over the years, we have witnessed a struggle in China between the political authority and self-governance efforts by professionals. The centralized authority has adopted a series of measures to constrain and undermine the professionalization processes and other nongovernment organizations that are outside its realm of political control. The ideology of centralization denies professionalism, and sees professional associations as a threat to the centralized authority. Indeed, professionals are forced to give up or adapt their values and judgments to political ceremonies. When a professional (i.e., a professor) has to participate in such political ceremonies under political pressures, he/she has to suspend professional judgment and expectations and play a facilitating role in such rituals and ceremonies. As such, professionalization processes are disrupted, marginalized, and become mere gestures rather than the basic values and norms that shape social relations and behavioral expectations.

In Chapter 1, I point out that there are two main themes to understand governance in China, the first is the relationship between the central and local governments, and the second is the relationship between the state and the populace. In China's long history, the former occupied a central place and the latter gained saliency only occasionally. Historically, the self-organization of grassroots society and the fact that top-down government bureaucracies did not extend below the county level greatly alleviated the pressures and burdens of governance in the empire. In the contemporary era of state building, in contrast, the state and society have established close, direct, and intensive interactions. On the one hand, local governments have provided organizational links between the state and the populace, with tremendous capacities for social mobilization; on the other hand, uneven regional development, bottom-up social pressures, and rightful resistance have all generated tremendous pressures on the centralized authority. The episodes of road construction, village elections, and collective actions discussed in the previous chapters show that Chinese society is not merely passively "being governed"; rather, grassroots China stubbornly insists on its participation in the political process, in its own ways and by its own logic. The people have played different roles on different occasions: Sometimes they were part of the resources being mobilized to pursue policy targets; sometimes they provided buffers to alleviate the adverse effects of state policies; and sometimes they provided mechanisms to resist or to rebel against the will of the state.

Chinese society has changed fundamentally in the post-Mao era, as has the world at large in which China is now actively participating. The authoritarian state has tried hard to hold on to its power, and so far, it has succeeded. But both the organization and ideology pillars that sustain the mode of party-state domination and the social ground upon which the power-holders stand are shifting. Decades of China's opening up to the outside world, with a multitude of channels for international exchanges of information, ideas, and institutional practices and with millions of citizens traveling around the world and bearing witness to lives and activities in other societies, will inevitably leave long-lasting marks on the future trajectory of change in China. Along with the advance of an increasingly pluralistic Chinese society and expanding capacities for self-organization, the theme of state–society relationships will become even more salient in China's governance and will play a significant role in shaping the direction of change in the future. To wit, the sources of fundamental change in China lie in its opening up to the outside world.

There is no doubt that contemporary China is at a conjuncture of historical significance in her search for a new mode of domination and in her move away from the legacies of bureaucratic monarchy and the party-state. Whatever path China may embark on during the next phase of its evolution, the quote from G. William Skinner, at the beginning of this chapter, is a somber reminder that China will have its own distinctive historical trajectory of change. To paraphrase Levenson (1965, vol. 3), to explain is not to excuse, nor is it to indict; to which I shall add that, it allows us to anticipate and to hope. It is my hope that the research reported in the book will help to shed light on the institutional arrangements and the mechanisms that have molded the patterned practice of governance in China and to make sense of the larger, historical context in which they have taken shape and of the course of change in the future. Obviously, whatever new institutions emerge in China's future, organizational challenges to governance discussed in this book will remain, but a new mode of domination and a new basis of legitimation will allow broader space for political imagination, experimentation, and a search for new solutions.

Glossary

biantong (变通) flexible adaptation

cengceng jiama (层层加码) downward acceleration of implementation pressures

cunzhishu (村支书) village party secretary

cunzhuren (村主任) elected village head

danwei (单位) workplace

danwei suoyouzhi (单位所有制) work unit-ownership system

daode zhiguo (道德治国) morality-based governance

dazibao (大字报) big-character poster

dingceng sheji (顶层设计) "top-level design"

duilian (对联) Chinese posters

jiancha yanshou (检查验收) inspection and appraisal

junxianzhi (郡县制) territorially-based prefecture and county institutions

keju (科举) civil examination institution

liandai zeren zhidu (联带责任制度) joint responsibility principle

shangfang (上访) higher authorities

shang you zhengce, xia you duice (上有政策, 下有对策) From above there are imposed policies, and from below there are evading strategies

she (赊) "take the goods first and make payments later"

tingyi (廷议) court debates

tuigeng huanlin (退耕还林) Sloping Land Conservation Program

weiwen (维稳) maintenance of social order

xingzheng fabaozhi (行政发包制) administrative subcontracting model

yalixing tizhi (压力型体制) pressure-centered government

yanguan (言官) official positions for criticism

yijiantiao (一肩挑)　"one-shoulder" policy (position of village party secretary and of the elected village head held by the same person).

yipiao foujue (一票否决)　one item veto rule

you hong you zhuan (又红又专)　red and expert

youxu jingzheng (有序竞争)　order-based competition

zheng-fa-wei (政法委)　(party's) political and legal commission

zhengji (政绩)　administrative achievements

zijin nuoyong (资金挪用)　illicit resource transfers

zuijizhao (罪己诏)　emperor's declaration of self-critique

References

Acemoglu, Daron and James A. Robinson. 2012. *Why Nations Fail*. New York: Harcourt Brace.

Aghion, Philippe and Jean Tirole. 1997. "Formal and Real Authority in Organizations." *Journal of Political Economy* 105(1):1–29.

Ahlers, Anna L. and Gunter Schubert. 2015. "Effective Policy Implementation in China's Local State." *Modern China* 41(4):372–405.

Ai, Yun. 2008. "Guojia Zhengce Zai Jicheng Zhengfu De Zhixing Guocheng [The Implementation of Family Planning Policies at the County Level]." *Paper presented at the Workshop on Empirical Research in Organizational Sociology*, Sun Yat-sen University, Guangzhou.

   2011. "Shangxiaji Zhengfu Jiang 'Kaohe Jiancha' Yu 'Yingdui' Guocheng De Zuzhixue Fenxi Yi a Xian 'Jihua Shengyu' Nianzhong Kaohe Weili [An Organizational Study of the Inspecting-Responding Process within the Chinese Government Hierarchy: A Case Study of the End-of-Year Assessment of Family Planning in County A]." *Shehui [Society]* 31 (3):68–87.

Alesina, Alberto and Enrico Spolaore. 2003. *The Size of Nations*. Cambridge, MA: The MIT Press.

Allison, Graham T. 1971. *Essence of Decision: Explaining the Cuban Missile Crisis*. Boston, MA: Little, Brown.

Baker, George, Robert Gibbons and Kevin Murphy. 2001. "Bringing the Market inside the Firm?" *American Economic Review* 91(2):212–18.

Bates, Robert H. 1981. *Markets and States in Tropical Africa: The Political Basis of Agricultural Policies*. Berkeley: University of California Press.

Bernhard, Michael. 1987. "The Strikes of June 1976 in Poland." *East European Politics and Societies* 1(3): 363–92.

Bian, Yanjie. 2018. "The Prevalence and the Increasing Significance of Guanxi." *China Quarterly* 235(3):597–621.

   2019. *Guanxi: How China Works*. Cambridge: Polity.

Binmore, Ken, Martin J. Osborne and Ariel Rubinstein. 1992. "Noncooperative Models of Bargaining." Pp. 181–225 in *Handbook of Game Theory* (Vol. 1), edited by R. J. Aumann and S. Hart. Amsterdam: Elsevier Science Publishers.

Birnbaum, Pierre. 1988. *States and Collective Action.* Cambridge: Cambridge University Press.

Blau, Peter M. 1963. *The Dynamics of Bureaucracy: A Study of Interpersonal Relations in Two Government Agencies.* Chicago, IL: University of Chicago Press.

Bourdieu, Pierre. 1986. "The Forms of Capital." Pp. 241–58 in *Handbook of Theory and Research for the Sociology of Education,* edited by J. G. Richardson. Westport, CT: Greenwood Press.

Brandt, Loren, Debin Ma and Thomas G. Rawski. 2014. "From Divergence to Convergence: Reevaluating the History behind China's Economic Room." *Journal of Economic Literature* 52(1):45–123.

Buchanan, James M., Robert D. Tollison and Gordon Tullock, eds. 1980. *Toward a Theory of the Rent-Seeking Society.* College Station: Texas A&M University Press.

Bulman, David J. 2016. *Incentivized Development in China: Leaders, Governance, and Growth in China's Counties.* New York: Cambridge University Press.

Bunce, Valerie. 1992. "Two-Tiered Stalinism: A Case of Self-Destruction." Pp. 25–45 in *Constructing Capitalism: The Reemergence of Civil Society and Liberal Economy in the Post-communist World,* edited by K. Poznanski. Boulder, CO: Westview.

Burbank, Jane and Frederick Cooper. 2010. *Empires in World History: Power and the Politics of Difference.* Princeton, NJ: Princeton University Press.

Burns, John P. 1988. *Political Participation in Rural China.* Berkeley: University of California Press.

Cai, Hongbin and Daniel Treisman. 2006. "Did Government Decentralization Cause China's Economic Miracle?" *World Politics* 58(July):505–35.

Cai, Yongshun. 2008. "Local Governments and the Suppression of Popular Resistance in China." *The China Quarterly* 193(1):24–42.

2010. *Collective Resistance in China: Why Popular Protests Succeed or Fail.* Stanford, CA: Stanford University Press.

Chan, Hon S. 2004. "Cadre Personnel Management in China: The Nomenklatura System, 1990–1998." *The China Quarterly* 179(September):703–34.

Chan, Hon S. and Jie Gao. 2018. "The Politics of Personnel Redundancy: The Non-leading Cadre System in the Chinese Bureaucracy." *China Quarterly* 235(September):622–43.

Chandler, Alfred D., Jr. 1994. *Scale and Scope: The Dynamics of Industrial Capitalism.* Cambridge, MA: Belknap Press of Harvard University Press.

Chen, Chih-jou Jay. 2009. "Growing Social Unrest and Emergent Protest Groups in China." Pp. 87–106 in *Rise of China: Beijing's Strategies and Implications for the Asia-Pacific,* edited by H.-H. M. Hsiao and C.-Y. Lin. London and New York: Routledge.

Chen, Jiajian, Qiongwen Zhang and Yu Hu. 2015. "Xiangmu Zhi Yu Zhengfujian Quanze Guanxi Yanbian: Yi Funü Xiao E Daikuan Xiangmu

Weili [Project System and Its Impact on the Relationship between Different Levels of Government: Taking Women's Small Loan Payments as an Example]." *Shehui [Society]* 35(5):1–24.

Chen, Tushou. 2013. *Guguo Renmin Yousuosi [Reflections of the People]*. Beijing: Sanlian Shudian.

Chen, Xi. 2012. *Social Protest and Contentious Authoritarianism in China*. New York: Cambridge University Press.

2017. "Origins of Informal Coercion in China." *Politics and Society* 45(1):67–89.

Chen, Xulu. 1992. *Jindai Zhongguo Shehui De Xin Chendaixie [The Evolution of Modern Chinese Society]*. Shanghai: Shanghai Renmin Chubanshe.

Chen, Yongfa. 1998. *Zhongguo Gongchan Geming Qishinian* [Seventy Years of the Chinese Communist Revolution] (2 vols.). Taipei: Lianjing Chuban Shiye Gongsi.

Cheung, Steven. 2008. *Zhongguo De Jingji Zhidu [The Economic Institutions of China]*. Beijing: Zhongxin Chubanshe.

Chong, Dennis. 1991. *Collective Action and the Civil Rights Movement*. Chicago, IL: University of Chicago Press.

Chu, Tung-tsu. 1962. *Local Government in China under the Ch'ing*. Cambridge, MA: Harvard University Press.

Chu, Tung-Tsu. 1965. *Law and Society in Traditional China*. Paris: Mouton.

Chung, Jae Ho. 2016. "China's Local Governance in Perspective: Instruments of Central Government Control." *China Journal* 75(January):38–60.

Chwe, Michael Suk-Young. 2001. *Rational Ritual: Culture, Coordination, and Common Knowledge*. Princeton, NJ: Princeton University Press.

Coase, Ronald H. 1937. "The Nature of the Firm." *Economica* 4(3):386–405.

1960. "The Problem of Social Cost." *Journal of Law and Economics* 3 (October):1–44.

Cohen, Paul A. 2010. *Discovering History in China: American Historical Writing on the Recent Chinese Past*. New York: Columbia University Press.

Colburn, Forrest D., ed. 1989. *Everyday Forms of Peasant Resistance*. Armonk, NY: M.E. Sharpe.

Coleman, James S. 1982. *The Asymmetric Society*. Syracuse, NY: Syracuse University Press.

1994. *Foundations of Social Theory*. Cambridge, MA: Belknap Press of Harvard University Press.

Committee, Document Office of the Party Central. 1986. *S Anzhongq Uanhuyi Ilai De Zhongyiaow Enjian Xuanbian [Selected Documents since the Third Plenum]* (2 vols.). Beijing: People's Publishing House.

Creel, H. G. 1964. "The Beginnings of Bureaucracy in China: The Origin of the Hsien." *The Journal of Asian Studies* 23(2):155–84.

Crozier, Michel. 1964. *The Bureaucratic Phenomenon*. Chicago, IL: University of Chicago Press.

Cyert, Richard Michael and James G. March. 1963. *A Behavioral Theory of the Firm*. Englewood Cliffs, NJ: Prentice Hall.

Dalton, Russell J. and Manfred Kuechler, eds. 1990. *Challenging the Political Order: New Social and Political Movement in Western Democracies*. New York: Oxford University Press.

Deng, Xiaonan, Jiaqi Cao and Ping Tianmaoshu, eds. 2012. *Wenshu, Zhengling, Xinxi Goutong: Yi Tangsongshiqi Weizhu [Documents, Decrees, and Information Flow: Research on Tang-Song Dynasties]* (2 vols.). Beijing: Peking University Press.

Deng, Yanhua and Kevin J. O'Brien. 2013. "Relational Repression in China: Using Social Ties to Demobilize Protesters." *China Quarterly* 215(September):533–52.

Dewatripont, Mathias and Eric Maskin. 1995. "Credit and Efficiency in Centralized and Decentralized Economies." *Review of Economic Studies* 62 (4):541–55.

Di, Jinhua. 2010. "Tongguo Yundong Jinxing Zhili: Xiangzhen Jiceng Zhengquan De Zhili Celüe Dui Zhongguo Zhongbu Diqu Maiiang 'Zhishu Zaoliu' Zhongxin Gongzuo De Ge'an Yanjiu [From Online to Offline: The Formation of Collective Action and Its Contributing Factors: A Case Study of a Protest in the Location of a Food Waste Treatment Facility]." *Shehui* (3):168–95.

Dikotter, Frank. 2010. *Mao's Great Famine: The History of China's Most Devastating Catastrophe, 1958–1962.* New York: Walker.

DiMaggio, Paul J. and Walter W. Powell. 1983. "The Iron Cage Revisited: Institutional Isomorphism and Collective Rationality in Organizational Fields." *American Sociological Review* 48(2):147–60.

Duara, Prasenjit. 1988. *Culture, Power, and the State: Rural North China, 1900–1942.* Stanford, CA: Stanford University Press.

Eaton, Sarah and Genia Kostka. 2014. "Authoritarian Environmentalism Undermined? Local Leaders' Time Horizons and Environmental Policy Implementation in China." *China Quarterly* 218(June, 2014):359–80.

Edin, Maria. 2003. "State Capacity and Local Agent Control in China: CCP Cadre Management from a Township Perspective." *The China Quarterly* (173 March):35–52.

Eisenstadt, S. N. 1968. "Introduction: Charisma and Institution Building: Max Weber and Modern Sociology." Pp. ix–lvi in *Max Weber on Charisma and Institution Building: Selected Papers*, edited by S. N. Eisenstadt. Chicago, IL: University of Chicago Press.

Ellickson, Robert C. 1991. *Order without Law: How Neighbors Settle Disputes.* New York: Cambridge University Press.

Elman, Benjamin A. 2013. *Civil Examinations and Meritocracy in Late Imperial China.* Cambridge, MA: Harvard University Press.

Evans, Peter. 1995. *Embedded Autonomy: States and Industrial Transformation.* Princeton, NJ: Princeton University Press.

Evans, Peter, Dietrich Rueschemeyer and Theda Skocpol. 1985. *Bringing the State Back In.* New York: Cambridge University Press.

Evans, Peter and James E. Rauch. 1999. "Bureaucracy and Growth: A Cross-National Analysis of the Effects of 'Weberian' State Structures on Economic Growth." *American Sociological Review* 64(5):748–65.

Fei, Xiaotong. 1992[1948]. *From the Soil: The Foundations of Chinese Society. A Translation of Fei Xiaotong's Xiangtu Zhongguo. With an Introduction and Epilogue by Gary G. Hamilton and Wang Zheng.* Berkeley: University of California Press.

Feng, Shizheng. 2011. "Zhongguo Guojia Yundong De Xingcheng Yu Bianyi: Jiyu Zhengti De Zhengti Xing Jieshi [The Origins and Transformation of National Mobilization in China: Toward a Holistic Approach]." *Kaifang Shidai [Open Times]* (1):73–97.

Feuchtwang, Stephan. 2001. *Popular Religion in China: The Imperial Metaphor.* New York: Routledge.

Finer, S. E. 1997. *The History of Government III: Empires, Monarchies and the Modern State.* London: Oxford University Press.

Freidson, Eliot. 1986. *Professional Powers: A Study of the Institutionalization of Formal Knowledge.* Chicago: University of Chicago Press.

Friedland, Roger and Robert R. Alford. 1991. "Bringing Society Back In: Symbols, Practices, and Institutional Contradictions." Pp. 232–63 in *The New Institutionalism in Organizational Analysis,* edited by W. W. Powell and P. J. DiMaggio. Chicago, IL: University of Chicago Press.

Friedman, Edward, Paul G. Pickowicz and Mark Selden. 1991. *Chinese Village, Socialist State.* New Haven, CT: Yale University Press.

Fudenberg, Drew and Jean Tirole. 1983. "Sequential Bargaining with Incomplete Information." *Review of Economic Studies* 50(2):221–47.

Fukuyama, Francis. 2004. *State Building: Governance and World Order in the Twenty-First Century.* Ithaca, NY: Cornell University Press.

Gamson, William. 1968. *The Strategy of Social Protest.* Homewood, IL: Dorsey.

Gao, Hua. 2000. *Hongtaiyang Shi Zenyang Shengqide: Yan'an Zhengfeng De Lailong Qumai [How the Red Sun Rose: The Origin and Development of the Yan'an Rectification Movement].* Hong Kong: Chinese University of Hong Kong Press.

Geertz, Clifford. 1978. "The Bazaar Economy: Information and Search in Peasant Marketing." *American Economic Review* 68(2):28–32.

Gibbons, Robert. 1998. "Incentives in Organizations." *Journal of Economic Perspectives* 12(4):115–32.

Gobel, Christian. 2011. "Uneven Policy Implementation in Rural China." *China Journal* (65 January):53–76.

Gouldner, Alvin Ward. 1964. *Patterns of Industrial Bureaucracy.* New York: Free Press.

Granovetter, Mark. 1978. "Threshold Models of Collective Behavior." *American Journal of Sociology* 83:420–43.

1985. "Economic Action and Social Structure: The Problem of Embeddedness." *American Journal of Sociology* 91:481–510.

Griffiths, Franklyn. 1971. "A Tendency Analysis of Soviet Policy-Making." in *Interest Groups in Soviet Politics,* edited by G. Skilling and F. Griffiths. Princeton, NY: Princeton University Press.

Grossman, Sanford and Oliver Hart. 1986. "The Costs and Benefits of Ownership: A Theory of Vertical and Lateral Ownership." *Journal of Political Economy* 94(4):681–719.

Gu, Baochang, Feng Wang, Zhigang Guo and Erli Zhang. 2007. "China's Local and National Fertility Policies at the End of the Twentieth Century." *Population and Development Review* 33(1):129–47.

Hamilton, Gary G. 1984. "Patriarchalism in Imperial China and Western Europe: A Revison of Weber's Sociology of Domination." *Theory and Society* 13 (3):393–425.

Hankiss, Elemer. 1989. "Demobilization, Self-Mobilization and Quasi-Mobilization in Hungary, 1948–1987." *East European Politics and Societies* 3:105–51.

Harding, Harry. 1981. *Organizing China: The Problem of Bureaucracy, 1949–1976*. Stanford, CA: Stanford University Press.

Hart, Oliver and John Moore. 1988. "Incomplete Contracts and Renegotiation." *Econometrica* 56(4):755–85.

Hart, Oliver. 1995. *Firms, Contracts and Financial Structure*. New York: Oxford University Press.

Havel, Vaclav. 1985. *The Power of the Powerless: Citizens against the State in Central-Eastern Europe*. Armonk, NY: M.E. Sharpe.

He, Baogang. 2007. *Rural Democracy in China: The Role of Village Elections*. New York: Palgrave.

He, Ping. 1998. *Qingdai Fushui Zhengce Yanjiu: 1644–1840 [Research on Tax Policies in the Qing Dynasty, 1644–1840]*. Beijing: Zhongguo Shehui Kexue Chubanshe.

Heberer, Thomas and Gunter Schubert. 2012. "County and Township Cadres in China as a Strategic Group: A New Approach to Political Agency in China's Local State." *Journal of Chinese Political Science* 17(3):221–49.

Heberer, Thomas and René Trapple. 2013. "Evaluation Processes, Local Cadres' Behaviour and Local Development Processes." *Journal of Contemporary China* 22(84):1048–66.

Hirschman, Albert O. 1970. *Exit, Voice, and Loyalty: Responses to Decline in Firms, Organizations, and States*. Cambridge, MA: Harvard University Press.

1982. *Shifting Involvement: Private Interest and Public Action*. Princeton, NJ: Princeton University Press.

Hou, Xudong. 2018. *Chong: Xin-Ren Xing Junchen Guanxi Yu Xihan Lishi De Zhankai* (The Spoils System: The Trust-Appointment Style and Emperor-Bureaucrat Relationship since the Western Han Dynasty). Beijing: Beijing Shifan Daxue Chubanshe.

Hsiao, Kung-Chuan. 1960. *Rural China: Imperial Control in the Nineteenth Century*. Seattle: University of Washington Press.

Huang, Philip C. C. 1990. *The Peasant Family and Rural Development in the Yangzi Delta, 1350–1988*. Stanford, CA: Stanford University Press.

2008. "Centralized Minimalism: Semiformal Governance by Quasi-Officials and Dispute Resolution in China." *Modern China* 34(1):9–35.

Huang, Ray. 1974. *Taxation and Governmental Finance in Sixteenth-Century Ming China*. New York: Cambridge University Press.

1981. *1587: A Year of No Significance*. New Haven, CT: Yale University Press.

2001. *Huanghe Qingshan: Huang Renyu Huiyilu [(Yellow River and Green Mountain: Huang Renyu's Memoir)*. Beijing: Sanlian Shudian.

Huang, Yasheng. 1995. "Administrative Monitoring in China." *The China Quarterly* (173 (September)):828–43.

2003. *Selling China: Foreign Direct Investment During the Reform Era*. New York: Cambridge University Press.

Huntington, Samuel P. 1968. *Political Order in Changing Societies*. New Haven, CT: Yale University Press.

Isamu, Ogata (尾形勇) and Hequan Zhang. 2010 [1991]. *Zhongguo Gudai De "Jia" Yu Guojia [Home and "Country" in Ancient China]*. Nanjing: Jiangsu Renmin Chubanshe.

Jensen, Michael C. and W. H. Meckling. 1976. "Theory of the Firm: Managerial Behavior, Agency Costs, and Ownership Structure." *Journal of Financial Economics* 3(4):305–60.

Jin, Guantao and Qingfeng Liu. 2011. *Xingsheng Yu Weiji: Lun Zhongguo Shehui Chaowending Jiegou [Prosperity and Crisis: The Structure of Super Stability in Chinese Soeciety]*. Beijing: Falü Chubanshe.

Kennan, John and Robert Wilson. 1993. "Bargaining with Private Information." *Journal of Economic Literature* 31(1):45–104.

Kerr, Steven. 1975. "On the Folly of Rewarding A, While Hoping for B." *Academy of Management Journal* 18(4):769–83.

Kipnis, Andrew B. 2015. "Modernity and the Chinese Moral Crisis." *China Journal* 75:121–27.

Kornai, János. 1979. "Resource-Constrained versus Demand-Constrained Systems." *Econometrica* 47(4):801–19.

1986. "The Soft Budget Constraint." *Kyklos* 39(1):3–30.

Kornai, János, Eric Maskin and Gérard Roland. 2003. "Understanding the Soft Budget Constraint." *Journal of Economic Literature* 41(4):1095–136.

Kostka, Genia and Jonas Nahm. 2017. "Central-Local Relations: Recentralization and Environmental Governance in China." *China Quarterly* (231 (September)):567–82.

Kuhn, Philip A. 1980. *Rebellion and Its Enemies in Late Imperial China: Militarization and Social Structure, 1796–1864*. Cambridge, MA: Harvard East Asian Series 49. Harvard University Press.

1990. *Soulstealers; the Chinese Sorcery Scare of 1768*. Cambridge, MA: Harvard University Press.

2002. *Origins of the Modern Chinese State*. Stanford, CA.: Stanford University Press.

Kung, James Kai-sing and Shuo Chen. 2011. "The Tragedy of the Nomenklatura: Career Incentives and Political Radicalism During China's Great Leap Famine." *American Political Science Review* 105(1):27–45.

Laba, Roman. 1986. "Worker Roots of Solidarity." *Problems of Communism* 35:47–67.

Laffont, Jean-Jacques and Jean-Charles Rochet. 1997. "Collusion in Organizations." *Scandinavian Journal of Economics* 99(4):485–95.

Lampton, David M., ed. 1987. *Policy Implementation in Post-Mao China*. Berkeley: University of California Press.

Lampton, David M. 1992. "A Plum for a Peach: Bargaining, Interest, and Bureaucratic Politics in China." Pp. 33–58 in *Bureaucracy, Politics, and Decision Making in Post-Mao China*, edited by K. G. Lieberthal and D. M. Lampton. Berkeley and Los Angeles: University of California Press.

Landes, David S. 2006. "Why Europe and the West? Why Not China?" *Journal of Economic Perspectives* 20(2):3–22.

Landry, Pierre F. 2008. *Decentralized Authoritarianism in China: The Communist Party's Control of Elites in the Post-Mao Era.* New York: Cambridge University Press.

Larson, Magali Sarfatti. 1977. *The Rise of Professionalism: A Sociological Analysis.* Berkeley: University of California Press.

Lazear, Edward and Sherwin Rosen. 1981. "Rank-Order Tournaments as Optimum Labor Contracts." *Journal of Political Economy* 89(5):841–64.

Lee, Ching Kwan. 1998. "The Labor Politics of Market Socialism: Collective Inaction and Class Experiences among State Workers in Guangzhou." *Modern China* 24(1):3–33.

Lee, Ching Kwan and Yonghong Zhang. 2013. "The Power of Instability: Unraveling the Microfoundations of Bargained Authoritarianism in China." *American Journal of Sociology* 118(6):1475–508.

Levenson, Joseph R. 1965. *Confucian China and Its Modern Fate: A Trilogy* (3 vols.). Berkeley: University of California Press.

Li, Cheng and David Bachman. 1989. "Localism, Elitism, and Immobilism: Elite Formation and Social Change in Post-Mao China." *World Politics* 42 (1):64–94.

Li, Feng. 2008. *Bureaucracy and the State in Early China: Governing the Western Zhou.* New York: Cambridge University Press.

Li, Hongbin and Li-An Zhou. 2005. "Political Turnover and Economic Performance: The Incentive Role of Personnel Control in China." *Journal of Public Economics* 89(9–10):1743–62.

Li, Rui. 1999. *Dayuejin Qinliji* (My Personal Experiences during the Great Leap Forward) (2 vols.). Haikou: Nanfang Chubanshe.

Lieberthal, Kenneth G. 1992. "Introduction: The 'Fragmented Authoritarianism' Model and Its Limitations." Pp. 1–30 in *Bureaucracy, Politics, and Decision Making in Post-Mao China*, edited by K. G. Lieberthal and D. M. Lampton. Berkeley: University of California Press.

Lieberthal, Kenneth and David M. Lampton, eds. 1992. *Bureaucracy, Politics and Decision Making in Post-Mao China.* Berkeley: University of California Press.

Lieberthal, Kenneth and Michel Oksenberg. 1986. *Bureaucratic Politics and Chinese Energy Development.* Washington, DC: U.S. Dept. of Commerce, International Trade Administration.

Lin, Nan. 1995. "Local Market Socialism: Local Corporatism in Action in Rural China." *Theory and Society* 24:301–54.

    2001. *Social Capital: A Theory of Social Structure and Action.* New York: Cambridge University Press.

Lindblom, Charles E. 1959. "The Science of 'Muddling Through'." *Public Administration Review* 19(2):79–88.

    1979. "Still Muddling, Not yet Through." *Public Administration Review* 39 (6):517–26.

Lipsky, Michael. 1980. *Street-Level Bureaucracy.* New York: Russell Sage Foundation.

Ma, Xiaoying and Leonard Ortolano. 2000. *Environmental Regulation in China: Institutions, Enforcement, and Compliance.* Lanham, MD: Rowman & Littlefield.

Mahoney, James and Kathleen Thelen. 2009. "A Theory of Gradual Institutional Change." Pp. 1–37 in *Explaining Institutional Change: Ambiguity, Agency, and Power*, edited by J. Mahoney and K. Thelen. New York: Cambridge University Press.

Maier, Charles S., ed. 1987. *Changing Boundaries of the Political: Essays on the Evolving Balance between the State and Society, Public and Private in Europe.* London: Cambridge University Press.

Manion, Melanie. 1985. "The Cadre Management System, Post-Mao: The Appointment, Promotion, Transfer and Removal of Party and State Leaders." *The China Quarterly* 102(June):203–33.

   2006. "Democracy, Cumminity, Trust: The Impact of Elections in Rural China." *Comparative Political Studies* 39:603–20.

Mao, Zedong. 1977a. *Mao Zedong Xuanji, Di Wu Juan [Selected Works of Mao Zedong]* (Vol. 5). Beijing: Renmin Chubanshe.

   1977b [1957]. "On the Correct Handling of Contradictions among the People." Pp. 363–402 in *The Selected Works of Mao Zedong* (Vol. 5), edited by Z. Mao. Beijing: People's Publishing House.

   1991. *Mao Zedong Xuanji* [The Selected Works of Mao Zedong]) (Vol. 2). Beijing: Renmin Chubianshe.

March, James G. 1962. "The Business Firm as a Political Coalition." *Journal of Politics* 24(4):662–78.

March, James G. and Herbert Alexander Simon. 1958. *Organizations.* New York: Wiley.

March, James G. and Johan P. Olsen. 1979. *Ambiguity and Choice in Organizations.* Bergen: Universitetsforlaget.

   1988. *Decisions and Organizations.* New York: Blackwell.

   1994. *A Primer on Decision Making: How Decisions Happen.* New York: Free Press.

Marx, Karl. 1963[1852]. *The Eighteenth Brumaire of Louis Bonaparte.* New York: International Publishers.

Mason, David S., Daniel N. Nelson and Bohdan M. Szklarski. 1991. "Apathy and the Birth of Democracy: The Polish Struggle." *East European Politics and Societies* 5:205–33.

McAdam, Doug. 1982. *Political Process and the Development of Black Insurgency, 1930–1970.* Chicago, IL: University of Chicago Press.

McAfee, R. Preston and John McMillan. 1995. "Organizational Diseconomies of Scale." *Journal of Economic & Management Strategy* 4(3):399–426.

McMillan, John. 1992. *Games, Strategies, and Managers.* New York: Oxford University Press.

Merton, Robert K. 1968a. "Bureaucratic Structure and Personality." Pp. 249–60 in *Social Theory and Social Structure*, edited by R. K. Merton. New York: Free Press.

   1968b. "On Sociological Theories of the Middle Range." Pp. 39–72 in *Social Theory and Social Structure (1968 Enlarged Edition)*, edited by R. K. Merton. New York: Free Press.

Meyer, John W. and Brian Rowan. 1977. "Institutionalized Organizations: Formal Structure as Myth and Ceremony." *American Journal of Sociology* 83(2):340–63.

Michels, Robert. 1968. *Political Parties: A Sociological Study of the Oligarchical Tendencies of Modern Democracy.* New York: Free Press.

Migdal, Joel S., Atul Kohli and Vivienne Shue. 1994. *State Power and Social Forces: Domination and Transformation in the Third World.* New York: Cambridge University Press.

Milgrom, Paul and John Roberts. 1988. "An Economic Approach to Influence Activities in Organizations." *American Journal of Sociology* 94: S154–S79.

1992. *Economics, Organization and Management.* Englewood Cliffs, NJ: Prentice Hall.

Mueller, Dennis C. 2003. *Public Choice III.* New York: Cambridge University Press.

Munro, Neil. 2012. "Connections, Paperwork or Passivity: Strategies of Popular Engagement with the Chinese Bureaucracy." *China Journal* 68 (July):147–75.

Nathan, Andrew. 2003. "Authoritarian Resilience." *Journal of Democracy* 14 (1):6–17.

Naughton, Barry. 1996. *Growing out of the Plan.* New York: Cambridge University Press.

Nee, Victor. 1989. "A Theory of Market Transition: From Redistribution to Markets in State Socialism." *American Sociological Review* 54:663–81.

O'Brien, Kevin J. and Lianjiang Li. 1999. "Selective Policy Implementation in Rural China." *Comparative Politics* 31(2):167–86.

2000. "Accommodating 'Democracy' in a One-Party Stat: Introducing Village Elections in China." *China Quarterly* 162:465–89.

2006. *Rightful Resistance in Rural China.* New York: Cambridge University Press.

O'Brien, Kevin J. and Rongbin Han. 2009. "Path to Democracy? Assessing Village Elections in China." *Journal of Contemporary China* 18(60).

Oi, Jean C. 1989. *State and Peasant in Contemporary China: The Political Economy of Village Government.* Berkeley: University of California Press.

1992. "Fiscal Reform and the Economic Foundations of Local State Corporatism in China." *World Politics* 45(1):99–126.

1995. "The Role of the Local State in China's Transitional Economy." *The China Quarterly* 144 (December)(1):1132–49.

1999. *Rural China Takes Off: Institutional Foundations of Economic Reform.* Berkeley: University of California Press.

Oi, Jean C. and Shukai Zhao. 2007. "Fiscal Crisis in China's Townships: Causes and Consequences." Pp. 75–96 in *Grassroots Political Reform in Contemporary China*, edited by M. Goldman and E. Perry. Cambridge, Mass.: Harvard University Press.

Oksenberg, Michel. 1974. "Methods of Communication within the Chinese Bureaucracy." *China Quarterly* 91:1–39.

Oliver, Pamela. 1980. "Rewards and Punishments as Selective Incentives for Collective Action: Theoretical Investigations." *American Journal of Sociology* 86:1356–75.

Oliver, Pamela, Gerald Marwell and Ruy Teixeira. 1985. "A Theory of the Critical Mass: I. Interdependence, Group Heterogeneity and the Produciton of Collective Action." *American Journal of Sociology* 91:522–56.

Olson, Mancur. 1965. *The Logic of Collective Action*, Edited by M. Cambridge. Cambridge, MA: Harvard University Press.

Orton, J. Douglas and Karl E. Weick. 1990. "Loosely Coupled Systems: A Reconceptualization." *Academy of Management Review* 15(2):203–23.

Ostrom, Elinor. 1990. *Governing the Commons: The Evolution of Institutions for Collective Action*. New York: Cambridge University Press.

Ouyang, Jing. 2011. *Celüe Zhuyi: Jie Zhen Yunzuo De Luoji [Tactics: The Logic of Operations in Jie Town]* . Beijing: Zhongguo Zhengfa Daxue Chubanshe.

Pang, Baoqing, Shu Keng and Lingna Zhong. 2018. "Sprinting with Small Steps: China's Cadre Management and Authoritarian Resilience." *China Journal* (80 July):68–93.

Parish, William L. and Martin King Whyte. 1978. *Village and Family in Contemporary China*. Chicago: University of Chicago Press.

Pei, Minxin. 2006. *China's Trapped Transition: The Limits of Developmental Autocracy* Cambridge, MA: Harvard University Press.

Peng, Yusheng. 2004. "Kinship Networks and Entrepreneurs in China's Transitional Economy." *American Journal of Sociology* 109(5):1045–74.

Perkins, Dwight Heald. 1988. "Reforming Chna's Economic System." *Journal of Economic Literature* 26(2):601–45.

Perry, Elizabeth J. 1989. "State and Society in Contemporary China." *World Politics* 42(July):579–91.

Perry, Elizabeth J. and Merle Goldman. 2007. *Grassroots Political Reform in Contemporary China*. Cambridge, MA: Harvard University Press.

    2011. "From Mass Campaigns to Managed Campaigns: 'Constructing a New Socialist Countryside'." in *Mao's Invisible Hand: The Political Foundations of Adaptive Governance in China*, edited by S. Heilmann and E. J. Perry. Cambridge, MA: Harvard University Asia Center.

Pieke, Frank N. 2009. "Marketization, Centralization and Globalization of Cadre Training in Contemporary China." *The China Quarterly* 200 (December):953–71.

Piven, Frances Fox and Richard A. Cloward. 1977. *Poor People's Movement: Why They Succeed, How They Fail*. New York: Vintage Books.

Pressman, Jeffrey L. and Aaron Wildavsky. 1984. *Implementation*. Berkeley: University of California Press.

Putnam, Robert. 1993. *Making Democracy Work: Civic Traditions in Modern Italy*. Princeton, NJ: Princeton University Press.

Qian, Yingyi. 1994. "Incentives and Loss of Control in an Optimal Hierarchy." *Review of Economic Studies* 61(3):527–44.

Qian, Yingyi and Barry R. Weingast. 1997. "Federalism as a Commitment to Preserving Market Incentives." *Journal of Economic Perspectives* 11(4):83–92.

Qian, Yingyi and Gérard Roland. 1998. "Federalism and the Soft Budget Constraint." *American Economic Review* 88(5):1143–62.

Qian, Yingyi, Gérard Roland and Chenggang Xu. 1999. "Why Is China Different from Eastern Europe? Perspectives from Organization Theory." *European Economic Review* 43(1):1085–94.

2006. "Coordination and Experimentation in M-Form and U-Form Organizations." *Journal of Political Economy* 114(2):366–402.

Qu, Jingdong, Feizhou Zhou and Xing Ying. 2009. "Cong Zongti Zhipei Dao Jishu Zhili: Jiyu Zhongguo 30 Nian Gaige Jingyan De Shehui Kexue Fenxi [From Overall Domination to Technical Governance: A Sociological Analysis Based on 30 Years of the Reform Experience]." *Zhongguo Shehui Kexue [Social Sciences in China]* (6).

Radner, Roy and Michael Rothschild. 1975. "On the Location of Effort." *Journal of Economic Theory* 10(3):358–76.

Research Office of CCP History, Henan Province. 2006. *Henan "Dayuejin" Yundong [The "Great Leap Forward" Movement in Henan]*. Beijing: Zhonggong Dangshi Chubanshe.

Research Office of CCP History, Shangdong Province. 2002. *Shandong "Dayuejin" Yundong [The "Great Leap Forward" Movement in Shandong]*. Rizhao: Rizhao Baoye Yinshua Youxian Gongsi.

Rong, Jingben (et al). 1998. *Cong Yalixing Tizhi Xiang Minzhu Hezuo Tizhi De Zhuan Bian: Xianxiang Liangji Zhengzhi Tizhi Gaige [From a Pressure System to the Institutions of Democratic Cooperation: Reform of Political Institutions at the County and Township Levels]*. Beijing: Zhongyang Bianyi Chubanshe.

Rooij, Benjamin Van. 2006. "Implementation of Chinese Environmental Law: Regular Enforcement and Political Campgaigns." *Development and Change* 37(1):57–74.

Rosenbaum, James E. 1984. *Career Mobility in a Corporate Hierarchy*. Orlando, FL: Academic Press.

Rothstein, Bo. 2015. "The Chinese Paradox of High Growth and Low Quality of Government: The Cadre Organization Meets Max Weber." *Governance* 28 (4):533–48.

Rubinstein, Ariel. 1982. "Perfect Equilibrium in a Bargaining Model." *Econometrica* 50(1):97–109.

1985. "A Bargaining Model with Incomplete Information About Time Preferences." *Econometrica* 53(5):1151–72.

Rude, George. 1981. *The Crowd in History*. London: Lawrence and Wishart.

Schell, Orvile. 1988. *Discos and Democracy*. New York: Pantheon Books.

Schubert, Gunter and Anna L. Ahlers. 2012. "County and Township Cadres as a Strategic Group: 'Building a New Socialist Countryside' in Three Provinces. " *The China Journal* (67 January):67–86.

Schurmann, Franz. 1968. *Ideology and Organization in Communist China*. Berkeley: University of California Press.

Schwartz, Benjamine I. 1985. *The World of Thought in Ancient China*. Cambridge, MA: The Belknap Press of Harvard University Press.

Scott, James C. 1985. *Weapons of the Weak: Everyday Forms of Peasant Resistance*. New Haven, CT: Yale University Press.

1989. "Everyday Forms of Resistance." in *Everyday Forms of Peasant Resistance*, edited by F. D. Colburn. Armonk, NY: M.E. Sharpe.

1998. *Seeing Like a State: How Certain Schemes to Improve the Human Condition Have Failed*. New Haven and London: Yale University Press.

Scott, Richard W. and Gerald F. Davis. 2007. *Organizations and Organizing: Rational, Natural, and Open Systems Perspectives*. Upper Saddle River, NJ: Pearson Education.

Selznick, Philip. 1949. *TVA and the Grass Roots: A Study in the Sociology of Formal Organization*. Berkeley: University of California Press.

1952. *The Organizational Weapon: A Study of Bolshevik Strategy and Tactics*. Santa Monica, CA: Rand Corp.

Shambaugh, David. 2007. "China's Propaganda System: Institutions, Processes and Efficacy." *China Journal* 57 (January):25–58.

2008. "Training China's Political Elite: The Party School System." *The China Quarterly* 196 (December):827–44.

Shen, Tong. 1990. *Almost a Revolution*. Boston, MA: Houghton Mifflin Company.

Shi, Tianjian. 1999. "Village Committee Elections in China: Institutionalist Tactics for Democracy." *World Politics* 51:385–412.

Shils, Edward Albert. 1975. *Center and Periphery : Essays in Macrosociology*, Edited by E. A. Shils. Chicago, IL: University of Chicago Press.

Shirk, Susan L. 1982. *Competitive Comrades: Career Incentives and Student Strategies in China*. Berkeley: University of California Press.

1993. *The Political Logic of Economic Reform in China*. Berkeley: University of California Press.

Shue, Vivienne. 1988. *The Reach of the State: Sketches of the Chinese Body Politic*. Stanford, CA: Stanford University Press.

Simon, Herbert. 1947. *Administrative Behavior: A Study of Decision-Making Processes in Administrative Organization*. New York: Macmillan.

Skinner, G. William. 1964. "What the Study of China Can Do for Social Science." *Journal of Asian Studies* 23(4):517–22.

Skinner, G. William and Edwin A. Winckler. 1969. "Compliance Succession in Rural Communist China: A Cyclical Theory." Pp. 410–38 in *A Sociological Reader on Complex Organizations*, edited by A. Etzioni. New York: Holt, Rinehart and Winston.

1971. "Chinese Peasants and the Closed Community: An Open and Shut Case." *Comparative Studies in Society and History* 13(3):270–81.

Skinner, G. William and Hugh D.R. Baker, eds. 1977. *The City in Late Imperial China*. Stanford, CA: Stanford University Press.

1985. "Presidential Address: The Structure of Chinese History." *Journal of Asian Studies* 54(2):271–92.

Skocpol, Theda. 1979. *States and Social Revolutions*. Cambridge: Cambridge University Press.

Song, Liansheng. 2002. *Zongluxian, Dayuejin, Renmin Gongshehua Shimo [The Beginning and End of the Great Leap Forward's People's Commune Movement]*. Kunming: Yunnan Renmin Chubanshe.

Spence, A. Michael. 1974. *Market Signaling: Informational Transfer in Hiring and Related Screening Processes*. Cambridge, MA: Harvard University Press.

Stark, David. 1989. "Introduction." Pp. 1–27 in *Remaking the Economic Institutions of Socialism: China and Eastern Europe*, edited by V. Nee and D. Stark. Stanford, CA: Stanford University Press.

Stinchcombe, Arthur L. 1965. "Social Structure and Organizations." Pp. 142–93 in *Handbook of Organizations*, edited by J. G. March. Chicago, IL: Rand McNally.

Strand, B. 1990. "Protest in Beijing: Civil Society and Public Sphere in China." *Problems of Communism* 39:1–19.

Su, Yang. 2011. *Collective Killings in Rural China During the Cultural Revolution*. New York: Cambridge University Press.

Sun, Liping and Yuhua Guo. 2000. "'Ruanying Jianshi': Zhengshi Quanli Feizhengshi Yunzuo De Guocheng Fenxi: Huabei B Zhen Shouliang De Ge'an Yanjiu [Both Hard and Soft: Process Analysis of the Informal Operation of Formal Power: A Case Study of Grain Collection in B Town, North China]." *Qinghua Shehuixue Pinglun Tsinghua [Sociology Review]* Special Issue:21–46.

Sun, Xin. 2015. "Selective Enforcement of Land Regulations: Why Large-Scale Violators Succeed." *China Journal* 74:66–90.

Tan, Qixiang. 1986. "Zhongguo Wenhua De Shidai Chayi He Diqu Chayi [Diversities in the Chinese Culture across Regions and over Time]." *Fudan Xuebao [Shehui Kexue Ban]* (2):4–13.

Tarrow, Sidney. 1989. *Struggle, Politics and Reform: Collective Action, Social Movements and Cycles of Protest*. Ithaca, NY: Center for International Studies, Cornell University.

Thornton, Patricia H and William Ocasio. 2008. "Institutional Logics." in *The Sage Handbook of Organizational Institutionalism*, edited by R. Greenwood, C. Oliver, R. Suddaby and W. R. Nord. Los Angeles, CA: Sage Publications.

Tian, Yi and Xu Zhao. 2008. *Taxiang Zhishui: Yige Xiangzhen De Sanshinian, Yige Guojia De "Yinmi" Caizheng Shi [Taxes in Towns: Thirty Years in a Town, a Country's "Secret" Financial History]*. Beijing: Zhongxin Chubanshe.

Tilly, Charles. 1986. *The Contentious French*. Cambridge, MA: Belknap Press of Harvard University Press.

———. 1990. *Coercion, Capital, and European States, Ad 990–1990*. Cambridge, MA: Blackwell.

———. 1995. "To Explain Political Processes." *American Journal of Sociology* 100 (6):1594–610.

Tirole, Jean. 1986. "Hierarchies and Bureaucracies: On the Role of Collusion in Organizations." *Journal of Law, Economics, and Organization* 2 (2):181–214.

———. 1993. "Collusion and the Theory of Organizations." Pp. 151–213 in *Advances in Economic Theory: Proceedings of the Sixth World Congress of the Econometric Society*, edited by J. J. Laffont. Cambridge: Cambridge University Press.

1994. "The Internal Organization of Government: Rethinking Political Decentralization." *Oxford Economic Papers, New Series* 46(1):1–29.

Townsend, James R. and Brantly Womack. 1986. *Politics in China (3rd Edition)*. Boston, MA: Little, Brown.

Treisman, Daniel. 2007. *The Architecture of Government*. New York: Cambridge University Press.

Tsai, Lily L. 2007. "Solidary Groups, Informal Accountability, and Local Public Goods Provision in Rural China." *The American Political Science Review* 101(2):355–73.

Tsai, Wen-Hsuan and Nicola Dean. 2013. "The CCP's Learning System: Thought Unification and Regime Adaptation." *China Journal* 69 (January):87–107.

Tullock, Gordon. 1967. "The Welfare Costs of Tariffs, Monopolies, and Theft." *Western Economic Journal*:224–32.

Viola, Lynne. 1987. *The Best Sons of the Fatherland: Workers in the Vanguard of Soviet Collectivization*. New York: Oxford University Press.

Wade, Robert. 1990. *Governing the Market: Economic Theory and the Role of Government in East Asian Industrialization*. Princeton, NJ: Princeton University Press.

Walder, Andrew G. 1986. *Communist Neo-Traditionalism: Work and Authority in Chinese Industry*. Berkeley: University of California Press.

1987. "*Communist Social Structure and Worker's Politics in China.*" Pp. 45–89, edited by V. Falkenheim. Ann Arbor: Center for Chinese Studies, University of Michigan.

1995a. "Local Governments as Industrial Firms: An Organizational Analysis of China's Transitional Economy." *American Journal of Sociology* 101 (2):263–301.

1995b. "Career Mobility and the Communist Political Order." *American Sociological Review* 60(3):309–28.

Walder, Andrew G., Bobai Li and Donald J. Treiman. 2000. "Politics and Life Chances in a State Socialist Regime: Dual Career Paths into the Urban Chinese Elite, 1949 to 1996." *American Sociological Review* 65(2):191–209.

2009. *Fractured Rebellion: The Beijing Red Guard Movement*. Cambridge, MA: Harvard University Press.

2019. *Agents of Disorder: Inside China's Cultural Revolution*. Cambridge, MA: Belknap Press of Harvard University Press.

Wang, Hansheng, Shiding Liu and Liping Sun. 1997. "Zuowei Zhidu Yunzuo He Zhidu Bianqian Fangshi De Biantong [Systems Operation and Systems Change] ." *Zhongguo Shehui Kexue Jikan [China Social Science Quarterly]* 21 (Winter):45–68.

Wang, Hansheng and Yige Wang. 2009. "Mubiao Guanli Zerenzhi: Nongcun Jiceng Zhengquan De Shijian Luoji [The Responsibility System of Policy Target Management: The Logic of Practice in Rural Governance]." *Shehuixue Yanjiu [Sociology Research]* (2).

Wang, Peng and Jingyi Wang. 2018. "How China Promotes Its Military Officers: Interactions between Formal and Informal Institutions." *China Quarterly* 234 (June 2018):399–419.

Wang, Shaoguang. 1995. *Failure of Charisma: The Cultural Revolution in Wuhan.* New York: Oxford University Press.

Wang, Ya'nan. 1981 [1948]. *Zhongguo Guanliao Zhengzhi Yanjiu [Research on the Chinese Bureaucracy].* Beijing: Zhongguo Shehui Kexue Chubanshe.

Wank, David L. 1999. *Commodifying Communism: Business, Trust, and Politics in a Chinese City.* New York: Cambridge University Press.

Wasserstrom, Jeffrey. 1991. *Student Protests in Twentieth-Century China.* Stanford, CA: Stanford University Press.

Weber, Eugen J. 1976. *Peasants into Frenchmen: The Modernization of Rural France, 1870–1914.* Stanford, CA: Stanford University Press.

Weber, Max. 1946. *From Max Weber: Essays in Sociology Translated, Edited, and with an Introduction by H. H. Gerth and C. Wright Mills.* New York: Oxford University Press.

1968. *The Religion of China: Confucianism and Taoism.* New York: Free Press.

1978. *Economy and Society: An Outline of Interpretive Sociology.* Berkeley: University of California Press.

Weick, Karl E. 1976. "Educational Organizations as Loosely Coupled Systems." *Administrative Science Quarterly* 21(1):1–19.

1982. "Management of Organizational Change among Loosely Coupled Elements." in *Change in Organizations: New Perspectives on Theory, Research and Society*, edited by P. S. Goodman. San Francisco, CA: Jossey-Bass Publishers.

White, Lynn T. III. 1989. *Politics of Chaos: The Organizational Causes of Violence in China's Cultural Revolution.* Princeton, NJ: Princeton University Press.

Whiting, Susan H. 2000. *Power and Wealth in Rural China: The Political Economy of Institutional Change.* New York: Cambridge University Press.

Whyte, Martin King. 1973. "Bureaucracy and Modernization in China: The Maoist Critique." *American Sociological Review* 38(4):149–63.

1980. "Bureaucracy and Antibureaucracy in the People's Republic of China." Pp. 123–41 in *Hierarchy and Society*, edited by G. M. Britan and R. Cohen. Philadelphia, PA: Institute for the Study of Human Issues.

Whyte, Martin King and William L. Parish. 1984. *Urban Life in Contemporary China.* Chicago, IL: University of Chicago Press.

Will, Pierre-Etienne. 1990. *Bureaucracy and Famine in Eighteenth-Century China.* Stanford, CA: Stanford University Press.

Williamson, Oliver E. 1975. *Markets and Hierarchies, Analysis and Antitrust Implications: A Study in the Economics of Internal Organization.* New York: Free Press.

1985. *The Economic Institutions of Capitalism: Firms, Markets, Relational Contracting.* New York: Free Press.

Wilsford, David. 1988. "Tactical Advantages Versus Administrative Heterogeneity: The Strengths and the Limits of the French State." *Comparative Political Studies* 21:126–68.

Wilson, James Q. 1975. "The Rise of the Bureaucratic State." *The Public Interest* 41:77–103.

1989. *Bureaucracy: What Government Agencies Do and Why They Do It*. New York: Basic Books.

Wu, Yi. 2007. *Xiaocheng Xuanxiao: Yige Xiangzhen Zhengzhi Yunzuo De Yanyi Yu Chanshi [Noises in a Small Town: Scenes and Interpretations of Political Processes in a Small Town]*. Beijing: Shenghuo Dushu Xinzhi Sanlian Shudian.

Xu, Chenggang. 2011. "The Fundamental Institutions of China's Reforms and Development." *Journal of Economic Literature* 49(4):1076–151.

Yan, Buke. 1996. *Shidafu Zhengzhi Yansheng Shigao [The Historical Evolution of the Literati and Officialdom]*. Beijing: Beijing Daxue Chubanshe.

2010. *Zhongguo Gudai Guanjie Zhidu Yinlun [An Introduction to the Official Ranking Institutions in Ancient China]*. Beijing: Beijing Daxue Chubanshe.

Yan, Yunxiang. 1996. *The Flow of Gifts: Reciprocity and Social Networks in a Chinese Village*. Stanford, CA: Stanford University Press.

2006. "Chaxugeju Yu Zhongguo Wenhua Zhong De Dengjiguan [The Mode of Differentiation and the Hierarchical Norm in Chinese Culture]." *Shehuixue Yanjiu* (4):201–13.

Yang, Dali L. 1996. *Calamity and Reform in China: State, Rural Society, and Institutional Change since the Great Famine*. Stanford, CA: Stanford University Press.

2004. *Remaking the Chinese Leviathan: Market Transition and the Politics of Governance in China*. Stanford, CA: Stanford University Press.

Yang, Guobin. 2009. *The Power of the Internet in China: Citizen Activism Online*. New York: Columbia University Press.

Yang, Jisheng. 2013. *Tombstone: The Great Chinese Famine 1958–1962*. New York: Farrar, Straus and Giroux.

Yang, Kuisong. 2013. *Renbuzhu De Guanhuai [Uncontrollable "Care"]*. Xining: Guanxi shifan daxue chubanshe.

Yang, Mayfair Mei-hui. 1994. *Gifts, Favors, and Banquets: The Art of Social Relationships in China*. Ithaca, NY: Cornell University Press.

Ying, Xing. 2001. *Dahe Yimin Shangfang De Gushi [The Story of Immigration Petitions in Dahe]*. Beijing: Sanlian Chubanshe.

Zald, Mayer N. and John D. McCarthy. 1987. *Social Movements in an Organizational Society*. New Brunswick, NJ: Transaction Books.

Zang, Xiaowei. 2017. "How Cohesive Is the Chinese Bureaucracy? A Case Study of Street-Level Bureaucrats in China." *Public Administration and Development* 37(3):217–26.

Zelin, Madeleine. 1984. *The Magistrate's Tael: Rationalizing Fiscal Reform in Eighteenth-Century Ch'ing China*. Berkeley, CA: University of California Press.

Zelizer, Viviana A. 1994. *The Social Meaning of Money*. New York: Basic Books.

Zhang, Jing. 2017. "Constructing the Idea of Organization: Thought Self-Check and Organizational Review of Cadres (1952–1960)." *Shehui* 37(5):59–77.

2018. *Jiceng Zhengquan: Xiangcun Zhiduzhu Wenti (Xiuding Ben) [Issues Related to the Grassroots Government System]*. Shanghai: Shanghai Renmin Chubanshe.

Zhang, Xuehua. 2017. "Implementation of Pollution Control Targets in China: Has a Centralized Enforcement Approach Worked." *China Quarterly* 231 (September 2017):749–74.

Zhao, Dingxin. 2001. *The Power of Tiananmen: State–Society Relations and the 1989 Beijing Student Movement*. Chicago, IL: University of Chicago Press.

Zhao, Dingxin, Ruixue Gong and Wan Hu. 2012. "'Tianmingguan' Ji Zhengji Hefaxing Zai Gudai He Dangdai Zhongguo De Tixian [The 'Mandate of Heaven' and Performance Legitimation in Ancient and Contemporary China]." *Jingji Shehui Tizhi Bijiao* (1).

2015. *The Confucian-Legalist State: A New Theory of Chinese History*. New York: Oxford University Press.

Zhao, Shukai. 2010. *Xiangzhen Zhili Yu Zhengfu Zhiduhua [Township Governance and Government Institutionalization]*. Beijing: Shangwu Yinshuguan.

Zhe, Xiaoye and Yingying Chen. 2011. "Xiangmuzhi De Fenji Yunzuo Jizhi He Zhili Luoji: Dui 'Xiangmu Jincun' Anli De Shehuixue Fenxi [The Mechanism and Governance Logic of the Hierarchical Operation of the Project System: Social Analysis of the Case of 'Projects Entering the Village']." *Zhongguo Shehui Kexue [Social Sciences in China]* (4).

Zhou, Feizhou. 2006. "Cong Jiquxing Zhengquan Dao 'Xuanfuxing' Zhengquan: Shuifei Gaige Dui Guojia Yu Nongmin Guanxi Zhi Yingxiang" [From an Absorbing Regime to a 'Suspended' Regime: The Impact of the Tax-for-Fee Reform on the Relationship between the State and Farmers]." *Shehuixue Yanjiu [Sociology Research]* (3).

2009. "Jinbiaosai Tizhi [the Tournament System]." *Shehuixue Yanjiu [Sociology Research]* (3):54–77.

2012. *Yiliweili: Cziaheng Guanxi Yu Difang Zhengfu Xingwei [In Pursuit of Interests: Fiscal Relationships and Local Government Behavior]*. Shanghai: Shanghai Sanlian Shudian.

Zhou, Li-an. 2007. "Zhongguo Difang Guanyuan De Jinbiaosai Moshi Yanjiu [Governing China's Local Officials: An Analysis of the Promotion Tournament Model]." *Jingji Yanjiu [Economic Research]* (7):36–50.

2014. "Xingzheng Fabaozhi [Administrative Subcontracting]." *Shehui [Society]* 34(6):1–38.

2017. *Zhuanxingzhong De Difang Zhengfu: Guanyuan Jili Yu Zhili (Di'er Ban) [Local Government in Transition: Officials' Incentives and Governance (Second Edition)]*. Shanghai: Gezhi Chubanshe.

Zhou, Xueguang. 1993. "Unorganized Interests and Collective Action in Communist China." *American Sociological Review* 58(1):54–73.

2010a. "The Institutional Logic of Collusion among Local Governments in China." *Modern China* 36(1):47–78.

2010b. "Can a Falling Leaf Tell the Coming of the Autumn? Making Sense of Village Elections in a Township and in China." Pp. 167–88 in *Growing Pains: Tensions and Opportunity in China's Tranformation*, edited by J. Oi, S. Rozelle and X. Zhou. Stanford, CA: Walter H. Shorenstrein Asia-Pacific Research Center, Stanford University.

Zhou, Xueguang. 2019a. "Lun Zhongguo Guanliao Tizhizhong De Feizhengshi Zhidu (Informal Institutions in the Chinese Bureaucracy: An Essay)." *Qinghua Shehui Kexue (Tsinghua Social Sciences)* 1(1):1–42.

2019b. "Huang Renyu Beilun Yu Diguo Luoji: Yige Cengzhi Wei Xiansuo [The Huang Renyu Paradox and the Logic of Empire: The Case of Civil Examination Institution]." *Shehui [Society]* 39(2):1–30.

2020a. "Social Media and Governance in China." Pp. 128–48 in *Fateful Decisions: Choices That Will Shape China's Future*, edited by J. Oi and T. Fingar. Stanford, CA: Stanford University Press.

2020b. "Dangzheng Guanxi: Yige Renshi Zhidu Shijiao Yu Jingyan Zhengju [The Relationship between Party and Government: A Personnel Management Perspective and Empirical Evidence]." *Shehui [Society]* (3):137–67.

Zhou, Xueguang and Yun Ai. 2010. "Duochong Luoji Xia De Zhidue Bianqian: Yige Fenxi Kuangjia" [Multiple Logics of Institutional Change: Toward an Analytical Framework]." *Zhongguo Shehui Kexue (Social Sciences in China)* (4):132–50.

Zhou, Xueguang and Yun Ai. 2016. "Bases of Governance and Forms of Resistance: The Case of Rural China." Pp. 443–60 in *The Sage Handbook of Resistance*, edited by D. Courpasson and S. Valls. Thousand Oaks, CA: Sage Publications.

Zhou, Xueguang, Yun Ai and Hong Lian. 2012. "The Limit of Bureaucratic Power: The Case of the Chinese Bureaucracy." *Research in the Sociology of Organizations* 34:81–111.

Zhou, Xueguang, Hong Lian, Leonard Ortolano and Yinyu Ye. 2013. "A Behavioral Model of Muddling through in the Chinese Bureaucracy: The Case of Environmental Protection." *The China Journal* (70 July):120–47.

Zhu, Zongbin. 2006. *Zhongguo Gudai Zhengzhi Zhidu Yanjiu (Research on China's Ancient Political System)*. Xi'an: Sanqin Chubanshe.

Zweig, David. 1989. "Struggle over Land in China: Peasant Resistance after Collectivization, 1966–1986." in *Everyday Forms of Peasant Resistance*, edited by F. Colburn. Armonk, NY: M.E. Sharpe.

Index

ad hoc taxes, in inverted soft budget
    constraint phenomenon, 193
administrative achievement projects. *See*
    zhengji gongcheng
administrative subcontract model, 13–14, 22
allocation of control rights, 58–59
    delegation and separation of rights, 60
    for environmental regulation, 66–67, 80,
        98
        for goal setting, 66, 68–70
        for incentive provision, 67, 70–75
        for inspection, 66–70
        principal–agent relationship and,
            78–80
        in subcontracting model, 67
    formal authority for, 58–59
    informal authority for, 58–59
    over goal setting, 59
    over incentive provisions, 59–60
    over inspections, 59
Anti-Bourgeois Liberalization Campaign,
    291–92, 295
Anti-Rightist Campaign, 289
appraisal mechanisms, collusion and,
    150–62
    information controls in, 152–57
    jiancha yanshou, 150
    manipulation of inspection mechanisms,
        156–57
    for Municipal Environmental Protection
        Bureau, 152
    in research settings, 151–52
    sudden attack strategies, 154–55

arbitrary power
    in bureaucratic state, 46–47, 306
    campaign-style mobilization and, 91–93
    of supreme leaders, 9
asymmetric formation, 11
attention mechanisms, 170
authoritarianism. *See also* totalitarian
    systems
    regional decentralization, 311
authority. *See also* charismatic authority
    in control rights theory, 58–59
    in village elections, relationships between,
        257–59, 267
    in Weberian bureaucracy, 34–35
        legal-bureaucratic, 34–35
        obedience to, 34
        patrimonial, 34–35, 38
        traditional, 35
authority relationships, collusion and,
    133–34

Bao Village, elections in, 245–47
behavioral flexibility, in collusion, 140
biantong (flexible adaptation), 16, 49
    collusion and, 135–36
Boulevard Village, elections in, 244–45
bounded rationality, 11
bureaucracy. *See also specific topics*
    impersonal, 147–50
    Merton's critique of, 236
bureaucratic bargaining
    commitment as element of, 112
    conceptual approach to, 129

339

For EU product safety concerns, contact us at Calle de José Abascal, 56–1°, 28003 Madrid, Spain or eugpsr@cambridge.org.

www.ingramcontent.com/pod-product-compliance
Ingram Content Group UK Ltd.
Pitfield, Milton Keynes, MK11 3LW, UK
UKHW010248140625
459647UK00013BA/1738